"This is that rare thing—a book that speaks equally to Christians and sceptics. Combining gripping historical narrative with a keen critique of contemporary debates, Dickson makes one of the most honest, challenging, and compelling cases for Christianity you will ever read."

—Teresa Morgan, Professor of Graeco-Roman History, University of Oxford

"*Bullies and Saints* is a commendably honest work that goes beyond simple apologetics: one that is all the more subtle in its effect for being often very apologetic."

—Tom Holland, author of *Persian Fire* and *Dominion*

"This is an important book. My father was a deeply religious man and in public life. Around him were copious efforts to throw a Christian cloak over a multitude of political judgements driven by secular ambitions and directions—often deeply harmful. He used to say that the task for a Christian in public life, or anywhere, is to act in a manner that would not deny others an experience of the cross. This book by John Dickson has taught me exactly what he meant. It is a book of the ages for this age. The worst efforts by many have obscured or distorted the message, using it for power, greed, lust, prejudice, and ignorance. Their historical and contemporary efforts have destroyed the access to faith for many. But throughout the centuries, and now, others have shone a light on Jesus's message of love, charity, kindness, selflessness and salvation—values and behaviours which are timeless. Decency is open to everyone of whatever faith or none. However, the fundamental belief of Christians that we are all made in God's image is a deep grounding. Why this is so is here in these pages."

—The Honourable Kim Beazley AC, Governor of Western Australia, Ambassador to the United States of America (2010–2016), former Leader of the Australian Labor Party

"I don't often hear people question these days whether or not Christianity is true. I hear them ask whether or not it's good. And that's the challenge John Dickson accepts in *Bullies and Saints*. His honest look does not dismiss the horrible evil committed in the name of Christ, then and now. And that's why you can trust this book. When we can be honest about the past, we can be discerning about the present. Whether or not you believe in Jesus, this book will test what you thought you knew and open your eyes to what might be possible."

—Collin Hansen, editorial director of The Gospel Coalition, host of the *Gospelbound* podcast, and coauthor of *Gospelbound: Living with Resolute Hope in an Anxious Age*

"*Bullies and Saints* is no simple apologia for the Christian church, or for Christianity as such. John Dickson offers a thoroughly frank account of Christian history, confronting some of the ugliest episodes in that story. But at the same time, he highlights and disproves the countless distortions and falsehoods that sceptics have so often levied against the faith. Such an honest accounting reinforces the view that Christianity is an essential foundation of our civilization. Dickson has written a very necessary book, which at the same time makes for enlightening and rewarding reading."
—PHILIP JENKINS, DISTINGUISHED PROFESSOR
OF HISTORY, BAYLOR UNIVERSITY

"This is a measured and masterful retelling of two thousand years of Christian history. Whatever your current beliefs, I recommend you grab a copy and let Dickson introduce you to the saints and bullies who have shaped our world. I learned from every page and now have a better understanding of infamous affairs like the Crusades and the Inquisition, as well as more knowledge of a thousand unsung heroes of the faith. Read it and weep, smile, question, cogitate, and sing."
—REBECCA MCLAUGHLIN, AUTHOR OF *CONFRONTING CHRISTIANITY*

"John Dickson is a scrupulous historian, a fair-minded judge, and a wonderful storyteller. *Bullies and Saints* is an invaluable, thoughtful, and at times rightly provoking consideration of the good and the bad, the beautiful and the ugly, in the long Christian story. In prose that is supple and easy, it captures the inevitable complexity and cross-grained contexts of all human endeavours, even divine human endeavours. And it understands profoundly that professing Christianity does not cure you of the human condition, with all its perplexing possibilities, all its heroism and terror, its majesty and its degradation. And yet there is a light that shines."
—GREG SHERIDAN, FOREIGN EDITOR OF *THE AUSTRALIAN*
AND AUTHOR OF *GOD IS GOOD FOR YOU*

"The problem of suffering and evil is one of the hardest problems that faces any worldview. Yet Christians face an even harder problem—to account for the horrors inflicted in the name of Jesus Christ, who taught the highest ethic ever seen and repudiated the use of violence to defend him and his message. When we think of the so-called Crusades and Holy Wars in the Middle Ages, must we agree with the late Christopher Hitchens that 'religion poisons everything,' or are there any redeeming features? Are there any saints among the bullies? Ancient historian John Dickson is eminently qualified to help us dig into the facts. He convincingly demonstrates that 'sacred violence' is not traceable to the first three centuries of the Christian era. With refreshing honesty, he opens our eyes to the fascinating divergent developments in succeeding centuries that led, on the one hand, to bullies, brutality and oppression and, on the other hand, to saints, charity, hospitals, and human rights. 'Bullies are common—saints are not.' If you wish to know the how and the why, as you should, then there is nothing for it but to buy and read Dickson's book and judge for yourself.

It is superbly well-informed historical analysis at its best. I unhesitatingly recommend it as essential reading for anyone wishing to engage with the hard questions arising from the evils of Christendom. Get it and share it!"

—JOHN C. LENNOX, EMERITUS PROFESSOR OF MATHEMATICS,
EMERITUS FELLOW IN MATHEMATICS AND PHILOSOPHY
OF SCIENCE, UNIVERSITY OF OXFORD

"This lively account of the history of the church brings bullies and saints across two thousand years to life. It challenges equally the glib assertions of those who would whitewash the evil in Christian history and those who would expunge its good. Erudite and immensely readable, it is a must for both the defenders and detractors of the faith."

—MICHAEL SPENCE, PRESIDENT AND PROVOST,
UNIVERSITY COLLEGE LONDON

"This challenging work from a well-qualified historian tackles one of the current issues facing the Christian church. Critics say Christianity (and often all religions) have done more harm than good. Dr. Dickson is not afraid to face this and to acknowledge in a confronting fashion the failings of the church over the centuries to live up to Christ's teaching. Nevertheless, his measured approach, argued (as a historian must) from the fine details of the documents of history, ends on a message of hope. This is a book for believers, doubters, sceptics, and downright enemies of the church to weigh up."

—ALANNA NOBBS, PROFESSOR EMERITA, DEPARTMENT OF
ANCIENT HISTORY, MACQUARIE UNIVERSITY

"I don't know another book like this—an honest guide through the labyrinth of two thousand years of both violence and virtue in the name of Christianity. Dickson, a qualified historian, explains the complexities of the past with disturbing even-handedness. The dirty washing of Christian history is laid out here for all to see, but we're also invited to consider beautiful actions, often by those unknown. I highly recommend this book, not just for its factual content and fair analysis, but also as a window for understanding the world today."

—PETER J. WILLIAMS, PRINCIPAL, TYNDALE HOUSE, CAMBRIDGE

"John Dickson would not know, until reading this, that his previous work has been as critical as the works of C. S. Lewis, Benedict XVI, and others to saving my adult Catholic faith. In his latest book he offers an engaging, honest, and personal account of why Christianity is good, without for a moment diminishing the manifest failures of some Christians to live up to the demands of their faith. I do not agree with everything John says, but I cannot recommend *Bullies and Saints* highly enough. You should buy it, read it, and ponder."

—MICHAEL QUINLAN, PROFESSOR OF LAW,
UNIVERSITY OF NOTRE DAME, AUSTRALIA

"This timely and courageous book openly engages with both the 'bullies' and the 'saints' of Christian history. Dickson grapples with the most horrific atrocities committed in the name of Christianity. Yet he does this not to whitewash them but rather to acknowledge them and to offer the kind of Christian self-critique Jesus demanded. In doing so, Dickson holds the church up to the standards of its founder—Jesus Christ. He offers a fruitful conceptual tool for understanding the ways in which, historically, Christians have—and have not—followed the teachings of Jesus. This is the metaphor of the 'beautiful tune,' which, as Dickson points out, the church has at times performed well, and at times performed poorly. But the melody, Dickson reveals, was never completely drowned out. This illuminating metaphor enables Dickson to reveal some of the historical outworkings of Jesus's teachings that are now the cornerstone of human rights, care for the sick and marginalised, and mass education. Dickson is not only a great historian but also—and this is uncommon among scholars—a great storyteller with the ability to communicate history beautifully and accessibly. This is what makes his writing so refreshing. He is humble, down-to-earth, and engaging. Christians and non-believers alike will find *Bullies and Saints* a compelling read."

—SARAH IRVING-STONEBRAKER, SENIOR LECTURER IN MODERN
EUROPEAN HISTORY, WESTERN SYDNEY UNIVERSITY

"In this deeply personally motivated book, John Dickson challenges his readers to face up to the long history of violence and retribution carried out by those who bear the name of Christ and his church, yet also offers a plea for the equally long history of self-giving for the sake of others. Rather like a long-distance guided railway journey, he visits key moments and individuals in the history of the western church, drawing on recent scholarship and on the writers of the time, refusing to let his audience dwell only on the beauty spots but clearly hoping that it is their example that will provide hope and inspiration for the future. While this may give sceptics from outside the church pause, it will best have served its purpose if it enables those within to come to a better understanding of the dark side of their own heritage and of the shadows it casts even over the present and to move forward in humility."

—JUDITH M. LIEU, LADY MARGARET'S PROFESSOR OF
DIVINITY EMERITA, UNIVERSITY OF CAMBRIDGE

"John Dickson has little problem acknowledging the 'log' in Christianity's eye. As an insider to the Christian tradition and as a trained historian, he articulates with a clarity beyond many popular critics just how much of an image problem the Christian Church has—there is hypocrisy in every century. And yet he also knows that Christianity has contributed uniquely to history, and its hospitals, schools, reformers, and advocates for human dignity have often managed to open the most jaundiced eye. Whether you believe we would be better off without Christianity or whether you have found it profoundly life-giving, *Bullies and Saints* is an invitation to look again at the Christian church's performance and to see if we cannot glimpse something of the founder's own loving character and concern for human well-being."

—Mark P. Ryan, Adjunct Professor of Religion and
Culture, Director of the Francis A. Schaeffer Institute,
Covenant Theological Seminary, St. Louis

"The blunt outrage of a serious historian keeps John Dickson wondering. How have the saints got it so wrong, so often? The tell-tale breakthrough for me came in the middle chapters of this book. Two generations on from Constantine we have the engaged reactions of four young men, close intellectual peers in a single decade. One, Julian, runs the Roman empire and means to get rid of the Christian revolution. The others are bishops or the like in backblocks Cappadocia. All four agree on the flashpoint. The government itself must act, not for the strong, but for the weak and therefore the so-called undeserving, however irrational that seems. John Dickson need not have worried so much. In the long run the revolutionary commands of Jesus have been profoundly built into our secular policy, in spite of church hypocrisy. Indeed, our zeal to expose such hypocrisy is itself a legacy of Jesus's teaching about the kingdom."

—Edwin Judge, Emeritus Professor of History,
Macquarie University, Sydney

"*Bullies and Saints* is an impressively even-handed account of Christianity's history, offering a subtle account of its paradoxes and ironies. It readily acknowledges Christians' role in many of the worst parts of the human story, while also detailing Christians' extraordinary collective good and Christianity's distinctive contributions. The book showcases Dr. Dickson's talent for deeply insightful scholarship that is engaging, accessible, and thoroughly enjoyable to read."

—Andrew Tuch, Professor of Law, Washington
University in St. Louis

"The old question, 'Is Christianity true?' has been replaced by the new one, 'Is Christianity good?' In this well-paced and eminently readable survey, Dickson sincerely grapples with the checkered moral history of the church. He takes Christian harm seriously, considering everything from the crusades to the child sex abuse scandal. Simultaneously, Dickson draws us into those unprecedented aspects of the church—its commitment to the powerless, for instance—that ought to awaken our curiosity. In the end, he defends the faith best, whether addressing its shame or its glory, by simply telling the truth."

—Rachel S. Ferguson, Director of the Liberty
and Ethics Center, Professor of Managerial
Philosophy, Lindenwood University Missouri

bullies

and

saints

bullies

and

saints

AN HONEST LOOK AT THE GOOD AND EVIL
OF CHRISTIAN HISTORY

JOHN DICKSON

**ZONDERVAN
REFLECTIVE**

ZONDERVAN REFLECTIVE

Bullies and Saints
Copyright © 2021 by John Dickson

Requests for information should be addressed to:
Zondervan, *3900 Sparks Dr. SE, Grand Rapids, Michigan 49546*

Zondervan titles may be purchased in bulk for educational, business, fundraising, or sales promotional use. For information, please email SpecialMarkets@Zondervan.com.

ISBN 978-0-310-11836-7 (hardcover)
ISBN 978-0-310-11937-1 (international trade paper edition)
ISBN 978-0-310-11936-4 (audio)
ISBN 978-0-310-11837-4 (ebook)

Art direction: Tammy Johnson
Cover Design: Studio Gearbox
Cover Images: © Heritage Pics; Agefotostock / Alamy Stock Photo
Interior Design: Mallory Collins

Printed in the United States of America

21 22 23 24 25 /LSC/ 10 9 8 7 6 5 4 3 2 1

JUL - 2 2021

For Ben and Karen
ΦΙΛΟΙ ΕΙΣ ΤΟΝ ΑΙΩΝΑ

Contents

Map of the Roman Mediterranean   xv

Map of Medieval and Modern Europe   xvi

Special Thanks to   xvii

Better off without Religion—A Prelude   xix

1. The Day I Lost Faith in the Church   1
   A Christian Massacre in the Year 1099

2. The Crusades in a Nutshell   8
   Holy Wars from the 1000s to the 1200s

3. The Beautiful Tune   23
   The Christian Ethic of the First Century

4. Log in the Eye of the Church   37
   Another Thing Jesus Said in the First Century

5. Good Losers   44
   Persecution of the Church from AD 64 to 312

6. Constantine and Religious Liberty   58
   The First Christian Emperor in the Early 300s

7. Constantine and the Birth of Charity   69
   Financial Changes to Roman Law in the Early 300s

8. Julian the Apostate   87
   An Emperor Winds Back the Clock on Christianity in the 360s

9. Muscular Christianity   96
   A Senator and Bishop in the Late 300s

10. Cappadocian Christianity   106
    Bishops, Healthcare, and Slavery in the Late 300s

11. Iconoclastic Christianity   116
    Christian Riots and the Closing of Pagan Temples from 380 to 415

CONTENTS

12. "Just War"   125
    A Theory of Christian War in the Early 400s

13. The Death of Rome and Growth of the Church   137
    Barbarians and Christians in Europe from 400 to 1100

14. Christian "Jihad"   147
    Forced Conversions in Europe in the Late 700s

15. The Greatest European You've Never Heard Of   155
    A "Renaissance" in the Middle of the "Dark Ages"

16. Knights of Christ   167
    The Prelude to "Holy War" in the Build Up to 1100

17. Prophets and Hypocrites   179
    Medieval Monasteries, Charities, and Reforms

18. The Eternal Empire of the East   197
    The Forgotten Byzantines from the 500s to the 1400s

19. Inventing the "Dark Ages"   210
    The Seeming Catastrophe of the 500s to 1200s

20. The Inquisition   218
    Heresy Trials from the 1100s to the 1500s

21. The Reformation "Wars of Religion"   236
    More Bloody Battles in the 1600s

22. The "Troubles"   248
    Confessional Conflict in the 1700s to 1998

23. Moral Reckoning   257
    Child Abuse in the Modern Church

24. Social Capital   265
    The Ordinary Work of the Contemporary Church

25. The "Log in the Eye" of Us All   275
    Hypocrisy in Every Century

The Beautiful Tune—A Coda   283

Notes   287

Scripture Index   319

Subject Index   321

Map of the Roman Mediterranean

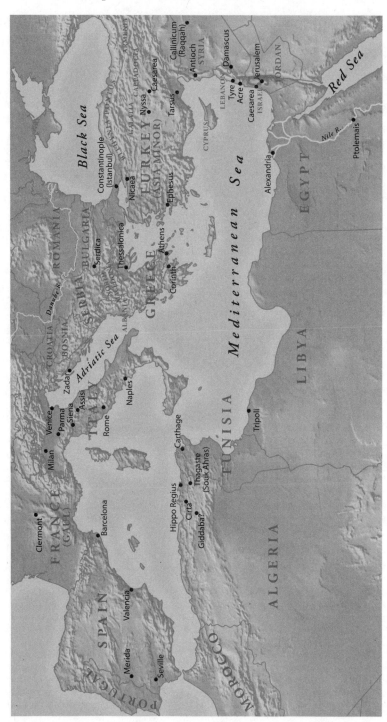

Map of Medieval and Modern Europe

Special Thanks to

Raley Payne, for invaluable research and editorial assistance.

Lyndie and David Leviston, for fresh eyes and welcome suggestions.

My friends at the Centre for Public Christianity, especially Simon Smart, Allan Dowthwaite, Natasha Moore, and Justine Toh, for years of thoughtful discussions about these matters.

The Department of Ancient History at Macquarie University, especially Professors Edwin Judge, Alanna Nobbs, and Dr Chris Forbes, for exemplifying the careful "secular" study of Christianity.

Bill Hurditch, Jana Robertson, Rob Clarke, and Dugald Mackenzie, for providing guidance for the entire Undeceptions project.

Professor Michael Quinlan at the University of Notre Dame, for reading the manuscript, kindly providing a commendation, and offering 3000+ words of suggested improvements.

St. Andrew's Anglican Church, Roseville, for the two-decade reminder that, despite the monumental failures of Christian history, there is still such a thing as the "holy catholic church."

Nicholas Purcell, Camden Professor of Ancient History, Faculty of Classics, University of Oxford, for sponsoring my visiting status in the faculty over the last few years, without which I could not have done the research for this book.

Dr Hagop Kiyork, for our intellectual strolls solving all the world's problems.

Meredith Dimarco, for fixing the aches and pains of seven months hunched over my desk writing this book.

Buff, Josh, Sophie, and Josie, for putting up with an obsessive husband and father.

Better off without Religion—A Prelude

In August 2008 I lost a debate that changed the way I think about the topic of this book.

I say "I" lost the debate. But it was a team effort. My role was mostly behind the scenes, promoting the event, providing one of the speakers—a well-known Oxford professor—and assisting with debate preparation for "my side." The motion under consideration was: *We'd be better off without religion.* I was supporting the *negative*, in case you were wondering.

It was obvious from the outset which particular religion was the key defendant. Islam, Hinduism, and Buddhism came away unscathed. Judaism took a few hits, mainly because of the "violent bits" in the Old Testament. But it was Christianity, the largest of the religions and chief spiritual bully, that took the most heat.

All 1,238 seats of the venue (Sydney's Recital Hall) were filled. The event was broadcast live on ABC Radio, the national broadcaster. As people entered the theatre they were polled to gauge how they felt about the topic before hearing the arguments. The idea was that they would be polled again at the end of the night to reveal the winner. In the very brief moment I had the microphone, just before the final poll, I asked the audience to think of one sincerely religious person in their life and ask whether the world really would be a better place without such faith. It is easy to form a mental image of *the historic church*, I said, that is cut off from the realities of the average congregation of harmless do-gooders down the street. My challenge had no effect on the outcome, of course. I am sorry to say that the *affirmative* overwhelmingly won *both* polls. It turns out this particular group of Australians believed that we *would* be better off without religion.

I came away that evening with a clear sense of something I had been pondering for several years. In Australia, the UK, and the USA—the three countries I have spent the most time in—we have experienced a significant shift in the perception of the value of religion, in general, and Christianity in particular. Twenty or so years ago a frequent complaint against the faith was that it was too moralistic, holier-than-thou, or goody two-shoes. Today it is just as common to hear people say that the problem with the church is that it is immoral, violent, and hateful. When renowned journalist and atheist Christopher Hitchens published his 2007 *God Is Not Great*, and gave it the provocative subtitle, *How Religion Poisons Everything*, he was tapping into an increasingly widespread feeling about religion throughout his native Britain and his adopted home of America. The book also did terrifically well in Australia.

There is also some good research on all this. In 2017 an Ipsos Poll surveyed twenty countries about their views of religion. One of the questions was: "Do you agree with the statement: *Religion does more harm in the world than good*?" In the US, 39 percent of respondents said they agreed with the statement. I find that remarkable. In a country usually regarded as one of the most religious on earth, almost four in ten people think religion is a negative force. Great Britain was worse—or *better*, depending on your view—with 61 percent of those surveyed agreeing with the statement. Spare a thought for Australia, where 63 percent of people think religion does more harm than good. Only Belgium (68 percent) had a more negative view of religion.[1]

A similar pattern can be seen in the UK-based Ipsos MORI survey "Rating Professions by Trustworthiness, 1993–2015."[2] Respondents were asked to rank sixteen professions according to "trustworthiness to tell the truth." Sadly, journalists and politicians were near the bottom by 2015. Unsurprisingly, doctors and teachers were at the top. Pollsters and civil servants were in the middle.

What about clergy? Interestingly, religious authorities came in seventh overall in the truth-telling stakes, with about 67 percent of Brits saying they trusted the men and women of the cloth. What is more revealing, though, is that there has been a steady decline in the public's level of trust in clergy in the twenty-two years the survey has been collecting data. Religious leaders have dropped four places and fifteen percentage points over the period. Scientists, by contrast, have climbed four places and sixteen percentage points, passing clergy in perceived trustworthiness in 2011. A similar study for Australia in 2015 found that just 39 percent of people saw ministers of religion as ethical and honest, ranking them twelfth out of thirty professions.[3]

In some ways I am surprised clergy rank higher in these polls than, say, journalists or politicians, who always appear in the bottom third. I would have thought that increasing secularization and the events of recent years would send priests and pastors to the bottom. These polls roughly coincide with the child sexual abuse scandals that have rocked the church around the world over the last twenty years. Between 2001 and 2003, *The Boston Globe*'s famous *Spotlight Team* blew open the story of the extent of child molestation and cover-ups in the Archdiocese of Boston. In the ten years prior, more than seventy priests had been credibly accused of the abuse of minors, and the church had settled cases "under an extraordinary cloak of secrecy."[4] At the time of the fourth of twelve explosive investigative articles (31 January 2002), the *Globe* reported that there were suspected pedophile priests still on active duty, often just quietly redeployed as hospital or prison chaplains. This is not an American or Roman Catholic problem only, as we will see in chapter 25.

To say that the church has an "image problem" does not quite capture it. Christianity has had two millennia to win the affection and confidence of the world. Yet, for a large number of us today, this venerable tradition deserves neither our love nor our trust. Christopher Hitchens spoke for many when he wrote:

> We believe with certainty that an ethical life can be lived without religion. And we know for a fact that the corollary holds true—that religion has caused innumerable people not just to conduct themselves no better than others, but to award themselves permission to behave in ways that would make a brothel-keeper or an ethnic cleanser raise an eyebrow. . . . As I write these words, and as you read them, people of faith are in their different ways planning your and my destruction, and the destruction of all hard-won human attainments that I have touched upon. Religion poisons everything.[5]

I imagine Christopher Hitchens would be deeply suspicious of the project of this book. (Sadly, he died of throat cancer in 2011.) I can hear him groaning: *As if* a Christian believer—even a mild-mannered Anglican one—would be willing to look into the darkness of Christian history and provide anything like a fair-minded account! *As if* a Christian "apologist" (I reject the word, but he would no doubt throw it at me) could admit that the "saints" can be as brazen "sinners" as anyone, and sometimes worse! I suppose only readers who finish this book will be able to judge if my imaginary Hitchens is correct. Any protestations I offer at this point are predictable and empty. I will simply admit that I have felt Hitchens's presence—ghostlike—in my study as I write this book.

Hitchens was also a hypothetical conversation partner as I co-wrote and co-presented the 2018 film, *For the Love of God: How the Church Is Better and Worse Than You Ever Imagined*. It is a sweeping survey of some of the best and worst in Christian history and today.[6] The documentary provided snapshots of the church, in three-and-a-half hours of colour, movement, and occasional humour (at least from my co-hosts). What follows is doubtless much less entertaining, but it attempts what would be impossible (and certainly inadvisable) on screen: a century-by-century retelling of the bullies and saints of Christian history, often in their own words, or at least in the words of those who loved or hated them.

This is not an academic work—it is not written for other researchers and teachers. But it does follow a crucial principle of intellectual history: the desire to submit our own imagined narratives to the actual evidence, that is, the *primary sources*, whether contemporary biographies, surviving letters, laws, inscriptions, or archaeology. There is quite a bit of that sort of thing in this book. For a subject like ours, this is crucial, because often our impressions of whether *we'd be better off without religion* are developed partly from personal experience (good or bad) and partly from second- or third-hand news reports, conversations in the pub, or documentaries on the History Channel. The evidence we will explore is mixed, but it is *evidence* that must inform our conclusions.

There is another thing I must stress from the outset. I will not be making any great distinction between the Roman Catholic Church and the Protestant Church or the Orthodox Church. There are significant theological differences between the traditions, as I will outline in chapter 21, but viewed historically, they are essentially the same social institution. It is all too easy for Protestants like me to distance themselves from some of the great evils of church history, such as Crusades and Inquisitions, by pointing out that *that was the Catholics!* On social media the other day, following something I said about the church of the Middle Ages, a vocal Presbyterian clergyman I know made exactly this point: Dickson collapses the church into one amorphous entity of his own self-loathing. But Protestantism, he said, should be kept separate. I suppose when your tradition popped up in the sixteenth century it is tempting to disown all the bad stuff between Jesus and Martin Luther. But that does not work for me. Not only have Protestants in their brief five-hundred-year history participated in all the same bigotry, hatred, and violence of their Catholic counterparts, this convenient line of reasoning leaves Protestantism in the strange position of having to admit that it has made almost no contribution to the historical fabric of western civilization, since all of the hospitals, charities, educational institutions, and distinctively Christian ethics of Protestantism are largely a continuation of traditions that thrived in Catholicism and Orthodoxy for the one thousand, five hundred years before. (My Presbyterian friend probably wouldn't mind that. For him, and other evangelical Christians, the important thing about Christianity is not any *social* contribution but the *theological* contribution Protestants made in clarifying the message of salvation *through faith alone*.) I say all this as a proud Protestant—if readers will accept an Anglican as a Protestant! My point, however, is that for the purposes of this century-by-century retelling of the bullies and saints of church history, there is no difference between the three great traditions of Christianity. Martin Luther, Ambrose of Milan, and Gregory of Nyssa are all leaders of "the church." We will meet these three, and many more, in the pages that follow.

I have used the expressions "the west" and "western civilization" a couple of times already. Let me make clear that this is not code for "white civilization" or for any contemporary longing for the recovery of a "Judeo-Christian society" of the past. I understand the recent worries about the way these terms have been co-opted for a conservative agenda. Yet, in history circles, it is just a given— irrefutably so—that *much* of the laws, ethics, philosophy, literature, and culture of the countries of Europe, Britain, Ireland, the United States, South America, Canada, South Africa, Australia, and New Zealand can be traced to concrete precedents—good and bad—in the Greco-Roman and Jewish-Christian societies that spread *westward* from Italy in the fourth to the sixteenth centuries. This is what I mean by "the west" and "western civilization." And as I will detail in chapter 18, none of this should downplay the remarkable achievements and contributions coming out of the *eastern* empire (Byzantium) and *Islamic* civilization in the Middle Ages.

From the time of the 2008 debate to the 2018 film and now to the writing of this book, I admit to feeling a deep sympathy, affinity even, for anyone who thinks Christianity has done more harm than good. There will be much to bolster that impression in what follows. At the same time, I cannot shake the conviction that the evidence demands we acknowledge that even in the darkest moments of Christian history (and today), the flame that Christ himself lit— "love your enemies, do good to those who hate you" (Luke 6:27)—had a habit of exposing the darkness from within and then reigniting itself throughout the church. This book is a tribute to both. Or to offer another metaphor to which I will return in chapter 3, Christ wrote a beautiful tune, which the church has often performed well, and often badly. But the melody was never completely drowned out. Sometimes it became a symphony.

It was during the filming of the 2018 documentary that I had a second profound experience that altered my perspective on the topic of this book. I can tell you the exact time and place. If you had polled me in that very moment, I too may have voted for the *affirmative* in the debate ten years earlier. In the first chapter, then, I want to take you to that dreadful spot, the site of a Crusader massacre and celebration. Then, after a brief history of the Crusades, roughly during the middle of the church's two-thousand-year history, we will wind back to the first century and explore what Christ himself hoped for his movement, before then trying to work out what went wrong—and right—as the centuries unfolded.

The Day I Lost Faith in the Church

A Christian Massacre in the Year 1099

Whoever for devotion alone, not to gain honour or money, goes to Jerusalem to liberate the Church of God can substitute this journey for all penance.

—POPE URBAN II

The title of this chapter is an exaggeration, but not a large one. I find myself in a dilemma. The formal creed of Christianity, known as the Nicene Creed, asks the faithful to declare their belief in "the holy catholic and apostolic Church" (by the way, "catholic" here just means *universal*, not Roman Catholic). In a very real sense, then, Christians are meant to have some kind of faith or spiritual confidence in the institution Christ established. He did himself say, "I will build my church, and the gates of Hades [death] will not prevail against it" (Matt 16:18). Yet, anyone who knows the story of Christianity through the centuries knows that the church has been anything but consistently "holy." Sometimes it has been the ally of Hades itself. As a long-time student of history, and an even longer church attender, I feel conflicted. I know where the bodies are buried in the graveyard of church history, yet I am also somehow meant to mouth the words of the Nicene Creed.

"Men Rode in Blood Up to Their Knees"

I have never felt this inner conflict more acutely than when I stood on the site of one of the greatest atrocities in religious history. I was in Jerusalem filming scenes about the Crusades, that series of unsuccessful "holy wars" in which European Christians sought to expel the infidel occupants of the Holy Land, that is, the majority Muslim population of the Middle East.

We were granted permission to film at the Al-Aqsa Mosque, the third holiest site in Islam, which sits on a massive plaza known as the Haram al-Sharif, or Temple Mount. Sharing the plaza is the Dome of the Rock, the beautiful golden dome that appears in every Jerusalem postcard. Almost thirty American football fields would fit into this giant 150,000 m² open-air court.

On 15 July 1099, something like ten thousand European Crusaders burst through Jerusalem's protective walls. Marching through the narrow streets of the city, they fought anyone who resisted. They made their way up to the Haram al-Sharif, where they discovered thousands of residents cowering in fear, hoping against hope that their sacred precinct would provide them with protection, practical and divine. But these fighting men, "pilgrims" as they called themselves, had been marching for two years. They had journeyed two thousand miles from France to Jerusalem. They had been besieging the city for a month. They were not about to let a victory go to waste. According to our records, the Crusaders whipped themselves up into a such an unholy frenzy that they slaughtered men, women, and children. They threw some victims over the plaza's high walls to their deaths three storeys below. They butchered the rest with swords, daggers, fire, arrows, and spears. They even gave chase to those who had climbed the roof of the Al-Aqsa Mosque and had them killed on the spot.[1] The blood reportedly filled the great promenade between the mosque and the dome. We have eyewitness accounts of the events. With gruesome glee and obvious exaggeration, Raymond of Aguilers, a leader of the First Crusade, wrote of this fateful day in the "ides of July":

Wonderful sights were to be seen. Some of our men cut off the heads of their enemies; others shot them with arrows, so that they fell from the towers; others tortured them longer by casting them into the flames. Piles of heads, hands, and feet were to be seen in the streets of the city. . . . It was a just and splendid judgement of God that this place should be filled with the blood of the unbelievers, since it had suffered so long from their blasphemies.[2]

As if this were not enough, old Raymond goes on to tell us that the next day, 16 July 1099, the pilgrims held a thanksgiving service in Jerusalem's Church of the Holy Sepulchre, just five hundred metres away from the site of the massacre the day before. "How they rejoiced and exulted and sang a new song to the Lord!" he tells us. "This day, I say, will be famous in all future ages, for it turned our labors and sorrows into joy and exultation." It is a confronting fact of history that a church originally designed to mark the place of the unjust and brutal crucifixion (and resurrection) of the humble man from Nazareth became the venue of jubilant songs and prayers to celebrate a ruthless military victory in Jesus's name.

Retelling these horrible details to camera as I stood in the sacred plaza outside the Al-Aqsa Mosque was the moment I sensed a loss of faith in the church. It was not simply that I had read the sources, rehearsed my lines, and now found myself standing in the hideous spot where it all happened. It was because directly in my line of sight as I delivered the lines, just a metre to the left of camera, was our Muslim guide and "minder" assigned to us to show us around the site and keep onlookers satisfied that we really did have permission to film in this spot. Her name was Azra, a Jerusalem Arab Muslim with perfect English. She watched me deliver my lines, over and over until I got them right (I am not a one-take wonder). By the time we got the take the director liked, I could see that Azra had a tear in her eye. I suddenly realised this is not just a gory piece of history. For Jerusalem Muslims—for many Muslims, actually— this event is a source of pain, shame, and even anger.

Not that Azra was at all bitter. As we were packing up, I said to her, "I'm so, so sorry. That must have been difficult for you to watch!" She was beautiful. "No, no," she replied, "It's fine. It's all fine." But I could tell it was not fine. The date, 15 July 1099, has left a nine-hundred-year-old wound in the soul of many.

Any triumphalist feelings I harboured about the historic church died that day. I could not get the juxtaposition out of my mind: Azra's quiet tear and

Raymond of Aguiler's ecstatic "splendid judgement of God." Declaring my belief in the "holy Church" could never have the same meaning again. I still say the words of the Creed, but they function as much like an aspiration as they do an affirmation of the history of Christianity through the ages.

I acknowledge that this experience at the Al-Aqsa Mosque was not wholly or strictly rational. Does it make sense for me to say "Sorry" to Azra? I was not there in 1099. I like to think I would never have taken part in the massacre of her Jerusalem forebears. I am not morally responsible for any of it. I certainly do not bear the guilt of it. All of this is true. So why does "Sorry" still seem like the right thing to say? I suppose it is because I am connected to my "team," just as Azra has a connection to her "team" ("family" might be the better metaphor). As someone representing Christianity in that moment, it was appropriate to feel some shame that blood was spilled *in the name of Christ*. And it was right to communicate that sentiment to Azra.

Were the Crusades Really "Religiously" Motivated?

All of this raises a connected matter. Were the Crusades a *religiously motivated* series of wars? It is tempting to hide behind the alternative explanations sometimes given: that the Crusades were really just a European land grab under the guise of religion; that they were part of a search for new resources; or even that they were a confected scheme to keep tens of thousands of otherwise out-of-work men occupied. Christopher Tyerman, the well-known authority on the Crusades from Oxford University in the UK, has rightly said, "Most of what passes in public as knowledge of the Crusades is either misleading or false."[3] And this applies just as much to *Christian* knowledge of the Crusades as it does to *secular* knowledge.

It is difficult to read the primary sources of the Crusades without being confronted by the strong religious motivations and aims expressed—the importance of defending co-religionists, upholding the honour of sacred sites, and bringing glory to Jesus Christ over the advancing "paganism" of Islam. Raymond of Aguilers, whom I quoted earlier, was actually a *chaplain* to the First Crusade. His specific role was to remind others of the spiritual mission inherent in these acts of violence. Speaking of the massacre in 1099, he declared, "This day, I say, marks the justification of all Christianity, the humiliation of paganism, and the renewal of our faith."[4]

This expression, "the renewal of our faith," is important for understanding the Crusades. It chimes with the perspective of the instigator of the First Crusade, Pope Urban II. I have to be careful here, because it is easy to offer simplistic accounts of these things—on both sides of the equation—and it is true there is a huge backstory to the rise of "holy war" in Christianity in the centuries before Urban (more on that later). Yet, it is clear the pope had a *spiritual* mission in mind when he officially called for the First Crusade, four years before that bloody breach of Jerusalem's walls.

Whatever Pope Urban's *political* ambitions—whether to exert a unifying force over a fractious Europe, or to join together western and eastern Christendom—it was his *theology* that undergirded his thinking. Urban longed to recover what he saw as the purity of the church of earliest times in matters of doctrine and morals. He believed the church needed a grand moment of repentance and unity if it was to experience the renewing grace of God. That moment presented itself to him when he received pleas for help from the faraway Byzantine Christian emperor Alexius I Comnenus (AD 1056–1118), whose kingdom lay on Islam's western front (basically what we call Turkey today).

Ever since its origins in the 600s, Islam enjoyed a highly developed and successful practice of "holy war." Muslim armies spread throughout the Middle East, Egypt, and on toward Europe. By the 1050s, Islamic forces had captured much of the old Byzantine Empire, and within a couple of decades they were knocking on the door of Alexius's capital, Constantinople (now Istanbul). Alexius promptly sent envoys to the pope (who lived in France in this period, not Rome) begging for assistance. Surely western Christianity would not stand to see the last remaining outpost of eastern Christianity swept away. Urban saw this as the moment he had been waiting for, when the church could redeem itself by assisting a fellow Christian (Greek Orthodox) kingdom and winning back the holy sites of Jerusalem, which had been occupied by the "unbelievers" since the year 637.

After a four-month preaching tour throughout France promoting his plan, Pope Urban officially called for the First Crusade in a sermon delivered outside the cathedral at Clermont, in central France, on 27 November 1095. The sermon itself is lost to us, but we have eyewitness accounts. We also have a few of

Urban's own letters describing the project. The central theme was clear: with full papal blessing, this war was not sinful but redemptive. Any pilgrim willing to go to the east, fight the Muslims, and reclaim Jerusalem for the Lord would receive pardon for sins and the promise of salvation. "Whoever for devotion alone, not to gain honour or money, goes to Jerusalem to liberate the Church of God," he declared, "can substitute this journey for all penance."[5] Urban writes of how he "imposed on them [the Crusaders] the obligation to undertake such a military enterprise for the remission of all their sins."[6] This is a remarkable new theology within Christianity: salvation is found in fighting the infidel. Apparently, the crowd that first heard Urban's sermon at Clermont responded in unison—perhaps led by the pope's assistants—*Deus lo volt*, "God wills it."

The religious nature of the First Crusade is clear. It is underlined by the key piece of theatre performed by all crusading soldiers who took the vow to win back Jerusalem. They each received a piece of cloth in the shape of a cross and sowed it onto their garments as a sign that they were obeying the words of Christ himself: "If any want to become my followers, let them deny themselves and take up their cross and follow me. For those who want to save their life will lose it, and those who lose their life for my sake, and for the sake of the gospel, will save it" (Mark 8:34–35). Any modern reader of this passage will protest that Jesus obviously meant that his disciples should be willing to *bear persecution* for his cause, all the way to their own death. It plainly does *not* mean that they should *fight* for his cause. But in France in the eleventh century the key public interpretation of this passage—and it *was* a favourite passage—was that able-bodied Christian men should bear the cross of fighting against the enemies of Christ. The very word "Crusade" comes from the Latin *crux* or "cross," referring to this ceremony of taking up the sacred emblem.

There was a time when I would dodge the criticisms relating to the Crusades and other low points in church history by saying that they were not really "done in Christ's name"—they were secular projects unrelated to theology. Obviously, I no longer think that. The more I have learned about the Crusades, the more I understand why so many people see these middle centuries between the decline of Rome in AD 500 and the birth of the modern world in 1500 as the "Dark Ages." They were a period of barbaric gloom, when the church reigned and people suffered. I do not hold that view, as I will explain in chapter 19, but I am certainly sympathetic toward those that do.

◆

Just how thoroughly I have changed my mind on these things will become apparent in the next chapter. This book is not exactly a chronological history of the church, or a history of the Crusades, but I think it is worth offering an overview of these "wars of the cross" lest I give the impression that what happened in the First Crusade was a five-year *aberration* in the otherwise good-natured story of the church. Once we have confronted these troubling middle centuries, we will press REWIND to the first century, examine the life and teaching of Christ briefly, and then press PLAY to see what happened in Christian history to make warfare against unbelievers (and worse) seem plausible to many medieval believers.

The Crusades in a Nutshell

Holy Wars from the 1000s to the 1200s

Lest we get on our high horse and think this is unique to some other place, remember that during the Crusades people committed terrible deeds in the name of Christ.

—PRESIDENT BARACK OBAMA, 2015

I have already talked about the First Crusade in some detail. Its themes and aims can, to some degree, stand as the model for later Crusades. It also represents a pivot point in the history of Christianity.

First Crusade (1096–99)

Before Pope Urban II's preaching campaign of 1095–96, warfare had an ambiguous status in Christian teaching. It was sometimes viewed as a necessary evil in a fallen world. And sometimes—especially in the early centuries—it was wholly rejected as a contradiction of the Gospel demand: "Love your enemies, do good to those who hate you" (Luke 6:27). I will discuss the backstory to Christian "sacred violence" later. For now, it is perhaps worth noting that historians typically speak about *five* different Crusades. This is, of course, a matter of convenience, an easy way to organise *our* thoughts on this subject. People in, say, the year 1203 did not talk about "Heading off to the Fourth Crusade"! Still, it is sometimes helpful to make our thoughts about history *neater* than the history itself.

Several armies of European volunteers, amounting to something like one hundred thousand men, heeded the call of Pope Urban II to assist the Christian Byzantine emperor Alexius I against Muslim aggression. They hoped to protect Constantinople and win back Jerusalem for Christ. The campaign was a stunning success, from the Crusaders' point of view. Even though only ten to fifteen thousand men reached Jerusalem in 1099, they were able to recapture the Holy City in a matter of weeks.

Part of the First Crusade's spiritual force, if I can call it that, came from a charismatic monk known as Peter the Hermit. His dishevelled appearance obscured a keen talent for recruitment and the management of soldiers, as well as a fiery preaching style. It is unclear whether he was the pope's appointee or just a successful independent zealot who supported the cause. He rallied up to thirty thousand men from France and Germany, both peasants and some elites. He personally led them toward the Holy Land, across the Rhineland in central Germany, down the Danube River to the Balkans, across to Constantinople, and then on toward Jerusalem via Syria. "His message was revivalist," explains Oxford's Christopher Tyerman, "peppered with visions and atrocity stories."[1] Peter himself was the source of several atrocities. As he marched through the Rhineland, he and his men slaughtered Jewish communities, partly for their supposed responsibility for the death of Christ centuries earlier and partly for their alleged complicity in recent Muslim attacks on Christian sites in Jerusalem (more perversely, it may also have just been fighting practice).[2] Anti-Semitism had a long history in Christianity, going back at least as far as the fourth century, but it rarely took the form of Peter's full-scale pogroms in 1096. There were massacres and/or forced conversions in Mainz, Cologne, Regensburg, and Prague. The majority of armies organised by Pope Urban apparently did not participate in such violent persecutions of Jews. And, curiously, various other

Christian armies attacked and defeated some of Peter's men for their indiscriminate violence.[3] But Peter remained a major figure in the First Crusade, even preaching a sermon—a pregame pep talk—on the Mount of Olives overlooking Jerusalem on the eve of the sacking of the city.[4]

I have already described the massacre that occurred on 15 July 1099 outside the Al-Aqsa Mosque. Suffice it to say that few were spared. Jews were burned alive in their synagogues. Muslims were cut to pieces or tortured by fire. One Jewish witness to the events speaks of the horror but notices *by way of concession* that at least the Crusaders did not rape the women, as other invaders had done: "We have not heard—thank God, the exalted—that the cursed ones known as Ashkenaz [Europeans] violated or raped women, as others do."[5] Talk about damning with faint praise!

Following the victory of July 1099, the Crusader leaders established several little European "kingdoms" in the region. They are known collectively as Outremer (from the French, "beyond the sea"). Most of the fighters went straight back home to Europe after the hostilities. They had little interest in living in the Holy Land. By the year 1100, just one year later, only about three hundred knights were left in southern Palestine. The principal Crusader ruler, Godfrey of Bouillon, stayed in Jerusalem and gave himself the title "defender of the Holy Sepulchre," a reference to the tomb or sepulchre of Jesus in Jerusalem. His successor, Baldwin I, went a bit further and took the implausible title "king of Jerusalem."[6]

Second Crusade (1145–49)

In 1144 there was a successful Muslim backlash against the Crusader stronghold of Edessa (on the border of Syria and Turkey, six hundred miles north of Jerusalem). The new pope, Eugenius III, declared a fresh campaign to defeat the enemies of Christ in 1145. He renewed all the same ideas and promises of Pope Urban II half a century earlier. German and French contingents responded. They were inspired by one of the foremost clerics of the age, Abbot Bernard of Clairvaux (AD 1090–1153), who helped establish the famous Knights Templar. He was already famous for preaching and writing about love and devotion to God. Now he proclaimed an extraordinary message of violence on behalf of

Christ: "But now, O brave knight, now, O warlike hero, here is a battle you may fight without danger [to the soul]," Bernard wrote in a letter to his followers sometime after 1145, "where it is glory to conquer and gain to die. Take the sign of the cross, and you shall gain pardon for every sin that you confess with a contrite heart."[7]

Despite the rhetoric, the Second Crusade was a spectacular failure, with the European forces variously defeated and destroyed in Asia Minor (Turkey) in 1147 and at Damascus in 1148. The "Kingdom of Jerusalem" was still in Christian hands, just. It would only be a matter of time before resurgent Islamic forces made a move against the Holy City.[8]

Third Crusade (1188–92)

Forty years after defeating the Crusaders at Damascus, Islamic forces turned toward Jerusalem. The jewel of the Crusader project hung in the balance. I say "jewel," but the European presence in the city had always amounted to a rather tinpot kingdom, and by the 1180s the region had fallen into disrepair and political instability. It remained a site of fervent religious pilgrimage for Christians from the west, but it was not somewhere many people wanted to live and raise a family.

This instability stood in sharp contrast to the powerful Islamic kingdom that arose in the twelfth century. One of the keys to earlier Crusader success had been the way Muslim tribes themselves were at war with each other. The Crusaders were able to exploit the disunity and instability. However, by the 1160s a massive, unified Islamic dominion had emerged from Egypt to Syria under the leadership of one of the most famous names in Islamic history, Salah ad-Din, or Saladin (AD 1138–93).

Saladin defeated the Jerusalem Christian forces in the Battle of Hattin in Galilee, a spot I have driven past many times on my way to Jesus's homeland in Galilee. Passing by the twin hills where this bloodbath occurred, I have often thought of Jesus preaching throughout the Galilean hills more than a thousand years earlier: "Blessed are the peacemakers, for they will be called children of God" (Matt 5:9); "Bless those who curse you, pray for those who abuse you" (Luke 6:28). In any case, on 4 July 1187, Saladin with thirty thousand men annihilated the European force at Hattin. It was the beginning of their Independence Day. We have a gruesome eyewitness account, written by Saladin's secretary Imad Ad-Din:

> Islam passed the night face to face with unbelief, monotheism at war with trinitarianism, the way of righteousness looking down upon error, faith opposing polytheism. . . . Humiliation was inflicted on the men of Sunday [that is, the Christians], who had been lions and now were reduced to the level of miserable sheep. I passed by them and saw the limbs of the fallen cast naked on the field of battle, scattered in pieces over the site of the encounter, lacerated and disjointed, with heads cracked open . . . [it continues in this vein for many more lines].[9]

The lurid account is no doubt designed to shock and entertain, but this was a genuinely crushing blow against the principal European force in Palestine. One eyewitness (Ibn al-Athir), passing the battleground a year later, described "the land all covered with bones, which could be seen even from a distance, lying in heaps or scattered around."[10]

With such a comprehensive victory, Saladin was quickly able to force the neighbouring Crusader towns and castles to surrender. Just three months later, on 2 October 1187, he took Jerusalem with a minimum of fuss. He chose to accept the Crusaders' offer to capitulate rather than taking the city by deadly force. With obvious joy and pride, Saladin wrote of his restoration of Islamic worship in the Holy City: "The servant [Saladin's preferred way to refer to himself] has restored the Al-Aqsa mosque to its ancient destination. He has placed imams in it who will there celebrate the true worship. The word of God has been exalted."[11]

The European reaction to all this was swift and furious. When news of the fall of Jerusalem reached the west, the kings and lords of France, Germany, and England *themselves* "took the cross," vowing to win back the city of Christ. Armies of over one hundred thousand fighting men sped off to Palestine, with the king of England himself, Richard I ("The Lionheart"), stepping foot on Acre, a port in northern Palestine, in April 1190.

Despite the massive fanfare and manpower of this Third Crusade, it was inconsequential. The forces of Richard and those of Saladin fought some exciting battles, enhancing the military reputations of both. But neither was able to achieve their ultimate aim. Richard wanted Jerusalem, but Saladin's forces prevented it. Saladin wanted the Europeans gone completely, but he was unable to oust them from various port towns. Saladin eventually made a treaty (2 September 1192), handing the Crusaders control of about sixty miles of the Palestinian coast, from Jaffa in the south to Acre in the north. Importantly, Saladin also agreed to allow Christian pilgrims safe passage from Jaffa to the Holy City, a road that everyone still drives today when travelling from the airport at Tel Aviv (Jaffa) to Jerusalem. King Richard sailed home in October that year, and Saladin died in Damascus with a fever five months later (4 March 1193).[12]

Fourth Crusade (1198–1204)

The uneasy compromise struck by Saladin and Richard would last less than a decade before the Europeans attempted another formal Crusade. This Fourth Crusade was unlike any of the previous three. Not only was it unsuccessful, it hardly even got started.

For Pope Innocent III (pope from AD 1198 to 1216), the stalemate between Richard and Saladin was simply not good enough. In the year 1201 numerous French barons heeded his call to try again to win back the Holy City from the Muslims. None of the kings of Europe wanted to be involved this time. That meant finances quickly became an issue. After setting out to the Holy Land, the crusading armies stopped in Venice. While there, they struck a deal with the city that changed the course of Crusader history. In return for Venice's material support, the Crusaders promised to help the Venetians conquer the port city of Zara (now Croatian Zadar) across the Adriatic Sea. This was something new for the Crusades. It was a reversion to the old "secular" warfare for territory. And, weirdly, Zara was a fellow *Christian* city under the auspices of a strong supporter of the Crusades, King Emeric of Hungary.

The campaign against Zara was successful, and this new Venetian-Crusader alliance then turned its sights on Constantinople. Remember, Constantinople was the capital of the Byzantine Christian Empire, the remnant of the Roman Empire in the east. These are the people who, in the person of Emperor Alexius

I, first begged Pope Urban II to come help defend eastern Christendom against Muslim aggressors. But many Europeans had been disappointed at the low level of support Constantinople had offered to the restoration of the Holy Land after the success of the First Crusade. So, there was some ill-feeling between the Latin Catholics and these Greek Orthodox Byzantines. Some in the Crusader leadership believed Constantinople *owed* them.

A significant number of Fourth Crusaders objected to taking Constantinople, and they abandoned the campaign in disgust. The leaders, however, and the majority of soldiers stayed to fight. On 13 April 1204 they breached the great city's walls and ransacked the place for the next three days. For the following half-century Constantinople was *Latin* and *Catholic*, when it had been the capital of everything Greek and Orthodox since the AD 300s.

The Fourth Crusade travelled no further toward its goals. It morphed into a merely pragmatic war over land and historic grudges. It somehow feels even grubbier than the previous Crusades. Many Crusaders felt the same.[13]

Fifth Crusade (1213–29)

Pope Innocent III continued advocating for Crusades despite the outcome of the Fourth Crusade. He and his appointees reiterated the importance of the original crusading goal (Jerusalem), and they emphasised the *redemptive* nature of "taking up the cross" to fight God's enemies. In 1212, Pope Innocent's propaganda campaign inspired a series of informal peasant adventures. One is commonly called the Children's Crusade. Huge numbers of landless peasants, working poor, women, and even children as young as six set out to the Holy Land in imitation of previous Crusades. Unfortunately, our records do not tell us what happened to them. Rumours spread that many were forced into slavery along the way, and worse. All we really know is that they had zero impact on events in faraway Palestine.

But the popular fervour inspired by Innocent's preaching may, in turn, have encouraged the pope formally to decree in 1213 another attempt to win back the Holy Land. Once again, the head of the western church promised "full forgiveness of sins" for all who, with a contrite heart, participated in the venture. Clergy were instructed to supply "volunteers." Special days of prayer and fasting were declared. Donations were invited. New taxes were imposed. Wide international diplomacy was conducted. And in 1215 a huge church council was convened, with one thousand, three hundred delegates in attendance from all over Catholic Christendom. The Fifth Crusade was official.

Innocent III died the following year, on 16 July 1216, but his successor, Honorius III, continued the momentum. In the summer of 1217 a series of flotillas packed with knights and fighting men launched out from various European ports.

Unlike earlier Crusades, the Fifth Crusade focused its energies in Egypt rather than Palestine. By this time Cairo had become the power base of Islam under the sultans of the Ayyubid kingdom founded by Saladin. The Crusader goal was still Jerusalem, ultimately, but nothing could be achieved without a show of force in Egypt.

It was during the battles in Egypt that Francis of Assisi (AD 1181–1226) made an appearance on the war front. Best known today as the founder of the Franciscan Order, which has nearly twenty thousand priests, Francis was one of the most charismatic and influential clerics of the Middle Ages. He journeyed to Egypt in 1219, warned the Crusaders they were destined to fail, and insisted that God wanted to convert the Muslims through his simple *persuasion*. He somehow convinced Crusader authorities to let him venture into enemy territory to "preach the gospel" of Christ's death and resurrection to Sultan al-Kamil himself. It did not work out as he hoped. More about that in chapter 17.[14]

The long Egyptian campaign resulted in an inauspicious stalemate and eventual Crusader withdrawal. It was punctuated by occasional bloodbaths on both sides, one deadly flooding of the Nile in late 1219, and an epidemic of (possibly) scurvy, which killed up to 20 percent of the Christian forces. After numerous negotiations and some heavy Crusader losses, the Europeans retreated from Egypt. Many returned home. Others headed up to Acre on the north coast of Palestine (still held by Christians) to explore other ways to achieve the Crusader goal.

The final treaty with Sultan al-Kamil was struck not by Crusaders, nor by the pope in Rome, but by a Frederick II (AD 1194–1250), the Holy Roman Emperor of the time. The term "Holy Roman Emperor" was the glorious title given to the secular ruler of the vast European lands from Italy to Germany. In this period the pope ruled church matters, and the emperor dealt with "worldly" matters—sort of. I call him the "secular" ruler, but that is probably anachronistic. In this period most officials were overtly devout, even if they often clashed with the pope. The Holy Roman Emperors were crowned by the popes (hence "Holy"), but they saw themselves, implausibly, as heirs to the fallen western Roman Empire from centuries earlier. More about all that in chapters 13 and 14.

Frederick II's relationship with the pope was strained, to say the least. But he was a keen Crusader. In 1227 he launched his own mini-Crusade (sometimes called the Sixth Crusade) within the larger Fifth Crusade. He was somehow able to exploit the Islamic factions in Syria and Egypt to extract a deal in 1229. According to the treaty, Jerusalem and Bethlehem were restored to the Europeans, as well as a large passageway to and from the coast. The Holy City was to be controlled by Christians, but, in a stroke of genius, the Temple Mount itself, the site of the Al-Aqsa Mosque and the Dome of the Rock, was to remain under local Muslim control. A goal that could not be reached by two centuries of intermittent bloodshed was suddenly achieved through negotiation.

The victory was short-lived. Jerusalem remained under European control for just fifteen years, from 1229 to 1244, when the city was captured by Turkish raiders allied to Egypt. Astonishingly, Jerusalem would remain in Muslim hands from 1244 until the British defeated the Ottoman Turks in World War I at the "Battle of Jerusalem" in 1917.[15]

We get a sense from all this of the intractable nature of the problems of Jerusalem and its surrounds today. The Jews predominated in this land from approximately 1000 BC until AD 135, when the Roman Emperor Hadrian temporarily ousted them from the land. From the mid-to-late second century until the seventh century, Jews and Christians shared the land under Roman rule, until the Muslim conquest in 637. Apart from the brief Crusader occupation in the eleventh century and then again even more briefly in the thirteenth century, Muslims enjoyed unchallenged rule over Jerusalem and Palestine until the arrival of the British (AD 1917–1948) and the establishment of the Jewish state of Israel (from 1948). This is not the book to discuss Middle Eastern politics, but a little background helps us appreciate the basis of various historical claims and the sheer magnitude of the problem.

After 1244 there were numerous other skirmishes in the Holy Land that were part of the crusading tradition. None was successful. Although Europeans held onto Acre on the north coast of Palestine for several decades following the Fifth Crusade, even this was lost in 1291, and crusading to the Holy Land became a thing of the past.

One odd event is worth retelling. About fifty years after the fall of Acre, a German Christian pilgrim was travelling by the Dead Sea in Southern Palestine (something typically permitted by Muslim rulers). He came across two elderly gentleman who turned out to be French Templars captured at Acre in 1291 half a century earlier. These men had been forced into the service of the sultan and become fully absorbed in Middle Eastern life. They married, had children, and settled in the Judean hills. They were completely unaware of events in the west. That was about to change. They and their families were promptly escorted back to France, where they were hailed as heroes. They received papal honours and a generous pension. They lived out their final days in France in relative comfort and peace.[16] They are a fitting symbol of the rather inglorious conclusion to the whole Crusader history. Dreams of conquest and the exaltation of Christ were reduced to the quaint domesticity of two elderly farmers.

There were numerous other military expeditions that went by the name—and theology—of a Crusade, where fighting God's alleged enemies was a guarantee of sins forgiven. Perhaps the most shocking is known as the Albigensian Crusades of 1209–1229 (fought against a very strange heretical group).[17] Numerous other "heresies" were also the target of Crusades, including Czech Hussites in the fifteenth century and Protestants in the sixteenth century. And I have said nothing about the Crusades against Muslim conquerors in Spain (AD 1147) or against "pagans" in the Baltic in the 1200s. These "wars of the cross" were far more frequent than they were successful.

The End of the Crusades

Happily, popes today do not launch Crusades. Indeed, on 12 March 2000 Pope John Paul II publicly apologised for the whole business. "We cannot *not* recognize the betrayals of the Gospel committed by some of our brothers, especially during the second millennium," the pope declared. "We ask forgiveness for the divisions between Christians, for the use of violence that some have resorted to in the service of truth and for the acts of dissidence and of hostility sometimes taken towards followers of other religions."[18]

That the Crusades are a thing of the past is clear. What factors led to their demise is more complicated. In a fascinating conclusion to his major work on the history of the Crusades, Christopher Tyerman insists that no genuine history of the Crusades can offer easy explanations for their conclusion. Nevertheless, there are a few agreed-upon features.

First, a partial explanation is found in the tradition of peace pursued by Francis of Assisi and others. The strange events surrounding Francis and his plea for peace and conversion were far from unique. As Tyerman notes, they reveal that "in the crusader camp and more generally among the intellectual elites there existed a Christian alternative to military crusading." Tyerman labels it "reasoned evangelism." Francis's hopeless mission to Sultan al-Kamil "expressed, however eccentrically, the desire of many to arrange an honourable end to their difficulties."[19] It was not any *secular* critique of church violence that brought down the Crusades. Indeed, many of the early modern humanist scholars in the 1400s, those usually credited with *secularizing* Europe, were enthusiasts for the Crusades, Tyerman points out. The Crusades were undermined from *within*. As I said earlier, the founding traditions of Christianity have a habit of periodically reasserting themselves in the life of the church. This certainly *eventually* happened in the case of the military conception of "taking up the cross."

A second factor in the decline of crusading was the rise of the Protestant Reformation in the sixteenth century, discussed in more detail in chapter 21. The reformers rejected the authority of the popes, and half of Europe followed their lead. Given that a Crusade needs a papal decree and blessing, large-scale Crusades became implausible. Even the mini-Crusades attempted against the Protestant cause in France, Germany, and England came to little.[20] Reformers like the German monk Martin Luther (AD 1483–1546) not only rejected the idea that human activities (whether warfare or charity) could merit God's blessing, they also tended to see warfare as the business of *secular* rulers.[21] In the Protestant view, clergy were not *mediators* between God and humanity. They were *teachers*. Once they had taught their people well, citizens and their rulers could be trusted to lead society in the ways of God. In his 1523 treatise *On Secular Authority*, Luther distinguished between the "kingdom of God" and the "kingdom of the world." He was not exactly advocating a separation of church and state, but his influential view certainly meant that many areas of civic life, including warfare, fell to secular authorities.[22]

Certain other intellectual movements, thirdly, were also important for the demise of Crusader ideology. The theory of "holy war" was only ever "loosely" based on ancient or medieval Christian writings, Tyerman notes, but "its justification looked increasingly awkward in the face of sixteenth-century scriptural theology and attacks founded on the New Testament."[23] He is talking about the new humanism that arose throughout Europe at this time. Humanism was an intellectual movement of the fourteenth to sixteenth centuries that revived an interest in the ancient texts of Greece and Rome and that developed more and more sophisticated literary techniques for properly understanding those classical texts. This sent Christian thinkers (both Catholic and Protestant) back to the original texts—whether classical or biblical—to examine what was really there instead of allowing centuries of tradition to obscure their view.

As humanism broadened to become more secular, local officials throughout Europe began to discount religion as a valid cause for war. This was not a pacifist tendency in secular (or religious) humanists; it was a reasoned judgment that matters of state were best decided on the basis of clear material and political concerns, not spiritual ones. The increasingly secular Europe of the seventeenth to the twentieth centuries was no less militaristic than the church had been in the centuries before. But with religious wars excluded, Europe could return to the older, more traditional, more universal grounds for warfare: power, honour, land, ideology, resources, and politics.

A fourth and final factor in the decline of crusading is often overlooked. The Crusades were mostly a failure. Popular imaginings about this period sometimes picture an almighty medieval church terrorising the defenceless Muslims of Turkey, Syria, Palestine, and Egypt and bringing them into brutal subjugation. In fact, apart from the surprising (and brutal) victory of the First Crusade in July 1099, the Crusaders were the losers. They were able to hold onto Jerusalem (and little else) between 1099 and 1187, and then again for just fifteen years between 1229 and 1244, but beyond that the central goal of the eastern Crusades never materialised. The truth is: Islamic forces *won*. Whatever the spiritual benefits of the Crusades—none, in my view—these Christian holy wars were not very good at winning wars! Jerusalem, the Dome of the Rock, and the great Al-Aqsa Mosque have been safe in Muslim hands—apart from the brief periods mentioned—from the 600s right through to modern times. The only event in a thousand years to interrupt regular prayers in the Al-Aqsa Mosque was COVID-19. As the *New*

York Times reported, "Now, the coronavirus pandemic has done what the intervening centuries [and all those Crusades!] had not: largely emptying the often crowded and chaotic spaces of Islam's third holiest site."[24]

Underscoring the general failure of the Crusades is the fact that, until recently, Muslims have retold the story of the Crusades not as a humiliating blight on Islam but as an example of Muslim strength over the western infidel. "Muslims had not hitherto shown much interest in the crusades, on which they looked back with indifference and complacency," wrote Cambridge University's famed medievalist Jonathan Riley-Smith. "They believed, after all, that they had beaten the crusaders comprehensively."[25]

Reviving the Crusades

How did the Crusades come to gain their reputation for successful bullying? It is generally agreed that a dramatic turn occurred in the 1890s, six hundred years after the last Crusaders were expelled from Palestine. In the late nineteenth century, the Constantinople-based Ottoman Empire faced a revolt from their Balkan territories and strong pressure from Britain and France to grant independence to Romania, Serbia, and Bulgaria. The superpower of the Islamic world was being rapidly reduced. The response from the Ottoman ruler Sultan Abdulhamid II (AD 1842–1918) was to declare that Europe had begun a new Crusade against Muslims. A few years later the first Muslim history of the Crusades was written (AD 1899). The author, Sayyid 'Ali al-Hariri, cited the Sultan in his introduction: "Our most glorious sultan, Abdulhamid II, has rightly remarked that Europe is now carrying out a Crusade against us in the form of a political campaign."[26] As Riley-Smith notes, "This was an entirely new development" in the Islamic consciousness.[27] But the idea caught on. Western *bullying* of the Islamic world—which was far more effective in modern times than it had been in the Middle Ages—was now regarded as a form of crusading. Ironically, this has perpetuated in the modern mind an impression that the original Crusades nine hundred years ago were—like today's politics—a successful suppression of Muslim power. They were nothing of the sort. The Crusades were violent and often misguided, from my perspective, but they were not successful.

The *legacy* of the Crusades is equally minimal. Most major wars in history leave an indelible mark on the winners and the losers. Resources change hands, ideologies are promoted or quashed, and new borders are drawn up. This cannot really be said of the eastern Crusades. With the exception of the island of Cyprus, which fell to Richard I in 1191 and has been mostly western and Christian pretty much ever since, "the western presence that had begun when the first Crusaders burst into Anatolia and northern Syria," writes Christopher Tyerman, "left few traces."[28] There are some wonderful archaeological sites to visit (I recommend the wonderful Crusader fortress at Caesarea, Israel), and there is a bitter historical memory about the Al-Aqsa Mosque slaughter of 15 July 1099, but there is not much else.

◆

At the National Prayer Breakfast in the United States in 2015, then-president Barack Obama caused a media storm by suggesting that, just as terrorist organisation Islamic State had committed modern atrocities, so Christians throughout history had done terrible things in the name of Christ—the Crusades chief among them. "Lest we get on our high horse and think this is unique to some other place, remember that during the Crusades," Obama said, "people committed terrible deeds in the name of Christ." Murderous extremism "is not unique to one group or one religion. There is a tendency in us, a sinful tendency that can pervert and distort our faith." The backlash was immediate and intense, particularly from the Christian conservative side of US politics, which insisted that Christianity was rarely, if ever, as relentlessly violent as Islam.[29]

The contrast claimed by Christian conservatives might be valid for the first few centuries of each religion. No one denies that Christianity was consistently marked by suffering and non-violent resistance from the time of Jesus through to the fourth century. Equally, no one—Muslim or otherwise—disagrees that Islam conducted victorious military campaigns from its very inception, from the time of Muhammad's own battles in Badr and Mecca in the 620s–630s to the Islamic conquests of Syria, Palestine, Egypt, North Africa, and Spain over the next century or more. We will soon see, however, that the fourth and fifth centuries of Christian history were a genuine turning-point. From that time on, President Obama's assessment that "people committed terrible deeds in the name of Christ" is shamefully true.

This is not a book of comparisons, tallying up the violence scores of religions. It is a book about the bullies and saints of Christianity. The fact is: the Crusades have left a mark that cannot be washed away. The most long-lasting impact of the Crusades has little to do with borders, Middle Eastern politics, or the relative size of the world's two largest religions. The real legacy of the Crusades is the way they stand as a symbol of the violent Dark Ages and of the church's all-too-human capacity for dogma, hatred, and violence toward enemies. Admitting this reality should be instinctive for genuine Christians, at least in theory, as I will try to explain in the next two chapters.

The Beautiful Tune

The Christian Ethic of the First Century

Love your enemies, do good to those who hate you, bless those who curse you, pray for those who abuse you.

—JESUS, SERMON ON THE MOUNT

One Friday morning in 2017, I hired a cello, paid for a two-hour lesson, and practiced my heart out for five straight days. The following Tuesday I had to be on stage "performing" the opening bars of Bach's incomparable *Prelude* to Cello Suite No. 1 in G Major. I am sure you know it. But if you don't, please feel free to put this book down immediately and go listen to something truly sublime, before returning to what is, by comparison, ridiculous!

I had never held a cello in my life, so it was a daunting experience, especially as I had to play in a gorgeous Sydney theatre, surrounded by lights and cameras, in front of the toughest audience of all, my friends and colleagues producing the documentary *For the Love of God*. Standing in the wings, watching me, was a well-loved Australian concert cellist, Kenichi ("Keni") Mizushima.

He peppered me with encouragement: "You can do it"; "Maybe just lift your elbow a little"; "That's not bad for five days"; that sort of thing. It was a contrast to the smirks I could see on my friends' faces in the empty auditorium.

I survived the experience. The incriminating evidence can be viewed online—where, more to the point, you can watch the marvellous Keni in action.[1] The goal of the scene, apart from creating some visual fun at my expense, was to illustrate a serious point. Disregarding Christianity on the basis of the poor performance of the church is a bit like dismissing Johann Sebastian Bach after hearing Dickson attempt the Cello Suites. Hearing me play, you could be forgiven for wondering whether Bach really knew how to write a tune. But most of us have a vague idea of how the original is meant to sound. So, we might suspend judgment about the melody itself and place the blame where it belongs, my playing. We know to distinguish between the *composition* and the *performance*. In the documentary we tried to drive this point home by allowing Keni to take over from me, showing us how the piece is meant to sound. It is delightful for the viewers, though excruciating for me. Keni makes me look truly awful.

I have often felt something similar when pondering Jesus Christ and the history of the church. Jesus wrote a beautiful composition. Christians have not performed it consistently well. Sometimes they have been badly out of tune. Occasionally they have played something entirely different. And when people turn to contemplate the original, Christ makes Christians look bad.

In this chapter I want to examine two of Christ's most distinctive *melody lines* (I will try not to push the analogy too much further). I want to explore two aspects of his teaching that have simultaneously resounded through the centuries and exposed Christian hypocrisy in all its awful discord.

Sermon on the Mount

Many of Jesus's sayings have become proverbial in the English-speaking world (friends confirm the same is true for Greek, Italian, German, Dutch, French, Romanian, Spanish, Swedish, Hungarian, and Russian):

"salt of the earth,"
"city on a hill,"

"love thy neighbour,"

"do unto others as you would have them do to you,"

"good Samaritan,"

"prodigal son,"

"blind leading the blind,"

"a cross to bear,"

"pearls before swine,"

"do not let the left hand know what the right is doing,"

"judge not, lest you be judged,"

"a wolf in sheep's clothing,"

"cast the first stone,"

"eat, drink, and be merry,"

"render unto Caesar what is Caesar's,"

"sign of the times,"

"go the extra mile,"

"shout from the rooftops,"

"log in the eye," and many others.

All of these originally came from the lips of Jesus, even if he does not always get the credit. Years ago I met with an Australian politician, in the education department, who told me how much he loved the leadership motto of John F. Kennedy, "To whom much is given, much is required." When I pointed out that Kennedy borrowed the words from Jesus of Nazareth (Luke 12:48), my politician friend was delighted to learn that the adage had an even more venerable origin.

Even the great Albert Einstein, who was no friend of formal religion, acknowledged his deep admiration for Christ's sayings: "I am enthralled by the luminous figure of the Nazarene," he remarked in a 1929 interview. "No one can read the Gospels without feeling the actual presence of Jesus. His personality pulsates in every word. No myth is filled with such life. No one can deny the fact that Jesus existed, nor that his sayings are beautiful."[2] There are, of course, people nowadays who "deny the fact that Jesus existed." It is a theme I have explored in detail elsewhere.[3] But few of us dispute that the words attributed to him—"or whoever wrote his script," as atheist Richard Dawkins quips—are, indeed, "beautiful." Even Professor Dawkins remarks, in a moment of friendly concession, that Christ's famous Sermon on the Mount "is way ahead of its time."[4]

The Sermon on the Mount, found in the New Testament's Gospel of Matthew, chapters 5–7, is perhaps the best-loved collection of Jesus's teachings. A similar, and independent, version of the same material is found in chapter 6 of the Gospel of Luke. Many of the now-proverbial expressions quoted a moment ago come from this mere two-thousand-word collection (whether from Matthew or Luke). Regardless of your faith or doubt, I highly recommend reading this portion of the New Testament, if only out of cultural curiosity. Very few speeches in history can claim to have influenced western culture more than this one. It is Christ's Cello Suites.

The Centrality of Love

Much of the Sermon on the Mount concerns the topics people often associate with Jesus: love, peace, humility, and so on. Consider this striking passage taking us to the heart of his ethical demands:

> Love your enemies, do good to those who hate you, bless those who curse you, pray for those who abuse you. If anyone strikes you on the cheek, offer the other also; and from anyone who takes away your coat do not withhold even your shirt. Give to everyone who begs from you; and if anyone takes away your goods, do not ask for them again. Do to others as you would have them do to you.
>
> If you love those who love you, what credit is that to you? For even sinners love those who love them. If you do good to those who do good to you, what credit is that to you? For even sinners do the same. If you lend to those from whom you hope to receive, what credit is that to you? Even sinners lend to sinners, to receive as much again. But love your enemies, do good, and lend, expecting nothing in return. Your reward will be great, and you will be children of the Most High; for he is kind to the ungrateful and the wicked. Be merciful, just as your Father is merciful. (Luke 6:27–36; see also Matt 5:38–48)

I regard these words as the most sublime ethical teaching ever given. Perhaps this is just confirmation bias on my part. But for several years now I have periodically posted a challenge on social media inviting sceptical friends to find a block of teaching from anywhere in the pre-modern world that matches Christ's emphasis on *love* and *mercy* toward everyone, including enemies. The challenge has not yet been met. Perhaps that is more bias.

I am not suggesting Jesus was the only moral teacher from antiquity to mention *love* within ethics. On the one hand, love certainly does not feature in the best-known moral codes of the *pagan* world (Babylon, Egypt, Greece, Rome). Universal love is not there in the proverbs of Egypt, the Code of Hammurabi, the ethics of Plato and Aristotle, the 147 maxims of Delphi, or the wonderful moral discourses of Seneca, Epictetus, or Plutarch. What we find, instead, in these Egyptian, Mesopotamian, and Greco-Roman moral teachings are things like justice, courage, wisdom, and moderation—the four cardinal virtues of western antiquity. There is hardly a mention of love, mercy, humility, or non-retaliation.[5] Humility, in particular, was largely viewed by the ancients *negatively*—as debasement or humiliation—rather than as a virtue, a topic I have written about at length elsewhere.[6]

Where we do find an emphasis on *love* is in Jesus's *Jewish* background. The Jewish Scriptures, or what Christians call the Old Testament, enjoin things like, "love your neighbour as yourself" (Lev 19:18). In context, this instruction is one of 613 commandments of the Old Testament. But one influential teacher from *just before* Jesus brought love to the fore. Rabbi Hillel (first century BC) characterized his Judaism as "loving peace and pursuing peace, loving people and drawing them near to the Torah [God's *instruction*]."[7] A humorous story—admittedly written several centuries after Hillel's death—is told about a "heathen," a Greek or Roman, who wanted to become a Jewish "proselyte" or convert. He first went to another famous rabbi of the same period, Shammai, but did not have much luck. So he went to Hillel and got a delightful answer:

> On another occasion it happened that a certain heathen came before Shammai and said to him, "Make me a proselyte on condition that you teach me the whole Torah while I stand on one foot." Shammai drove him out with the builder's cubit which was in his hand. When he went before Hillel, he made him a proselyte. He said to him, "What is hateful to you, do not do to your neighbor. That is the whole Torah. The rest is commentary. Go and learn."[8]

You may notice the similarity between Hillel's statement, "What is hateful to you, do not do to your neighbor," and the statement of Jesus quoted earlier: "Do to others as you would have them do to you" (Luke 6:31; Matt 7:12). This is the famous Golden Rule. It is often pointed out—when I throw out my social media challenge—that even if Jesus's emphasis on the *love of enemies* is difficult to find in other philosophies, the Golden Rule is a universal ethical insight. I hope I am not being stubbornly pro-Jesus when I say that I am not so sure. Hillel offers only the *negative* formulation of the Golden Rule. He asks his convert to *abstain from doing the wrong* that he does not wish done to himself. We might call this the *Silver* Rule. Jesus offers a *positive* formulation of the principle. His disciples—a word that simply means *students*—are to do the good they wish to be done to them. That is the *Golden* Rule.

The revered Jewish scholar of the life of Jesus, Professor David Flusser of the Hebrew University in Jerusalem, memorably wrote about Jesus's *intensification* of Jewish traditions. Jesus was a Jew—few things about him are more certain—but in his teaching he was a radical and a reformer. "Those who listened to Jesus' preaching of love," Flusser observes, "might well have been moved by it. Many in those days would have agreed with him. Nonetheless, in the clear purity of his love they must have detected something very special. Jesus did not accept all that was thought and taught in the Judaism of his time. Although not really a Pharisee himself, he was closest to the Pharisees of the school of Hillel, who preached love, but he pointed the way further to unconditional love—even of one's enemies and of sinners. As we shall see, this was no sentimental teaching."[9]

Flusser makes the crucial point that Jesus not only *intensified* an already existing Jewish emphasis on love but that he presented this intensification as an extension of his own life and mission: "It was not simply his total way of life that urged Jesus to express loving devotion to sinners; this inclination was deeply linked with the purpose of his message. From the beginning until his death on the cross, the preaching of Jesus was, in turn, linked to his own way of life."[10] It may sound like we have strayed into theology. But for Flusser, this is simply a historical observation (Flusser was a Jew, not a Christian). *Love of enemies* was central to Christ's teaching, not as an arbitrary moral innovation but as a reflection of the entire course of his life. The narrative of all four New Testament Gospels inches inexorably towards Jesus's self-sacrifice. The arrest, trial, and crucifixion of Jesus get roughly the same space in the Gospels as the Sermon on the Mount (about two thousand words). This is where the "love of enemies" finds its clearest expression. Jesus willingly gave his life on a cross, not as a martyr for a cause but as a Saviour taking the place of sinners.

Readers who are acquainted with Christian preaching will recognise all this as the central Christian doctrine of *salvation*, found in all brands of Christianity—Catholicism, Orthodoxy, and Protestantism. Christ took upon himself the sins of all humanity, so that all who entrust themselves to God might find forgiveness and mercy. In the death of Christ we see God's own "love of enemies." Instead of condemning the undeserving, God has mercy on them through Christ's sacrifice. As the apostle Paul put it twenty-five years after Jesus, "But God proves his love for us in that while we still were sinners Christ died for us" (Rom 5:8).

My intention here is not to lay stress on the "salvation message." I want to make the *historical* point that we can draw a straight line from Jesus's teaching about love to the climax of his story in dying (as he saw it) for the sake of sinners. The love ethic is not arbitrary, in other words. It is not a mere intensification of one command among many. Nor is it merely the altruistic instinct that evolved in the human species (alongside all the other less friendly instincts). It is Christ's special legacy in the world. He was *possessed*, we might say, with a sense of God's love for all, including enemies, and *that* is why he felt he had to die for them. This divine mercy must be the central ethic for his students, he taught, because it is *who God is*. Disciples are to love (others) as they have been loved (by God in Christ). This is the logic behind the climactic words of the passage quoted earlier. Having urged his students to "love your enemies" and "do good to those who hate you," Christ ends with, "for he [God] is kind to the ungrateful and the wicked. Be merciful, just as your Father is merciful" (Luke 6:35–36).

The point was not lost on his first followers. Within a generation of Jesus, one of his disciples, John, put this teaching plainly to the newly established Christians of Asia Minor (or what we call Turkey): "We know love by this, that he laid down his life for us—and we ought to lay down our lives for one another" (1 John 3:16). Again, "Whoever does not love does not know God, for God is love. God's love was revealed among us in this way: God sent his only Son into the world so that we might live through him. In this is love: not that we loved God but that he loved us and sent his Son to be the atoning sacrifice for our sins. Beloved, since God loved us so much, we also ought to love one another" (1 John 4:8–11).

Here is the central moral logic, the original melody, of Christianity. God's love must animate the Christian's love for all. The obvious fact that this *moral logic* did not translate into a consistent *moral history* is the dilemma at the heart of this book.

Imago Dei

There is a second melody line that should be held in mind as we assess the church's performance. It is intimately connected to the first, and it influenced the way many of us, whether believer or sceptic, talk about our fellow human beings.

From the beginning Jews and Christians insisted that every man, woman, and child is created in the *imago Dei*, the "image of God." As a result, everyone possesses equal and inestimable worth. When the US Continental Congress affirmed on 4 July 1776 that "all men are created equal, that they are endowed by their Creator with certain unalienable Rights," the framers were consciously repurposing this biblical teaching for the political setting. In fact, the original draft written by Thomas Jefferson, one of the more *secular* of the American founders, described this as a "sacred truth."[11] The same is true of the *Universal Declaration of Human Rights* ratified by the United Nations in Paris on 10 December 1948. Its opening lines insist upon "the inherent dignity and . . . equal and inalienable rights of all members of the human family"; and "All human beings are born free and equal in dignity and rights. They are endowed with reason and conscience and should act towards one another in a spirit of brotherhood."[12]

Sceptical readers may bristle at the suggestion that such grand declarations of the secular west were influenced by the Bible. The church's record on human rights makes this particularly hard to swallow. But the *historical* connection is difficult to avoid, given the prominence of the language of *humanity's sacred dignity* in Christian discourse over the previous two thousand years. "I don't doubt that Jesus Christ in particular brought about a revolution in thinking of people as equal in the sight of God," observed Samuel Moyn, Professor of Law and History at Yale and the author of a volume on the origin of modern human rights.[13] "Later, this idea of moral equality became an ideal of political equality. And there's no doubt that that's caused the world to change drastically."[14] Moyn is not trying to award trophies to the Christian faith. He is not a professing Christian, and he is actually highly critical of church history. "While Christians did a lot to introduce the idea of the equality of all individuals," he remarks, "they also did a lot to obstruct the progress of that idea."[15]

The notion of the "image of God" lies at the heart of the Christian view of human dignity. The expression itself appears just a handful of times in Scripture, but it inspired centuries of philosophical and ethical reflection. It first appears on the opening page of the Bible, in the account of creation:

Then God said, "Let us make humankind in our image, according to our likeness; and let them have dominion over the fish of the sea, and over the birds of the air, and over the cattle, and over all the wild animals of the earth, and over every creeping thing that creeps upon the earth."

So God created humankind in his image,
in the image of God he created them;
male and female he created them.

God blessed them, and God said to them, "Be fruitful and multiply, and fill the earth and subdue it; and have dominion over the fish of the sea and over the birds of the air and over every living thing that moves upon the earth." (Gen 1:26–28)

As the Bible's *opening* statement about human beings, the expression "image [or likeness] of God" must be *core* to the biblical evaluation of men and women.[16] So what does it mean?

The words "image of God" refer, in part, to humanity's *authority* to have "dominion" over creation.[17] This fits neatly with evidence from the ancient Near East that monarchs were sometimes thought to be a living "image" of divinity.[18] The difference in Genesis is that the concept is *democratized*. It emphatically refers to *all* men and women. The former Chief Rabbi of Britain, the much-celebrated intellectual Lord Professor Rabbi Jonathan Sacks (what a title!), wrote in his 2020 book *Morality*, "That is what makes the first chapter of Genesis revolutionary in its statement that every human being, regardless of class, colour, culture or creed, is in the image and likeness of God himself. In the ancient world it was rulers, kings, emperors and pharaohs who were held to be in the image of God. What Genesis was saying is that we are all royalty. We each have equal dignity in the kingdom of faith under the sovereignty of God."[19]

The expression also describes human beings as God's *children*. The next time we read of the "image of God," its familial meaning is obvious:

> When God created humankind, he made them *in the likeness of God*. Male and female he created them, and he blessed them and named them "Humankind" when they were created.
>
> When Adam had lived one hundred thirty years, he became the father of a son *in his likeness, according to his image*, and named him Seth. (Gen 5:1–3, emphasis added)

The parallelism is unmistakable. Just as Adam had a child in his likeness and image, so every man and woman bears God's image. To be made in the *imago Dei* is to be regarded by the Creator as offspring. The expression does not refer to any particular *capacity* in human beings. It describes our *relation* to the Creator.[20] All human beings, regardless of their ability or usefulness, are equally and inestimably precious because they are considered *children of the Creator* and therefore *our own kin*.

As "theological" as all this may sound, it has immediate social implications. It means that I am to treat other human beings as having infinite dignity as offspring of the Creator. The Bible makes this connection almost immediately. Genesis 9:6 says that no one should murder another person, "for in his own image God made humankind." In the New Testament, Jesus's half-brother, James (yes, Jesus had a half-brother), insists that we should not even "curse those who are made in the likeness of God" (Jas 3:9).[21]

Like so many other Jewish concepts, the *imago Dei* lies behind much of Jesus's own teaching, even though he does not use the expression. He describes God as the "father" of humanity—and this applies even to *disobedient* humanity, according to his famous parable of the Prodigal Son (Luke 15:11–32). Christ's students were to reflect their Father's likeness in their treatment of others, as we saw earlier in the chapter: "Be merciful, just as your Father is merciful" (Luke 6:36). In his Sermon on the Mount the same thought is close at hand in his remarkable teaching that our treatment of neighbours is *equal to* (or at least parallel to) our worship of God:

> So when you are offering your gift at the altar [a common Jewish act of worship in the temple], if you remember that your brother or sister has something against you [i.e., you have wronged them], leave your gift there before the altar and go; first be reconciled to your brother or sister, and then come and offer your gift. (Matt 5:23–24)

The rationale for an instruction like this is that we cannot claim to honour the Creator if we are dishonouring one of his other offspring, our siblings. A similar thought is present in two striking sentences in a later New Testament letter from the apostle John: "for those who do not love a brother and sister whom they have seen, cannot love God whom they have not seen. . . . Those who love God must love their brothers and sisters also" (1 John 4:20–21).

Throughout this book we will encounter numerous later Christians explicitly citing this concept of the *imago Dei* as the rationale for caring for the poor, burying the dead, starting hospitals, and even freeing slaves. And we will also see the church doing much "to obstruct the progress of that idea," as Samuel Moyn put it.

A New View of Humanity

There is value in comparing this Judeo-Christian view of the human being with the "pagan" or Greco-Roman view at the time of Christianity's birth. The comparison highlights something that is often difficult to see today. In the contemporary world there is no practical difference between the *Christian* estimation of humanity and the *secular humanist* estimation—the two ideas are historically related. It is easy for us to assume that such a high view of the person, regardless of their talents or contributions, is the *default* view through every age. That simply is not the case.

Consider the following letter, dated 17 June 1 BC. A Roman soldier named Hilarion is stationed in the Egyptian port city of Alexandria. He writes home to his wife Alis, promising to send her some of his pay soon, asking her to look after their child, and, poignantly, reassuring her that he has not forgotten her. Some aspects of family life have not changed. In passing, though, Hilarion tells Alis that, if she happens to be pregnant, she should discard the baby when it comes:

> Hilarion to his sister Alis, many greetings, also to my lady Berous and Apollonarion. Know that I am still in Alexandria; and do not worry if they [the army] wholly set out, I am staying in Alexandria. I ask you and entreat you, take care of the child, and if I receive my pay soon, I will send it up to you. Above all, if you bear a child and it is male, let it be; if it is female, cast it out. You have told Aphrodisias, "Do not forget me." But how can I forget you? Thus I'm asking you not to worry. The 29th year of Caesar, Pauni 23 [17 June 1 BC].[22]

Talk of casting out a child at birth—in a throw-away line in an otherwise normal family letter—is shocking to modern readers. I have read this letter to many audiences over the years, and the feeling in the room is palpable. But in ancient times, this was neither shocking nor illegal. It was not even immoral. Disposing of newborns was regarded as a method of family planning. Throughout the Greek and Roman world, excess children were frequently discarded, especially if the parents felt they could not afford another mouth, or if the child was deformed or disabled, or, as in the above case, if it was a girl.[23]

Sometimes removing a child involved direct "infanticide," killing and disposing of the newborn. More commonly, it involved a practice known euphemistically as *expositio* or "exposure." The greatest of ancient Greek philosophers, Aristotle (384–322 BC), had advised, "As to exposing or rearing the children born, let there be a law that no deformed child shall be reared."[24] The child was simply left outside, whether on a street corner, in the marketplace, or even at the rubbish dump. The child might, of course, be picked up by other parents who would raise it as their own. Sadly, it could also be taken by professional traffickers, killed by an animal, or simply fall victim to the elements.

Hilarion would be arrested on the spot today. But in his context he was not a moral "monster." He held the widespread *rational* view that a child's value depended not on some intrinsic, ineffable worth but on its capacities or usefulness to the family. The outrage we feel toward the practice of exposing infants just illustrates the very different assumptions we work with today. In the ancient Greek and Roman world there was little ethical reflection on this practice. Jews of the time spoke out against it, of course. In fact, we know of one high-profile Jewish critic of *expositio*, a teacher named Philo, who happened to be living in Alexandria at exactly the time Hilarion was stationed there.[25] Christians were likewise vocal about it, preaching and writing against the practice, and even collecting abandoned infants and caring for them as their own. (Hundreds of thousands of people are alive today—descendants of rescued foundlings—as a result of this ancient Christian practice.[26] More about all this in chapters 7 and 10.)

In public lectures on these themes I have occasionally asked audiences to imagine being the friend of Hilarion in 1 BC and trying to convince him why it is *wrong* to "cast out" a newborn simply because the parents do not want it. We might instinctively start talking about *equality* and *inalienable rights*. But Hilarion would probably look at us, bemused. In cool-headed fashion, assuming he had read some Greek philosophy, he might turn it back on us: On what basis can you claim that a barely self-aware newborn is *equal* to other humans? Isn't that just an arbitrary doctrine? Would you say that all *animals* are equal? Does all *art* have the same worth? Are all *tools* equally valuable? Hilarion might press us further: For what other dimension of life would we argue that items with obviously different capacities and utility all share the same worth? Nature herself has made some people smarter, stronger, better, and, therefore, more useful. The more usefulness, the greater the value. The logic is inescapable. We should prefer the strong and beneficial, and let Nature take care of the rest.[27]

Ancient Jews and Christians had no difficulty explaining why every man, woman, and child was inherently and equally valuable. Human beings, they said, bear the *image of God*. The Creator regards them as his offspring. The church did not consistently live out this conviction, as we will see, but the doctrine did lead to some remarkable historical developments, including—after three hundred years of trying to persuade Rome—a complete ban on killing infants in a law of AD 374.[28]

Philosopher and atheist Raimond Gaita helpfully highlights the unusual spot secular westerners find themselves in today. "If we are not religious, we will often search for one of the inadequate expressions which are available to us to say what we hope will be a secular equivalent of it." He gives examples:

"human beings are inestimably precious," they possess "inalienable dignity," and so on. But "these are ways of trying to say what we feel a need to say when we are estranged from the conceptual resources we need to say it. . . . Not one of them has the simple power of the religious way of speaking."[29] Gaita does not accept the religious way of thinking—that human beings are made in the image of God. He simply acknowledges that secular philosophy has thus far struggled to match its simplicity and force. For two thousand years western cultures have grown used to thinking of human beings as bearing God's image and therefore as possessing *inestimable* and *equal* worth. Now that such "God talk" makes many of us awkward, we struggle to find coherent ways to express the same lofty view of humanity.

It will be important to hold in mind these twin aspects of Christianity's moral logic throughout this book. For one thing, it is clear that "love of enemies" and "the image of God" drove much of what was unique in the history of Christianity, as even the most begrudging historians and philosophers will acknowledge. The church is at its best, in history and today, when it performs these melody lines contained in its founding documents. Then again, reminding ourselves of the moral logic of Christ and the New Testament makes the story I am going to tell all the more tragic. The bigotry, selfishness, and violence of the church, whether in the Crusades, Inquisitions, wealth accumulation, or the horrors of child abuse, are not only departures from broad humanitarian principles. They are a betrayal of the specific mandate Christ gave his movement.

It is true that secular standards today often make Christians look bad. Jesus Christ makes them look especially bad. And, curiously, he demanded that his followers be the first to admit this.

Log in the Eye of the Church

Another Thing Jesus Said in the First Century

Why do you see the speck in your neighbor's eye, but do not notice the log in your own eye?

—JESUS, SERMON ON THE MOUNT

When the documentary I mentioned in chapter 1 first came out in 2018, I attended numerous cinema screenings to promote the film. My co-hosts and I would introduce the movie, let people watch the ninety-minute cinema cut, and then field audience questions. Almost without fail, each evening someone would raise their hand and ask: *Aren't you letting the team down a bit by airing the church's dirty laundry in public?* That's not exactly how the question was worded, but it was certainly the sentiment. Some Christians in our audiences were disappointed that we had featured so many examples of the church's failures. Christ had said his followers would be marked by "love," and here *we* were suggesting the church was frequently characterised by hatred, bigotry, and violence. Whether at these tos-and-fros at public screenings or on social media afterwards, people would accuse us of trying too hard to appeal to the sceptical "woke" crowd by bad-mouthing God's own people.

My answer to this challenge was always the same. It is true that Jesus called for *love* above all things, but it is also true that the first lesson he gave to his disciples was that they should be willing to admit their own *failure* to love, their own moral bankruptcy.

"Blessed Are the Poor in Spirit"

Jesus's teaching about love in the Sermon on the Mount is well known. Less well known is his somewhat pessimistic view of human nature. Consider just two statements:

> If you then, who are evil, know how to give good gifts to your children, how much more will your Father in heaven give good things to those who ask him! (Matt 7:11)

> On that day many will say to me, "Lord, Lord, did we not prophesy in your name, and cast out demons in your name, and do many deeds of power in your name?" Then I will declare to them, "I never knew you; go away from me, you evildoers." (Matt 7:22–23)

The word "evil" is jarring to modern ears. We usually reserve it for the Hitlers of the world. But it is pretty common in Jesus's teaching, where it basically means *immoral* or *wicked*. And he uses it of *everyone*, whether his opponents or his closest followers. It is one of the great differences between Jesus's perspective and ours: he spoke of human beings as characteristically flawed; we talk like we are characteristically good. This basic outlook can be seen in the opening two lines of the Sermon on the Mount:

> When Jesus saw the crowds, he went up the mountain [hence: Sermon on the *Mount*]; and after he sat down, his disciples came to him. Then he began to speak, and taught them, saying:
> "Blessed are the poor in spirit, for theirs is the kingdom of heaven.

"Blessed are those who mourn, for they will be comforted." (Matt 5:1–4)

The expressions "poor in spirit" and "those who mourn" both refer to recognising the lamentable moral condition of humanity, including within Christ's own "disciples" or students. Well-known biblical scholar Don Carson explains, "Poverty of spirit is the personal acknowledgement of spiritual bankruptcy. It is a conscious confession of unworth before God. As such, it is the deepest form of repentance."[1] It is remarkable that the richest ethical discourse in the western tradition (more of my bias again) begins with a call to admit our spiritual and moral bankruptcy.

I had an interesting conversation about all this with a thoughtful journalist from Australia's national broadcaster. He told me he liked *some* of the ethical teachings of Jesus—the bits about love and peace—but he was deeply wary of any talk of human guilt and divine mercy. He worried this could crush the human spirit, especially in children (he and his wife were about to have their first child). They would grow up, he feared, in a cloud of guilt that obscured their abilities and intrinsic value. He preferred the notion that we all have within us everything we need to live honourable lives. I explained that I think the shoe is on the other foot. Imagine growing up in a family where the expectation is that you are good through and through. You will make the "first 15" (a rugby union reference), always stay out of trouble, get straight As at school, and quickly repair any personal failures. I suggested that *this* was the recipe for crushing a child's spirit. Such a performance-based mentality, where worth is tied to achievement, cannot prepare us for the inevitable failures of life. Much better, it seems to me, is to raise our children in the full knowledge of their gifts *and* their flaws and in the knowledge that they are loved regardless of performance.

Christ did not teach that we are hopeless failures destined only to be immoral, but he did insist that recognising our flawed humanity is the first step toward seeing his "kingdom." Adopting this outlook is like growing up in a family that simultaneously has high hopes for you—*who could deny Christ's hopes for Christians!?*—but also trains you from the outset to acknowledge fault and to trust that your membership in the family depends on love, not achievement.

None of this "theology" may be true. Some readers will think it is mumbo jumbo. That is fine. At this point I am only concerned to explain why admitting moral poverty *amongst Christians* is such an important feature of Christ's own teaching. Back in 2012, British intellectual and atheist Francis Spufford announced that he had *inadvertently* (that's almost how he describes it) "found Christianity." His book, titled *Unapologetic: Why, Despite Everything, Christianity Can Still Make Surprising Emotional Sense*, caused a stir at the time. Among the many interesting things he writes concerning his journey from anti-Christian snob to bumbling, half-believing Anglican is his description of coming to realise his own "tendency to lurch and stumble and screw up by accident" and his "active inclination to break stuff, 'stuff' here including moods, promises, relationships we care about, and our own well-being and other people's."[2] To his great surprise, confronting all this was far from crushing. It was liberating:

> I've found that admitting there's some black in the colour-chart of my psyche doesn't invite the blot of dark to swell, or give a partial truth more gloomy power over me than it should have, but the opposite. Admitting there's some black in the mixture makes it matter less. It makes it easier to pay attention to the mixedness of the rest. It helps you stop wasting your time on denial, and therefore helps you stop ricocheting between unrealistic self-praise and unrealistic self-blame. It helps you be kind to yourself.[3]

According to Christ, only when his followers face their "poverty of spirit," what Spufford calls the "black in the colour-chart," will they become conscious also of the "blessedness" of "inheriting the kingdom of God." It is one of the many paradoxes of Jesus's teaching. It is frequently misunderstood by Christians as well as sceptics.

No less paradoxical is the next insight of Christ's opening words in the Sermon on the Mount. Only those with a healthy sense of the human propensity to muck things up are in a position fairly to lament the immorality out there in the world. That is the meaning of the line: "Blessed are those who *mourn*, for they will be comforted." The language Jesus employs here recalls a specific passage in his Jewish Bible, or Old Testament. The book of Isaiah, written centuries earlier and known to everyone in Jesus's first audience, contains a passage that likewise speaks of "comforting" those who "mourn" (Isa 61:1–9). In context, however, it is not about the regular sadness that affects our lives; it is about lamenting the injustices we see around us, the "robbery and wrongdoing" of the world, as Isaiah 61:8 puts it, and then wishing the Almighty would do something about it. This is no doubt what Jesus means here by "mourning": the grief one feels when looking at the evil of the world. In other words, the demeanour Christ expected of his followers as they look at the immorality in others is one of sorrow. Sorrow. Not the judgmentalism for which the church is sometimes notorious. But a humble melancholy that *first* sees its own moral poverty and *only then* grieves the "robbery and wrongdoing" of others.

The Carpenter's Log and Speck

These two opening lines of Christ's teaching—one about admitting personal evil, the other about lamenting external evil—chime with one of his best-known sayings, from near the end of the Sermon on the Mount:

> Do not judge, so that you may not be judged. For with the judgment you make you will be judged, and the measure you give will be the measure you get. Why do you see the speck in your neighbor's eye, but do not notice the log in your own eye? Or how can you say to your neighbor, "Let me take the speck out of your eye," while the log is in your own eye? You hypocrite, first take the log out of your own eye, and then you will see clearly to take the speck out of your neighbor's eye. (Matt 7:1–5; see also Luke 6:37–42)

The command "Do not judge" does not add another item of ethical behaviour. It begins to draw Christ's moral teaching to a close by describing *the posture* of those who join his movement. Jesus has certainly reached the ethical heights in the preceding paragraphs: peacemaking, humility, truth-telling, sexual purity, love, non-violence, charity, simplicity in prayer, and shunning greed all make an appearance. The temptation for those who have accepted such sublime teachings is to look down on those who have not! Jesus, however, insists that his students must resist this urge. "Judge not" is the only proper attitude of those who accept his teaching. "The taboo about being 'judgemental,'" Spufford wryly remarks, "wasn't formed in our culture in reaction to religion; it isn't part of the great journey into the secular light." Rather, it is "a little piece of inherited Christianity, a specifically Christian prohibition which has turned proverbial and floated free of its context, origins all forgotten."[4]

Exposing judgmentalism in religious folks is a deeply Christian tradition, in theory.

Christ underlines the point with one of his most famous metaphors: the log in the eye. Here we catch a glimpse of his upbringing. A passing line in one of the Gospels tells us that his father, Joseph, was a carpenter (Mark 6:3). The word is *tektōn*, which refers to something closer to a "builder," that is, someone who works with stone and metal as well as wood.[5] Still, Jesus will have spent much of his teenage years assisting his father in making and mending timber products, such as doors, fences, and farming equipment. And one thing carpenters know well is the painful experience of getting a bit of sawdust in the eye. How many times must Jesus have gotten a "speck" in his eye and asked his father to help him get it out, or the other way around! At some point he must have realised what an excellent picture this is of our moral outlook.

One thing you cannot do when you have something in your eye, even a tiny particle, is see clearly. Jesus speaks here of getting an entire "log" in the eye. He was fond of rhetorical hyperbole—this one is almost humorous. The point about the log in the eye is that his students are meant to be more conscious of their own wrongdoing (a "log") than the wrongdoing of others (a "speck"). Again, atheist-turned-Anglican Francis Spufford puts it with panache:

> The religion certainly can slip into being a club or a cosy affinity group or a wall against the world. But it isn't supposed to be. What it's supposed to be is a league of the guilty. Not all guilty of the same things, or in the same way, or to the same degree, but enough for us to recognize each other.[6]

The basic posture of a Christian in the world should be one of humble melancholy, accepting their card-carrying membership in the "league of the guilty." We first see the evil in ourselves and only then lament the evil in the world.

This is my answer to the Christian who complains that I am "letting the team down" by airing the church's dirty laundry in public. It was the Master of the church himself who said I should worry more about my own sins than the sins of others. The same Lord who called his followers to pursue love, peacemaking, purity, and all the rest also insisted, in the same sermon, that Christians should be quick to admit personal fault and slow to condemn the faults of others.

It is no exaggeration to say that this aspect of Christ's teaching is one of the reasons I do not lose hope in Christianity, even when my faith in the "holy church" sometimes wobbles in the face of the church's record. If Christ had said that his followers would only ever be examples of love and integrity—the "shiny people" in a dark world—I am not sure how I would maintain confidence in the wisdom of the Founder. I doubt I could bear the weight of the accumulated counterevidence of the centuries.

All of this is why I feel free, despite the occasional grumpy question from Christians, to write a book about the *bullies* and *saints* of Christian history. There will be plenty of time to explore the positive contributions of Christianity—the myriad ways Christians put love into practice—but I cannot see how any of that material would make sense to thoughtful readers without facing the systemic failures of Christians to live Christianly. Think of this book as an exercise in noticing the "log" in the eye of the church.

Good Losers

Persecution of the Church from AD 64 to 312

They were covered with wild beasts' skins and torn to death by dogs.

—TACITUS, AD 115

In the world today we have a confronting picture of the two faces, the Jekyll and Hyde, of church history. There is the humble servant cheerfully bearing pain rather than inflicting it, and there is the morality policeman eager to bully the culture for the cause of "righteousness." This second figure is often associated with US evangelicals, but Australian conservatives are often described in similar terms, and this is meant to be one of the least Christianized countries in the west. Right now, actually, my homeland is in the middle of a fracas over "religious freedom," an expression that is often interpreted by the general public as the freedom to discriminate against minorities. One major newspaper recently led with the headline, "Religious Discrimination Bill Gives Australians 'Right to Be a Bigot.'"[1] The article is not exactly a model of fair reporting—and I would argue that wide religious freedom is necessary for a healthy secular democracy—but it does highlight the way many in the media think about the "bully" church.

Persecution Today

But things are different elsewhere. In China, the Middle East, and parts of Africa right now, Christians have no legislative or social clout, and they frequently face grave opposition from the dominant culture. Christians, it turns out, are among the most persecuted minorities in the world today, as a British government report recently revealed.[2] The statements of church leaders in these contexts are confronting. They do not whinge, plot, or even plead for help. They exhibit a strange resolve to hold the truth of Christianity while pursuing the path of love and non-retaliation toward their oppressors. They seem like good losers.

In December 2018, for example, one hundred Christians from the underground house church movement in Chengdu, China, were arrested and detained. Most were released shortly afterwards. The leader of the group, Wang Yi, was secretly tried at the Chengdu Intermediate People's Court and sentenced to nine years detention, the longest sentence given to a house church pastor in a decade (I have personally met others detained for just a year or two). In a letter smuggled out to the west shortly after his detainment, Pastor Yi describes his philosophy. "The gospel demands that disobedience of faith must be non-violent," he writes. "The mystery of the gospel lies in actively suffering, even being willing to endure unrighteous punishment, as a substitute for physical resistance. Peaceful disobedience is the result of love and forgiveness. The cross means being willing to suffer when one does not have to suffer. For Christ had limitless ability to fight back, yet he endured all of the humility and hurt. The way that Christ resisted the world that resisted him was by extending an olive branch of peace on the cross to the world that crucified him."[3]

For readers who are not plugged into the global Christian scene, a letter like this, and the events that prompted it, may seem remarkable, perhaps even implausible. Certainly, where I live, news of a "persecuted church" seems like an oxymoron. The reputation of the church in the west is such that it is difficult for many to imagine that a large proportion of Christians today live in precarious circumstances, let alone that the leaders of those churches advocate "compassion" toward interrogators and insist on "extending an olive branch of peace" to persecutors. As a result, the persecution of Christians is rarely reported in the mainstream media, even though it remains one of the most widespread human rights abuses in the world today.

How can these two pictures of the one movement coexist? Or to ask the question in a more linear historical manner: How could a movement that acted like Pastor Yi for its first three hundred years end up looking and sounding like the morality police? The next several chapters will answer that question.

Massacred in the "Circus" of Rome

The church under Roman rule, from Emperor Tiberius (AD 14–37) to Emperor Constantine (AD 306–337), specialised in what you might call "losing well." Christians accepted that the *state* had the right to use force against evildoers, but it held that they themselves had no such right. Christians were almost entirely pacifist in outlook (I say *almost* because there is mixed evidence about how the church responded to soldiers who wanted to be Christians, as I will explain in chapter 12). The very structure of their faith—grounded in Christ's sacrifice—forbade revenge and demanded compassion, even toward enemies. In those days the church was more likely to be mocked for its devotion to philanthropy and martyrdom—literally mocked for these things—than for bigotry or violence. In those days you could never have imagined that Christians would one day appear as the bullies.

The New Testament book of Acts gives us front-row seats to the expansion of troubles for Christianity in the first three decades.[4] Less well known is what happened immediately after that period. The expansion of the church from AD 60 to 300 has been described to me by well-known classical historians as almost "miraculous." I myself wrote a long doctoral thesis on Christian mission in the early Roman Empire, and I am frankly at a loss to explain the success of Christianity in the face of Roman opposition.[5] I can tell you what Christians *did* and *where* they went, but I cannot account for the end result. The Ancient History Department at Macquarie University where I did my studies was not interested in *theological* speculations about the matter (concerning *God's* involvement in the movement). Historically speaking, it is all pretty mysterious.

In any case, we have clear evidence that churches were thriving in Rome itself within fifteen years of the death of Jesus in Jerusalem. By the late AD 40s, Christian debates in the city had even come to the notice of the Emperor Claudius, who expelled some of the ringleaders of the "disturbance."[6] Less than twenty years later, expulsion morphed into genuine persecution. This is a theme that has admittedly been exaggerated by Christians over the years, as they have retold stories of endless persecutions and unconquerable faith. Recent writers have tried to correct the myth by minimising the evidence almost beyond recognition. One notable example is the English New Testament scholar Candida Moss in her 2013 *The Myth of Persecution: How Early Christians Invented a Story of Martyrdom*.[7] The title is a little clickbait-y. Dr. Moss knows as well as anyone that while Christians were not *routinely* persecuted by the Romans, we have good evidence that they were formally repressed on several occasions in this early period, and the experience left an indelible mark on the Christian consciousness.[8]

In AD 64 Emperor Nero convicted "vast numbers" of Christians in Rome. The Roman statesman and chronicler Cornelius Tacitus left us a brief but brutal account. "They were covered with wild beasts' skins and torn to death by dogs," he calmly reports, and "they were fastened on crosses, and, when daylight failed were burned to serve as lamps by night." And just when you thought it couldn't get worse: "Nero had offered his Gardens for the spectacle, and gave an exhibition in his Circus [a games arena], mixing with the crowd in the habit of a charioteer."[9] Tacitus himself was no fan of Christianity. He thought of it as a "pernicious superstition" and a "disease," which all started when "Christus, the founder of the name, had undergone the death penalty in the reign of Tiberius, by sentence of the procurator Pontius Pilatus." Still, Tacitus could admit that some Romans began to feel a bit sorry for the Christians.

Nero's actions were the first state-sponsored violent suppression of Christians, just thirty years after Jesus. This is about the time when many of the New Testament texts, Gospels and letters, were written.[10] One text, penned by the apostle Paul to the fledgling churches of Rome just a few years before Nero's violence against them, urges believers to prepare for opposition by recalling the ethos of Jesus: "Do not repay anyone evil for evil, but take thought for what is noble in the sight of all. If it is possible, so far as it depends on you, live peaceably with all. Beloved, never avenge yourselves, but leave room for the wrath of God. . . . Do not be overcome by evil, but overcome evil with good" (Rom 12:17–21). The first Christians believed that God would one day deal with the oppressors, but they themselves were forbidden to take matters into their own hands.

A few years ago I stood in what remains of Nero's Circus. The site now lies within the walls of the Vatican (there's something poetic about that). I thought about these ancient Christians to whom Paul had written his letter. I wondered how they processed the words "overcome evil with good" when Nero started to crucify and burn them for a spectacle.[11]

Anonymous Pamphlets in Bithynia

We have excellent evidence from fifty years later of widening state action against Christians in the important Roman province of Bithynia-Pontus, in the north of modern Turkey. By the year 112 it had become the norm in this region to pursue, interrogate, and even execute Christians. We only know this because the provincial governor, the thirty-nine-year-old Pliny the Younger, wrote to Emperor Trajan seeking his advice on how to proceed. We have that letter, along with more than one hundred of his other letters.[12] Pliny was almost feeling bad that he had to round up so many locals. He begins the letter, "It is my custom to refer all my difficulties to you, Sir, for no one is better able to resolve my doubts and to inform my ignorance." It turns out that Pliny had never tried Christians before; he seems to have inherited the policy on taking up his position. "I do not know the nature or the extent of the punishments usually meted out to them," he writes, "nor the grounds for starting an investigation and how far it should be pressed."[13]

The problem has become significant, Pliny tells us, because locals are now informing on Christians by circulating anonymous pamphlets naming names: Demetrius the leatherworker is a Christian, Junia the seamstress was seen at church, and so on. Why would locals denounce their neighbours in this way? "From several hints in the letter," notes Robert Wilken of the University of Virginia, "it is possible to infer that the charge was brought by local merchants, perhaps butchers and others engaged in the slaughter and sale of sacrificial meat."[14] When people became Christians, they stopped sacrificing animals in the pagan temples, and sometimes they even stopped buying the meat that was taken from those temple sacrifices to the marketplace to be on-sold (the meat was now deemed by Christians and Jews to be "tainted"[15]). Conversion to Christianity threatened the local business.[16] And the numbers were growing. Pliny frets that "a great many individuals of every age and class, both men and women, are being brought to trial." As a good Roman, he has no interest in overstepping the boundaries of justice. He does not want to kill people willy-nilly. He outlines for the emperor his interim policy:

> For the moment this is the line I have taken with all persons brought before me on the charge of being Christians. I have asked them in person if they are Christians, and if they admit it, I repeat the question a second and third time, with a warning of the punishment awaiting them. If they persist, I order them to be led away for execution; for, whatever the nature of their admission, I am convinced that their stubbornness and unshakeable obstinacy ought not to go unpunished.[17]

He adds that he has worked out a way to distinguish between real Christians and false ones. "I considered that I should dismiss any who denied that they were or ever had been Christians when they had repeated after me a formula of invocation to the gods and had made offerings of wine and incense to your statue, and furthermore had reviled the name of Christ, none of which things, I understand, any genuine Christian can be induced to do."[18] He found this "unshakable obstinacy" unreasonable and insolent.

Pliny is at a loss to know exactly what crime Christians have committed. He even attempted "to extract the truth by torture from two slave-women, whom they call deaconesses."[19] This is an interesting piece of early evidence that leaders in the church of this period could be slaves and women. We do not know what exactly these slave women did in their local churches, but it is clear Pliny thought they were representative leaders of the movement. Yet, he found "nothing but a degenerate sort of cult carried to extravagant lengths."[20]

From other interviews, Pliny has discerned only three things about Christians: they sing to Christ, take moral vows, and eat together. Pliny provides one of our earliest descriptions of a church service:

They also declared that the sum total of their guilty or error amounted to no more than this: they had met regularly before dawn on a fixed day to chant verses alternately among themselves in honour of Christ as if to a god, and also to bind themselves by oath, not for any criminal purpose, but to abstain from theft, robbery and adultery, to commit no breach of trust and not to deny a deposit when called upon to restore it. After this ceremony it had been their custom to disperse and reassemble later to take food of an ordinary, harmless kind.[21]

We also possess Emperor Trajan's reply to Pliny.[22] It is a brief but clear approval of Pliny's policy: "You have followed the right course of procedure, my dear Pliny," he writes. "These people must not be hunted out; if they are brought before you and the charge against them is proved, they must be punished." This means executed or, in the case of people with full Roman citizenship, sent to Rome for trial before the emperor.

Pliny died in office the following year (AD 113). From a lovely memorial inscription prepared by friends back in Rome we know that he left money in his will to establish public baths in his honour, money to support one hundred of his former slaves, and an annual dinner in his name.[23] He was the quintessential "Roman gentleman,"[24] even if Christians throughout this region must have feared him as a murderer.

We have some Christian letters from this time and place. Perhaps the most significant comes from outside the New Testament collection, composed right about the time of Pliny. Ignatius was the bishop of the churches of Antioch in Syria. Sometime during the reign of Emperor Trajan (AD 98–117), he was arrested and ordered to stand trial in Rome—an indication that persecution had reached quite far east in the early second century. Accompanied by ten soldiers, Ignatius was taken on the several-month overland journey through Turkey then on to Greece before arriving in the capital, where he was executed, most likely fed to wildcats in the Colosseum.[25] Throughout his journey he was permitted to write to Christians in various towns along the way. Seven of his letters survive. They are filled with the call to "love," a word that appears no fewer than sixty-four times in the collection.[26] In his letter to Christians in Ephesus, he pleaded:

Pray continually for the rest of humankind as well, that they may find God, for there is in them hope of repentance. Therefore allow them to be instructed by you, at least by your deeds. In response to their anger, be gentle; in response to their boasts, be humble; in response to their slander, offer prayers; in response to their errors, be steadfast in the faith; in response to their cruelty, be civilised; do not be eager to imitate them. Let us show by our forbearance that we are their brothers and sisters, and let us be eager to be imitators of the Lord.[27]

Almost a hundred years after Jesus had proclaimed "love your enemies, do good to those who hate you," it is clear that this was still the melody Christians were expected to sing.

Losing Well, and Other Victories

We know of various other Roman persecutions of Christians in the second and third centuries, and the pattern is pretty much the same. Around the year 215, for example, the proconsul (a governor) of the Roman province of Carthage in North Africa, named Scapula, launched a local campaign to suppress the church. We know this because we have a public letter written to Scapula by the leading Christian intellectual of the province, the brilliant former lawyer and rhetorician Quintus Septimius Florens Tertullian (AD 160–225). Tertullian's four-page letter refers in passing to the torture and execution of ordinary believers. He reminds the governor that Christians number in the thousands in the province. He threatens a mass turnout before his court. Christians had done it before, in one of the first non-violent peaceful protests in recorded history, and they were willing to do it again.[28] What would the governor do then? Torture and kill them all? "What will you make of so many thousands, of such a multitude of men and women, persons of every sex and every age and every rank, when they present themselves before you?" he asks. "How many fires, how many swords will be required? What will be the anguish of Carthage itself, which you will have to decimate?"[29]

Tertullian's boldness is striking. Ancient Christians were not timid. They did not adopt a posture of peaceful resistance through a kind of slave mentality of the bullied. Nor was their religion an opiate that dulled them to social realities here and now. In fact, reading the early sources, it is clear they actually felt like they were the *victors*! They believed that true power to change the world lay not in politics, the judiciary, or the military but in the message of Christ's death and resurrection. Whatever we make of a "miraculous" resurrection all these years later, the first Christians really believed it. And they saw it as the proof and pledge that God vindicated the suffering Jesus and will also one day vindicate his suffering church.

This is what made Christians good, even cheerful, losers—the thought that they had *already won*! Their role was simply to remain true to the way of Christ, seeking to transform the world through prayer, service, persuasion, and suffering. Tertullian radiates this sentiment in the opening lines of his letter to Scapula:

> We are not in any great perturbation or alarm about the persecutions we suffer from the ignorance of men; for we have attached ourselves to this sect, fully accepting the terms of its covenant. . . . For our religion commands us to love even our enemies, and to pray for those who persecute us, aiming at a perfection all its own. For everyone loves those who love them; it is peculiar to Christians alone to love those that hate them.[30]

Three decades after Tertullian, a brief but more widespread persecution occurred during the short reign of Emperor Decius (AD 249–251). This led to the execution of numerous prominent Christians, including Bishop Alexander of Jerusalem, Bishop Babylas of Antioch, and even Bishop Fabian of Rome.[31] With such high-profile deaths, the Romans were no doubt hoping to discourage the masses from even contemplating Christianity. According to Christians at the time, it had the opposite effect. People were intrigued to find out more about this faith, and soon many of them found themselves convinced it was the truth.[32] The good losers were winning.

The "Great Persecution"

Something unprecedented happened fifty years after the killing of these three prominent bishops. At the dawn of the fourth century, seemingly out of nowhere, Rome launched its greatest ever campaign of violence against the church. Christianity had been growing dramatically since its beginnings in

Galilee and Judea. By the 200s it had reached into almost every part of the Roman Empire, including France (Gaul), North Africa, and Spain, in sufficient numbers to become hugely annoying to authorities, prompting these periodic campaigns of violence just mentioned. A new policy was required.

Intellectual power for a new policy against the Christians came from the celebrated Greek philosopher Porphyry (AD 234–305). He was one of the outstanding intellects of the era and the most powerful critic Christians faced in ancient times. Raised in the cosmopolitan trade city of Tyre in Phoenicia, on the northwest coast of the modern state of Israel, Porphyry was uniquely placed to take on the Christians. He was an "easterner," deeply aware of the history and traditions of the Jews and Christians in Palestine, and yet comprehensively educated in the best of Greco-Roman philosophy, literature, and religion. And he used all this to great effect by producing several works intended to undermine Christian Scripture and theology, including *Against the Christians* and *Philosophy from Oracles*.[33] Porphyry was Richard Dawkins, Christopher Hitchens, and Sam Harris rolled into one.

One of Porphyry's works, *Philosophy from Oracles*, is a full-scale defence of traditional pagan religion, which simultaneously downgrades Jesus to the level of a "pious man" who was "deemed worthy of immortality after death."[34] Several scholars today believe this was a work specifically commissioned by the emperor, Diocletian (AD 245–312), to provide the philosophical rationale needed to revive the ancient traditions and suppress Christianity.[35]

Porphyry openly argued that Christians were a *public menace*, since they dishonoured the very gods who had preserved the health and wealth of the empire for centuries: "How can these people [Christians] be thought worthy of forbearance?" Porphyry ominously asked. "They have turned away from those who from earliest times are referred to as divine among all Greeks and barbarians. And to what sort of penalties might they not justly be subjected who are fugitives from the things of their fathers?"[36] The argument was clear: the gods had protected Rome since ancient times; anyone who abandoned the gods forfeited the right to imperial protection.

By the year 303 things reached fever pitch. Buoyed by the arguments of public intellectuals like Porphyry and a governor named Hierocles,[37] Emperor Diocletian issued a series of four edicts designed to crush Christianity. In this he was fully supported by his assistant emperor in the east, Galerius (AD 250–311).

Roman politics was complicated at this time. The empire had been divided into two: a western region and an eastern region, each with its own "Augustus" (senior emperor) and "Caesar" (junior emperor). Diocletian was theoretically only the *eastern* Augustus (with Galerius as his Caesar), but everyone recognised his seniority. The point here is that he was able to promote an empire-wide suppression of Christians known to historians today as the "Great Persecution." It was unlike anything that had come before in intensity, duration, and geographical spread.

The first edict, dated 23 February 303, decreed that churches should be demolished and their Scriptures burned. We have a remarkable state record, a literal transcript, of the interrogation of church leaders at Cirta in North Africa, dated to within months of the first edict: 19 May 303. The Roman guardian of the city, the "permanent priest and curator," was Mutatius Felix. He was tasked with investigating church leaders and property in the region. In the record, he interviews several church leaders, including Paul the bishop and various others, deacons and readers. He is particularly interested in "codices," the books of Christian Scripture, which were to be destroyed. Two deacons, Marcuclius and Catullinus, refuse to play along. They hand over just one book and advise that the other books are with various members of the church, elsewhere in the city. Felix is not impressed. The official transcript records:

> Felix the permanent priest and curator said . . . : "Why have you given only one codex?"
>
> Catullinus and Marcuclius said: "We have no more, as we are subdeacons; but the readers have the codices."
>
> Felix said: "Show me the readers!"
>
> Marcuclius and Catullinus said: "We don't know where they live" [surely, a little white lie].
>
> Felix said to Catullinus and Marcuclius: "If you do not know where they live, tell their names."
>
> Catullinus and Marcuclius said: "We are not traitors. Here we are, have us killed."
>
> Felix said: "Let them be taken into custody."[38]

That is the last we hear of brave Catullinus and Marcuclius. It was probably the last anyone heard of them.

Felix continued his interviews in Cirta, which are also detailed in the transcript. Going from house to house, he had more luck with other readers and deacons, listed as Edusius, Junius, Victorinus, Felix the tailor (true story), Proictus, Victor the grammarian (a teacher of Latin literature), Euticius, and finally Coddeo, who was not home at the time, we are told, but whose wife also complied with the order and brought out six codices. In total, Felix the Curator walked away with twenty-seven codices of Scripture from this one church, a priceless treasure now lost to the world (along with thousands of other manuscripts lost in the Great Persecution).

According to the emperor's edicts, Christians were also forbidden to assemble. Freed slaves who confessed Christ were re-enslaved. And any believers in the upper echelons of society, including in academic posts, lost their positions and social rank. The measures were harsh, but the effect was limited, even after a second and third edict along similar lines. Christianity refused to die.

A fourth edict issued in the year 304 brought things to a head. The law mandated that *every* citizen should participate in sacrifices to the traditional Greek and Roman gods. Anyone who refused, as Christians must, was to be tortured until they relented, or else they were executed. The measures were not carried out with equal vigour everywhere in the empire. Asia Minor, Palestine, Egypt, and North Africa bore the brunt. That is where the majority of Christians lived. The western regions of Gaul/France and Britain, however, were hit less hard. It continued, especially in the east, for eight long years (AD 303–312). Diocletian had abdicated in 305, but his assistant emperor, Galerius, became "Augustus" and continued the persecution apace. Galerius suffered an agonizing illness in 311 and issued an edict of toleration toward the Christians, in which he even asked Christians to pray for him (30 April 311). But his successor, Maximinus Daia (AD 270–313), had no qualms continuing the persecution in the east. During these eight years there was a large number of Christian martyrs throughout all ranks of society.[39] It was the ultimate test of Christian resolve.

The Keys to Christian Resolve

We have a few Christian texts written in the middle of the Great Persecution. One of them comes from a professor of rhetoric at the academy of Nicomedia in northwest Turkey, which had recently become the imperial capital. His name was Lucius Lactantius (AD 240–320). He was one of numerous Christians in this period who had attained a secular academic position. When the persecution broke out in 303, Lactantius was forced to resign his post, and he fled to the relative safety of the west. While in hiding he wrote *The Divine Institutes*, which was an attempt to defend the truth of Christianity against the arguments of educated Roman detractors, such as the great Porphyry. As someone living and teaching in the imperial city when Diocletian planned and launched the Great Persecution, Lactantius was well placed to push back against Christianity's critics.[40]

In a section of the *Institutes* titled "True Worship," Lactantius contrasts the "logic" of Christian ethics with the rationale found in Greco-Roman moral theories. He explains that Christianity emphatically connects *devotion to God* with *compassion toward humanity*. Why? Because human beings bear the *imago Dei*. "Whatever you grant to man," he says, "you also grant to God, since man is the likeness of God." If we owe love to our Creator, we also owe love to his children, our own creaturely siblings. "If we have all been given the breath of life by one and the same God," he continues, "we must all be brothers, and closer than brothers too, being brothers in spirit rather than in the flesh." This "sibling relationship is why God instructs us to do evil never and good always."[41] This demands mercy and forgiveness, never revenge:

> The just man will never forgo the chance to act mercifully. He is to answer a curse with a blessing; he himself should never curse, so that no evil word may proceed out of the mouth. He should also take great care never to create an enemy by fault of his own, and if there is someone so aggressive as to do harm to a good and just man, the good and just man should put up with it in a forgiving and self-controlled fashion, exacting no revenge of his own but leaving it to the judgment of God.[42]

Lactantius tends to couch his language in the philosophical terms his readership expected (and that he no doubt enjoyed), but the biblical rationale for his thinking—the "image of God" and "love of enemy"—is clear. God loves all his creatures, so Christians must love even their persecutors.

I will mention Lactantius again in the next chapter, when we explore his remarkable argument—*contra* Porphyry—that all citizens should be granted "religious liberty." It was an argument known one thousand, five hundred years later to American's founding father of religious liberty, Thomas Jefferson (AD 1743–1826). For now, I want to draw a single, irresistible conclusion. Both the *founding documents* of Christianity (the New Testament) and the *founding centuries* of Christian history (AD 30–312) provide a clear portrait of what we might call "normative Christianity." A key aspect of that norm is the resolve to love *even enemies* because they, too, bear the image of God. Whatever we must say about later bad behaviour—and I will say a lot—it is obvious we will not find an explanation of the church's hatred and violence in the *origins* of the movement.

For the first three centuries Christians seemed like "good losers." They believed they had already received the greatest reward—God's love through Christ's death and resurrection. And they were sure that his story of suffering followed by vindication was also theirs. They would win—they *had* won—even when they lost. All that was required of them, as they waited for God's kingdom, was prayer, service, persuasion, and endurance of hardship. Jesus had given them a beautiful tune, and they were going to sing along.

One benefit of knowing all this, as I have said before, is that it provides a *standard* by which we can rightly judge all future behaviour of the church. If we know the melody, we can usually pick when someone is out of key. And the first hints of discord occurred almost immediately after the Great Persecution ended. No one could have predicted what was about to happen, least of all the Christians. Out of the blue, at the height of the church's suffering, the most powerful man in the world announced he was a Christian.

6

Constantine and Religious Liberty

The First Christian Emperor in the Early 300s

All who have the wish to observe the religion of the Christians may hasten to do so without any worry or molestation.

—EMPEROR CONSTANTINE

In a 2018 *Washington Post* article titled "The Church Is Tempted by Power and Obsessed with Sex," national affairs columnist David Von Drehle offered a kind of *curriculum vitae* of the corruptions of Christianity from the beginning to today. He mentions some of the highlights explored in this book: the Inquisition, Reformation wars, the trial of Galileo, and, of course, the recent child sexual abuse scandals and their cover-ups. "Church leadership, from the popes all the way down," he tells us, "hasn't been able to tell right from wrong." And it all began, he thinks, with the unholy marriage of church and empire: "Since its alliance with the Roman Emperor Constantine in the fourth century, the Catholic hierarchy has been tempted by power."[1] Von Drehle is half right.

The Conversion of Constantine

In the year 312, almost three hundred years after Christ, Flavius Valerius Constantinus, soon to be known as Constantine the Great, announced his allegiance to the God of the Christians. So far as we can tell, the change of mind followed a remarkable victory over his imperial rival Maxentius.

As I said in the previous chapter, Roman politics was complicated at this time, with a senior emperor (Augustus) and a junior emperor (Caesar) in both the east and the west. Understandably, all four rulers jockeyed for prime position, and they probably all longed to be sole ruler over the lot. Maxentius was Constantine's most powerful rival in the west. Already in Rome, Maxentius was rumoured to have reigned like a despot. According to one near-contemporary source, he even demanded that highborn wives of some senators periodically sleep with him. Some of these women were apparently Christians, and they committed suicide rather than go to the man's bed.[2] His rule, however, was about to end.

In October AD 312, after numerous victories in the west, Constantine and his army entered Italy and confronted the forces of Maxentius at the Milvian Bridge, which crosses the Tiber about 5km north of Rome. Constantine's victory was total, and Maxentius himself was drowned in the famous river.

The victory at Milvian Bridge on 28 October 312 would be just another battle among thousands in Roman history were it not for Constantine's startling announcement that he had won the encounter with the assistance of *Jesus Christ*. According to his own account given directly to the scholar-bishop Eusebius of Caesarea—whose writings are preserved—in the days before the confrontation with Maxentius, Constantine had been reflecting on the inadequacies of the Greco-Roman gods and pondering the devotion of his own father Constantius I to a single deity. Constantius I was not a Christian, but he was a philosophical monotheist.

Around noon one day, so Constantine reports, the soon-to-be emperor saw a sign of pure light in the sky in the shape of a cross. It was inscribed with the words *in hoc signo vinces* or "in this sign conquer"! Constantine fell asleep that evening confused and disturbed by what he had seen. He was visited in a dream. "In his sleep," Eusebius tells us, "the Christ of God appeared to him with the same sign which he had seen in the heavens, and commanded him to make a likeness of that sign which he had seen in the heavens, and to use it as a safeguard in all engagements with his enemies."[3] He obeyed the dream. It worked. Within a week, he had defeated the more numerous forces of Maxentius. The western region was now Constantine's.

Another writer from the same time, Lactantius, whom we met in the previous chapter, only reports the dream, not the daytime sign in the sky.[4] It is difficult to know what to make of it all. Yet, rereading my copy of Eusebius just now, I am inclined to give him the benefit of the doubt. There is a clear air of hesitation in his retelling. He admits he only feels comfortable recounting the incident because the emperor himself had "confirmed his statement by an oath."[5] Personally, I think Eusebius reports the story as he received it. It is Constantine's version of events, or perhaps his interpretation of events, that I find difficult to believe. That said, one of the preeminent experts on Constantine, the British historian Arnold H. M. Jones, insists, "There is no reason to doubt the *bona fides* of either Eusebius or Constantine":

> What Constantine probably saw was a rare, but well-attested, form of the "halo phenomenon." This is a phenomenon analogous to the rainbow, and like it local and transient, caused by the fall, not of rain, but of ice crystals across the rays of the sun. It usually takes the form of mock suns or of rings of light surrounding the sun, but a cross of light with the sun in its centre has been on several occasions scientifically observed. The display may well have been brief and unspectacular, but to Constantine's overwrought imagination it was deeply significant.[6]

Whatever we make of the strange happenings in late October AD 312, this was a genuine and totally unexpected turning point in the history of the world. The most persecuted people in the empire now had the most important patron imaginable, the great "Augustus" of the western Roman Empire—soon to be the sole emperor of east and west (AD 324). A people used to mockery and social exclusion (and worse) were now invited into the very centre of power. And, perhaps most bizarrely, the Christian sign of humble self-sacrifice was now a formal part of the Roman war machine.

Eusebius adds that he himself inspected the new Roman "standard" (the banner that armies fought under) that Constantine fashioned to celebrate his new religion: "A long spear, overlaid with gold, formed the figure of the cross by means of a transverse bar laid over it," he writes. "On the top of the whole was fixed a wreath of gold and precious stones; and within this, the symbol of the Saviour's name, two letters indicating the name of Christ by means of its initial characters." This is the famous Chi-Rho symbol: *chi* is the first Greek letter in "Christ" and is drawn like an "X," and *rho* is the second letter (the "r") and is drawn like our "P." Placed over each other in the manner Eusebius describes, it looks like ☧. (The same symbol would later appear on imperial coins.) Eusebius concludes: "and these letters the emperor was in the habit of wearing on his helmet at a later period. . . . The emperor constantly made use of this sign of salvation as a safeguard against every adverse and hostile power, and commanded that others similar to it should be carried at the head of the armies."[7]

It is difficult to convey just how strange this turn of events will have seemed to everyone, Christians included. Just a year earlier Christianity had been outlawed, on pain of death. Now it was showered with imperial protection and benefaction. One priest a few years later was so thrilled finally to have a Christian emperor that he gave a speech in the presence of Constantine declaring that the emperor was—I can hardly bring myself to type the words—"destined to share the empire of the Son of God in the world to come." I can almost hear the gasps from the other clergy in attendance. I am happy to report that Constantine was indignant and told the man to stop speaking and go back to praying for the emperor instead.[8] Good advice.

Legalizing Christianity

Some would say this is the moment when everything went wrong in Christian history. This is when the church's fixation with power and its air of entitlement burst forth like the release of a tightly coiled spring. It was the moment of revenge for the once-bullied *bully*.

Roman historians today tend to be more cautious about these things, noting that, while Constantine's embrace of Christianity was a definite turning point for the church, the egregious excesses of church power, wealth, and violence developed much later (as I will detail). Indeed, many of Constantine's reforms were reversed just twenty-five years later by one of his successors, Emperor Julian (ruled AD 361–363). As we will see in chapter 8, Julian ejected Christians from positions of power, stopped them from teaching in the academies, and took measures to revive pagan religion throughout the empire. Fancying himself a bit of a philosopher, Julian even published works against the Christians.

The long reign of Constantine the Great (AD 306–337) did not cause the immediate moral collapse of the church, as columnist David Von Drehle suggested in the *Washington Post*. It did, however, open the door to some lamentable compromises with power and privilege, coupled with some happy developments for Roman society generally. Like so much of human history, the story is complicated and sometimes contradictory.

The first and most obvious thing Constantine did was to extinguish all oppression orders against the Christians and declare Christianity wholly legal. He prepared with his eastern counterpart, Emperor Licinius, what is known as the "Edict of Milan." It was not strictly an edict, and it was not issued at Milan! But it gets its name from the fact that the details of a new approach to religion were hammered out at a meeting of the two emperors in Milan. The policy was then issued in the name of both emperors—Constantine's name first—at Nicomedia near Constantinople (northwest Turkey) on 13 June 313. The Edict of Milan guaranteed tolerance for all faiths. The remarkable document begins, "We believed that we should give both to Christians and to all men the freedom to follow religion, whichever one each one chose." This is "so that whatever sort of Divinity there is in heavenly regions may be gracious and propitious to us and to all who live under our government." Another paragraph of the edict almost reads like a modern secular text:

> Freedom and full liberty has been granted in accordance with the peace of our times, to exercise free choice in worshipping as each one has seen fit. This has been done by us so that nothing may seem to be taken away from anyone's honour or from any religion whatsoever.[9]

Christianity was not made the official religion of the empire in this period; it was merely granted legal status *equal* to that of the still-dominant pagan religions. Constantine openly favoured Christianity as his personal religion, just as every emperor before him had sponsored his preferred deity or deities. But paganism was *mostly* left to its own devices—to flourish or fail—throughout Constantine's twenty-five-year rule.

Freedom of Religion

Where did Constantine get this idea of *religious liberty for all*? Most of us, all these years later, take for granted that the state will grant complete freedom in spiritual matters. But for most of history, in most parts of the world, this simply was not the case. Religion was seen as too important to the health of society *not* to be regulated. The significance of religion lay mainly in that it secured prosperity for the state and victory over enemies, so long as the gods were duly honoured by the people. This was the logic, as I said earlier, behind the philosopher Porphyry's justification of state suppression of the church: by displeasing the traditional gods, Christians endangered everyone.

We do not have to speculate about where Constantine got his relatively "enlightened" views about religion outlined in the Edict of Milan. Two Christian thinkers had made a striking case for religious liberty well before Constantine defeated Maxentius and proclaimed himself a Christian. One of them was in the distant past, but his writings were still well known. The other became one of Constantine's confidantes. I have mentioned both before.

A century before Constantine, the rhetorician-turned-theologian Tertullian (AD 160–225) wrote to Scapula, the proconsul of Carthage, to make clear that Christians were not afraid of persecution and would continue to love their enemies, come what may (as we saw in the previous chapter). Part of Tertullian's argument is that Christians have a completely different understanding of the nature of religion. Worship is not a matter of culture or politics but of the mind and will. Tertullian makes clear that he has no time at all for pagan religion. Intellectually, he is quite intolerant of pagan religion. But he insists that everyone should worship as they see fit:

> We are worshippers of one God, of whose existence and character Nature teaches all men; at whose lightnings and thunders you tremble, whose benefits minister to your happiness. You think that others, too, are gods, whom we know to be devils. However, it is a fundamental human right, a privilege of nature, that every man should worship according to his own convictions: one man's religion neither harms nor helps another man. It is assuredly no part of religion to compel religion—to which free-will and not force should lead us.[10]

Tertullian's language of a "right" to "free" worship sounds very modern, but it is *ancient* and *Christian*.

A similar argument was made by another Christian thinker, and this thinker directly influenced Constantine. I mentioned previously the arguments about love offered by Lactantius (AD 240–320) in his *Divine Institutes*, written shortly after he had to abandon his academic post in Nicomedia at the outbreak of the Great Persecution (AD 303–312). He survived the years of suppression and was restored to favour when Constantine rose to power. In fact, in 317 Constantine invited him to be the personal tutor of his eldest son and heir, Crispus. Lactantius was suddenly extremely influential.

Lactantius's *Institutes* was an attempt to rebut pagan criticisms of Christianity and to outline why the Bible's conception of *the Good* is philosophically and morally superior to anything offered in the Greco-Roman world. Part of his argument was that Christianity is a *religion of the mind* rather than a cultural feature or an extension of the state. His lengthy chapter on "Justice" is probably the first attempt in western history to offer a sustained argument for reciprocal tolerance of all religions. If we are looking for an intellectual source of the Edict of Milan, it is Lactantius.[11]

Lactantius reasoned that *coerced* religion was the opposite of *true* religion, and so it was illogical. He pointed out that if one has to use force to advance one's religion, the arguments in favour of that religion must be pretty weak: "If the reasoning is sound," he said, "let them argue it! We are ready to listen." Violence shows you have already lost, he argues. Christians, on the other hand, are happy to die for their faith, since they know they have already won the Truth. Here is a small excerpt from his extensive treatment:

> There is no need for violence and brutality: worship cannot be forced; it is something to be achieved by talk rather than blows, so that there is free will in it. . . . No one is detained by us [Christians] against his will—anyone without devotion and faith is no use to God; but when truth detains, no one departs. If they [pagans] have any confidence in their truth, let them teach it to us: let them talk, let them just utter, let them have the nerve, I say, to engage in debate of some such sort with us. Religion must be defended not by killing but by dying, not by violence but by endurance. . . . There is nothing that is so much a matter of willingness as religion.[12]

Lactantius offers a "true theory of toleration," writes Elizabeth dePalma Digeser in the *Journal of Roman Studies*. "He understands that both Christians and the followers of the traditional religions strongly disapprove of and disagree with the other, but he also argues that neither group should use force against the other. And he advocates forbearance in order to achieve a greater good."[13] The argument is deeply rooted in Lactantius's Christian understanding of God's way of relating to men and women, as a father to his children rather than as a monarch to subjects. If love is the goal—love for God and neighbour—religion can never be a matter of force.[14]

Christians would not always maintain this commitment to freedom of religion. There are periods in history when Christian rulers banned "false" worship and forced the conversion of subjects. In fact, eighty years after Lactantius, a pagan orator named Libanius would plead before Theodosius I for Christian tolerance of pagan shrines and officials. He used Lactantius's own arguments (about the centrality of persuasion) *against* Christian zealots. He reminded them that "in their very own rules"—i.e., in the teachings of earlier Christians—"persuasion meets with approval and compulsion is deplored." Thus, if you "resort to force . . . you would obviously be breaking your own rules."[15] Christians broke those rules often enough in the centuries that followed.

Anti-Pagan Religious Reforms?

Constantine *mostly* left pagan religion to its own devices. But there are some exceptions. First, Constantine ended the sacrifices of the imperial cult. As weird as it sounds to modern ears, for centuries there was a system of temples and priests throughout the empire dedicated to paying homage to the emperors as quasi-divinities. Constantine ended this imperial cult almost immediately.[16]

Second, in a letter of 23 May 318, Constantine publicly scolded those who used "magic arts." He ruled against magic designed to hurt people, but he allowed magic designed to help people or improve crops. He reasoned that even if magic is morally wrong (for a Christian), no one is injured in cases of "white" magic.[17]

Third, in another letter of AD 323—a decade after his conversion—Constantine castigated a major pagan sacrifice in Rome, the Lustral Sacrifice purifying the city. His complaint was not directed against the sacrifice itself but against officials who had compelled Christians to participate. He threatened beatings and fines if it happened again.[18] He was not a warm and fuzzy Christian ruler!

The temptation to overthrow pagan religion must have been great in AD 324, when Constantine defeated the eastern Augustus, Licinius, to become the sole ruler of the Roman Empire.[19] Yet, we have a public letter from Constantine written in the wake of his victory. In it he explains that he will *not* remove traditional practices. His reasoning is intriguing. He freely admits in the letter that he would "indeed have earnestly recommended such removal [of paganism] to all men," but he knows that such worship would "remain fixed in the minds" of some—since religion is a matter of conscience—which would "discourage the hope of any general restoration of mankind to the way of truth." In other words, banning paganism would backfire and work against his hope that all people become Christians. "For it may be," he muses, "that this restoration of equal [religious] privileges to all will prevail to lead them [pagans] into the straight path. Let no one molest another, but let everyone do as his soul desires."[20]

This letter of 324 is astonishing in context. Licinius, as co-emperor, had been the co-author of the Edict of Milan a little over a decade earlier. Sometime around AD 320, however, he turned against the Christians in his eastern provinces. He purged his royal court and the civil service of believers, shrewdly making pagan sacrifice a test of office. He banned Christian worship in buildings within the city (ostensibly as a public health measure). He placed travel restrictions on bishops and even executed some of them.[21] To some in this three- or four-year period, it must have seemed like things were reverting to the bad old days of the Great Persecution of 303–312. But it was relatively short lived. Constantine and Licinius clashed over territorial disputes, and Licinius was soon deposed, leaving Constantine sole ruler. And *this* is the context for the letter just quoted, reassuring the eastern provinces that, despite his love for the Christian religion, Constantine refuses to inflict on pagans what Licinius had just inflicted on Christians: "Let everyone do as his soul desires."

No one would describe Emperor Constantine as a model of enlightened pluralism when it comes to religion—or anything else for that matter! Yet Constantine, and the church around him, remained broadly committed to the ideals of the Edict of Milan. This legislation of tolerance toward all faiths was a remarkable development in the history of politics.

From Emperor Constantine to Thomas Jefferson

Leaping forward many centuries, the ideas of Tertullian and Lactantius, and the Edict of Milan, would be employed by one of the most famous names in the modern progress toward freedom of religion. Thomas Jefferson, the third President of the United States, is often regarded as the political founder of America's concept of "religious liberty." He led the debate in the *Virginia Statute for Religious Freedom* in 1786, the forerunner of the first amendment's guarantee that "Congress shall make no law respecting an establishment of religion, or prohibiting the free exercise thereof."[22] Jefferson's direct influences were recent political philosophers such as John Locke and perhaps various eighteenth-century Baptist thinkers.[23] But we also know that Jefferson was aware that the west's *first* argument for religious liberty went back to Lactantius and Tertullian.

Jefferson's private book collection contains copies of both Lactantius and Tertullian. Robert Louis Wilken of the University of Virginia was granted access to the Jefferson collection in preparation for his 2019 book, *Liberty in the Things of God: The Christian Origins of Religious Freedom*. It turns out that in Jefferson's private copy of his *Notes on the State of Virginia, query XVII* (on religious freedom), he had written out *in Latin* the very passage from Tertullian quoted earlier: "[I]t is a fundamental human right, a privilege of nature, that every man should worship according to his own convictions: one man's religion neither harms nor helps another man. It is assuredly no part of religion to compel religion—to which free-will and not force should lead us."[24]

It gets better. Professor Wilken requested to see Jefferson's personal copy of Tertullian. "When the book was brought up from the stacks," he reports, "I held in my hand a small leather-bound volume published in Cambridge, England, in 1686. As I turned the pages and came to chapter 2 of *Ad Scapulam* [the letter *To Scapula*], to my astonishment, I saw that Jefferson had underlined the passage and put a large X in the margin."[25] Wilken does not argue that Jefferson was directly influenced by Tertullian and Lactantius, only that this great Enlightenment statesman and US President knew that the modern world was not the first to insist on religious liberty.

◆

Constantine's conversion and his Edict of Milan could have done enormous, lasting good (they did *some* good, as we will see). The principles of *compassion for all* and *freedom of religion* found in the New Testament, Tertullian, Lactantius, and many others might have speedily transformed the empire into a very different place. Constantine did often act as evangelist in chief, but his proselytizing tendency did not translate into force in the empire.[26] Not at first. Before exploring some of the measures that elevated Christians over others, I want to outline one important way *everyone* benefited from Constantine's conversion: he greatly enhanced the church's charitable services.

Constantine and the Birth of Charity

Financial Changes to Roman Law in the Early 300s

*Give to the blind, the sick, the lame and the destitute; if you don't,
they die. Men may have no use for them, but God has.*

—LACTANTIUS

When the people of the cross collided with the Roman war machine in the conversion of Emperor Constantine, the result was mixed. On the one hand, there was a remarkable, if unstable, policy of toleration of viewpoints. It did not last. Some of the other "benefits" of Constantine's conversion, described below, gave the church its first taste of privilege and entitlement, setting the stage for the vast global superpower known as "Christendom," the domain of Christ. It would be unhistorical to see this as all bad. Some of it was very good. But it would also be a mistake to deny the growing *log* in the eye of the church.

I want to give a lot of space to the concessions and gifts Constantine gave to the church. The reason for this will become clear. Many of the legal and cultural changes made during his twenty-five-year reign explain both the *best* and *worst* of Christianity for a millennium or more. For example, certain tax breaks allowed the church to become the principal source of social welfare in the west for the next fifteen hundred years. On the other hand, the political influence given to bishops eventually made some of them as wealthy and powerful and sometimes as wicked as any Roman senator. Constantine's raft of pro-Christian measures lit a fuse that exploded—in slow motion over many centuries—into the innumerable saints and bullies of Christian history.

Building Programs

One enormous benefit to Christians following Constantine's conversion was very practical. The emperor ordered that damaged, demolished, or confiscated church buildings "should be restored without any question whatsoever to these same Christians, that is, to their corporation and assembly."[1] This decree pertained only to *public* church properties, not to individual houses of Christians.

Especially interesting is Constantine's insistence that the financial restoration of church buildings should not come at the expense of non-Christian citizens. Some buildings had been seized by state officials in the persecution and then on-sold or gifted to others. In handing back these properties, citizens were to be reimbursed by the state.[2] Constantine did not want the restoration of churches to penalise the pagan majority.

Constantine also set out on a new prodigious building program. This will not have surprised anyone. For centuries emperors had made their own mark on cities with extravagant redevelopment projects, many of which were religious in nature. For example, Emperor Augustus (63 BC–AD 14) had built the famous Roman Forum, along with the nearby Temple of Mars Ultor (the Avenger), both still viewable in Rome today. On the way out of the Forum toward the Colosseum, tourists can also gaze at the magnificent Arch of Titus, built by Emperor Titus (AD 39–81) to commemorate the Roman victory over the Jews and their temple in Jerusalem in AD 70. In antiquity, leaders saw themselves as builders in chief.

One of Constantine's major projects was moving the capital of the empire eight hundred miles east of Rome to the city of Byzantium. He promptly renamed it—after himself—Constantinople, modern Istanbul. He ordered the construction of great churches throughout the city, as well as numerous residences, administrative centres, recreational facilities, and the enormous infrastructure that goes with such projects—roads, aqueducts, sewerage systems, and so on.

One thing that may have surprised people, including Christians, was Constantine's desire to build vast monuments in faraway Jerusalem and surrounds, where very few Roman citizens, not even Constantine himself, ever visited.[3] In AD 326 he permitted his mother, Helena—a devout supporter of Christians—to visit the Holy City and to recommend the construction of new monuments to Christ. The two most spectacular buildings, still standing today, are the Church of the Nativity in Bethlehem, commemorating the birthplace of Jesus, and the Church of the Anastasis (Resurrection), better known today as the Church of the Holy Sepulchre. The latter was constructed directly on top of a first-century tomb that local Christians at the time insisted was the very sepulchre, or tomb, of Jesus. Modern archaeological research does indeed confirm the presence of a first-century tomb cut into an ancient quarry beside a garden just a hundred or so feet outside the AD 30 wall of Jerusalem.[4] I take history tours there each year, and it is extremely difficult to help people see past the hyper-religiosity of the grand labyrinth of buildings (run now by five different denominations) and imagine a quiet garden tomb just beyond the hustle and bustle of the ancient city. Not everyone "feels the presence of Jesus" in the spot, but everyone sees the impact of Constantine.

Bishops as Magistrates

In a strange innovation, the emperor gave certain judicial powers to bishops, that is, to the clerical *overseers* (that's what the word "bishop" means) responsible for the priests and churches of a given region. Despite Rome's best efforts in earlier centuries, Christians probably made up at least 10 percent of the fifty million people of the empire by the year 300. Bishops, therefore, were in spiritual and moral authority over *many* people.[5]

Christians had long allowed church leaders to settle various civil disputes between believers, just as the New Testament had urged (1 Cor 6:1–6). In a highly dysfunctional and hierarchical Roman legal system—which Christians were often shut out of—this was a godsend to the mostly lowly complainants within church circles. On 23 June 318, just five years after his conversion, Constantine wrote this Christian practice into law: bishops could formally try a range of cases, including the freeing of slaves. In fact, the law stated that litigants in the secular courts could transfer their case to the church courts to be tried before bishops.[6] The law was originally well motivated, but it was open to abuse, as subsequent church history would show.

A Gift of Bibles

Constantine made way for some highly significant theological and social developments, both positive and negative. For one thing, he sponsored a big Bible-copying project. It was the least he could do. One of Diocletian's first decrees against the Christians at the outbreak of the Great Persecution in 303 was to destroy the Christian Scriptures. This was devastating for Christians. Unlike much Greek and Roman religion, churches were more like schools or philosophical clubs than religious cults, a point forcefully argued by the well-known Roman historian Edwin Judge.[7] Getting rid of Christian books was a blow to the heart of the movement. Some manuscript copies predating the Great Persecution have survived—copies of the Gospels and Paul's letters—but we might have had thousands if it were not for Diocletian's strategy. In any case, Constantine reversed this. Not only did he give Christians the freedom to make their own copies, he paid for fifty spectacular copies of the Bible to be made and brought to his imperial capital. It is clear from his letter mandating the production of these Bibles that he had no involvement in the content of the Scriptures—contrary to modern conspiracy theories—but his gift was hugely significant.[8]

Scribal copying was astonishingly expensive. I interviewed Brendan Haug, the curator of the Papyrological Collection at the University of Michigan, which houses some of history's most precious manuscripts—more than fifteen thousand. Kept within a vault, within a vault, within a vault, the department houses thirty double-sided pages of the earliest papyrus copies of the letters of the apostle Paul, dating to a hundred or so years before Constantine. In the course of our conversation, Brendan told me that this manuscript of Paul's letters, known as P46 and originally made up of 104 pages in total, would have had a production cost equal to three years' salary of an average worker.[9] And that's just to reproduce Paul's letters, which make up less than 10 percent of the Bible. A Bible would have cost the equivalent of thirty years' salary. What's more, the materials and labour that went into Constantine's fifty Bibles were infinitely superior to those of the earlier P46 (Google "Images of Papyrus 46" and "Images of Codex Sinaiticus" to see the contrast). The math is mind-blowing. Nothing, of course, could have made up for the loss of manifold biblical manuscripts during the Great Persecution, but Constantine's gift of fifty Bibles was a benefaction of lasting significance.

Council of Nicaea (AD 325)

Constantine made a tangential contribution to theology. Following the atrocities and civil unrest of his predecessors, Constantine wanted his empire to enjoy "a life of peace and undisturbed concord," as he put it.[10] However, he inherited a problem that threatened to tear the church itself apart, a doctrinal dispute about the status of Jesus Christ that could only be settled by a universal meeting of Christian leaders held in the city of Nicaea (northwest Turkey) in May–July of AD 325. This so-called Council of Nicaea produced a summary of Christian doctrine known as the Nicene Creed. It is the universal statement of belief accepted by Catholics, the Orthodox, and mainline Protestants to this day. The real history of the council is much less entertaining than the version told in Dan Brown's bestselling 2003 novel *The Da Vinci Code*.[11]

The fictional story of the Council of Nicaea suggests that Constantine wanted to elevate the humble man Jesus to God status as an instrument of state control. The truth of the matter is that Constantine had no role in the debate beyond sponsoring the six-to-eight-week conference and giving his welcoming address. It is unlikely he even understood the subtleties and significance of the arguments. The debate revolved around the recent views of a Christian priest in Alexandria named Arius, who had proposed that Jesus was a bridge between humanity and divinity, *not* the full incarnation of God himself. This was an innovation. Ever since the first century, Christians had referred to Jesus *as God*. They took Old Testament passages that referred to the Creator and applied them directly to Jesus.[12] They sang hymns to Jesus as Lord of heaven and earth.[13] And they occasionally came right out and declared that Jesus was God.[14] But this puzzled philosophically minded pagans who wondered how on earth *absolute Infinity* (God) could be related to *finitude* (a Jew named Jesus). Arius's solution was to say that Jesus was not *actually* God but a godlike creature. He put his ideas in a poem titled *Thalia* ("Banquet") and in popular songs to be sung in churches and elsewhere.[15]

Arius's ideas spread. At some points in the next thirty years "Arianism" could have become the majority position.[16] Constantine just wanted to stop all the arguing.[17] Somewhere between two hundred and fifty and three hundred and twenty church officials, mainly bishops, attended the Council of Nicaea. Only *two* voted in favour of Arius's proposal. The rest affirmed, "We believe in one Lord, Jesus Christ," as the resulting Nicene Creed puts it, "the only Son of God, eternally begotten of the Father, God from God, Light from Light, true God from true God, begotten not made, of one Being with the Father."

Constantine's Humanitarianism and Anti-Semitism

Constantine did far more than busy himself with specifically religious matters. First, Constantine mandated a weekly day off for everyone. Apart from the Jewish idea of a Sabbath day (the fourth of Moses's famous Ten Commandments), regular, scheduled rest was virtually unknown in the ancient world. Peasants worked all the time, and elites worked as little as they could. Constantine mandated a civic day off, based on the Jewish biblical model but applicable to all. The law is dated to the summer of AD 321.[18] It must have been a great summer for those who had never known a regular day off. We owe the western notion of a weekend to Moses and Constantine.

Second, despite remaining brutal by our standards, Constantine ended certain formal punishments, which he believed to be an affront to righteousness. He outlawed crucifixion.[19] And on March AD 316 he also ruled that the crimes of convicted criminals should no longer be branded or tattooed on the face, since the face "has been made in the likeness (*similitudo*) of heavenly beauty," the first reference to the "image of God" in secular law.[20] Instead, criminals should be marked on the hand or thigh. Similarly, in AD 325 he tried to ban gladiatorial games. "Bloody spectacles displease Us," his decree begins. "We wholly forbid the existence of gladiators."[21] This seems to have taken immediate effect in the east, but it was decades before blood sports were stamped out in Rome and the west. That story deserves to be told.

It was not until AD 404, long after Constantine, that a total ban on gladiatorial games was achieved. And it was a lone Christian who made it happen. Telemachus was a pious monk from one of the eastern provinces. He brought down a centuries-old industry with one dramatic act. Today we think of monks as odd solitary figures who do little beyond praying and chanting. In the third and fourth centuries, monks were one of Christianity's greatest public assets: they were otherworldly but also active on the streets with charity; they were relatively learned but also utterly penniless; they were severe on sin but also somehow successful at recruiting sinners.[22] In any case, travelling to Rome one day, Telemachus took Christian preaching against blood sports to a whole new level. He turned up at the stadium, leapt over the guardrail, and raced into the arena to stop the fighting. "The spectators were indignant," one source tells us, "and stoned the peacemaker to death." When news of this reached Emperor Honorius, he declared Telemachus a "martyr" and finally put an end to a five-hundred-year tradition.[23] The celebrated eighteenth-century historian Edward Gibbon quipped that "Telemachus' death was more useful to mankind than his life."[24] Gibbon never missed an opportunity for a joke at religion's expense. I would reply that it was precisely Telemachus's life that inspired him to face death for the cause of humanity.

Third, Constantine changed family law in humane ways.[25] On 31 January 320 he overturned the long-held Roman law penalizing those who never married or couples who never had children. Such people were excluded from various inheritance laws and laws about receiving gifts. Constantine ended all that, ruling that singles and the childless "shall have an equal status" and, further, that "the same provision shall be effective with respect to women."[26] He also made divorce more difficult under Roman law. In a period when divorced women were at a distinct disadvantage, this was a godsend to many (women more than men). The new law explicitly stated, "nor indeed shall a husband be permitted to divorce his wife on every sort of pretext." If the husband is found to have divorced his wife on trivial grounds, "he must restore her entire dowry, and he shall not marry another woman. But if he should do this [i.e., marry another woman after divorcing on trivial grounds], his former wife shall be given the right to enter and seize his home by force and to transfer to herself the entire dowry of his later wife in recompense for the outrage inflicted upon her."[27] In another series of proclamations in 313, 315, and 322, Constantine also tried to remove the economic impulse to abandon infants in the practice of *exposure* (discussed in chapter 3). The law stated: "If any parent should report that he has offspring which on account of poverty he is not able to rear, there shall be no delay in issuing food and clothing."[28] Constantine used churches as the welfare distribution centres for this program.[29]

A fourth kind of law, I am afraid to say, was anything but humanitarian. Constantine legislated against Jews. He banned Jews from owning Christian slaves on the absurd religious grounds that it was improper "that those whom the Saviour had ransomed should be subjected to the yoke of slavery by a people who had slain the prophets and the Lord himself."[30] The Christian slave in that case was granted freedom. Jews were also not allowed to circumcise their non-Jewish slaves. If they were found to have done so, not only would they lose their slaves; they would be "visited with capital punishment." Leaving aside the tragedy that slavery itself remained a blind spot for most of the church for many centuries (a subject for chapter 10), it is impossible not to see in this legislation the first institutionalized "Christian" anti-Semitism. Christianity had begun as a Jewish renewal movement. Within three centuries a Christian emperor cast the Jewish people as second-class citizens and the "slayers of Christ." This anti-Semitic law was ratified on 8 May 336, almost exactly one year before Constantine's death. The law was an ominous sign of things to come in the decades and centuries that followed.

The Church and Taxation

Perhaps Constantine's most significant legislative changes concerned financial policy and tax relief. These had a huge impact on the church and society. It deserves our attention for the rest of the chapter.

A small but significant financial change occurred on 3 July 321, when Constantine ruled that "[e]very person shall have the liberty to leave at his death any property that he wishes to the most holy and venerable council of the Catholic Church."[31] The word "catholic" here, by the way, just refers to the *whole* church. Anyway, this law allowing untaxed bequests to churches, a thing already permitted for other corporations, would eventually have a huge impact on the church's ability to be self-sufficient, and more! Over time—and, of course, no other organisation has had *more* time—the property holdings of the church would become unfathomably large. What seemed like a small tax concession in the summer of 321 would become one of the church's chief sources of income (property) and a principal cause of understandable criticism.

Another financial benefit was the clergy's exemption from "public offices." Many middle-class citizens of the empire were required to perform government services of various kinds. We might think of it as a form of taxation. This could involve giving lodging to visiting soldiers and officials, providing supplies to the city, or even sitting on municipal councils. These public offices were often onerous, particularly when they involved taking time out of one's regular employment. I guess modern equivalents might be the compulsory jury duty in Australia or national service in Israel; France recently announced that all sixteen-year-olds must do a month of service training (in first aid, for example), after which they are encouraged to do three months volunteering for the public good. In any case, in the spring of 313, just six months after his victory at Milvian Bridge, Constantine wrote to the proconsul of Africa, Anulinus, ordering that the clergy of the province "should be kept absolutely free from all the public offices. . . . For when they render supreme service to the Deity, it seems that they confer incalculable benefit on the affairs of the State."[32]

Clergy were not the only people in Roman society to be released from such civic duties. All pagan priests, professors, physicians, and leaders of Jewish synagogues enjoyed the same privilege. Constantine was now just extending it to Christian clergy.[33] Constantine's logic in connection with churches was that the activities of the clergy—which included visiting the sick, distributing charitable gifts, and preaching these things into existence—were already a valuable public office. These exemptions were formalised more broadly around the empire in a series of laws over the next fifteen years.[34]

There was a brilliant catch. Wealthy citizens capable of performing significant public services were explicitly forbidden to enter the clergy, lest they use the church as a loophole to escape this form of taxation: "no decurion (a middle- to high-ranking citizen) or descendant of a decurion or even any person provided with adequate resources shall take refuge in the name and the service of the clergy"; and, moreover, the clergy must be chosen only from among those "who have slender fortunes."[35] This law survived at least a generation beyond Constantine and was reiterated in legislation of AD 364.[36] In this period Roman law still had a somewhat patronising view of Christian clergy, says Princeton's Peter Brown: "The bishops and clergy were privileged precisely because they were not expected to be the equals of the rich."[37] Times would soon change, of course!

One of Constantine's laws reveals the rationale for giving churches the privileges enjoyed by other imperial associations and cults. Legislation dated 1 June 329, fifteen years after the emperor's conversion, ratifies the prohibition against the wealthy becoming clergy. In so doing, the law makes a clear distinction between the role of the rich and the role of the church: "the wealthy must assume secular obligations [through their taxes and public offices], and the poor must be supported by the wealth of the churches."[38] In other words, well-to-do citizens should attend to matters of state, while Christians should continue to assist the poor. The church was granted tax-free status because it was effectively the empire's charity arm. This was something entirely new.

Charity in Greek and Roman Society

We take for granted today that charitable services are widely available. This was not the case in the ancient world. The notion that rich citizens had a moral obligation to care for the destitute was almost non-existent in Greece and Rome in this period. I say *almost* non-existent because we do find the occasional references in our sources to individuals who practised humanitarian forms of care in their communities.[39] Yet, charity formed no part of the major moral discourses of the era, whether in Plato, Aristotle, Epicurus, Seneca, Epictetus, or Plutarch. Consider the famous Maxims of Delphi, a hugely popular distillation of the "good life" in 147 pithy commands. The maxims include such gems as "Help your friends," "Return a favour," "Honour good people," "Respect yourself," "Don't trust fortune," "Despise no one," and the very sage "Stop yourself killing." But there is nothing close to "Redress poverty," "Share with the destitute," or anything like that.[40]

One reason for this dearth of ancient references to charity is practical: there was not much to go around, so it made little sense to share what excess you had beyond your circle of family, friends, or clients. There were also more theoretical reasons. Poverty was often seen as a punishment of the gods or, in a less religious mode, as a balancing principle of the universe. The world is on an endless loop or cycle—so many believed—and the "rational principle" of the cosmos has a habit of redressing the injustices of former run-throughs. A generation before Constantine, the hugely influential neo-Platonic philosopher Plotinus (AD 205–270) put it like this:

> The rational principle does not look only at the present on each occasion but at the cycles of time before, and also at the future, so as to determine men's worth from these, and to change their positions, making slaves out of those who were masters before, if they were bad masters; and, if men have used wealth badly, making them poor. . . . We must conclude that the universal order is for ever something of this kind.[41]

Plotinus was one of the more high-minded philosophers of the era. Yet even he could imagine that the destitute somehow *deserved* their destitution (he says the same thing about sexual assault, but I thought it best not to give the full quotation). Within such a view, there just was not much to motivate people to care for those outside their circle of loved ones.

Plato, in the fourth century BC, had insisted that while virtuous citizens struck down in hard times may be assisted by the wider community, the "unworthy poor" should be banished. The wise legislator, he said, will do well to banish beggars from their cities "to the end that the land may be wholly purged of such a creature."[42] Officials in imperial Rome followed Plato's sage advice. During times of famine, the Roman senate ordered non-citizens *out* of the city. Grain allowances were never to be given to the great mass of poor in the city but *only* to citizens who could show their bronze or lead *tessera*, the equivalent of a citizen's ID or passport.[43]

Wealthy "benefaction" was, of course, an important feature of ancient Roman life. Emperors and other elites would bestow gifts on the citizenry—and only citizens—including buildings, monuments, and public games, as well as food supplies in times of shortage. The word for this was *euergetism*, "do-gooding," and it was closely linked to the virtue of *philotimia*, "love of honour." Public benefaction in ancient times was not *charity* on the basis of human need, but a *social contract*. The benefactor shared resources with less-well-off citizens in return for public honour. This civic *euergetism*, writes Peter Brown of Princeton, "contained no element of compassion for the poor."[44] For this reason, Christian writings from the period frequently criticised this weird dimension of Greco-Roman ethics, insisting that kindness designed to bring a reward or honour did not deserve the title "charity," or love.[45]

The Birth of Christian Charity

Teresa Morgan is Professor of Graeco-Roman History at the University of Oxford. She wrote the standard volume on mainstream ethics in the Roman world.[46] In a 2019 interview I asked her what she regards as Christianity's most distinctive contribution to ancient life. She said *charity*:

> Christians are taught that God loves them absolutely, and that on that basis they can trust in God, they can love God, and, because they are given such an abundance of love, they can afford to love one another with enormous, unreserved generosity. That is a completely different model of relations with your fellow human beings, and how your relationship with God affects your relationship with human beings, from anything in ancient religious think-ing in general, apart from Judaism. It is certainly completely different from anything that is in popular moral consciousness. And with that idea of love goes care of the vulnerable. This is a world with no social safety nets. But Christians create social safety nets. They are the people who are notorious for looking after the widows, the poor, the orphans, the people who in most of society are just slung out onto the street.[47]

Professor Morgan notes in passing an important feature of the origins of charity in the western world: it was Jewish before it was Christian. Passage after passage in the Jewish Scriptures, or the Christian Old Testament, calls on the faithful to assist the poor stranger, the fatherless, and the widow.[48] Some texts go so far as to suggest that the excess of the "haves" actually *belongs* to the "have-nots" by divine right.[49] And there is clear evidence from the Roman period that Jews looked after one another so effectively that "no Jew ever has to beg," as one emperor put it.[50]

Jesus and the first Christians were all Jews. Caring for the poor was assumed. Yet, as with so many other things, Jesus *intensified* or *universalized* Jewish practice. In his provocative parable of the Good Samaritan (Luke 10:30–37), he tells how a Jewish man was robbed and left for dead on the road between Jerusalem and Jericho—an ancient road still visible and walkable today. A temple *priest* walks past, unwilling to assist. A *Levite* (a priestly assistant) does the same. Then a *Samaritan* turns up. He stops and cares for the man: he bandages his wounds, pays for lodging in a local inn, and returns later to check on the patient and to pay for any further expenses. Today the proverbial "good Samaritan" is known for similar acts of charity. But the key to the story in Jesus's day is that Samaritans were the ethno-religious *enemies* of the Jewish people. By making a Samaritan, not a fellow Jew, the hero of his parable, Jesus was simultaneously critiquing his own people for not living up to God's commands and insisting that compassion must be shown across ethnic and religious boundaries. He ends the parable with a stark: "Go and do likewise."[51] Christians did *go and do likewise*. They took the Jewish tradition of charity and showered it on Jew and pagan, believer and unbeliever alike. Consider the following pieces of evidence from these early centuries.

In the 40s and 50s of the first century, the apostle Paul conducted what might be the first international aid project in recorded history, collecting donations from non-Jewish Christians in Greece and Asia Minor (Turkey) for the famine-ravaged people of Judea.[52] The great apostle Peter had earlier urged Paul, as he launched out on his empire-wide mission, to please "remember the poor" (Gal 2:10). Paul did just that. Some of his most beautiful teachings remind Christians in wealthier regions of what drives charity: "For you know the generous act of our Lord Jesus Christ, that though he was rich, yet for your sakes he became poor, so that by his poverty you might become rich. . . . I do not mean that there should be relief for others and pressure on you, but it is a question of a fair balance" (2 Cor 8:9, 13). Again, we can see the beautiful tune at play: Christ's sacrificial love for us inspires practical love for others. The apostle John makes an almost identical point toward the end of the first century: "We know love by this, that he laid down his life for us—and we ought to lay down our lives for one another. How does God's love abide in anyone who has the world's goods and sees a brother or sister in need and yet refuses help?" (1 John 3:16–17).

The earliest Christian description of a church service—after the New Testament era—comes from the famed public advocate for the faith Justin Martyr (AD 100–165). He outlines the five regular elements of the meeting: readings from the writings of the apostles, instruction from a designated leader, a thanksgiving meal of bread and wine, public prayers, and, finally, a collection for "orphans and widows, and those who, through sickness or any other cause, are in want, and those who are in bonds."[53] In approximately the same period, we catch a glimpse of the kind of exhortation Christian leaders gave to the wealthy in their churches. The *Shepherd of Hermas,* composed in Rome around 150, declares: "Instead of fields, buy souls that are in distress, as anyone is able, and visit widows and orphans, and do not neglect them; and spend your wealth and all your possessions, which you received from God, on fields and houses of this kind."[54]

By the year 250, long before Christianity's official legal acceptance, the church in Rome was doing its best to support an extraordinary number of impoverished people on a daily food roster. A letter from Bishop Cornelius of Rome to a church official in faraway Antioch mentions in passing the various ministers and activities of the church, including: "forty-six presbyters [i.e., priests or teachers], seven deacons . . .," and so on, and then "above fifteen hundred widows and persons in distress, all of whom are supported by the grace and loving-kindness of the Master."[55] One thousand, five hundred people in a welfare program is a body of people equal to the largest artisan associations in Rome.[56]

Christians continued these programs in the most difficult of circumstances. Around the same time—middle of the third century—a pandemic hit the Mediterranean world that ravaged cities for a decade. Historians call it the Cyprian Plague, named after the Christian bishop of Carthage in North Africa whose writings provide our clearest firsthand evidence of the nature of the disease: "the bowels, relaxed in constant flux, discharge the bodily strength," Cyprian writes at the outbreak of the pandemic (AD 252); "a fire originated in the marrow ferments into wounds . . . the intestines are shaken with a continual vomiting . . . the eyes are on fire with the injected blood. . . ."[57] You get the idea. Some have speculated that Cyprian is describing a *filovirus* such as Ebola.[58]

Whatever the medical details of the Cyprian Plague, we have confronting evidence that Christians at the time felt duty bound to care for the sick. Often, families abandoned their loved ones at the first sign of sickness. They might not have understood infection control, but they certainly knew that contact with the sick meant almost certain death. A letter from the same time over in Alexandria (on the Mediterranean coast of Egypt) grimly reports the panic that filled the city when the plague hit: "those who were in the first stage of the disease they would thrust away, and fled from their dearest. They would even cast them in the roads half-dead, and treat the unburied corpses as vile refuse, in their attempts to avoid the spreading and contagion."[59] The letter was written by the Alexandrian bishop, Dionysius (AD 200–264). He praises those Christians, certainly not all Christians, who overcame their fears and followed the way of Christ in the pandemic:

> Our brethren, for the most part, were careless of themselves and with exceeding love and filial kindness clung to one another, visiting the sick without regard to the danger, diligently ministering to them, tending to them in Christ; being infected with the disease from others, they drew upon themselves the sickness of their neighbours, willingly taking over their pains. In this manner the best, at any rate, of our brethren departed this life, including certain presbyters and deacons, and some of the laity.[60]

As our world passes through its own pandemic—I am writing in late 2020—I certainly do not endorse Dionysius's rejection of "social distancing" measures, which, to my mind, are an essential aspect of care. Nevertheless, there is something heroic, if naïve, in what he reports. It seems that two hundred years after Jesus, Christians were still reading the parable of the Good Samaritan, which also contains a reference to washing wounds and carrying the injured, and heeding its call to "Do likewise."

One final piece of evidence comes from fifty years later, right at the outbreak of the Great Persecution (AD 303–312). It provides an intimate detail of the charitable programs of one church in the town of Cirta (North Africa). Roman officials entered the church at Cirta hoping to confiscate hidden valuables. In chapter 5 I quoted from the transcript of the interviews, in which state officials confiscated and destroyed twenty-seven codices (books) of Christian Scripture. They were also looking for any items of monetary value. I suppose they imagined that churches might be a bit like pagan temples, which often did contain treasures in vaults, and sometimes even functioned as banks.

The church of Cirta did have several precious objects, mainly vessels for use in the church service. They are listed in the report: two golden chalices, six silver chalices, seven bronze candlesticks, and so on. Then follows an almost humorous catalogue of less valuable articles, clothing from the church's storeroom for the poor. We read of "82 women's tunics, 38 capes, 16 men's tunics, 13 pairs of men's shoes, 47 pairs of women's shoes, 19 peasant clasps." Further inspections of the building found a dining room: "four jars were found there and six pots," says the transcript.[61] Roman authorities *had* uncovered the real "treasure" of the church: its program of charity.

The last few pages have provided only a fragment of the evidence we possess for the explosion of charity among the first Christians in the years after Jesus and before Constantine's conversion. When the emperor eventually freed churches from persecution and then exempted them from taxation, he was setting loose the largest charitable movement the world would ever see. It is an aspect of Christian behaviour that has never disappeared. Even during the most opulent, negligent, and violent periods of church history, redressing poverty remained central to the church's calling in the world. It remains so today, even though much of the west's welfare is now also provided by the state and other secular humanitarian agencies.

The explosion of charity in the fourth century is one clear way in which Christ's teaching has impacted the history of western society. This was "a world before our world," as Peter Brown puts it in the final line of his magisterial volume on wealth and charity in antiquity, but it is "a world from which so many of our own views on wealth and poverty have derived."[62] Constantine's exemptions for the church in the early 300s—which foreshadowed comparable legislation in most western countries ever since—only enabled churches to do more charitable work. Tax breaks might have made the work a little less heroic, but they also made it more widespread. Even today, in a country like Australia, most of the top fifty charities by revenue are Christian charities.[63] Christ's "Go and do likewise," together with Constantine's "churches shall be exempt," remade our world in important ways.

A Final Word about Constantine

The emperor fell desperately ill shortly after Easter in AD 337. He travelled to the spa town of Helenopolis, hoping to find refreshment. When it was obvious that he was in terminal decline, he journeyed to Nicomedia and asked the bishop there to baptize him. It might seem odd that Constantine was baptized twenty-five years after his conversion, but in the fourth century this was not unusual. Baptism was sometimes regarded as the *seal* of one's faith rather than an initiation. As a "catechumen" or student of the faith, Constantine was still considered a Christian throughout his reign. In any case, he took off his purple robes, replaced them with the simple white of a disciple, and was baptized by the bishop of Nicomedia. A few days later he died, before being buried in Constantinople.

It is, of course, impossible to psychoanalyze a figure like Constantine seventeen centuries after his death. His motives and inner life remain obscure to modern historians. Yet there is a remarkable feature of his Christian rhetoric that goes some way toward explaining his approach to faith and how it might have impacted citizens of the empire. In his much-studied *Constantine and the Conversion of Europe*, Cambridge University's Arnold H. M. Jones noted that the emperor spoke of God mainly as a God of power. His favourite expressions were: Mighty One, Highest God, Lord of All, and God Almighty. "Only rarely does he speak of him as the Saviour," Jones notes, "and never as loving or compassionate." From Constantine's surviving letters, speeches, and decrees, it appears that "his relations with his God were regulated by fear and hope and not by love."[64]

Compared to the consistent language of *love* dominating the first three hundred years of Christian literature, Constantine's rhetoric about God was grand and austere. This might not be good Christian theology, but it was excellent *imperial religion* and well suited to the aspirations of the Roman people. Many good Romans would have been attracted to this way of thinking and speaking about Christianity. And many Christians happily sang along.

Constantine did not transform the church in his lifetime. The *romanisation* of Christianity and the *Christianisation* of Rome were long processes. But everyone in the 330s knew that something was dramatically changing: crosses were appearing on the Roman military standards, and coins in the marketplace were being stamped with ☧, the first two letters of "Christ." The meaning was impossible to ignore, and the opportunities hard to turn down. Christians began to dare to believe that Christ was beginning to reign over the earth.

Constantine's record is a strange combination of peacemaking and violence, of humanitarian reform and bigotry, of legislated religious freedom and growing intolerance toward Jews and pagans. The conversion of Constantine to the way of Christ opened the door to the church's own conversion to the ways of the world, to the ways of power, wealth, and even violence, in the name of Christ. The Christendom that slowly emerged provided the world with both unprecedented gifts and unspeakable evils. The once good losers would sometimes become very bad winners.

But before the church revealed its full blessings and gravest sins, it experienced a near-complete reversal of Constantine's legacy. Twenty-five years after the first Christian emperor, one of his successors would seek to sideline Christianity and revive paganism's supreme place in the empire. Had he succeeded, western history might have looked very different. I am talking about the whirlwind reign of Emperor Julian.

Julian the Apostate

An Emperor Winds Back the Clock on Christianity in the 360s

The worship of the gods is on a splendid and magnificent scale, surpassing every prayer and every hope.

—EMPEROR JULIAN

I n the AD 330s, 40s, and 50s, everything seemed to be going the church's way. Successive emperors and co-emperors (Constantine II, Constantius II, Constans I, Gallus Caesar) continued in the tradition of Constantine the Great. They tolerated paganism (mostly) and cemented Christianity's place in the empire. Yet, it is a sign of just how fragile this transition period was that a young, bright emperor in the early 360s could rapidly reverse Christianity's fortunes. Bishops woke up one day to find themselves shut out of the halls of power and their people put squarely on the back foot. The old religions would once again take centre stage.

Emperor Julian's Pagan Revival

Flavius Claudius Julianus (AD 332–363) was born in Constantinople in the last years of Constantine's reign. He was, in fact, Constantine's nephew and the cousin of the great intervening senior emperor, Constantius II, who ruled from 337 to 361. Although raised in a Christian household, Julian abandoned his faith at age twenty. He had read widely in both Christian and pagan literature, as was the norm among Christian intellectuals of this time. In fact, it was one of his Christian tutors, George of Cappadocia, who had introduced him to the works of the classical pagan tradition. Reflecting later, Julian would describe George's library as "very large and complete and contained philosophers of every school." Indeed, when Julian became emperor in 361, he demanded that George's entire library, every single volume, be brought to him, on pain of "the severest penalty" to the poor man charged with the task.[1]

In any case, after studying for a time in Athens and elsewhere, Julian zealously embraced Greek philosophy and literature, initiated himself into venerable religious cults of Greece, and was a devotee of "theurgy," a magical practice designed to unite the human soul with the divine. He even published a "Hymn to the Mother of the Gods" (i.e., Cybele): "Grant to the Roman people in general that they may cleanse themselves of the stain of impiety [i.e., Christianity]; grant them a blessed lot, and help them to guide their Empire for many thousands of years!" his hymn pleads. "Grant me virtue and good fortune, and that the close of my life may be painless and glorious, in the good hope that it is to you, the gods, that I journey!"[2] We will see in a moment that he did not quite get the "painless and glorious" death he prayed for.

When Julian became emperor in AD 361 at age thirty, he set about dismantling the position of the church in society. He did not persecute the "Galileans," as he called them, in the manner of earlier emperors. But he used every other available means. He flushed Christians out of his imperial court, rescinded the tax exemptions of Constantine, banned Christian academics from teaching (more on that in a moment), and published tracts ridiculing them. He also did everything he could to revive the glories of the old religion, building and refurbishing temples, sponsoring pagan priests in various cities, and, in the words of Rowland Smith of the University of Newcastle upon Tyne, "overtly discriminated in favour of pagan individuals and communities in his appointments and judgments."[3] His "measured" approach to oppressing Christians is captured well in a brief letter to an imperial administrator named Atarbius: "I affirm by the gods that I do not wish the Galileans to be either put to death or unjustly beaten, or to suffer any other injury; but nevertheless I do assert absolutely that the god-fearing must be preferred to them."[4]

It seems that Julian was true to his word: he did not order the violent persecution of Christians. He did, however, sometimes turn a blind eye. In the city of Alexandria in northern Egypt in the first year of his reign, a massacre of Christians took place. Apparently prompted by Christians mocking the pagan gods in public, a mob "assailed the Christians with whatever weapon chanced to come to hand, in their fury destroying numbers of them in a variety of ways . . . [the text lists the gruesome methods]." They then descended on the main church of Alexandria and dragged Bishop Georgius outside. They "fastened him to a camel, and when they had torn him to pieces, they burnt him together with the camel." The usually fair-minded Socrates Scholasticus, the Christian scholar who records the event, half-acknowledges that Georgius had it coming: for "he had been exceedingly obnoxious to all classes, which is sufficient to account for the burning indignation of the multitude against him."[5] A pagan writer from the period, Ammianus Marcellinus, also tells us that Bishop Georgius was "forgetful of his calling, which counselled only justice and mildness" (a nice description of Christianity on a good day!). He adds that even local Christians "burned with hatred for Georgius."[6] He must have been a piece of work! In any case, my point is that when Emperor Julian heard about the killings, which involved many more victims than Georgius, he did almost nothing about it. He wrote to the city scolding them for disorderly conduct that was beneath the dignity of so great a city.[7] There were no further consequences, and no one was brought to justice.

On one occasion Julian blamed the Christians for a destructive fire in the great temple to Apollo at Daphne near Antioch. He had the great church of Antioch closed as punishment, even though our pagan source—Ammianus again—concedes the rumour was untrue.[8] On another occasion the emperor seized all the property and goods of the church of Edessa (a long-Christian city near the Syrian-Turkish border) and, with dripping sarcasm, explained that he was really just helping Christians achieve their own high ideals: "Since by their most admirable law they are bidden to sell all they have and give to the poor, in order to aid those persons in that effort, I have ordered that all their funds, namely, that belong to the church of the people of Edessa, are to be taken over that they may be given to the soldiers, and that its property be confiscated to my private purse."[9]

Just when I find myself almost admiring Julian's wit and verve, I recall that his most famous action against the Christians was designed to deal a decisive blow to their intellectual progress in Roman society. On 17 June 362 he decreed that all "masters of studies"—the equivalent of schoolteachers and university lecturers—had to be approved directly by him.[10] Julian was effectively banning Christian instructors from all schools. (Christians would return the compliment one hundred and sixty years later, when Emperor Justinian would sack *pagan* professors, as discussed in chapter 18.) Julian explained his measures in a letter on the matter. He thought it was shameful to have professors of the divine traditions of the Greeks who did not themselves affirm the Greek divinities: "what is that but the conduct of hucksters," he wrote. "I think it is absurd that men who expound the works of these [Greek] writers should dishonour the gods whom they used to honour."[11] A number of Christian professors in prominent positions had to resign. One was the celebrated Victorinus at the academy of Rome, whose very public conversion to Christianity a decade earlier had caused a sensation. Another was the gifted Armenian philosopher Prohaeresius at the venerable academy of Athens.[12] (Many are unaware today that longsuffering Armenia was the first nation to embrace Christianity officially[13]). Today's perception of the church as opposed to "secular" scholarship does not fit with our ancient evidence. Christian philosophers were, in fact, one key factor in the church's success among pagan elites. That's what Emperor Julian was trying to stop.

Julian's Pagan Welfare Program

The other thing Julian tried to stop was Christianity's virtual monopoly on charitable services among the destitute. This emperor provides some of the best evidence we have for the pervasiveness of church-run welfare programs in the fourth century. On the one hand, Julian castigated Christians for their "philanthropy." On the other, he tried to emulate them by establishing similar programs in pagan temples, explicitly based on the church model. In a letter to an unknown pagan priest—a kind of *director* of priests—Julian writes about the disease of Christianity, and its antidote:

> We must pay special attention to this point, and by this means effect a cure. For when it came about that the poor were neglected and overlooked by the [pagan temple] priests, then I think the impious Galileans [Christians] observed this fact and devoted themselves to philanthropy. And they have gained ascendancy in the worst of their deeds through the credit they win for such practices. . . . The Galileans also begin with their so-called love-feast [open meals], or hospitality, or service of tables—for they have many ways of carrying it out and hence call it by many names—and the result is that they have led very many into atheism.[14]

Julian frequently calls Christians "Galileans" to mark their origins in the backwaters of Palestine. He also calls them "atheists" because they deny the noble gods of Greece and Rome. In any case, the emperor wants pagan priests to be active in charitable works, just like the Christians. He wants to beat the church at its own game.[15] In a speech before the Roman senate, Julian berated the noblemen for allowing their women to sponsor Christianity's efforts to feed the poor: "Every one of you allows his wife to carry everything out of his house to the Galileans, and when your wives feed the poor at your expense they inspire a great admiration for godlessness [i.e., Christianity] in those who are in need of such bounty."[16]

The theme is even clearer in another of Julian's letters, to Arsacius the high priest of Galatia, the year before the emperor's death. In it, the emperor marvels at the rapid return of pagan religion, which he had brought about in the last year. Then he laments that, nonetheless, Christianity continues to thrive because of its charitable services. His solution is to demand the establishment of a similar welfare program in the traditional temples:

> No one a little while ago would have ventured even to pray for a change of such a sort or so complete within so short a time [a reference to his own work in the last twelve months or so]. Why, then, do we think that this is enough, why do we not observe that it is their [Christians'] benevolence to strangers,

their care for the graves of the dead and the pretended holiness of their lives that have done most to increase atheism? I believe that we ought really and truly to practise every one of these virtues. And it is not enough for you alone to practise them, but so must all the priests in Galatia, without exception. Either shame or persuade them into righteousness or else remove them from their priestly office.[17]

There is passing reference in the above quotation to a dimension of Christianity's charity in ancient times that is often overlooked (and I failed to discuss it in chapter 7). Julian mentions the Christians' "care for the graves of the dead." He is referring to the extraordinary *burial services* of the church in the second to the fourth centuries.

The Church as a Burial Society

Tourists to Rome nowadays often visit one of the several major underground catacombs on the outskirts of the ancient imperial capital. To us all these years later, they seem rather creepy—miles of caves with row after row of niches cut into the walls where the dead were laid to rest. But to ancient people these were a godsend.

One of the great terrors of ancient life was the thought of dying without a proper burial. To be left to the elements or wild beasts was horrific. And that is exactly what happened if you were not wealthy enough to afford a burial site or if you had not paid your monthly fees to a funerary union, whose purpose was to collect your body upon death and guarantee you a decent burial. They would even collect your body if you died on a faraway business trip. Documentation for such unions has survived, so we know they were not cheap: the joining fee alone was the equivalent of about a month's wages for a day labourer, and the monthly dues were about half a day's wages.[18]

The Christian solution was to offer their own free burial service, part of which can still be glimpsed in the vast catacombs of Rome. Literally hundreds of thousands of people were buried there. A few years ago I walked through the Catacomb of Priscilla in Rome, filming a scene for a documentary. What is striking—once you get used to the creepy atmosphere—is the sense of "family" expressed in this burial system. You were laid to rest amongst your fellow believers, young and old, rich and poor alike. Traditional Roman burial grounds, just like traditional Roman life, usually observed strict boundaries between the classes, separating nobles from the plebs with a wall, fence, or border stones. Not so in the Christian catacombs. We can tell that some wealthy Christians were buried there. Tomb designs and funerary art make that obvious. But there is a surprising absence of any separation between rich and poor. An important archaeological analysis by John Bodel in 2008 observes, "The novelty in the catacombs is that the two forms of burial [rich and poor] are integrated with each other and housed within the same undefined space." What we see is "a heterogeneous mixture of persons of different wealth and status with no distinctively unifying beliefs about the representation of privilege in burial." A Christian catacomb was thus "a world of its own, without normal parameters."[19]

The church's "care for the graves of the dead," as Emperor Julian put it, was not a mere practical necessity. Christians saw it as a fitting expression of one of the most basic thoughts in the Jewish-Christian view of reality: every man, woman, and child was made in the image of God, as we saw in chapter 3. In his account of the faith written for Roman intellectuals, Lactantius (AD 240–320) contrasts the opinion of certain pagan philosophers with the demands of Christianity:

> The last and greatest duty of piety is burial of strangers and paupers, something which those [pagan] experts in justice and virtue have never discussed. . . . What is in the balance is an idea. We will not therefore permit a creature made in God's image to fall prey to wild beasts and birds: we will return it to the earth whence it came; unknown to us he may be, but we will fulfil his kinsmen's duty.[20]

It is an interesting argument. The Christian duty to grant even strangers and paupers a proper burial might not provide any practical *benefit* to the departed. But it pays due honour to the idea that human beings are creatures made in God's image, valuable to the Father of creation, if not to anyone else.

Julian's Last Gasp

Julian detected that such Christian charities were a key to the growth of the church—to the "increase in atheism"—and so he tried to launch his own welfare system. In the letter to Arsacius quoted a moment ago, the emperor advises that he has provided the equivalent of millions of dollars from the imperial treasury to ensure its success:

> I have but now made a plan by which you may be well provided for this; for I
> have given directions that 30,000 modii of corn shall be assigned every year
> for the whole of Galatia [= 59,400 dry gallons, weighing more than 2 tons],
> and 60,000 pints of wine [= 28,000 litres]. I order that one-fifth of this be
> used for the poor who serve the priests, and the remainder be distributed by
> us to strangers and beggars. For it is disgraceful that, when no Jew ever has
> to beg [because of the Jewish welfare system], and the impious Galileans
> support not only their own poor but ours as well, all men see that our people
> lack aid from us.[21]

Julian's program was short-lived. On 26 June 363, as his armies progressed toward their goal of invading Persia in the east, he was hit by an arrow and died later that evening. His sudden death signalled the end of the campaign to revive paganism and to send Christianity back into obscurity. His welfare program in the temples never took off. Who knows what happened to the money and resources dispatched to Arsacius!

One of our ancient sources, admittedly written by a gloating Christian named Theodoret of Antioch, says it was reported that Julian clutched his wound on the battlefield, "filled his hand with blood, flung it into the air and cried, 'Thou hast won, O Galilean'!"[22] Whatever the truth of this report, Julian's death did mark the day the "Galilean" won.

Julian's immediate successor was his own general, Jovian. He died the following year (AD 364), apparently overcome by the fumes of his charcoal stove, but not before officially reversing Julian's anti-Christian policies. The empire, again split, was left to Valentinian in the west and his brother Valens in the east. Valentinian's decade-long reign (AD 364–375) has been described as "tolerant of pagans and most heretics,"[23] and overlapped with the first year of the bishopric of Ambrose of Milan (AD 374), a man who, as we shall see, was *not* renowned for tolerance.

By the late 300s the Christian emperors and churches would not risk another Julian. Christians would climb the social ladder and declare their vision for society from the palace rooftops. In previous generations bishops were forbidden to be chosen from among the elites of society. Pretty soon, however, church leaders were being parachuted in from the Roman Senate itself. And they would act like it.

Muscular Christianity

A Senator and Bishop in the Late 300s

The gap between the Forum and the church, which had seemed considerable a generation before, came to be closed.

—PETER BROWN, PRINCETON

The most unfortunate trends in the centuries leading up to the Crusades have their roots—or at least their premonitions—in the changes that began to take place when Constantine invited the church to dine at his table. This is not to buy into the cliché that Constantine caused the moral collapse of the church. Neat patterns like that may help us to picture a story, but they rarely correspond to the lumpiness of history. As I hope I have shown, many of the things Constantine did were improvements on what came before. A humanizing trajectory seemed possible, even after the great interruption of the reign of Julian. But things were variable.

The Roman Empire remained predominantly pagan for at least a century after Constantine. But the growing success of the church in evangelization and in the soft power of imperial influence led to the once-bullied slowly becoming the bullies. In the course of time, after some significant transition points, the Saviour's cross would seem like a perfectly plausible emblem on the shoulder of a medieval swordsman.

One major transition figure appeared toward the end of the 300s. Just like Constantine at the beginning of that century, this figure also "reigned" for about twenty-five years. He was not an emperor, however. He was the first Roman senator turned bishop. Bishop Ambrose (AD 339–397) is an amazing historical figure: elite statesman, experienced legislator, friend of emperors, as well as Christian convert, poet, and preacher. Before we get to Ambrose, I need to say something about the way Christians had been climbing up the social ladder in the decades leading up to him.

The Christian Social Ladder from AD 50–350

The church in the centuries after Constantine became rich and powerful. There are deep and subtle paradoxes to get our heads around here. The obvious one is: How did the champion of the poor end up amassing untold wealth?

The church itself was generally lower class. There were exceptions, even in the first century. Writing to the Corinthians back in AD 56, for example, the apostle Paul remarked, "Consider your own call, brothers and sisters: not many of you were wise by human standards, not many were powerful, not many were of noble birth" (1 Cor 1:26). "Not many," of course, suggests *a few*. And the few must have really stood out in the early period.

Evidence from about fifty years after Paul (around AD 112) enhances our picture of the social spectrum of the early Christians. At the beginning of the second century, Governor Pliny of Bithynia complained to Emperor Trajan (as we saw in chapter 5) that Christianity had "infected" a "great many individuals of every age *and class*."[1] If there was an increasing number of Christians from "every class," Roman snobs in the following century still characterised the church as the "dregs" of society. One day around the year 200, three elite men, Minucius, Caecilius, and Octavius, were strolling along the beach at Ostia, a lovely port city twenty miles southwest of Rome. (By the way, the town is beautifully preserved and well worth a visit). Octavius had recently become a Christian. When the topic of religion came up, his learned friend Caecilius shared his thoughts about the movement. He had both *theological* criticisms and *social* ones. Minucius recorded Caecilius's tirade for posterity: Christians are "a reprobate, unlawful, and desperate faction," he said. And "having gathered together from the lowest dregs the more unskilled, and women," the church was a "profane conspiracy." They "despise the temples as dead-houses, they reject the gods, they laugh at sacred things; half naked themselves, they despise honours and purple robes. Oh, wondrous folly and incredible audacity!"[2]

Christianity did not draw its members only from the "lowest dregs." Octavius himself was living proof. And, in any case, burial inscriptions in the Roman catacombs and cemeteries of this period (third and fourth centuries) reveal a surprising array of occupations for believers: there are artisans, tradesmen, minor civic officials, women silk weavers, a mirror-maker, barbers, horse-groomers, and—I kid you not—a comedian named Vitalis, whose inscription tells how "from jokes I gained a handsome house and income." And he fretted, "O death, you do not appreciate jokes."[3]

The rhetoric against Christians as mere "dregs" who "despise purple robes" probably derives from the church's reputation in this period as the defender of the poor. In our secular liberal society today, that sounds like an honour, but it was not intended as a compliment in a culture that dogmatically connected your social worth with your nobility and wealth. But things slowly changed.

Constantine's gifts and tax breaks to the church in the years following 312 simultaneously boosted Christianity's charitable work and enhanced its financial independence and sway. It was only a matter of time before the nobility accepted the church and the church accepted the nobility. Princeton's Peter Brown wrote the standard volume on "wealth, the fall of Rome, and the making of Christianity in the West" (the subtitle of his book). He thinks the transition was inevitable: "Of all the developments in the history of late Roman Christianity, the entry of the rich and powerful into the church was, in many ways, the most predictable." While churches continued to be associated with the poor, and were frequently dismissed as the simple poor, the fact is, Brown explains, the church in the first decades of the fourth century was by now mostly "well-to-do plebs"—what we might call lower middle class—and they remained open at *both ends* of the social spectrum: the destitute *and* the nobles were welcome. So, "by the year 350," says Brown, "the rich were already there, waiting in the wings, as it were, to make their presence felt in the churches."[4]

The subtleties and paradoxes mount. The church did not suddenly become a *thug* just because it had tax exemptions and wealthy patrons. Most other civic societies and pagan temples enjoyed similar privileges. And the church remained the sole dispenser of charity in the Roman world. As I was recently reminded in a polite argument with an Oxford scholar and defender of Christianity (who shall remain nameless), the greater the church's wealth and power, the more civic *good* the church was able to do for the millions of people on the edges of Roman society. That cannot be denied. As I was forced to admit to my interlocutor, the popular equation *wealthy church = compromised Christianity* is simplistic.

Six years after Constantine's death, in the period when the rich were still "waiting in the wings," an ecclesiastical council sought to make it difficult for the wealthy to enter their leadership. Constantine had already forbidden elites to join the clergy back in AD 320, as we saw. But in the year 343 bishops gathered at Serdica in modern-day Bulgaria, three hundred miles northwest of the imperial capital of Constantinople, to express their own disapproval at the rich becoming bishops without first serving for "an extended time" in more lowly positions. Bishop Ossius took to the floor (yes, we have detailed minutes of this business meeting from seventeen centuries ago!). He proposed: "I think it necessary that you treat this most carefully: if it happens that either a rich man or a jurist from the forum, or an administrator, shall have been asked for as a bishop, he shall not be ordained before he has discharged the function of lector [Bible reader] and the office of deacon and the ministry of presbyter [priest] . . . [so that] his faith, his modesty, his dignity, and reverence can be proved." Happily, the whole council replied in unison, "This is pleasing," and the rule was entered into canon, or church, law.[5] For a time, at least, it seems bishops themselves were nervous about the danger of wealth and power creeping into their ranks.

The ruling did not last. As the fourth century rolled on, it became clear that Christianity was fully legal and here to stay. The wealthy slowly walked out of the wings of the church and into the centre. This was not just because they wanted to get ahead. In this period you could get ahead more easily by joining one of the other—more numerous—civic or religious associations.

Peter Brown argues that what elites found in Christianity was "a social urban lung . . . a certain lowering of the sense of hierarchy and a slowing down of the pace of competition."[6] Rome was a place of fierce competition *among* the elites and *between* elites and non-elites. The church offered a form of society "with a gentler face," as Brown puts it.[7] In time, the wealthy would repay the church for the breath of fresh-air it provided by contributing their money and influence to its cause. Thirty years after the bishop's council at Serdica just mentioned, the church at Milan would get its first Roman senator and local governor *as its bishop*. It is an important evolution in the history of Christianity.

Ambrose: Roman Senator and Christian Bishop

It was, perhaps, inevitable that some of the Christian elite "waiting in the wings" would eventually assume church *leadership*. And, without doubt, the richest and most powerful person to make that move was Aurelius Ambrosius, Saint Ambrose (AD 339–397). In 374 he became the bishop of the important northern Italian city of Milan (now more famous for fashion than religion). If Constantine at the beginning of the fourth century was a turning point for the legal position of the church in the empire, the conversion and ordination of Ambrose toward the end of that century signalled a new era of elite power inside the church and, therefore, a fresh vision of the church's role in society. As a former Roman senator and governor, Ambrose has sometimes been described as the epitome of the proud, elitist, moralising bishop. That may be true. But in this period such a figure could not yet be a cliché. Ambrose was the first.[8]

Ambrose is famous in church history for several reasons. He left a great body of writings, five thick volumes in the modern editions, which have been studied ever since. In fact, the Catholic Church today regards Ambrose as one of the four traditional "Doctors (i.e., teachers) of the church," along with Jerome (AD 342–420), Augustine (AD 354–430), and Pope Gregory the Great (AD 540–604). Yes, all men! Only recently were women added to this illustrious list.[9] Ambrose is also widely known for his role in the conversion of the greatest western intellectual of the period—Christian or otherwise—Saint Augustine (AD 354–430), whose works are revered by both Catholics and Protestants today.

But I am particularly interested in the way Ambrose represents a major social or political development in Christianity. Not only did his consecration as bishop make clear that elites would now be welcomed into the highest ranks of church authority, Ambrose himself showed the way to a new *muscular* form of Christianity, one that was not afraid to boss people around for Jesus, for the good of society!

Ambrose came to Milan as imperial governor in the year 370. An aristocrat, politician, and orator fluent in both Latin *and Greek* (not common in this period), he was already a devout Christian. Within three years the Christians of Milan lobbied to make him their bishop. This was something new and surprising. Ambrose—and the wider church leadership—accepted the invitation, and in AD 374 he was parachuted straight into the bishop's role without having been a deacon or priest beforehand. While Ambrose retained some of his wealth and land holdings, becoming a bishop in this period still involved taking a pay cut and a big step down the social ladder. There is no reason to interpret his move cynically. There were still more pagans in the empire than Christians in this period.

Ambrose's eloquence in the pulpit, his personal donations to the church coffers, and his huge emphasis on caring for the poor made him extremely popular. Here was an upper-class Roman who was also a "man of the people." His efforts to make his churches a kind of alternative society in Milan paved the way for a new conception of the role of the bishop as a "public Christian." He was a cross between a holy man and a city mayor. His personal festive robes have likely survived to this day. They are stored in the Basilica of Saint Ambrose in Milan. They are like nothing in church history before: a precious silk garment and a damask cloak with scenes from a lion hunt woven into the fabric.[10] (It is worth Googling "robes of Saint Ambrose.").

As Ambrose's stature in Milan grew and his church increased in numbers, he began to flex his muscles in this increasingly important city. In the 380s he began to use his influence to sideline the Arians (those who rejected the theology of the Council of Nicaea). In 381 he summoned an Arian leader named Palladius to his residence and interrogated him, just as a governor would interrogate a criminal—something he had no doubt done before as governor. There were even stenographers in the hall taking down every incriminating word.

A couple of years later (AD 383), the imperial court resided in Milan. Officials asked Ambrose to free up one of the churches of the city for the use of the Arians. Ambrose refused. He explained that churches were not mere civic halls. They were places of worship. There was a tense standoff in Milan for several months. Roman authorities eventually gave in, not just because of Ambrose's background and personal gravitas but because the bishop had rallied the Christians of the city into large public protests. Crowds filled the streets and the churches, and they sang anti-Arian songs, which Ambrose himself had composed. Here is a verse from one of them (translated from the Latin into rhyming English):

> O Jesu, Lord of heavenly grace,
> Thou brightness of thy Father's face,
> Thou fountain of eternal light
> Whose beams disperse the shades of night.[11]

With songs, preaching, and political manoeuvres, the former-senator-now-bishop was able to push Arianism to the margins of society.

Ambrose began to speak out publicly *against* various imperial measures and even dared to contradict the emperor himself. For example, in AD 388 in the faraway Roman border town of Callinicum (Raqqah, Syria), Christians attacked a Jewish synagogue at the instigation of their local bishop. They burnt it to the ground (more on Christian riots in chapter 11). When news of the destruction of the Callinicum synagogue reached the emperor, now Theodosius I (reigned AD 379–95), the emperor ordered the punishment of the arsonists and the immediate rebuilding of the synagogue at the church's expense. Fair enough, too! But Ambrose caught wind of this—he was kept informed about most imperial machinations—and he demanded that the emperor cease and desist. Theodosius was a regular attender at Ambrose's church in Milan, and the bishop wryly asked in public, "Are the Jews to inscribe the façade of their synagogue with the inscription: 'The temple to impiety, built out of booty taken from the Christians'?"[12] Ambrose lists the churches that Jews had burnt down during the reign of Emperor Julian twenty-five years earlier: two at Damascus, he says, and others in Gaza, Ascalon, and Beirut.[13] No one was punished for those crimes, he remarks. Christians had to rebuild the structures themselves. It would thus be a betrayal of Christ to force the church now to rebuild the synagogue. Ambrose went further: Theodosius's order was "like that given by Julian"![14] Ambrose's words—which can be read in full in his widely published *Epistle* 74—are chilling in their vindictiveness toward Jews and in their audacity toward the emperor. Theodosius acquiesced. The emperor obeyed the bishop.

Ambrose flexed his muscles again two years later. In 390 Theodosius had ordered a retaliatory massacre of seven thousand civilians in the Greek city of Thessalonica. On receiving the shocking news, the bishop of Milan called Theodosius to account and banned him from receiving communion until the emperor repented, publicly! Theodosius attended church in Milan for months without wearing his imperial robes—a big deal for an emperor—until Ambrose was satisfied and readmitted him to the faithful.[15] This may smack of the high-handed behaviour we associate with popes in the late Middle Ages, but it was an entirely new thing in Ambrose. It was a gamble on Ambrose's part, not just a power play. In this case—but not in all cases—the bishop's sheer moral authority and popular appeal won the day.

Ambrose's Christian Society

Ambrose's persona as a "man of the people" was the key to many of his successes in the (now imperial) city of Milan. In addition to his vigorous preaching ministry, he rallied his clergy to step up and become "public Christians" themselves. Most other priests and bishops throughout Italy were middling men compared to Ambrose. Few of them would have thought that their role included exercising civil influence. The traditional tools of the church had been prayer, service, preaching, and suffering. That had worked out pretty well. But in his work "On Duties" (AD 388), Ambrose laid out a vision of the bishop as active in society for its good. While Christians were not yet a majority in the empire, they were the most influential single association. They had considerable property holdings and major benefactors (and a sense of divine calling, of course!). They also drew from all layers of society, from slaves to senators. Ambrose's idea was that all these things should be used to mend what was broken in Roman society. The church was to gather together the competing classes, especially the forgotten classes, into one new humanity under Christ. Ambrose helped other clergy flex their own (considerably smaller) muscles to the same end. On one occasion he encouraged the bishop of nearby Pavia to refuse the efforts of local tax officials to seize a wealthy woman's large donation to the church.[16] One can definitely see a growing sense of entitlement on the part of the church in Ambrose's day.

Ambrose set his vision of an alternative society against a very popular view of the church among pagans at this time. Many non-Christians had long said that the ills of the empire—military losses, a divided empire, stalled wealth— were proof that the gods were unhappy with the decline of traditional Roman religion. Ambrose replied that such ills were, in fact, the result of human sin and the abandonment of justice. The church, therefore, and not the pagan temples, had the true answer to Roman troubles. Only the church, he said, attended to humanity's sorrows, sins, and fractures. "For her own benefit the church owns nothing, except her faith," Ambrose said in an oration rebutting the pagan high official Symmachus. "These rents and these revenues the Church gives away. The possessions of the church are expenditure on the poor." By contrast, he challenges, "Let them [pagans] count up how many captives the temples have ransomed [i.e., slaves they have freed], what nourishment they have offered to the poor."[17]

One of the first tests of Ambrose's approach to the church in society was his insistence in AD 383–384 that the statue of the goddess Victory (Nike in Greek) should be removed from the Roman Senate House. This was like asking for the removal of the Statue of Liberty in New York or Nelson's Column in London. It brought him into direct conflict with the high official Symmachus, who argued that removing the goddess would be an affront to the memory of Rome and to the gods that had upheld Rome for centuries. Ambrose countered that there are plenty of opportunities for pagans to worship their false gods in their own temples, but idolatry should not be present in the Senate House. The argument went back and forth in print and in public orations. Ambrose finally won, convincing Emperor Valentinian II to remove the statue.[18]

The removal of Victory from the seat of Roman politics was yet another signal that the old ways were fading and that the Roman state intended to back Christianity all the way. "One should not underestimate the 'gentle violence' brought to bear on upper-class society," writes Peter Brown, "by the permanent presence of a Christian court, even when the politics of the emperors (and their choice of public servants) tended to remain religion blind."[19] Ambrose's muscular Christianity—his "gentle violence"—was beginning to win.

A key point to observe in all this is that Ambrose felt that he and his clergy were wholly justified in sidelining pagans and heretics, in amassing church wealth, and in exercising wide civic influence. They alone were effecting society's cure by establishing Christ's new humanity in the world. Becoming a "bully" for Jesus (to put it perhaps unfairly) was for the benefit of all. And given the church's reputation as the champion of the poor, many in the broader population welcomed this more muscular Christianity.

Ambrose's twenty-plus year episcopal career (AD 374–397) was as significant for the making of the Christian west as Constantine's conversion had been two generations earlier. It was the real "turning point in the Christianization of Europe," says Peter Brown.[20] In Saint Ambrose, "the gap between the Forum and the church, which had seemed considerable a generation before, came to be closed."[21] It is not that elites suddenly took over the church or that the church suddenly became mainly elite. It is rather that the church grew into a unique "association," never before seen in the segmented Roman world. It was a public space where all the different layers of society were bound together into a single family. It was a new humanity.

By the end of Ambrose's career, as the fourth century rolled into the fifth, Christianity was beginning to think of itself *for the first time* as the "majority." That probably wasn't numerically true for another half-century, but it was certainly the mood of the church. In Ambrose's own words, Christianity was like the waxing moon in a dark night: "at last it gleams with all the splendour of its radiant brightness."[22] Christ was beginning to "reign on earth," through the church. It is an outlook that would inspire both bullies and saints in the centuries to follow.

Before outlining some of the worst *bullying* that occurred in this time of transition, I want to pause and, in the next chapter, consider some *saintly* figures in precisely the same period. At the very time Ambrose was flexing his muscles in the west, three extraordinary bishops two thousand miles to the east were preaching on behalf of the poor, denouncing the practice of slavery, and establishing the world's first public hospital.

Cappadocian Christianity

Bishops, Healthcare, and Slavery in the Late 300s

*Whenever a human being is for sale, therefore, nothing less than
the owner of the earth is led into the sale-room.*

—GREGORY OF NYSSA

The problem with focusing on a larger-than-life individual like Ambrose
(AD 339–397) is that he can stand in our minds as the exemplar of *everything* the church stood for at this time: removing senate statues, defending the
destruction of synagogues, demanding a seat at the table of influence, and even
pushing emperors around. I chose to detail certain aspects of Ambrose's career,
perhaps at the expense of being entirely fair to him, because many historians
see him as a turning point in the self-confidence of the western church in the
late 300s.

But there are caveats. One is that Ambrose's muscular Christianity pushed
a humanitarian ethic into the centre of imperial life, with lasting benefits for
the vulnerable of Roman and European society. It is one of the paradoxes of

history, as we will see time and again in this book, that strident Christianity, for all its ugliness, did tend to establish charities, build schools, and provide what Peter Brown calls "a social and moral urban lung." Churches were simultaneously "places of moral zero tolerance" and "places of forgiveness, which implied the breaking of boundaries." They were intellectually intolerant but socially philanthropic, a fact "vividly concretized, on a day-to-day basis, by the breaking of social boundaries through outreach to the poor."[1]

There is another major caveat. Numerous other bishops, at the same time as Ambrose, were focusing less on politics and more on the old work of preaching sermons to the faithful, defending Christianity from pagan intellectual attack, and standing up for the weakest of society. And they did this without the structural power a senator-turned-bishop could wield. Stunning examples are found in three famous bishops in Cappadocia (modern central Turkey), two thousand miles to the east of Milan. They are known as the Cappadocian fathers: Gregory of Nazianzus (AD 330–390) and two brothers, known as Basil of Caesarea (AD 330–379) and Gregory of Nyssa (AD 330–395). At least one letter survives from Basil to Ambrose, so it is clear they knew about each other, even if the Cappadocians never met their princely western counterpart.[2]

Trinity, Charity, and the First Hospitals

The Cappadocian fathers are best known today—in theological circles—for their defence of the doctrine of the Trinity. Being highly educated in Christian and secular learning, they were periodically called upon to write essays and give orations expounding the mystery of the Father, Son, and the Holy Spirit.

But they were also passionate defenders of the poor and sick. Gregory of Nazianzus's *Oration 14*, "On Love for the Poor," is arguably the most systematic explanation of the centrality of charity ever composed. It is ten thousand words of biblical, theological, and logical argumentation driving home the point that "love for the poor" is supreme. There is a lovely rhetorical build up through successive paragraphs. "Faith, hope, and love are a fine thing," he begins, before offering a sentence or two on that topic. "Hospitality is a fine thing," he adds, with a sentence or two more. "Zeal is a fine thing . . .," "Humility is a fine thing. . . ." You get the idea.

A thousand or so words into the oration, he reaches his point: "We must regard charity as the first and greatest of the commandments since it is the very sum of the Law and the Prophets," and "its most vital part I find is the love of the poor along with compassion and sympathy for our fellow man. We must, then, open our hearts to all the poor and to all those who are victims of disasters from whatever cause."[3] From this paragraph he launches into a wealth of argumentation designed to leave the apathetic rich with nowhere to hide.

These are not mere words. Gregory Nazianzus's *Oration 14* was composed in connection with the construction in AD 368–372 of a huge welfare complex down the road on the outskirts of Caesarea, the modern town of Kayseri in central Turkey. The complex was known as the *Basileias*, named after Gregory's good friend Basil of Caesarea (AD 330–379). Basil oversaw the creation of history's first dedicated welfare centre and public hospital. Roman armies, of course, enjoyed hospital services. The rich could always employ doctors. The temples of the healing god Asclepius allowed people to sleep at their shrines and receive prayers and attention from the priests in return for donations and public acclamations of Asclepius's greatness. But there was no such thing as free medical care available for all, until Basil.

Basil's idea, what he called his *Ptocheion* or "Poorhouse," employed live-in medical staff who cared for the sick, drawing on the best traditions of secular Greek medicine. The "healthcare centre" (there is no other way to describe it) included *six* separate departments: one for the poor, another for the homeless and strangers, a house for orphans and foundlings (the church in the fourth century was still collecting exposed infants), a completely separate section for lepers, rooms for the aged and infirm, and a hospital proper for the sick.[4]

Basil was one of those Christians, drawing on the ancient Jewish tradition, who believed that if you had resources and withheld them from those in need, you were actually *stealing* from them. In a blistering sermon on Jesus's parable of the Rich Fool (Luke 12:13–21), Basil declared, "The bread that you hold back belongs to the hungry. The coat that you guard in a chest belongs to the naked. The shoes that you have left wasting away belong to the shoeless. The silver that you have buried in the ground belongs to the needy. In these and other ways you have wronged all those you were able to provide for."[5] Basil's sermon would resound through the centuries. In fact, this very paragraph would turn up as an authoritative citation nine hundred years later in the influential analysis of "Charity" by Thomas Aquinas (AD 1225–1274).[6]

Basil died in 379. His friend Bishop Gregory Nazianzus gave the funeral oration. In it, Gregory describes the healthcare centre, now ten years old, as a virtual city. "Go forth a little from this city and behold the new city, the storehouse of piety, the common treasury of the wealthy. . . . Others had their cooks and rich tables and enchanting refinements of cuisine, and elegant carriages, and soft flowing garments," Gregory says. "Basil had his sick, and the dressing of their wounds, and the imitation of Christ, cleansing leprosy not by word but in deed."[7]

The Basileias was the first public hospital in history, but it inspired many others. "Hospitals quickly expanded throughout the Eastern Empire in the late fourth and fifth centuries," writes Gary Ferngren, Professor of History at Oregon State University, "with bishops taking the initiative in founding them."[8] This eastern part of the empire, what we call the Byzantine Empire, had a history all its own, quite untouched by the barbarian takeover of Rome and the collapse of the Roman provinces of Gaul (France) and elsewhere in the 400s and 500s. For a thousand years after Basil, this Byzantine Christian society, which stretched from Turkey to Syria and from Palestine to Egypt, would flourish commercially, artistically, academically, and in widespread charity. More about that in chapter 18.

In the west—in Rome, France, and so on—hospitals were slower coming. Yet, already by 390 the old imperial capital saw the establishment of the first western equivalent of the Basileias. It was founded by perhaps the wealthiest woman in the empire, Fabiola. She belonged to one of the historic founding families of Rome. She survived an abusive husband, gained the emperor's permission to divorce, and, at some point, embraced Christianity. Feeling convicted about her wealth, she discarded her jewels and silken clothes and wore instead the dress of a *plebeian* and the robe of a slave. She became the friend and confidante of Jerome of Bethlehem (AD 345–420), one of the most learned and saintly scholars of the church. It is from two of Jerome's letters to Fabiola, and from his eulogy upon her death in 399, that we know something of her activities.

Fabiola sold her vast property holdings and distributed everything to the poor. Part of this involved founding what Jerome called "an infirmary." It has all the hallmarks of Basil's operation twenty years earlier, including the importance of washing wounds with one's own hands (an unthinkable thing for a highborn Roman woman): Fabiola "gathered into it sufferers from the streets,"

Jerome reports, "giving a nurse's care to poor bodies worn with sickness and hunger—maimed noses, lost eyes, scorched feet, leprous arms, swollen bellies. How often she carried on her own shoulders poor filthy wretches tortured by epilepsy! How often did she wash away the purulent matter from wounds which others could not even endure to look at! She gave food with her own hand, and even when a man was but a breathing corpse, she would moisten his lips with drops of water."[9]

The fame of Fabiola's institution spread from Italy to Britain. In time, many other well-documented hospitals arose in the west, just as they did in the east, all of them established by local bishops, priests, or monks. We have Basil and Fabiola to thank for an institution we now take for granted.[10]

It may be more accurate to say that we have Basil's older sister, Macrina (AD 327–379), to thank for the whole show. The few biographical details we have about Macrina leave the impression of a remarkable woman, whose intellect and example were the dominant force in Basil's and his brother Gregory's lives.[11] She had been taught to read by her mother, and she exerted herself in her studies. When her fiancé suddenly died, she refused all other suitors and devoted herself to the contemplative Christian life. Early on she educated her younger brothers and instilled in them the love of learning for which Basil and, especially, Gregory would become famous. Years later, when Basil returned from his formal studies at the elite academy of Athens, Macrina convinced him not to pursue an academic career but instead to give himself to the service of God and the church. He obeyed, and the outcome would alter history. Although wealthy, Macrina also sold her estate and gave everything to the poor, living out her years in a community of other contemplative women who studied, prayed, and worked a farm to sustain themselves. Together, these women also rescued infants who had been left abandoned. They raised the children within the community.[12] This, too, must have contributed to Basil's—and Gregory's—sense of what a useful life looks like. After Macrina's death in late 379, Gregory wrote a *Life of Macrina* in which he repeatedly describes her as "the great one" and his most important teacher. He mentions how, when she died, many young women grieved loudly: "They were those whom she had taken up when they had been thrown along the roads," he says, "and tended and fostered and led by the hand to the holy and spotless life."[13] In another work, Gregory speaks of his lengthy conversation with his sister just before her death. In it, he "casts Macrina in the role of Socrates in a philosophical dialogue with him as her student," write Lynn Cohick and Amy Brown Hughes in *Christian Women in the Patristic World*.[14] This was quite a compliment coming from the man many regard as eastern Christianity's most gifted intellect. Let me, then, say a bit more about Macrina's and Basil's little brother, Gregory.

The dates of Gregory of Nyssa (AD 335–395) correspond almost precisely to those of Ambrose of Milan (AD 339–397). He even became a bishop about the same time (Gregory in AD 371, Ambrose in AD 374). Gregory of Nyssa was one of the intellectual giants of early Christianity. We do not know if he attended the famed academy of Athens with his brother, Basil—who, as I mentioned in chapter 8, was a classmate of the future emperor and sceptic Julian the Apostate. But, somehow, Gregory eclipsed Basil in philosophical sophistication and rhetorical style. His *Catechetical Lectures*, designed to instruct newcomers in the faith, display an almost unbelievable subtlety and rigour.[15] He wrote many other works, and his thought remains a topic of research in the history of philosophy today. There is even an *International Colloquium on Gregory of Nyssa* that meets every few years.[16]

As a local bishop, Gregory of Nyssa also preached weekly sermons. One of these sermons left us with history's first full-throated attack on the practice of slavery. Christianity, of course, has a complicated history with slavery. I should say something briefly about Christianity and slavery before returning to Gregory's famous sermon.

Christianity and Slavery

It is well known that the leaders of the modern abolition movements were often outspoken Christians with overtly religious arguments, people like Thomas Clarkson (AD 1760–1846) and William Wilberforce (AD 1759–1833) in Britain, and William Lloyd Garrison (AD 1805–1879) and Frederick Douglass (AD 1818–1895) in the United States. Abolitionism was *not* a secular movement. "If the abolition of slavery had been left to enlightened secularists in the eighteenth century," says Professor Rowan Williams of Cambridge and the former Archbishop of Canterbury, "we would still be waiting."[17] That may be too harsh, but Williams has a point. It is a mistake to imagine that the push to end slavery in the eighteenth and nineteenth centuries was a *secular* project as opposed to a *religious* one. There was religion on both sides, to be sure. The difference is: the arguments *against* slavery were almost entirely religious or quasi-religious, whereas the arguments *for* slavery were economic, scientific, and pragmatic, as well as religious. The preeminent American authority on slavery, David Brion Davis, Sterling Professor of History at Yale University, titled his sweeping history of the subject, *In the Image of God*. In it he points out that "[t]he popular hostility to slavery that emerged almost simultaneously in England and in parts of the United States drew on traditions of natural law and a revivified sense of the image of God in man."[18]

The great American campaigner and former slave Frederick Douglass was scathing about churches that supported slavery—and there were many. In his public lectures on both sides of the Atlantic, he described them as the "bulwark of American slavery." To Douglass, slave-supporting churches and theologians were especially culpable, partly because they provided moral cover for an evil economic system, and partly because they were contradicting their own central doctrine that the Creator loves all those "stamped with the likeness of the eternal God," as he put it in a letter to William Lloyd Garrison.[19] It is clear from his speeches that he believed he was calling such churches not *forward* to a "progressive" vision of life but *back* to their foundational doctrine that all men and women share a "common Creator" and deserve filial love and respect.[20] Christian tolerance of slavery was an inexcusable blindspot for many Christians, Douglass and others argued, but it was not an outcome of Christianity. Let me set all this in a more ancient context.

It is true that the New Testament nowhere tells Christians to put an end to slavery. In fact, it tacitly tolerates slavery when it urges slaves to work hard for their masters, and also urges masters to treat slaves justly and fairly, because "you also have a Master in heaven" (Col 3:22–4:1). This is not quite *approval* of slavery. It is instruction on how to live within a seemingly unchangeable Roman system. An analogy might be the instruction in the New Testament to honour and obey the emperor (1 Pet 2:17). This tacitly tolerates pagan hereditary dictatorships, but it would be wrong to think of it as an endorsement of the system.

The New Testament does, however, explicitly condemn "slave traders" as "unholy and profane" and "contrary to the sound teaching" (1 Tim 1:9–11). It urges slaves to gain their freedom if they are able, and it insists that no one should choose to become a slave (1 Cor 7:21–23), as sometimes happened in the ancient world for economic reasons.[21] Almost unbelievably, we have very early evidence from just after the New Testament (AD 96) that Christians sometimes sold themselves into slavery in order to donate the sale price to the destitute.[22] Christians in the second and third centuries also took innovative measures to moderate slavery from within. By AD 115, for example, churches were establishing dedicated funds to pay for the manumission (formal release) of slaves. This ministry grew to become a significant aspect of Christian charity in the first few centuries.[23] Partly in recognition of this ministry, Constantine granted bishops the authority to manumit slaves at church expense in a decree of 18 April 321. This bestowed on former slaves the full rights of Roman citizenship.[24]

Sadly, things rarely went further. Christians did not overthrow slavery, even when they gained the theoretical power to do so, from about the sixth century. The absence of any clear New Testament command to abolish slavery, combined with the ubiquity of the system throughout Roman and barbarian society, meant that most Christians, in most parts of the world, accepted slavery as an unfortunate necessity in a fallen world. Rowan Williams might be right that it was Christianity that "lit a long fuse of argument and discovery [about slavery], which eventually explodes" in the eighteenth and nineteenth centuries.[25] But we can all agree that the fuse was *too long*.

Gregory of Nyssa versus Slavery

This is what makes Gregory of Nyssa's speech against slavery fifteen hundred years before Frederick Douglass so remarkable. It is a bright beam of light in the dark history of humanity and the church. His argument is the obvious one— obvious to us now, anyway. Human beings are made in the *image of God*. They are, therefore, equally and inestimably precious and cannot *belong* to anyone. This is precisely the premise that would win the day for abolition in eighteenth-century England and nineteenth-century America. Gregory of Nyssa saw this connection in the fourth century. Here is a portion of his remarkable sermon:

> You condemn man to slavery, when his nature is free and possesses free will, and you legislate in competition with God, overturning his law for

the human species. The one made on the specific terms that he should be the owner of the earth, and appointed to government by the Creator—him you bring under the yoke of slavery, as though defying and fighting against the divine decree. By dividing the human species in two with "slavery" and "ownership" you have caused it to be enslaved to itself, and to be the owner of itself. For what price, tell me? What did you find in existence worth as much as this human nature? What price did you put on rationality? How many obols [coins] did you reckon the equivalent of the *likeness of God*? How many staters [more expensive coins] did you get for selling the being *shaped by God*? God said, *let us make man in our own image and likeness* (Gen 1, 26). . . . Whenever a human being is for sale, therefore, nothing less than the owner of the earth is led into the sale-room. But has the scrap of paper, and the written contract, and the counting out of obols deceived you into thinking yourself the master of *the image of God*? What folly![26]

I have often wondered how different history might have been if Gregory of Nyssa, rather than Ambrose of Milan, had risen to chief prominence in the empire and gained the ear of the emperor. Gregory preached this sermon in about the year 380, right around the time Ambrose was cross-examining heretics, leading protests to prevent imperial use of church buildings, and complaining over Christians having to pay for a synagogue they burned down.

I do not mean to be harsh on Ambrose. I hope my Catholic readers will forgive such talk about one of their canonized saints. But there is an important lesson here for me as I study history. It is one that I have often recalled while writing this book. Sometimes the darkest and brightest moments of church history happen at the same time. This probably does not apply to the first three centuries, which seem to me like one long harmonious performance of Christ's original melody. But certainly from the fourth century—and obviously today—we often find beauty and discord together at the same time, though not always in equal proportion. Gregory and Ambrose were both great men. For me, one embodied the very essence of Christ's teaching. The other was as quintessentially Roman as he was Christian. For better and worse—and I do mean *both*—it was Ambrose who set the model for church-state relations in the west for the decades and centuries to come.

There would be many other Macrinas, Gregories, and Basils in church history. They can be heard bellowing from the side lines, and sometimes from the centre, urging Christians to remember the beautiful tune. We will meet many more of them in the following pages. There were also many Ambroses, brilliant and gifted men—yes, sadly, mostly men—who pushed for a more *muscular* Christianity. They did more than pray, persuade, serve, and suffer. They wanted to shape society—for good—by all necessary means. And, sadly, that sometimes even included riots and violence *for Jesus*, as we will now see.

Iconoclastic Christianity

Christian Riots and the Closing of Pagan Temples from 380 to 415

No person shall be granted the right to perform sacrifices; no person shall go around the temples; no person shall revere the shrines.

—EMPEROR THEODOSIUS

In the middle of writing this book, an African American man named George Floyd was killed by police during an arrest in Minneapolis, Minnesota, in the United States. His death triggered a protest movement against police brutality and racial injustice across the US and other parts of the world, including my hometown of Sydney. Protests in some US cities turned violent, prompting the US President Donald Trump to threaten to deploy the military to quell the riots. In a photo opportunity few will forget—it made Australia's evening news—the president offered a display of strength by standing in front of a historic church across the road from the White House, which had been damaged in the protests. He raised a Bible in one hand, somewhat awkwardly, and posed for photos. The message seemed clear: this leader stood for Christianity, and perhaps God stood with him.

Plenty of Christian leaders—on the left and right—criticised President Trump's actions. But the politicization of Christianity was hardly new. One Australian theologian, Dr Robyn J. Whittaker, wrote a piece in *The Conversation*, a news site offering academic commentary, asking "Has he done anything that powerful 'Christian' leaders haven't done for centuries? The answer is no. Co-opting Christianity in the service of power is almost as old as Christianity itself. We have been left with a legacy in Western Christianity of powerful rulers claiming God for their cause," she observes. "It is telling that, in the new Western empire, no American president has been elected without explicitly signalling his Christian faith."[1]

We can probably exclude the first three hundred years of Christianity from Whittaker's pessimistic account. But she has a point. It was not long after Constantine that hopes of an era of "freedom of religion" were dashed. "The 'hands-off' policy of Constantine with regard to paganism itself," writes Princeton's Peter Brown, "was flatly contradicted by the social revolution he himself had furthered."[2] It is just one of the many paradoxes and ironies we have to face in the history of this period. Constantine at the beginning of the fourth century made Ambrose at the end of that century a possibility, even an inevitability. And, as I have said, Ambrose represented a new "muscular Christianity" that had all of the *political confidence* of a Roman senator and all of the *righteous sense of mission* that was native to Christianity. It was a powerful fusion, with definite historical consequences.

Riots for Jesus

By the late fourth century, Christians were increasingly willing to exercise more than the "gentle violence" of pastoral politics.[3] I have already mentioned the burning down of the synagogue at Callinicum (Raqqah, Syria) in 388. Similar Christian mobs and arson attacks are reported in numerous sources for this period.

The great Egyptian city of Alexandria was already well known in antiquity as a place of rioting. One contemporary source bluntly describes Alexandria as "a city which on its own impulse, and without ground, is frequently roused to rebellion and rioting."[4] Christians were there in large numbers by the fourth century. The nearby district of Upper Egypt was one of the centres of the monastic movement, where communities of monks—both men and women, living separately—practised mutual ownership, manual labour, self-sufficiency, study, daily prayers, and wide charitable programs amongst the poor of the region.[5]

I am sorry to say that monks could also form a very effective angry mob. Tensions in Alexandria between Christians, Jews, and pagans had been steadily rising through the fourth century (recall the massacre of Christians in the first year of Julian's reign, AD 361). Now toward the end of the 300s, "there were some two thousand monks within striking distance of the great temples of Alexandria," writes Peter Brown.[6] And in the year 391, the monks *struck*!

The Alexandrian bishop, Theophilus, had asked Emperor Theodosius for permission to repurpose a disused pagan temple as a church. (With the rise of Christianity, there were many such disused temples.) Permission was granted. Restoration work on the building uncovered some basement rooms and items of pagan worship. The local non-Christian population regarded this as a desecration of the old religion, and a riot erupted. Clubs and swords were used against Christians. "Our side far outweighed the other in numbers and strength," says the principal Christian source informing us of these events, "but was less savage due to the mild character of our religion." (How I want to believe that!) "As a result, many of ours were wounded in the repeated conflicts, and some were even killed."[7] Crowds of non-Christians flooded into the great temple of Serapis, one of the architectural marvels of the ancient world, and they took Christians hostage. The mob barricaded themselves in, and a long, tense standoff began.

It is curious that our source, written by the Christian Rufinus of Aquileia, pauses at this point to give a detailed description of the magnificence of the temple and its statue of Serapis. He might have despised the rituals, but he admired the style. He then tells how one of the soldiers, a Christian, hacked away at the great statue. All hell broke loose. The monks and the Christian mob (one and the same thing, really) started attacking the structure. They somehow completely destroyed the temple, which housed some treasures and a library. It was an international event: "the razing of the most splendid temple of antiquity sent a shock through the empire," writes Philip Amidon, the modern translator of the works of Rufinus.[8]

The death of George Floyd mentioned a moment ago triggered a renewal of the Black Lives Matter movement and a wave of statue toppling across America (and, to a lesser extent, England and Australia), a "symbolic revolt against the histories of slavery and colonialism," said the *New York Times*.[9] Confederate statues fell, of course. But so did monuments to George Washington and Thomas Jefferson. In London, a statue of Winston Churchill was attacked by protestors who demanded that it be brought down. In Sydney, police had to guard a threatened memorial to Captain James Cook, the English sailor who "discovered" the eastern seaboard of Australia in 1770. Back in the US, various government buildings, including courthouses, were also targeted by rioters. The events have been a helpful reminder—for me, at least—of the way mass movements can develop a "righteous mind" that expresses itself in violence against monuments of a dark past. I do not mean to equate the political outrage of 2020 with the Christian iconoclasm of the fourth century. But good historical understanding involves trying to see things from the perspective of those you are studying. It is probably important to note that Christian rioters in Alexandria and elsewhere believed they were purifying public spaces of a dark cultural past.

Emperor Theodosius—to return to my specific point—apparently approved of the destruction of the Serapis monument; he possibly even encouraged it. He was an ardent Christian, keen to show his preference for Christianity. But he also announced a pardon for any citizens who had killed Christians during the siege and riots. We are told in our source that he did this in the hope that pagans "might be the more readily induced to embrace Christianity."[10] I find it hard to imagine such events—especially the destruction of the Serapis shrine—would induce anyone to think more highly of the Christian faith, but it apparently did![11] In any case, the iconoclasm continued. Monks in Egypt and elsewhere launched a campaign of destruction of pagan shrines. Worshippers themselves were left unharmed—at least in theory—but the "reign of Christ" meant the eradication of these monuments to Satan.

All the while, to return to a familiar paradox, the monks continued their large-scale charitable activities. They built hospitals and food distribution centres, and they mercifully buried the dead. Indeed, just a few years later, during a barbarian invasion, these same rioting monks were providing locals with an ambulance service, recovering and nursing the injured.[12]

Hypatia, a Secular Martyr?

Twenty-five years later, Alexandria would become the site of one of the most infamous examples of Christian zealotry and violence I have ever studied. At the beginning of the fifth century, the most famous teacher of mathematics and philosophy in Alexandria was a woman named Hypatia. She was the gifted daughter of another local academic named Theon. In AD 415 she was murdered by Christians.

The story of Hypatia is often told as a tale about a brilliant and influential *woman* who, because she taught *secular* philosophy (Neo-Platonism, to be precise), was hated by the church. A Christian mob confronted her at the behest of their bishop, Cyril, stripped her naked, and brutalised her to the point of death before burning her remains on the Egyptian shore. The church was sending a message: We will not tolerate *women* or *education*. The incident marked the beginning of centuries of Christian misogyny and anti-intellectualism. At least, this is the way the tale has been told since the eighteenth-century Enlightenment, including in the 2009 film *Agora* starring Academy Award winning actress Rachel Weisz as Hypatia. A similar account is found in the 2017 volume *A Darkening Age* by former high school classics teacher and journalist Catherine Nixey.[13]

The most authoritative work on the topic to date is *Hypatia: The Life and Legend of an Ancient Philosopher*, by Edward J. Watts, Professor of History at the University of California. Like most professional historians, Watts laments the way the life of a uniquely brilliant ancient philosopher has been reduced to a grim story about her death and what it supposedly tells us about religion. Hypatia was killed by a mob of Christians. That much is true. But Edward Watts is adamant that the awful fate of Hypatia had nothing to do with her *being a woman* or *being educated*. It even had little to do with religion.

As the chief intellectual of the city, Hypatia was asked by the Roman governor, Orestes, to help calm tensions between the local government and the recently appointed bishop of Alexandria named Cyril. Governor Orestes and Bishop Cyril did not get along, in part because Orestes was thought to have backed Cyril's rival for the role of bishop, a man named Timothy. The large Jewish community of Alexandria also opposed Cyril and supported Timothy. Cyril seems to have got a lot of people offside. He was an imperious leader. Later church tradition declared him a "saint," but I am not sure I would have liked to cross him.

Tensions broke out in the year 414 at—of all things—a dance performance in the theatre of Alexandria. The Jewish community present at the performance noticed one of Cyril's key public supporters in the audience, a local Christian teacher named Hierax. The Jews stirred up opposition against Hierax, whom they assumed was there to cause trouble. The governor sided with the Jewish community and ordered Hierax to be tortured *right there in the theatre*. All of this outraged Bishop Cyril, whose resentment toward Governor Orestes and the Jewish community deepened.

This is the context in which Governor Orestes sought the wise counsel of the local star philosopher Hypatia. It was felt that her wisdom and public profile might be able to smooth over tensions between Cyril and the government and between Jews and Christians. "Hypatia seemed like the ultimate neutral arbiter," says Watts.[14] Unfortunately, Cyril interpreted her role as support for Orestes *against* him. In response, one of Cyril's supporters, Ammonius, got carried away one day and threw a rock at the governor and hit him in the head. Luckily, a crowd of locals, including Christians, rushed the governor to safety. But the governor had Ammonius arrested and tortured. He died of his injuries. Cyril promptly (and implausibly) declared the monk Ammonius a martyr for the faith. It was obvious to most, however, including to the Christian source that recorded all this, that Ammonius was just a hot-headed thug.[15]

Governor Orestes and many other leading Christians in Alexandria decided to stop attending any church service at which Bishop Cyril was presiding. This is the other detail often overlooked. Orestes himself was a baptised Christian. He was trying to hold the city together before it descended into (further) chaos.

But any hope Governor Orestes had that Hypatia could help him establish a peace was soon dashed. A rumour spread among zealous supporters of Bishop Cyril that Hypatia had "bewitched" the governor. *That* is why Orestes and other local elites had stopped attending church. It all made perfect sense! In March 415 a group of Cyril's advocates led by a man named Peter confronted Hypatia. It is unlikely they set out to kill her, Watts says.[16] But the confrontation spun out of control. In the words of our best primary source, "dragging Hypatia from her carriage, they took her to the church called Caesareum, where they completely stripped her, and then murdered her with tiles. After tearing her body in pieces, they took her mangled limbs to a place called Cinaron, and there burnt them."[17]

The slaughter of the revered Hypatia outraged people across the empire. Having read the primary and secondary sources about the incident, I too am stunned and ashamed that confessing Christians could do such a thing.

The Hypatia incident reminds us that Christian faith does not prevent people from engaging in shameful acts of violence. While Cyril himself probably did not order an attack on Hypatia, "he was ultimately responsible for creating the climate that caused it," concludes Edward Watts.[18] In his efforts to consolidate his influence in the city, the bishop fostered an atmosphere of bigotry and distrust.

What Hypatia's Death Tells Us (and Doesn't)

Does the life and death of Hypatia tell us anything more broadly about the church's disdain for *women* and *secular knowledge*? The answer is *no*. First, as I just mentioned, the governor himself was a Christian and a deep admirer of Hypatia. In fact, many leading Christians in the city supported Orestes and Hypatia against their own bishop.

Second, Christians around the empire were just as outraged at the death of Hypatia as the general population was, perhaps more so. Indeed, the reason we have firm contemporary details of the event is that *Christians* joined in the wide condemnation of Cyril and his supporters. One leading Christian intellectual of the time, Socrates Scholasticus (AD 380–450), wrote a sober account of events, in which he praised Hypatia's learning and condemned the killers and the bishop. She "made such attainments in literature and science, as to far surpass all the philosophers of her own time," Socrates says. "All men on account of her extraordinary dignity and virtue admired her." He then turns to tell the sorry tale:

> It was calumniously reported among the Christian populace that it was she who prevented [Governor] Orestes from being reconciled to the Bishop [Cyril]. Some of them therefore hurried away by a fierce and bigoted zeal, whose ringleader was a reader named Peter, waylaid her returning home, and dragging her from her carriage . . . [he describes the murder as quoted above]. This affair brought not the least opprobrium, not only upon several, but

also upon the whole Alexandrian church. And surely nothing can be farther from the spirit of Christianity than the allowance of massacres, fights, and transactions of that sort.[19]

Any claim that the killing of Hypatia was connected to Christian opposition to *women* or to *pagan learning* must explain why our earliest and best evidence for the event is a *Christian* source that lauds Hypatia as the intellectual superior of all other (male) philosophers.[20]

Just as relevant is the fact that many of Hypatia's students were Christians. We know of the Libyan aristocrat Synesius and his brothers Eutropius and Alexander. Then there is the philosopher Athanasius, and a friend of Synesius named Olympius.[21] Synesius actually went on to become bishop of Ptolemais, five hundred miles south along the Nile. We have seven admiring letters from Synesius to Hypatia, in which he speaks to her as his "mother, sister, teacher and benefactor."[22] He died the year before Hypatia's murder in 415. His brother Eutropius, also a former student of Hypatia, succeeded him as bishop.

The death of Hypatia was an obscene tragedy, but it did not stop the intellectual progress in Alexandria, right up to the Islamic period (Egypt was taken by Muslims in AD 642). Indeed, as Watts notes, "Fifth- and sixth-century Alexandrian Platonists were some of the most prolific and influential teachers antiquity would ever see."[23] And some of them were Christians, such as the legendary mathematician, grammarian, and philosopher John Philoponus (AD 490–570), whose Greek works were preserved by Arab Christian scholars, passed onto Islamic civilization, and then were brought back into the west by Muslims in the Middle Ages. The writings of Philoponus would eventually influence early scientists such as Galileo (more about that in chapter 18).

The Closing of Pagan Temples: A Very Brief History

We are now in a period when Christian tolerance for the old ways was being exhausted, sometimes at the unofficial level of riots and sometimes at an official level. We can see a clear evolution—or devolution—in imperial policy throughout the fourth century and into the fifth. After Emperor Julian's brief campaign to sideline Christianity in AD 361–363, fresh laws from successive Christian emperors began to clamp down on pagan rituals.[24] Emperor Gratian (AD 359–383) refused to accept the long-established title of *Pontifex Maximus*, or high priest. He thereby effectively withdrew state sponsorship of pagan temples.[25]

The real turning point came with Theodosius in the 390s. He had earlier permitted prayers, incense, and various other rituals to revere the gods in the temples,[26] but later in his reign—perhaps under the influence of Ambrose—he declared the sacrifices illegal and the temples closed. He decreed, "No person shall be granted the right to perform sacrifices; no person shall go around the temples; no person shall revere the shrines." According to this law of 16 June 391, any imperial officials found to have engaged in such activities would be fined "fifteen pounds of gold."[27]

The laws finally banning pagan worship in the Roman Empire were not always scrupulously followed, and various administrative mopping-up operations would follow in later regimes. However, "next to the conversion of Constantine himself," writes John Curran of the Queen's University, Belfast, the ban on pagan worship in AD 391 "was the most significant legal point in the history of fourth-century Rome."[28] Fifty-four years after the death of Constantine the Great, and three hundred and sixty years after Jesus Christ, the old Greco-Roman religions were officially illegal.

You could mark AD 400 or thereabouts in your mental timescale of western history as the moment when Christianity had successfully pushed Greco-Roman religion to the margins, and soon into obscurity. The transformation was slow, but it ended up being total. One clear indication of this today is that everywhere in the west we assume the "monotheism" of Christianity, not the "polytheism" of the Greeks and Romans. Even our celebrated atheists today publish books against *God,* not the *gods*. This perspective only gained ascendency, from Syria to Britain, from the fifth century onwards.

With Christians slowly becoming the majority in the empire, and imperial officials looking to bishops for guidance in the affairs of state, some very important developments occurred in rapid succession. One of the most significant of these was the theological justification for state violence. This is the fascinating and disconcerting topic of our next chapter.

"Just War"

A Theory of Christian War in the Early 400s

The wise ruler will grieve at being faced with the necessity of waging just wars.

—BISHOP AUGUSTINE OF HIPPO

Early in season one of the classic series *The West Wing*, President Bartlet frets about the correct response to a Syrian attack on a US military plane carrying his beloved personal physician and fifty-seven other US medical personnel. A fiery exchange erupts between the president, who is a devout Catholic struggling with feelings of revenge, and his more experienced chief of staff, Leo McGarry:

Bartlet: We are doing nothing.
Leo: We're not doing nothing. Four high-rated military targets . . .
Bartlet: And this is good?
Leo: Of course it's not good; there is no good. It's what there is. It's

how you behave if you're the most powerful nation in the world. It's proportional, it's reasonable, it's responsible, it's merciful. It's not nothing. It's what our fathers taught us.

The title of the episode is "A Proportional Response," which is a key tenet of the ancient theory of "just war." And while I am not sure which "fathers" Leo is referring to in the episode, in the real world it was one particular *church father* who laid out the original theory.

In the previous chapter I mentioned the riotous activities of monks (and other Christians) in Alexandria toward the end of the fourth century and the beginning of the fifth. Most of that could be described—*though not excused*—as mob hysteria in a period of great social and religious change. Such outbursts were not frequent, nor were they part of a broader church policy. Violence in this period never featured in Christian rhetoric. That was about to change.

In the fifth century church leaders began to devise a distinctively Christian account of *state* violence. One of the most politically consequential intellectual developments in the first millennium of Christianity came from one of the most capacious minds of the period. Saint Augustine started to theorize about "*just* war."[1]

As more and more Christians filled administrative positions in the empire, and more and more bishops gained access to the imperial "ear" (on the model of Ambrose of Milan), it was perhaps inevitable that Christian intellectuals would be invited to offer guidance to rulers on how a Christian regime is meant to conduct its wars. This involved some elaborate thinking. How does the religion of "love your enemy," the religion of a *cross*, provide advice to the most successful military machine the world had ever seen?

Christians and Warfare in the First 400 Years

War was perhaps the most venerable feature of Roman culture. Throughout the entire period we have been exploring, emperors were almost continually waging war on multiple fronts, in Persia to the east, in the Baltics to the north, and in Germany to the west. Conquest was a central part of the Roman consciousness from at least the third century BC Punic Wars in North Africa.

For Christians, however, thinking about warfare was new and foreign. The Old Testament contained stories of holy war, but Jews themselves in this period had long believed that Joshua's conquest was unique, designed to secure the land of Israel at its foundation. It was not a model for broader conquest, except inasmuch as it provided the rationale for defending Israel's borders.[2] In Christian theology from the second to the fourth centuries, these Old Testament wars were usually interpreted allegorically. They were known to be genuine historical battles, but their meaning for Christians was entirely symbolic, having to do with Christ's victory over sin and death or the believer's battle with their own unruly soul.[3]

Making things worse—or better, depending on our perspective—the New Testament offered no guidance whatsoever for conducting wars. The apostle Paul had used the metaphor of the "armor of God," in which "righteousness" was a "breastplate," "faith" was a "shield," and the "word of God" was a "sword" (Eph 6:10–17). But it was impossible to interpret such images in these centuries in any concrete way. Paul had elsewhere taught that the pagan state had a right to "bear the sword" to punish wrongdoers (Rom 13:3–5). But he commanded Christians themselves—in the passage immediately before—to "Bless those who persecute you. . . . Do not repay anyone evil for evil. . . . Never avenge yourselves, but leave room for the wrath of God" (Rom 12:14–19). Above all, Christ's death on the cross at the hands of the Romans provided the ultimate critique of violence and a model of patient endurance in the face of suffering.

In the next few centuries, from 100 to 400, Christian thinkers opposed torture, capital punishment, and, for the most part, even participation in the army. We find the occasional literary reference around 200 to individual Christians serving as Roman soldiers.[4] From about the same time, there is a mosaic inscription on the floor of a church in Megiddo, Israel—the oldest yet found—that mentions a Roman "centurion" named "Gaianus." Presumably, he was a Christian benefactor.[5]

On the other hand, a detailed church manual from this time (AD 200) known as *The Apostolic Tradition of Hippolytus* lists the professions that disqualify people from receiving formal instruction in the faith—which, by the way, involved one class once a week for three years! The blacklist includes gladiators, hunters in the arena (who kill beasts for pleasure), officials and trainers for gladiatorial shows, military commanders who are obliged to execute others, and magistrates who also deal out capital punishment. The manual seems to allow regular soldiers to receive teaching (at least, they are not explicitly excluded), but if a fully instructed and baptised Christian "wishes to become a solider, let him be cast out. For he has despised God."[6]

Even a century later, around the year 300, Lactantius wrote straightforwardly, "A just man may not be a soldier, nor may he put anyone on a capital charge."[7] And, finally, rule number twelve of the Council of Nicaea, made in the presence of Constantine himself, declared that Christians who returned to being soldiers are like "dogs who return to their vomit," and if such a soldier changes his mind (again) and comes back to the fold, he must attend a further three years of classes about the faith.[8] It seems that nothing in Christianity's founding documents and founding centuries prepared the church for a marriage between Christian theology and state violence.

Enter the gifted rhetorician turned Christian bishop, Aurelius Augustinus, known today as Augustine (AD 354–430). His thinking on matters of church and state provided the breakthrough Christian regimes needed to find a way to conduct warfare in a manner that might be acceptable to the crucified and risen Lord.

Saint Augustine

Born in AD 354, Augustine grew up in the Roman province of North Africa (modern Algeria). His father was a pagan and his mother a devout Christian. He abandoned any interest in Christianity at seventeen years of age, took a lover with whom he bore a child, and placed his trust in his famed mastery of Latin language and literature. He searched for renown and fortune as a professor of rhetoric, winning teaching posts in the cosmopolitan cities of Carthage, Rome, and Milan (AD 375–385).

During this period Augustine read classical philosophers Cicero and Plotinus, who awakened a desire in him to know the truth of humanity's place in the cosmos. After a lengthy dalliance with an ascetic philosophy known as Manichaeism, he started to come under the influence of Christians in Milan. He soon came to the view that Manichaeism was a stale and doctrinaire philosophy, and Christianity was intellectually vibrant and expansive—almost the opposite of the modern impression.

An elderly Christian philosopher named Simplician (AD 320–400) was particularly influential for Augustine. Simplician was the tutor of Bishop Ambrose. He had also earlier been a friend of the revered pagan philosopher Victorinus, who had stunned Rome in the 350s, at the height of his career, by announcing he wanted to be a Christian. The not-yet converted Augustine was intrigued to discover from Simplician that the great Victorinus, "skilled in all the liberal teachings, who had read and criticized so many works of the philosophers, a teacher of so many noble senators, a man who, as a mark of his distinguished career as a teacher, had deserved and received a statue in the Roman Forum," *could end up a Christian!*[9] As someone obsessed with rhetoric and literature, Augustine had always found the Bible vulgar and simple. Now he was wondering if perhaps truth could be found beyond the hallowed turf of high Latin poetry and prose.

Around this time Augustine came under the influence of the preaching of Bishop Ambrose in Milan. At first Augustine was simply impressed by Ambrose's rhetorical power and personality. Eventually he came to feel that those "plain" Scriptures contained what all humanity had been searching for. In a villa garden one day in the middle of the summer of 386, he heard what he thought was a child repeatedly singing *tolle lege,* "take up, read." Wondering if it was a sign, he picked up a nearby copy of the letters of the apostle Paul from the New Testament. He opened at random and read the words, "Put on the Lord Jesus Christ, and make no provision for the flesh, to gratify its desires" (Rom 13:14).[10] Those words might not sound like much to modern ears, but for Augustine, "Indeed, immediately with the termination of the sentence, all the darkness of doubt were dispersed, as if by a light of peace flooding into my heart."[11]

Augustine felt he had discovered the answer to a philosophical question of his age: How might a rational human being live *beyond* animal passions, in full accordance with the rational soul of the universe? The answer Augustine found in the Gospels and letters of Paul, and which he would spend the next forty-five years expounding, was contained in that line from the book of Romans: Jesus Christ, the perfect embodiment of divinity, offered himself on our behalf, rose again, and poured out his Spirit into a Christian's life, so that by "putting on the Lord Jesus Christ" we might rise above fleshly instincts and rightly desire what is true and good. In what many consider history's first psychological autobiography, Augustine sums up humanity's place in the universe in the opening lines of his *Confessions*: "To praise Thee is the wish of every person who is but a part of Thy creation. Thou dost bestir them so that they take delight in praising Thee: for Thou hast made us for Thee and our heart is unquiet till it finds its rest in Thee."[12]

Augustine was baptised by Ambrose in Milan in AD 387. He was made a priest in 391 and then a bishop in 395 in the important commercial port city of Hippo Regius (modern Annaba, Algeria). He spent the rest of his relatively long life (he died at 76) thinking, teaching, and writing. Augustine's life and thought remain the subject of entire units of study in mainstream universities and seminaries around the world to this day.

Freeing Slaves in North Africa

Before exploring Augustine's influential theory of just war, I should make clear that he was also an intensely pastoral bishop. Almost three hundred of his letters survive, published today in six volumes.[13] They reveal a man deeply involved in the lives of others, concerned for their spiritual and material well-being. He also oversaw significant charitable services, with church farms producing food for the poor and church funds used to free slaves. As I explained in chapter 10, Christians sought to moderate slavery from within. Sadly, we do not know of anyone, apart from Gregory of Nyssa (AD 335–395), who mounted a full-scale critique of slavery. But Christians did feel obliged to assist slaves, when they could, especially when there were sufficient funds to buy someone's freedom. Many early Christians, of course, were themselves slaves or ex-slaves, including one of the bishops of Rome, Callistus, in the early 200s.[14]

Augustine faced a special problem in Hippo. Slave-traders, especially from Galatia in Asia Minor (Turkey), were using his city as a convenient port to ship slaves from north Africa to various destinations throughout the empire and beyond. Augustine had been deploying church funds in the normal way for years. But by the 420s, things were getting out of hand, and Augustine's churches were stretched to the limit.

In a letter to his friend Alypius, a bishop in the nearby city of Thagaste (modern Souk Ahras in Algeria), Augustine reports that large numbers of men, women, and children were being kidnapped and on-sold through Hippo's port.[15]

Parents had sold their children to the slavers, he says. A woman in Hippo had created a lucrative trafficking business by luring women from the wooded hill country of Giddaba (modern Chettabah), south of Hippo, on the pretext of purchasing timber from them, before imprisoning them, beating them, and selling them. One monk from the Hippo monastery was abducted and sold as a slave. Another man, one of the church's tenant farmers growing produce for the poor, sold his own wife into slavery, "stirred solely by this feverish pestilence (of greed)," Augustine says. Making matters worse, bands of thugs were now roaming the North African countryside abducting people and selling them to the traders. "They seem to be draining Africa of much of its human population," Augustine laments, "and transferring their 'merchandise' to the provinces across the sea."[16]

The most extraordinary part of this letter tells how Augustine's parishioners one day took the matters into their own hands. A large ship was in port, about to set sail with its human cargo. A member of the church, "a faithful Christian," says Augustine, "knowing our custom of missions of mercy of this kind, made this known to the church." Immediately, members of the church raided both the ship and a nearby holding cell. "About 120 were freed by our people," he reports. Once in a safe place, the slaves told their stories to the church, and "hardly a person could keep himself from tears on hearing all the various ways by which they were brought to the Galatians by trickery or kidnapping." Some were able to be returned to their families. Others were being housed and fed at the church. Still others had to be sheltered in the homes of local Christians around Hippo, "for the church could not feed all those whom it freed." Augustine's fear at the time of writing was that things were getting tense in the city. The slave traders had friends in high places, and they were beginning to agitate to get all their "merchandise" back. The rescue operation was not exactly legal, and Augustine worried that things were about to get bad for local Christians. Part of Augustine's motivation in writing to Alypius was to ask him to do what he can, during his stay in Italy, to get influential people to help. He ends the letter with a warning. If these things can happen in Hippo, "where in God's mercy the great vigilance of the church is on the watch so that poor people can be freed from captivity of this sort," imagine, he says, "how much similar trafficking in unfortunate souls goes on in other coastal areas"![17]

Augustine was not an abolitionist. In his mind, the system was an unhappy permanent feature of a fallen world. All that can be done about it is urge masters to treat their slaves well, use church funds to purchase people's freedom, and occasionally raid slave ships.

This brief glimpse into Augustine's pastoral thought is worth holding in mind as we turn to explore his influential ideas about "just war."

The City of God

For my purposes, only one of Augustine's many books demands our attention. *The City of God* was written in the wake of the worst catastrophe in Roman history. On 24 August AD 410 the so-called Visigoths (Germanic tribes) led by Alaric somehow managed to breach the Italian defences and do the unthinkable: they sacked Rome. After a long siege that cut off the city's food supply, the barbarians burst through the great walls of the city and penetrated, street by street, attack by attack, right into the great Forum itself, ransacking buildings and monuments along the way. One survivor of the attack wrote to a friend telling of the "shrill sound of the war-trumpet and the shouts of the Goths." Fear gripped the city, and "everything was thrown into confusion and disorder," he says. "In every home there was lamentation, and terror was spread through all alike. Slave and noble were on the same footing: all saw the same image of death."[18]

After several days of pillaging, and having more than made their point, the Visigoths advanced toward southern Italy, only to retreat back out of Italy after Alaric died of an illness within months of conquering Rome. These barbarians were better at conquering than maintaining stable rule.

Still, many were asking how the city could fall. It is difficult for us, all these years later, to appreciate what a disorienting cultural catastrophe this was. It is true that the empire had a second capital (Constantinople) and that the eastern part of the Roman Empire (the Byzantine Empire) would last for another thousand years, falling to the Ottomans only in 1453. But the sacking of the city of Rome by "barbarians" was an international event without parallel in its thousand-year history. Three days of public mourning were proclaimed in Constantinople, but little else was done to help the western capital. (Much was done to fortify the great walls surrounding Constantinople, lest the same thing happen there.)

Who was to blame for this catastrophe? For many, the obvious answer was *the Christians*. The old gods had sustained the Roman people for a millennium, and now, within a century of the first Christian emperor, the historic capital of the empire was defeated. Pagan critics, of whom there were still many in the early fifth century, were adamant that the gods had abandoned the people because the people had abandoned the gods. What lay ahead was darkness, the "dark ages."

Augustine met this challenge head-on by producing one of the most remarkable pieces of cultural (and theological) analysis in western history, with a whopping four hundred thousand-plus word count (three or four times the size of this book). *The City of God*, written in instalments between AD 416 and 422, turned the criticism of the pagans on its head. It presented a detailed, subtle, and devasting critique of the ethics, politics, and religion of the "earthly city" of Rome, in contrast to the reign of Christ, the true eternal city of God, which was humanity's only hope.

The City of God was not a simplistic argument for replacing the Roman Empire with an *earthly* Christendom, as if Christianizing state institutions would bring peace on earth. Augustine was too realistic—some would say pessimistic—to believe that. He believed that conversion to Christianity would bring *some* improvements to society, especially to the poor and marginalised, but "he would have been greatly astonished by the medieval canonists [later church lawyers] who interpreted him to imply that the empire ought to be run by bishops with the pope at their head," writes Oxford's Henry Chadwick. Augustine knew the weaknesses of Christians too well. He loved the church, but "the failures of its members, both clerical and lay, gave him moments of dark gloom."[19] I know the feeling.

This is the context in which we are to understand Augustine's thinking about "just war," the use of state violence in a manner that would approximate the ideals of a "city of God." His thoughts on this topic are not a major feature of his massive tome, and they were offered more as part of his critique of Roman values than as a political policy for Christian rulers to follow. Nevertheless, Augustine is arguably the most influential thinker—Christian or otherwise—for the next eight hundred years, so his treatment of this particular subject would have an impact out of all proportion to the space he devoted to it. Later thinkers would simply assume that wars could be *just* and then try to ensure that the wars they wanted to wage fell somewhere within the bounds of Augustine's doctrine.

An Outline of "Just War"

By Augustine's time in the early fifth century, it had become a practical impossibility to keep Christians out of the army; there were just too many Christian citizens, and some of them had risen to become generals. In AD 418, in the very period he was writing *The City of God*, Augustine wrote to Boniface, the tribune of Africa and a Christian, "Do not suppose that no one can please God who as a soldier carries the weapons of war."[20] So long as fighting is absolutely necessary and peace remains the goal, warfare can be good: "Your will ought to aim at peace; only necessity requires war in order that God may set us free from necessity and preserve us in peace. For we do not seek peace in order to stir up war, but we wage war in order to acquire peace."[21]

Ten years later (AD 427) Augustine felt compelled to write again to Boniface, subtly urging military intervention to protect Roman towns in North Africa from being attacked by marauding bands of Sahara tribesman: "What am I to say about the plundering of Africa that the African barbarians carry out with no opposition, while you are tied up in your difficulties and make no arrangement by which this disaster might be averted?" Who would have thought, he wryly asks, that under the gaze of the great Boniface these Saharan Berbers "would now have become so venturesome, would have made such advances, would have ravaged, robbed, and devastated such large areas full of people?"[22] This is something new: a Christian leader directly urging state powers to fight.

The broad principles of Augustine's *just war* theory can be pieced together from both *The City of God* and these various letters from the period. He utterly rejected the usual Roman justifications for war: enlarging the empire, protecting honour, removing iniquitous nations, or assuming that Roman subjugation was itself a kind of "peace."[23] Henry Chadwick, the great interpreter and biographer of Augustine, summarises Augustine's thoughts on just war. Military force can be *just* when:

1. its goal is to establish mutual peace between the parties;
2. it is waged only in self-defence or to recover stolen property;
3. soldiers exercise maximum restraint in hostilities (a proportional response);

4. fighting is conducted "with such respect for humanity as to leave the opponent without the sense of being humiliated and resentful"; and

5. prisoners of war are preserved, not (as so often happened) executed.[24]

It is clear that Augustine saw warfare—even *just* warfare—as a tragic necessity in the "earthly city," which can only ever be *partially* Christianized through the principles laid down.[25] In a moving passage toward the end of *The City of God*, Augustine writes:

> But the wise man, they say, will wage just wars. Surely, however, if he remembers that he is a human being, it is far more true that he will grieve at being faced with the necessity of waging just wars. If they were not just, he would not have to wage them, and so there would be no wars for the wise man. For it is the iniquity of the opposing side that imposes on the wise man the obligation of waging just wars; and this iniquity should certainly be lamented by human beings.[26]

In Augustine's view, even *just* wars are not "holy." And they are certainly not happy, even in victory.

Still, Augustine's arguments were to have an influence out of all proportion to his brief concessions about the necessity of state violence. Whatever Augustine's hopes, the monumental influence of his writings in the west in the coming centuries meant that he opened the way to Christian "holy war," culminating in the Crusades.

Most of the events that follow in church history, good and bad, find some precedent in the events and ideas of the first half-millennium of Christianity. Later ecclesiastical bullying can already be glimpsed in the muscular vision of church-and-state first exemplified in Ambrose. The church's infamous bigotry toward "sinners" is forecast in the monkish riots against pagan shrines. The flood of wealth that flowed into medieval church coffers (and contemporary megachurches) finds its source in the donations, land gifts, and tax exemptions granted to churches by successive fourth-century emperors. And the largescale "holy wars" against Muslims and heretics in the eleventh–fifteenth centuries were, with just a little bit of imagination, rationalised on the basis of Augustine's theory of *just war.*

Equally, through all of these centuries, the church was the only source of charity, the only defender of the weak, and the deepest wellspring of periodic reform and renewal, on the model of Jesus Christ. Augustine himself embodies the paradox of church history. He was responsible for establishing a theological justification for state violence *at the very same time* he was trying to liberate slaves. This is true of every age. For every Cyril of Alexandria (the bishop when Hypatia was murdered) there was a Basil of Caesarea (who established the first hospital). For every Christian warlord hacking his way through pagan Europe there was a humble preacher standing in his way preferring to die than to kill. We will meet both of these, and more, in the next few chapters.

The Death of Rome and Growth of the Church

Barbarians and Christians in Europe from 400 to 1100

Stop fighting, lads! Give up the battle! For we are taught by the trusty witness of Scripture, that we render not evil for evil, but contrariwise good for evil.

—BISHOP BONIFACE, AD 754

The centuries following the sacking of Rome in AD 410 are simultaneously complex and straightforward. The complicated bit is the history and politics, as the mighty Roman Empire in the west crumbles in less than a century. The easy bit—sort of—is the story of the church, which continues to display the same muscularity and charity we have seen in the previous decades.

Adding to the confusion is that there are really two imperial stories to tell: a western story and an eastern story. The Roman Empire in the west fell into disarray following the barbarian successes in Italy, North Africa, Gaul (France), and Spain. The kingdoms that then arose, even the barbarian ones, told themselves they were the continuation of the Roman Empire. But this was mostly a fiction designed to bring comfort and a sense of legitimacy.

The story of the eastern empire is totally different. We call it the Byzantine Empire now, since Byzantium was the original Greek name of Constantinople (modern Istanbul), which Constantine had made his capital and a "new Rome" back in 330. This Byzantine Empire is really just the vibrant eastern continuation of the actual Roman Empire. The collapse of Rome was experienced as a catastrophe everywhere *west* of Italy. But if you were fortunate enough to live in the *east*—in Asia Minor (Turkey), Syria, Judea, or Egypt—life carried on. The most cosmopolitan half of the empire was still in decent shape.

Westerners today rarely know much about the eastern side of world history, but there is a stunning story to tell. It is a story about wealth and stability, learning and religion, architecture, art, and charity—as well (of course) as ongoing wars. The contrast with their poor Christian cousins in the west could hardly be greater.

Yet, one thing linked these two imperial narratives: the church. Christianity continued to grow in both environments, *influencing*, and being *influenced by*, the dramatic events of the period. In the next five chapters I want to offer a brief account of what happened in the west in the five hundred years or so following the collapse of Rome. Then, in chapter 20 I will offer a brief history of the well-kept secret that is the Byzantine Empire. This will form a good mental bridge from the ancient world to the modern world, via the so-called Dark Ages in between.

The Dread of the Goths

Various Gothic tribes had been bearing down on the Roman world—east and west—for a century or more. As we have seen, the Visigoths led by Alaric eventually sacked the city of Rome in AD 410. Then they left. "Their numbers and military capacity might win the battles," Peter Brown says, "but they were in no position to win the peace."[1] After Alaric's men (following his death) returned north, Roman citizens in the west tried to rebuild or reimagine their glorious culture, and there was a succession of false starts and half-emperors. In the vacuum, the church increasingly looked like the most stable game in town. Interestingly, Alaric had left untouched the two giant Roman basilica churches connected with the apostles Peter and Paul. The buildings must have stood as a sign of Christianity's enduring presence and leadership.

Any semblance of western imperial stability ended in the late fifth century: the barbarian warrior Odoacer deposed the boy emperor Romulus Augustulus in 473 (a date sometimes regarded as the official end of the western empire); 20 years later, in 493, a new Gothic leader named Theodoric united various barbarian tribes to form the Ostrogoths, who finished what the earlier Visigoths could not. After killing Odoacer, they overtook Italy, established their own rule, and ended the western empire for good. They presented their regime as "the Roman empire continued,"[2] but that was a hard story to sell. People today who speak of "the Dark Ages" usually date it from this moment, right up until the fourteenth-century Italian Renaissance. We will explore all that in chapter 19.

The barbarian ruling classes were "perched insecurely on top"[3] of the great mass of Romans in Italy. Most locals got on with trying to live their lives, pay their taxes, and hope for better days. It's what conquered people usually do. The Gothic warrior-aristocracy maintained surprisingly good relations with the church in Rome. That church now owned major buildings and estates in the east of the city, at the famous Lateran Palace where the bishop of Rome lived, as well as in a former imperial park known as the "Vatican" on the west bank of the Tiber. Constantine had donated these lands and constructed churches there one hundred and fifty years earlier. "Vatican" today means *Catholic HQ*, but in this period it was an out-of-the-way suburb on the edges of the city.

In the uncertain times of the fifth century, Romans increasingly looked to church figures, especially the bishop of Rome, that is, the "papa" or pope, as a source of social authority with a legitimacy reaching back into previous centuries. The model of the bishop as a kind of mayor, exemplified by Ambrose a century earlier, was now wholly accepted by the populace, especially since many bishops were, in fact, from the senatorial class. And they processed to their churches just as Roman consuls of earlier times had processed through the city, "greeted by candles, scattering largesse to the populace, wearing the silken slippers of a senator."[4] The "princes" of the church were the new senatorial class.

This was true even in faraway Gaul (France) in the late fifth century, at the very time the western extremities of the empire were crumbling. There, the learned Roman aristocrat and statesman Sidonius Apollinaris (AD 430–486) had been made bishop in Clermont, the same town from which Pope Urban would launch the Crusades six hundred years later. Sidonius was "one of the last great representatives of classical culture in Gaul"[5] and a beloved philanthropist and supporter of monasteries. His move from Roman statesman to bishop was in many ways a comedown. But he threw himself into the role, preaching, writing, and visiting the parishes of his district. He left us a vivid picture of his ministry in the hundred or so letters that survive.[6] His region was overcome by the Visigoths in 475, and he himself was imprisoned for a time, before being allowed to return to his post in 476. In a bishop like Sidonius, the entire community, high and low, was joined together. In a curious twist, the poor old bishop was eventually reduced to a pittance by two pushy priests in his diocese who somehow wrangled their way into controlling most of the church estates. Often in this period priests complained about the power and wealth of their bishop. But, whether through weakness or sweetness, the opposite was the case with Sidonius.[7]

In any case, in these fractured conditions, as Rome crumbled and Europe groaned, the last non-Christians in the former western Roman Empire rallied to the Christian Church as the source of stability, charity, and, of course, spiritual comfort.[8] You could almost say that by the end of the fifth century, *to be a good Roman* was to be a *Christian*. And in a manner of speaking, we have the Goths to thank (or blame) for that.

The Rise of the Franks

At about the same time as Sidonius, the church was beginning to make inroads into pagan parts of Europe.[9] Roman-controlled Gaul had fallen to the Franks (Germanic peoples of northern France) around AD 486. Shortly afterwards, the king of the Franks, a man called Clovis (AD 466–511), suddenly declared his allegiance to Christianity and was baptised around the year 500.

Why exactly Clovis converted, we do not know. His wife Chlothild had been a Christian for some time, and we know that bishop Remigius of Reims (also known as Rheims) was in Clovis's ear about "the virtues and duties of a Christian ruler."[10] But whether it was external persuasion that converted

Clovis or his own political calculation about which was the most powerful deity—or both—is impossible to tell. Either way, it marked the beginning of the vast Merovingian Kingdom that went on to rule much of western Europe for the next two hundred and fifty years, until the Carolingian kingdom of Charlemagne in the eighth and ninth centuries.[11] Both the Merovingians and the Carolingians ended up being fierce supporters of the church—and I mean *fierce*. We are now in the period popularly known as the "Dark Ages." But there were also quite a lot of fun things going on. It was not all ignorance and violence, as we will see in the coming pages.

This was an era of great teaching "missions" into remaining pagan lands. Pope Gregory I, "the Great" (AD 540–604), for example, sent a local Roman monk named Augustine (not to be confused with the earlier Augustine), together with a band of forty assistants, to evangelize the people of England. Augustine was successful. The pagan King Æthelbert of Kent (AD 589–616) embraced Christianity, and Augustine himself became the first Archbishop of Canterbury—a title that had none of the prestige of today's Archbishop of Canterbury, who is the figurehead for eighty-five million Anglicans/Episcopalians around the world. (I should also give a shout out to the "Celtic" Christians, who had already made some inroads into England and Ireland as early as the third century, long before Pope Gregory's plan.[12])

Bishop Eligius: Goldsmith and Liberator of Slaves

A generation after Augustine of Canterbury, the Frankish lands produced a remarkable figure, Bishop Eligius (AD 590–660) of Noyon in northern France. Eligius is hardly known today, but, in his time, he was one of the most beloved men in Europe. His fame was twofold: he made jewellery and he freed slaves.

Born in Chaptelat near Limoges in southwest-central France, Eligius was trained as a master goldsmith. Because of his skill, he soon came to the attention of Clothar II, king of the Franks, one of the successors of Clovis. Clothar—then his successor Dagobert—employed Eligius to oversee the crafting of all the royal precious metals and jewellery. It was a highly distinguished position, and Eligius earned great wealth. His biography was written by his contemporary and friend Dado, the bishop of Rouen, from whom we get vivid descriptions of Eligius's dress: "having belts composed of gold and gems and elegantly jeweled purses, linens covered with red metal and golden sacs hemmed with gold and all of the most precious fabrics including all of silk." At the same time, Eligius was extremely devout and would constantly have a religious book "propped open before his eyes so that even while labouring he might receive divine mandates."[13]

One of those divine "mandates" shaped the rest of his life. Eligius was captivated by Christ's call to assist the downtrodden. Jesus had given himself for the world, and we are to do the same; that is the logic of life. He soon took to gifting the gold and jewellery he wore. His sumptuous attire ended up functioning like a bank or mobile charity. Wherever he found people in distress, he plucked off gems and precious metals from his garments and gave them away. He would leave on a business trip looking like royalty and return wearing "a hairshirt next to his flesh" or "the vilest clothing with a rope for a belt."[14]

Perhaps his most striking act of charity, for which he earned renown throughout Europe, was purchasing and freeing slaves. In seventh-century Gaul, the remnant of the Roman slave system still existed, but so did the slave practices of the Goths and pagans. Eligius could not bear to see another person in bondage. "He had this work much at heart," says Dado. "Wherever he understood that slaves were to be sold he hastened with mercy and soon ransomed the captive." He did not discriminate but liberated "both sexes and from different nations." He "freed all alike, Romans, Gauls, Britons and Moors but particularly Saxons who were as numerous as sheep at that time." And if he ran out of cash because of the sheer number of people for sale, "he gave more by stripping what he had on his own body from his belt and cloak to the food he needed and even his shoes so long as he could help the captives." He asked for nothing in return. If they wanted to stay with his community, he found them accommodation and a means of living. If they wanted to return to their own lands, "he would offer them what subsidy they required" for the journey.[15]

Eligius soon entered the priesthood and became a forceful preacher throughout France. In 641 he was made the bishop of Noyon, sixty miles north of Paris. But he never stopped feeding the poor and freeing slaves, using his own personal wealth and redirecting church funds for his projects. He was not just what we would call a "social justice advocate." He was also a zealous "evangelical," eager to extend the message of Christ into new regions, preaching and building new monasteries and churches. His biography speaks of pagans in Flanders and Antwerp "receiving him with hostile spirits and adverse minds." Yet, he persisted. He "gradually began to insinuate the word of God among them by the grace of Christ," and, eventually, a great multitude "left their idols and converted."[16] His converts were taught to sing the same tune he did: "You would see many people hurry to repent, give up their wealth to the poor, free their slaves and many other works of good in obedience to his precepts."[17]

Understandably, Eligius's death in 660 was a major event. Even the Frankish queen, Balthild of Ascania, rushed to see his body. She kissed it and wept aloud in front of the vast crowd. She demanded that his body be released to her, to be buried in her local monastery in Chelles. The uproar in Noyon was so great that she acquiesced to the will of locals. "So the corpse was brought to burial with all the city doing homage in tears."[18] It was a freezing and torrential winter's day (December 1), but nothing stopped the crowds. Even the queen refused a royal carriage and walked with the mourners to the grave.

Bishop Boniface: Persuader and Martyr

One generation after Eligius, and two generations after Augustine of Canterbury, England was sending out its own missionaries to the still-pagan lands in the north of Europe. An academic and monk named Boniface (AD 675–754) set out in 716 on an unsuccessful preaching campaign to Frisia (present-day Netherlands).[19] After travelling to Rome to receive papal blessing for his work from Pope Gregory II, he returned to the region in 719 and enjoyed quite a lot of success convincing Germanic warrior tribes to follow Jesus Christ. That was no easy thing! Over the next few decades—with the support of Rome—Boniface established Christian communities in Fritzlar, Ohrdruf, Ochsenfurt, and other German towns. It was an extraordinary work, for which he is remembered as the "apostle of Germany."

Boniface's method was *persuasion*. We have a lovely letter addressed to him from his friend and adviser Bishop Daniel of Winchester (AD 724). In it, Daniel outlines the way Boniface should go about trying to convert the pagans—through gentle teaching and argument. The letter begins, "To the venerable and beloved prelate Boniface, Daniel, servant of the people of God. I rejoice, beloved brother and fellow priest, that you are deserving of the highest prize of virtue. You have approached the hitherto stony and barren hearts of the pagans, trusting in the plenitude of your faith, and have laboured untiringly with the ploughshare of the Gospel preaching." Daniel goes on to give advice about various arguments to use against pagan polytheism, but his key point throughout is that Boniface "should strive to refute this and to convince them by many documents and arguments. These and many similar things you ought to put before them, not offensively or so as to anger them, but calmly and with great moderation." He closes the letter with "I pray for your welfare in Christ."[20] Boniface will need those prayers!

Another letter to Boniface in the same year (AD 724) came from Pope Gregory II (not to be confused with Gregory I). In it, the pope rejoices that "through the broadcasting of your preaching, the unbelieving people are being converted." The focus again is emphatically on the power of persuasion to change hearts:

> We give thanks to the power of the Lord and pray that He, from whom all good proceeds and whose will it is that all men shall come to a knowledge of the truth, may work with you and may lead that people out of darkness into light by the inspiration of His might. Let no threats alarm you, no fears cast you down, but holding fast to your faith, proclaim the Word. . . . For God who desires not the death of the sinner, but rather that he turn from his wickedness and live, will in all things give the increase. May God keep you in safety.[21]

Some readers will dislike the proselytizing zeal of Boniface, Daniel, and Pope Gregory (I and II). That's fine. My point is that the major mission campaigns into pagan Europe in the 600s and 700s were waged with the *old* Christian weapons of persuasion, service, prayer, and suffering. This is not to say there were not also some awful bishops who "were primarily political figures," writes Ian Wood in his history of the Merovingian Empire. There were even some that "behaved more like warriors than ecclesiastics." Yet, Wood concludes, "the behaviour of a few individuals should not overshadow the standards of the Church as a whole."[22] Boniface embodied these ideal standards, which included a willingness to suffer, rather than to harm, for the cause of Christ. It is something he would soon learn to put into practice the hard way.

Boniface was appointed Archbishop of Mainz (near Frankfurt) in 746, only to resign the post a few years later because he wanted to resume preaching in Frisia, where thirty years earlier he had unsuccessfully begun his work. The return did not go to plan. He was killed by local bandits in 754. While camped on the bank of the Boorn River in the north of the Netherlands, "[a] vast multitude of foes, armed with spears and shields, rushed with glittering weapons," his biography records. And when his own band of protectors drew their weapons to fight, he apparently yelled, "Stop fighting, lads! Give up the battle! For we are taught by the trusty witness of Scripture, that we render not evil for evil, but contrariwise good for evil."[23] It is nice to know that some Christian leaders, seven hundred years after Christ, were still singing the beautiful tune.

The response from Boniface's attackers was not as he might have hoped: "quickly the mad tumult of pagans rushed in upon them with swords and all the equipment of war, and stained the saints' bodies with propitious gore." The biography of Boniface's life—including this scene—was written just five or six years after his death by the English contemporary and priest, Willibald. The basic facts are widely accepted, and the peace-loving approach of Boniface's dying speech fits perfectly with what we know of the man from his ninety or so letters that have survived.[24] In the 700s he was everyone's model of how a missionary *should* live and die.

Over the course of about four centuries (AD 500 to 900), Europe was slowly being converted to Christianity through preaching, the establishment of churches and monasteries, and the appointment of bishops to oversee the work. The collapse of the Roman Empire in the west was a distant memory. The church was establishing itself as the principal source of cultural, intellectual, and spiritual energy.

The gentle, sacrificial approach to missionary activity exemplified by Augustine of Canterbury, Eligius, Boniface, the Gregories, Daniel, and others was not the only kind we know about in Europe in these Middle Ages. In AD 751/2, right around the time of Boniface's death, the Merovingians were displaced by the Carolingian dynasty as kings of the Franks. The most famous of these kings was Charles the Great, or Charlemagne (AD 742–814). In recognition of his political power and religious zeal, Charlemagne was crowned as "emperor" by Pope Leo III in Rome on Christmas Day in the year 800. This launched what we call the "Holy Roman Empire." This was neither the *actual* Roman Empire, nor a reference to the increasingly powerful church in Europe. The Holy Roman Empire was a succession of European kings, with constantly moving borders, which was *mostly* devoutly loyal to the Roman Church. It survived until 1806.[25]

Beginning with Charlemagne in the late 700s, this state devotion to the church led to some extravagant acts of coercion and violence, as well as to a "renaissance" of learning and culture. That paradox is the focus of the next two chapters.

Christian "Jihad"

Forced Conversions in Europe in the Late 700s

Faith is a voluntary thing and not a matter of coercion. A person can be drawn into the Faith, not forced into it.

—ALCUIN OF YORK, AD 796

I will never forget the Friday evening I made a fool of myself defending Christianity to an acquaintance in a noisy pub in Sydney. My interlocutor was a self-made Balmoral businessman (Google "Balmoral Beach, Sydney" and you will have an idea of what I mean). He asked what I did for a living. I explained that I *think, write*, and *speak* about historic Christianity. This usually either kills or ignites conversation. He responded by listing all the things that were wrong with the faith. Science had discredited belief in God, Christians were mostly hypocrites, and so on. I was happy to engage in friendly to-and-fro for a few minutes. Then he offered his climactic critique. Christianity had only spread throughout the world in those first few centuries *by force*. I asked him if he was remembering his religions correctly. He assured me he was. "Lots of books have been written about this," he said, in an expression that caught my interest. "The church converted nations with a sword." Apparently, it was baptism or death. *That* is how the early church grew.

Something went *off* in my head, and I am not proud of it. I laughed at his claim. I raised my voice. I reminded him I had a couple of degrees in this stuff. I quoted authors he had never heard of. And as the words were leaving my mouth, I could almost hear the whispers of the New Testament in my ear, "Always be ready to make your defense to anyone . . . yet do it with gentleness and reverence" (1 Pet 3:15–16). I was neither gentle nor reverent. The look on his face said it all. He excused himself and walked off to find a more pleasant conversation. Fair enough.

I am embarrassed about that evening for two reasons. Obviously, I was being a jerk, and I no doubt added to this sceptic's dataset of haughty Christians. But there is a second awkwardness. His time period might have been out by several centuries, but he was not *entirely* wrong. There is no hint of coerced conversions in the first few centuries of Christianity. In that period, there is clear evidence that church leaders preferred to be good losers than bad winners, as we saw in chapter 5. But behind my friend's exaggeration was a half-truth from several scattered periods of Christian history. The myth of forced conversions to Christianity is like most myths: there is *some* truth to it.

Christian Jihad

Something changed in northern Europe in the late eighth and early ninth centuries under Charlemagne (AD 742–814). Already during the Merovingian Kingdom under Clovis and his successors, it was normal for missionaries to follow after military conquests, establishing monasteries and churches in the new lands from which they could launch preaching and charitable missions among pagans.[1] The Carolingian Kingdom, including Charlemagne, inherited this general policy, with a couple of major differences.

Charlemagne, whose court was at Aachen (west Germany), was an even more ardent supporter of the church than the Merovingians had been. For his efforts, the pope would crown him the first "Holy Roman Emperor." The concept was straightforward. Charlemagne was chosen by God to revive the glories of the Roman Empire in the west *and* to defend and promote the cause of the church (hence "holy"). To be clear, the Vatican in no way *directed* Charlemagne. No one directed Charlemagne! But it did provide him with the social legitimacy he craved. Even more than Constantine four hundred and fifty years earlier, Charlemagne really seems to have had a sincere sense of divine calling. Yet, as we have seen, devotion to Jesus Christ is no guarantee of following his melody lines.

Charlemagne felt that it was his duty to bring "salvation" wherever God gave him dominion. He was a typical European warrior-king with a heartfelt desire to channel that skill for the glory of God as he saw it. He instituted wide-ranging law reform in favour of Christianity. The *Admonitio generalis* or "General Admonition" was a raft of legislative measures articulating "the king's responsibility for the people of God," observes Rosamond McKitterick, Professor of Medieval History at Cambridge, "and the need for everyone in the kingdom, and especially the secular and ecclesiastical elites, to work towards creating order and a polity worthy of salvation."[2] His method was similar to that of Clovis, supporting the building of monasteries and churches throughout his realm. But there was more. Among the "Saxons," Charlemagne adopted what has been described as a Christian "jihad."

The Saxons were a Germanic warrior people in what is now northwestern Germany.[3] Charlemagne waged a brutal thirty-year campaign against them, from 772 to 804. He wanted to incorporate them into his growing Frankish Empire, which would eventually encompass much of Europe. The task proved very difficult, as the Romans had earlier found with these northerners. Charlemagne's seeming successes among them were quickly reversed in Saxon rebellions. The sheer quantity of eighth-century weapons, shields, and chain mail found by archaeologists in this region offers grim testimony to the scale of the conflict.[4]

Charlemagne responded to these setbacks with brutality. In 782, for example, he ordered the beheading of more than four thousand, five hundred Saxons on a single day. Later in the war, after further agreements followed by rebellions, Charlemagne "removed ten thousand men who had been living with their wives and children," says his courtier and biographer, Einhard. He "dispersed them here and there throughout Gaul and Germany in various small groups."[5] Deporting large numbers of fighting men (with their families) to distant parts of the realm was a shrewd tactic. And it eventually worked. By

804, after nearly thirty years of fighting, the Saxons were subdued. They were also *converted*. Einhard records, "Thus, that war which had lasted for so many years ended on the terms laid down by the king and accepted by the Saxons; namely, that they would reject the worship of demons, abandon their ancestral pagan rites, take up the Christian faith and the sacraments of religion, and unite with the Franks in order to form a single people."[6]

Sometime before the full subjugation of the Saxons, Charlemagne had published a notorious set of laws titled the *Capitulatio de Partibus Saxoniae* or *Ordinances for the Region of Saxony*. Among the special rules for the unruly Saxons was this one: "If any one of the race of the Saxons hereafter concealed among them shall have wished to hide himself unbaptized, and shall have scorned to come to baptism and shall have wished to remain a pagan, let him be punished by death."[7] There is debate among specialists about whether these laws were intended to *bring about* conversion, or were a means of punishing regions that had formerly promised (pretended) to submit to Charlemagne's religion and rule.[8] Either way, it is the kind of coercive Christianity that my friend in the pub rightly despised. Robert Flierman of the University of Utrecht puts it starkly: "Saxon religious conformity was secured through a chilling maxim: baptism or death."[9]

Adding insult to injury, Charlemagne immediately imposed on every Saxon household "tithes," that is, religious taxes. This created a double blow: cultural destruction *and* a financial yoke. This, indeed, has all the hallmarks of a Christian "jihad," says Yitzhak Hen of the Hebrew University in Jerusalem, whose stimulating article on the topic is titled "Charlemagne's Jihad."[10]

Conversion and Coercion before Charlemagne

Charlemagne's policies among the Saxons were undeniably awful. They are evidence of a deadly experiment in "missionary" expansion in the late 700s. I admit I have found myself shaking my head as I write these paragraphs.

Yet, the forced conversion of the Saxons does not quite establish the point my sceptical friend wanted to make. Charlemagne's approach is a notorious *outlier* in the Christian tradition. As Yitzhak Hen himself observes, Charlemagne's decree for Saxony "has no precedent in the history of the Christian mission."[11]

Even leaving aside the high ideals of Jesus, the New Testament, and the couple of centuries that followed, there is also the Edict of Milan in 313, which declared the "freedom and full liberty . . . to exercise free choice in worshipping as each one has seen fit."[12] A century later, the most influential western Christian thinker for a millennium, Saint Augustine the bishop of Hippo (AD 354–430), laid down the principle that "[n]o one is to be compelled to embrace the faith against his will."[13] He believed in a theory of "just war," as we saw, but *converting pagans* was not one of its principles.

The same policy was followed by the pope himself in the sixth-century mission to England. Pope Gregory I (AD 540–604) wrote to an abbot named Mellitus, who was on his way to assist Augustine of Canterbury in the establishment of Christianity in the British Isles. In the letter, the pope expresses his longing to see the country converted to Christ, but he insists that the pagan temples themselves should not be damaged—the idols may be removed, but the buildings should not be destroyed. He gives the reason: so that pagans would not be resentful, and so that they might be more open to receiving the true worship of God. He also recommends that pagans be allowed to continue their ancient ritual of sacrificing large numbers of oxen to their gods, except that they should now be urged to do so "to the refreshing of themselves to the praise of God, and render thanks to the Giver of all things for their abundance."[14]

And then, of course, there was Boniface (AD 675–754) and his team, mentioned in the last chapter. He was the epitome of mission through persuasion and martyrdom among Germanic peoples in the decades immediately before Charlemagne's "jihad."

Charlemagne's Daring Critic

Most significant of all are two letters we have from one of Charlemagne's most trusted advisers. He attempted to convince the king to revert to a policy of persuasion. Perhaps the greatest European you've never heard of is the English church deacon and intellectual, Alcuin of York (AD 735–804). He was a leading biblical scholar and teacher of the liberal arts (rhetoric, logic, arithmetic, astronomy, and so on). He deserves a chapter of his own, which he will get when we finish this one. In 796—when he was absent from the royal court—Alcuin tried to modify Charlemagne's approach toward the Saxons and toward the newly conquered Avars of Austria-Hungary. He had a two-pronged approach. First, he wrote to his friend and fellow courtier Meginfrid, hoping that he would act as "Alcuin's go-between to the king."[15] Alcuin reminds Meginfrid of the entirely voluntary nature of true faith. "First, the Faith should be taught and thus the sacraments of baptism should be understood, and then the Gospel teachings should be delivered," he wrote. "A person can be drawn into the Faith, not forced into it. . . . Even after people have received the Faith and baptism, their weaker minds should be offered gentler commands."[16]

Alcuin admits that the Saxons are the "toughest of the tough," but he insists that forced conversion, baptism, and "tithes" are not in keeping with the spirit of Christianity. Indeed, he says that if the "light yoke and the easy burden of Christ" had been preached to the Saxons with the same zeal that tithes had been extracted from them and punishments dealt out to them, "then perhaps they would not be shrinking back from the sacrament of baptism."[17] Teachers of the faith, whether among the Saxons or the new lands of the Avars, must not be state tax agents. Instead, Alcuin says, they ought to follow "the examples of the Apostles: let them be preachers not plunderers."[18]

Alcuin had a second line of approach. In the same year (AD 796) he wrote a much softer letter directly to Charlemagne raising the same concerns. The Alcuin specialist Mary Garrison of York University recently described the Yorkshireman as "the only person who could contradict Charlemagne."[19] Even still, Alcuin begins modestly and with flattery. He praises Charlemagne for his concern for the salvation of the world. Then, as Yitzhak Hen puts it, "Alcuin drops the bomb, slowly and very carefully."[20] Mission is not about coercion and extracting tithes, but persuasion through "gentle teaching":

> Now in your wise and godly concern may you provide good preachers for the new people, sound in conduct, learned in the faith and full of the teaching of the gospel, intent on following the example of the apostles in the preaching of the word of God. For they gave their hearers milk, that is, gentle teaching. . . . New converts to the faith must be fed on gentler teaching as babies on milk, lest minds too weak for harder teaching vomit what they have imbibed. Careful thought must also be given to the right method of preaching and baptizing, that the washing of the body

in baptism be not made useless by lack in the soul of an understanding of the faith.[21]

In an astonishing turnaround, Charlemagne actually halted his harsh policy toward the Saxons, publishing a new code on 28 October 797—the *Capitulare Saxonicum*—which removed any mention of *baptism or death* and made numerous concessions to local pagan customs, so long as they did not directly contradict Christianity. In the long run, Alcuin was proved right. The *voluntary* approach to mission was more effective. Saxony would eventually fully embrace the faith and would become a leading centre of Christianity in the centuries to come.

There were other times of coerced conversion in church history—occasionally in Spain, for example—but Charlemagne's policy is the clearest and most infamous. And it provides a good example of one of the key things I keep learning as I study history. For all of its periodic degradations, the Christian Church has a habit of reforming itself. In this particular case, church law (canon law) would settle the matter in the *Decretum*, a handbook of church legislation compiled around the year 1140 by the Italian monk Gratian. Canon III states: "Others are to be invited to the faith not by harsh means, but by gentle words." Citing Pope Gregory I (AD 540–604) as the authority, the canon continues: "Those who sincerely wish to lead people who stand outside the Christian religion into a proper faith shall strive to do so by gentle means rather than by harsh means, lest adversity alienate the mind of those whom a reasonable argument would have been able to attract."[22]

This ruling was followed up in the next century by Thomas Aquinas (AD 1225–1274), probably the most influential western Christian thinker since Saint Augustine back in the fifth century. In his massive *Summa Theologiae*, a multivolume statement of the Christian faith, Aquinas writes with typical precision: "Unbelievers are by no means to be compelled to the faith, in order that they may believe, because to believe depends on the will." He adds that, while wars with pagan nations can legitimately be fought "to prevent them from *hindering* the faith of Christ," such wars must "not indeed be for the purpose of *forcing* them to believe, because even if they [Christians] were to conquer them [pagans], and take them prisoners, they should still leave them free to believe, if they will."[23]

✦

There were certainly many dark spots in early medieval Christianity, just as there are today. Yet, there is also a strong tradition of self-critique and reform within Christianity. Christians have at times participated in all that is worst in human nature, but their founding documents, and the traditions of their founding centuries, almost always find a way to reassert themselves in the darkness—to shine a spotlight on the evil and inspire fresh efforts to follow the way of Christ. That was certainly the case in the Christian missions of Europe: it was Alcuin's view, not Charlemagne's, that won the day.

The influence of Alcuin of York went far beyond his advocacy for persuasion over violence. This is a man who almost singlehandedly brought Europe into its first great "renaissance." Alcuin deserves his own chapter in this history of bullies and saints.

The Greatest European
You've Never Heard Of

A "Renaissance" in the Middle of the "Dark Ages"

Nothing is more essential to government, nothing more helpful in leading a moral life, than the beauty of wisdom, the praise of learning and the advantages of scholarship.

—ALCUIN OF YORK

In his 2011 Pulitzer Prize-winning book, *The Swerve: How the World Became Modern*, the Shakespeare scholar from Harvard, Stephen Greenblatt, offered a compelling story about the way the heroic Italian scholar named Poggio Bracciolini (AD 1380–1459) tore away the veil of ignorance that the church had cast over the medieval world.[1] According to Greenblatt, the church had for centuries sought to suppress the literary classics of Greece and Rome. Christians were worried that these pagan texts might undermine their hold over Europe. "Working with knives, brushes, and rags," we are told, "monks often carefully washed away the old writings—Virgil, Ovid, Cicero, Seneca, Lucretius—and wrote in their place the texts that they were instructed by their superiors to copy." [2] But Poggio would not be deterred. He was the ultimate humanist book hunter, determined to rescue what the "superstitious, ignorant, and hopelessly lazy" monks sought to hide. As a good early secularist, Poggio believed that monasteries were "the dumping grounds for those deemed unfit for life in the world."[3]

Then one fateful day in 1417, while riffling through the neglected scrolls of some dreary German monastery, Poggio made a discovery that would change the world (in Greenblatt's story). It was a manuscript of the ancient Latin philosopher-poet Lucretius (first century BC). The epic poem of seventy-four hundred lines advocated for the Epicurean philosophy, which insisted that the gods play no significant role in the world, that death is not to be feared, and that rationality would lead us to peace amidst suffering and disorder. No wonder the church was afraid of such a text! "Ordering his scribe to make a copy," says Greenblatt, "Poggio hurried to liberate it from the monastery," thereby "releasing a book that would help in time to dismantle his entire world."[4] For centuries, the church had "attacked, ridiculed, burned, or—most devastating— ignored and eventually forgotten" the rationalist tradition of Lucretius and his fellow Epicureans.[5] But Poggio's rediscovery was a secular miracle, a "swerve," in which the natural course of events—in this case, the church's attempt to suppress knowledge—was averted, and a new path was opened up for the world. That path was the Italian Renaissance of the fourteenth and fifteenth centuries, and the birth of modern learning.

The story Greenblatt narrates is enthralling. It chimes well with the oft-told saga of a relentless "dark ages" of ignorance that began with the collapse of Roman society around AD 500 and continued for the next eight hundred years until the 1300–1400s. Only then did the Italian humanists of the Renaissance revive the study of ancient classical literature and set Europe on a trajectory of artistic and scholarly renewal.

Greenblatt's story is partly true, which is to say that it is mostly false. The core detail of *The Swerve* is reasonable enough: Poggio discovered a copy of Lucretius's *On the Nature of Things* in a German monastery in 1417. Little else is historical. The Epicurean poem was important to Renaissance scholars when it was found, but the Renaissance had been going for more than half a century by then. In no sense was *On the Nature of Things* the "swerve" that made us "modern."

As many reviewers have pointed out,[6] Greenblatt offers an account of the Middle Ages that is unrecognisable to specialists of the period. At the heart of the book is a clue to its own falsehood: scholars like Poggio Bracciolini knew full well that if you were going to find a precious ancient manuscript anywhere, it would be in a Christian monastery, where texts like that of Lucretius had been preserved, studied, and copied since at least the time of Charlemagne, six hundred years earlier. In fact, as the great medievalist Brian Tierney of Cornell University has pointed out, "more than 90 percent of the works of ancient Rome that we know nowadays exist in their earliest form in a Carolingian manuscript," that is, in a text studied and copied by *Christian* scholars from the era of Charlemagne (eighth and ninth centuries). Their meticulous endeavours "form the basis of nearly all modern editions" of classical Roman literature.[7] We can perhaps accuse medieval monks of *hoarding* the ancient classics for themselves, but we cannot accuse them of hiding these texts, let alone trying to destroy them.

Light in the Dark

In the previous chapter I left us with the image of Charlemagne, in the late 700s, brutalising the Saxons before moderating his policy under the (probable) influence of Alcuin of York. But there is a crucial aspect of the Carolingian Empire that must be mentioned. Charlemagne established a massive educational program of schools and other centres of learning that made the work of later scholars like Poggio Bracciolini possible in the first place. Key here was Charlemagne's passionate sponsorship of the most learned men of the era, people like the bishop scholar-poet Theodulf of Orléans (in central France), Paul the Deacon, and Alcuin of York. With the help of these figures, Charlemagne raised up generations of educated clergy, court officials, and professional scholars. They established what scholars today call the "Carolingian Renaissance," six hundred years before the Renaissance of Poggio and his friends. As medievalist Mary Garrison of the University of York wryly remarks, "Alcuin, not the rediscovery of Lucretius in early modern times, was the true 'swerve' in Western culture."[8]

In the late 700s, right around the time Charlemagne was bullying the Saxons up north, the king was also trying to lift Europe up to a highpoint of legal, literary, artistic, and scholarly flourishing.[9] And if the amount of formal poetry is any indication of a culture's aesthetic confidence, the Carolingian Renaissance leaves our current day for dead.[10]

The "Wisdom" Approach to Learning

Alcuin of York (AD 735–804) is arguably the greatest European you've never heard of. This is not because of his efforts to persuade Charlemagne to adopt a gentler mission among the Saxons. It is because he was the architect of the educational reforms that spread throughout Europe in the centuries after him. He was vastly knowledgeable and an administrative genius, and he applied these twin talents to inspire a school system that reshaped Europe.[11] Shortly after Alcuin's death, a chronicler described him as "the most learned man anywhere to be found."[12]

Alcuin was born in York sometime around 735. By this time York had gained a reputation as a place of learning. The head of the cathedral school at York at this time was the gifted Ælberht, later the Archbishop of York. He insisted that his students learn more than just how to read the Bible and calculate the dates of the church calendar (the focus of many earlier schools). He wanted them to learn *for learning's sake*, and only then to apply what they knew to understand the things of God. Alcuin went to the York school as a boy. As the son of semi-noble parents, he was expected to get the best education available and then to contribute to society.

Alcuin excelled in his studies beyond all others, and he developed an intense love for the Christian faith. Both things would animate his long career. Alcuin became a teacher in the school and was chosen to accompany Ælberht on trips to the Continent, even to faraway Italy, collecting new books or new manuscripts of old books, Christian and classical. The library at York Cathedral became the pride of the country, containing both theological and secular works. Eventually, when his mentor Ælberht became archbishop in 766, Alcuin became head of the York school—perhaps the most prestigious school in the world—around the age of thirty. He was also ordained as a church deacon soon afterwards, a sign that he intended to direct his prodigious intellectual talent in the service of Christ.

York Cathedral adopted an educational philosophy known as "wisdom-theology."[13] It is not as creepy as it sounds. It is an idea that goes back to biblical times. Wisdom-theology says that God made the universe through his genius, or wisdom. As a result, the world functions not in a haphazard manner but in accordance with deep rational principles, which, by God's grace, our trained human wisdom can discover (at least in part). The idea is first expressed in the Old Testament book of Proverbs, chapter 8, centuries before Christ. In practice, this educational perspective means that learning about God's world is *in itself* an act of worship, because it is searching out the signs of God's own wisdom imprinted on creation. Learning about the motion of the planets, animals, logic, and so on was a fulfillment of the ancient biblical command to "love the Lord your God . . . with *all your mind*" (Mark 12:30, emphasis added). As a result, the education at York was very broad, taking in grammar, logic, mathematics, music, and much more.

The approach at York was not completely new. It was a recovery of an older approach to learning found everywhere in the early church.

Schooling in the Ancient Church

Critics often claim that the ancient and medieval church shunned "secular knowledge" and devoted itself exclusively to learning about the Bible and speculating about theology. The occasional statement of a church father is plucked out of context and presented as evidence. A good example is Saint Jerome (AD 342–420), one of the most influential Christian teachers back in the fourth and fifth centuries. Jerome was raised with the best pagan Roman education, only to reject classical literature in his thirties (in AD 374) after having a dream in which an angel accused him of preferring Cicero, the great Latin writer, to the Gospels. "Thou art a Ciceronian," the angel said, "not a Christian; for where thy treasure is, there will thy heart be also."[14] For the next fifteen years, Jerome refused to read pagan authors. He devoted himself instead to Bible translation and to writing commentaries and Christian essays. During this period, he wrote his oft-quoted line (oft-quoted by skeptics), "What communion hath light with darkness? What concord hath Christ with Belial [the Devil]? What has Horace in common with the Psalter? Virgil with the Gospels and Cicero with the Apostle?"[15] This sounds like a theological rejection of secular learning.

But Jerome returned to the classics around 389, until his death thirty years later in 420. During this mature period, especially in his letters to educated men and women and to church authorities, he often embellished his instruction and advice with citations from Cicero, Horace, Virgil, and other pagan writers. In an important essay on Jerome years ago, Arthur Stanley Pease of the University of Illinois described Jerome's attitude as moving through three phases: (1) the narrowly conservative Roman devotion to the classics of his upbringing and early adulthood; (2) the radical disillusionment and rebellion against the classics following his famous dream; and finally (3) the "true and ripe liberalism" of his last three decades, when Jerome could seamlessly expound a line of the New Testament and illustrate it with a line from Virgil's epic *Aeneid*.[16]

The "wisdom-theology" approach to knowledge was the norm among Christian theologians in the period following the New Testament, whether in the second century (Justin Martyr, Clement of Alexandria), third (Tertullian of Carthage, Origen of Alexandria), fourth (Gregory of Nazianzus, Basil of Caesarea, Gregory of Nyssa, Lactantius of Nicomedia), fifth (Augustine of Hippo, Jerome of Bethlehem), or the sixth century (Boethius and Cassiodorus of Rome). A quick Google search of these names will reveal that all of them valued secular learning as a window—if often an opaque window—into God's wisdom imprinted on the world.

It was not just the church's star intellects who appreciated education in ancient times. We know that at least as early as the second century, anyone wanting to become a disciple—remember, "disciple" just means *student*—had to undergo a period of rigorous instruction. Given that the church mainly drew people from the lower classes in the early period, our evidence is truly surprising. In Rome around the year 200, for example, if you wanted to become a baptised member of the church, you were required to do *three years* of schooling with an authorised teacher, once a week, outside of the weekly church service. That is a minimum of 144 hours of lectures (granting four weeks off a year) just to get started in the faith. Exceptions could be made for star pupils.[17]

This *catechesis* (Greek for "instruction") could also be sped up. In Jerusalem in the 300s there was a faster, more intense approach to catechetical studies: three hours of lessons each day, six days a week, for the seven weeks leading up to Easter. For this we have the eyewitness report of a highborn woman named Egeria, who visited Jerusalem (from Gaul or perhaps even Spain) in the fourth century: "They are all taught during those forty days, that is, from the first hour to the third hour, because catechesis is done for three hours. The dismissal from the catechesis having been done at the third hour, the bishop is immediately led from there with hymns to the Anastasis (i.e., the Church of the Holy Sepulchre) and the dismissal takes place at the third hour; and so they are taught for three hours a day for seven weeks, for in the eighth week, what is called Great Week, there is no time for them to be taught."[18] That is 126 hours of lessons. And remember, this is just to be baptised.

We also have good evidence about the *content* students were to learn. For the first five weeks the instruction is focused on the text of the Bible, especially Genesis, the Old Testament Law, and then the New Testament Gospels and Epistles. The material was heavily "apologetic," stressing the ways God's truth surpasses the claims of pagan philosophy and religion, as well as Judaism. In weeks six and seven, students are introduced line by line to the Nicene Creed, a dense three-paragraph summary of God the Father as Creator, God the Son as Redeemer, and God the Holy Spirit as the church's life-giver.[19] If I were to quote some of the catechetical lectures that survive from this time (the lectures of Bishop Cyril of Jerusalem), you might be astonished—as I was—at the level of literary and philosophical sophistication church leaders in this period demanded of their hearers.[20]

Modern Christians might criticise these ancient policies: If people want to follow Jesus, it could be argued, they should be able to be baptised on the spot, without any man-made imposition of study! Sure. Then again, this ancient educational program grew out of two important historical factors. First, Christians in this period were a minority surrounded by a dominant pagan culture. There was a lot of unlearning as well as learning to do. Second, Christians had discovered the hard way that if believers do not have a deep foundation in the content of the faith, they will not survive the pressures of persecution. As happy as I am not to have to invite my inquiring neighbours today to 126 hours of lectures to understand the faith, I feel that segments of the modern church have lost something of the rigour of their ancient counterparts.

With that, let me return to Alcuin in faraway England and Europe in the 700s and to his attempts to revive a spirit of learning in the church and society.

Studying with Alcuin

Alcuin was not a novelty in church history, but his contribution did come at a crucial time for Europe. Following the barbarian victories over the Romans in Gaul in the 500s, Europe did suffer a century or more of civic turmoil, as the Merovingians then Carolingians jockeyed for power and worked to expand and consolidate their kingdoms. Formal Roman-style education in this period did not disappear,[21] but it did become an elite luxury, something usually only expected of courtiers, bishops, and monks. The relative stability of Charlemagne's long reign over Europe in the late 700s provided the perfect conditions for a recovery of a broader educational project.

Alcuin came to the attention of Charlemagne on one of his journeys from England to Europe. The king knew talent when he saw it. At a meeting in Parma (northern Italy) in 781, Charlemagne urged Alcuin to come to his court and act as both a personal adviser and a kind of secretary of education. Alcuin agreed. A few years later, he moved to the court, which settled in Aachen in west Germany. From there, and later from a monastery in Tours in France, Alcuin directed a large educational program in the monasteries and cathedrals of Europe.

The letters and laws of Charlemagne in this period laid down clear demands: "Since it is our concern that the condition of our churches should always advance towards better things," he wrote in 786, "we strive with vigilant zeal to repair the manufactory of learning, almost destroyed by the sloth of our forefathers, and summon whom we can, even by our own example, to master the studies of liberal arts."[22] Indeed, Charlemagne did try to lead by example, asking Alcuin and others to teach him Latin, Greek and various other subjects. They had limited success, according to Charlemagne's own chronicler. The king slept with tablets and notebooks under his pillow so he could practise his writing at all hours, "but his effort, begun too late, achieved little," the chronicle reports.[23]

The king's famous education legislation of 789, known as the General Admonitions (*Admonitio generalis*), proclaimed: "Let the clergy join and associate to themselves not only children of servile condition but also the sons of free men. And let schools be established in which boys may learn to read."[24] It was a watershed law for the history of the west. About seventy such schools in this period were sufficiently active to leave a record of their activity.[25] Some of them (including the schools at Fulda, Tours, St. Gall, Auxerre, Liege, Metz, Laon, Salzburg, and Rheims) became famous throughout Europe, attracting many students. In some of these centres, "students could account for between 26 and 49 percent of the adult population," reports John Contreni of Purdue University in the US. Many of the children in these schools would become prominent in church and secular life in the 800s, including Remigius of Auxerre (AD 841–908), an expert in ancient Greek and Latin literature and the teacher of the hugely influential tenth-century reformer, Odo of Cluny (AD 879–942), whom we will meet in chapter 17.[26]

The emphasis of the Carolingian Renaissance was clearly on educating *boys*. But girls were not excluded. A letter of Hincmar (AD 806–882), the archbishop of Rheims, recommends that girls not be taught in the same place as boys, indicating that girls did indeed receive schooling.[27] And from the surviving two hundred-plus letters of Alcuin himself—many of them written to women—it is clear that he took a personal interest in teaching girls. Astronomy, in particular, became something of a fad among the ladies of the Carolingian court.[28] There is, in fact, "plenty of evidence to support the notion of widespread literate activity among noblewomen in the Frankish Empire," writes Steven Stofferahn in an essay on the topic. We have a brief letter from an anonymous schoolgirl to her teacher, "Mistress Felhin," asking permission to stay up all night with another schoolgirl, "reading and singing on behalf of our Lord."[29] A catalogue from the cathedral library of Cologne from the year 833 records books on loan to a number of laywomen in the community.[30] And there is clear evidence of women scribes in at least nine Frankish towns.[31]

The focus was not on elites only. Poor children also sometimes attended these schools. The law of 789 itself—just quoted—mentions "children of servile condition." And Charlemagne's biographer, Notker of St. Gall (himself a product of Alcuin's school system[32]), reports that the king personally ordered poor children into schools and, on occasion, even inspected their progress. The king would turn up at the school to review their "letters and poems"—a terrifying prospect for the students. At one of these inspections, the children of low rank outdid the nobles "with all the savours of wisdom, more than anyone could have hoped for." The king rebuked the wealthy children for their laziness and pleasure seeking. One child from that poor cohort became a court secretary and writer.[33]

Alcuin insisted upon the seven "liberal arts." The first three subjects made up the *trivium* or threefold-way: Grammar (Latin), formal Logic, and Rhetoric, or the study of the rules of persuasion. After completing the *trivium*, students could enter the *quadrivium* or fourfold-way: Arithmetic, Geometry, Music, and Astronomy. Alcuin liked to quote a passage of Scripture to illustrate how foundational these seven fields of study were to the wise life: "Wisdom has built her house; she has set up its seven pillars" (Prov 9:1). "No one," said Alcuin, "shall arrive at perfect knowledge save he be uplifted thither by these seven pillars or steps."[34]

Alcuin also demanded the highest quality handwriting from his students and fellow scholars. That might not sound like much, until you Google "Carolingian Minuscule" and look at images of the beautiful and uncannily recognisable script. The penmanship he standardised became the basis of modern non-cursive handwriting in the west. It is also the basis for the computer font I am using as I type these words (Times New Roman).

The seven liberal arts promoted by Alcuin were very much the *precursor* to the serious scholarship that Ælberht, Alcuin, Theodulf of Orleans, Paul the Deacon, and many others expected of themselves and all who became teachers and scholars after them. Once the liberal arts had been mastered, students could move onto the serious subjects: history, natural history (physical sciences), and, of course, theology. A handbook for clergy from this time makes clear that young priests were expected to have mastered the seven liberal arts, as well as some philosophy, before embarking on their theological and pastoral education.[35] Other advanced subjects included medicine and the law.[36] Alcuin once wrote to Charlemagne that nothing is more important for life and leadership "than the beauty of wisdom, the praise of learning and the advantages of scholarship."[37]

Studying grammar, logic, rhetoric, mathematics, music, astronomy, and all the rest was considered an act of devotion to the all-wise God. It was learning about the "wisdom" the Creator had imprinted upon the world. For Alcuin and his circle, and all those they inspired, this involved knowing not just the Bible and the church fathers, such as Augustine, Gregory the Great, Jerome, and Ambrose, but also all of the ancient Greek and Roman (classical) authors they could get their hands on. From Alcuin's own catalogues, letters, and the surviving manuscripts from this period, we know this included Plato, Aristotle, Galen, Pliny the Elder, Horace, Cicero, Seneca, Virgil, Livy, Ovid, and about sixty other authors.[38] The breadth of learning is remarkable. I have a PhD in ancient history from a well-resourced state university, but I confess that I have not read all of the authors these medieval masters absorbed. I certainly cannot quote them at will—as Alcuin routinely does in his poems and letters, from memory!

There may only have been about three hundred to five hundred separate titles in the best Carolingian libraries.[39] But we know of the copying and production of at least seven thousand books in the workshops of the 800s. Given that our evidence is fragmentary and random for this period, the real number must have been much higher, perhaps fifty thousand books.[40] The story of "dark ages" when the church suppressed knowledge is a fiction developed in modern times, as I will explore in chapter 19. The tale is rarely contradicted today because so few of us learn about medieval Europe. Why would we bother—it was "the Dark Ages"!?

The monumental influence of Alcuin and the other scholars of the Carolingian court is described well by Rosamond McKitterick, Professor of Medieval History at Cambridge University:

> This vibrant new culture of the late eighth and the ninth centuries provided the essential foundation for European culture thereafter. It must be stressed, though, that the Franks were Rome's heirs. They made Roman and Christian ideas and techniques of art and scholarship their own. The Christian church provided both the spiritual and moral framework, and the specific educational and liturgical needs which the Carolingians strove to fulfil. Yet the Franks in the Carolingian period were also intensely creative: they built on what they had inherited and made vigorous use of it to create something new and distinctively Carolingian that provided the bedrock for the subsequent development of medieval European culture.[41]

The ambitions of Alcuin and the Carolingian Renaissance received fresh impetus in later church directives. Pope Gregory VII decreed in 1079 that every cathedral in Christendom should establish a school for its region. And the universal church councils of 1179 and 1215 reiterated the demand, adding an economic requirement "that even penniless students could be taught."[42] The tradition of advanced education established by Alcuin—grammar, logic, rhetoric, arithmetic, geometry, and astronomy, and *then* history, science, and theology—set an educational pattern in Europe, on and off, for the next thousand years. And the classical education movement in the US today is still modelled on this framework. Finally, the first European "universities" in the 1100s, in Bologna, Paris, Oxford, and Cambridge, all owe a debt to the educational ambitions of the medieval church.[43] Indeed, universities like Oxford, whose motto remains *Dominus illuminatio mea*, "the Lord is my light," stand as concrete testimony to a tradition of education going back to Alcuin, and before him to the church fathers, and before them to the classics of Greece and Rome. Alcuin, with his royal patron Charlemagne, was, indeed, the real "swerve" in western culture.

One thing the medieval church cannot be accused of is ignoring the life of the mind. I venture to say that a gifted senior student in the School of Tours in the year 800 could give a modern English-speaking university student a run for their money in matters of grammar and syntax, fluency in a second language, the rules of formal logic, rhetoric, poetry, and even observational astronomy (i.e., calculating the movements of the heavenly bodies). And their handwriting would be vastly superior!

Yet, all that knowledge could not save the church from falling victim to its own stupidity over these same centuries. One element of the "Dark Ages" narrative that cannot be denied is that in its effort to convert the warrior-cultures of pagan Europe, the church itself was transformed into the biggest bully of all. This is the sorry tale I must tell in the next chapter.

16

Knights of Christ

The Prelude to "Holy War" in the Build Up to 1100

But the knights of Christ may safely do battle in the battles of the Lord, fearing neither the sin of smiting the enemy nor danger of their own downfall.

—BERNARD OF CLAIRVAUX

One of the peculiarities of Christianity, from the beginning, was its relative lack of *specific cultural badges* people had to wear in order to be Christian. The religion had its theological and moral convictions, of course, as well as its set text, the Bible. But it did not have a sacred language that adherents were encouraged to learn. It had no dietary laws or dress code. It was not wedded to particular times and places—pilgrimage to sacred sites had little significance in Christianity compared to other traditions. There were no particular careers Christians should avoid, apart from immoral ones. Nor were there categories of people—racial, credal, or even moral—with whom believers were not to associate or share a meal. Christ himself had been known as "a friend of tax collectors and sinners" (Luke 7:33–34).

The church had no distinctive ethnic profile, either. It started amongst Semitic peoples (Galilean and Judean Jews), but within twenty years it was embraced by Indo-Europeans in Asia Minor, Greeks, and Italians. Within two hundred years it had spread amongst Arabs, North Africans, Gauls (the French), the Spanish, and the Celts of Britain. Even today, roughly equal numbers of Christians live in Europe (26 percent), Latin America and the Caribbean (24 percent), and sub-Saharan Africa (24 percent).[1] And the largest cohort of professing Christians in the US is women of colour.[2] Already by the second century, Christians were making this point in their interactions with the pagan world. A text from AD 150 declares, "we live in both Greek and barbarian cities, as each one's lot was cast, and follow the local customs in dress and food and other aspects of life."[3]

All of this is a strength and a weakness. On the one hand, it has made Christianity an easily transportable faith. It is just as much at home in Africa or China as it is in France or the US. This is no doubt partly why it became history's first—and now largest—"world religion."[4] On the other hand, the relative lack of fixed social patterns in Christianity, combined with its missionary zeal, is one of its deepest vulnerabilities. Christians are prone to adopting local norms and accommodating themselves to the local context. The capacity and desire to *fit in* to a host culture makes them susceptible to the temptation to sacrifice some of their own ideals in an effort to win friends and influence people. (None of this is to deny that Christians have also sometimes universalized their local expressions of Christianity and imposed them *colonially* upon Christians in other parts of the world.)

The New Testament itself simultaneously celebrates Christianity's social flexibility *and* warns Christians against the temptation to be shaped by local society. "To the Jews I became as a Jew, in order to win Jews," wrote the apostle Paul to the Corinthians in about AD 55, "To those outside the law I became as one outside the law (though I am not free from God's law but am under Christ's law) so that I might win those outside the law. To the weak I became weak, so that I might win the weak. I have become all things to all people, that I might by all means save some" (1 Cor 9:20–22). The mention of remaining "under Christ's law"—a reference to Christ's teaching or original melody lines—is the part of this equation that Christians sometimes overlook. And Paul explicitly warns against such moral accommodation in his letter to the Roman churches about a year later: "Do not be conformed to this world, but be transformed by the renewing of your minds" (Rom 12:2). That is the theory.

But such warnings have, frankly, been insufficient to prevent the church from "conforming to this world" in myriad ways. Christianity's cultural flexibility can, as I say, leave it vulnerable to modification. In seeking to accommodate itself to a local setting, it can compromise its own moral logic. Something like this happened on a grand scale in the Middle Ages. As the church sought to win pagan warrior cultures to the faith, whether in France, Germany, or Scandinavia, it somehow managed to transform Jesus into the ultimate "warlord" and his church into the "knights of Christ." Let me tell that story.

The Conversion of the Church

A key theme in chapters 13–15 was the way the Roman Empire in the west died, even as the Christian Church survived and thrived, converting Gauls, Franks, and Saxons, and establishing countless monasteries, churches, and schools throughout Europe. The church proved itself to be more than simply "Roman." Its spiritual leadership remained in Rome, of course, but the wider church was a strange international and transcultural force. It was simultaneously active in politics wherever it went—for better or worse—but it was somehow immune to the passing fortunes of any particular regime, whether Roman, barbarian, Merovingian, or Carolingian. Christianity was frequently adopted as a "state religion," but it did not live and die with any state. Indeed, frequently in the Middle Ages Christian states went to war against each other—as they also did centuries later in the First and Second World Wars—but they did not think they were fighting each other's "religion." There is perhaps no clearer sign of the conversion of Europe than that its Christian states could wage war against each other without any sense that one faith was being exalted over another!

Christianity was highly successful beyond the frontiers of the Roman world, from which it had begun. But success was a two-edged sword, bringing challenges and demanding compromises. Just as the conversion of the Roman emperor in the early 300s unexpectedly transformed the church into an active player in the wealth and power of an empire, so the conversion of the warrior aristocracy of Gaul, England, and parts of Germany brought fresh "negotiations" with a way of life at least as old as Rome. The church converted many, and it found itself converted in the process.

Clovis, king of the Franks (AD 466–511), mentioned in chapter 13, provides one example of the Christian negotiation with power. He declared himself a Christian and was publicly baptised around the year 500. But in no sense did his Christianity appear to involve love of enemies or turning the other cheek. He came to power in a series of brutal victories over Roman strongholds in Gaul and elsewhere, and he maintained his power for three decades in a similar fashion. The early Christian tradition of being persecuted for the faith, of being a good loser, probably never entered his mind.

We have surviving letters between Clovis and local bishops. They tell an interesting story. For example, shortly before the year 500, Bishop Remigius of Reims wrote to the king urging him to fulfil his duty towards the poor and outcast: "Let justice issue from your mouth. Expect nothing at all from the poor and strangers. Let your court be open to all, so that no one shall depart from there downhearted. Whatever paternal property you possess, free captives with it and release them from the yoke of servitude." So far so good. Remigius also flatters the king for his accomplishments, even though Clovis was a famously brutal commander: the king is "the noted lord, greatly esteemed for his merits." Remigius then asks Clovis to keep Christian bishops close at hand: "You must summon to your side counsellors who can enhance your reputation. Your bounty should be pure and decent and you should pay respect to your bishops and always have recourse to their advice; and if there is good agreement between you and them, your province will better endure."[5]

The correspondence is an unsettling mix of sage Christian preaching and sucking up. Here we see the church—in the person of a key bishop on the frontiers of Christianity—*converting* and *being converted by* an ancient warrior aristocracy. I do not doubt the spiritual intentions of Bishop Remigius. Nor can I ignore his eagerness to hitch his wagon, the *church's* wagon, to the prevailing culture of the day.

Another letter from the same period is, to my mind, more chilling in its possibilities. Bishop Avitus of Vienne (southeast France) urges King Clovis to take his newfound Christianity into the regions he intends to conquer. The surviving letter cuts off just before mentioning the details of Clovis's military plans, but it is clear the bishop sees this as a great opportunity, divinely orchestrated, to spread Christianity deeper into pagan Europe. He praises the king for his recent baptism, his successes, and his "justice" (Clovis was better known for mercilessness). He then changes his tune: "There is one matter I would have improved." Through Clovis's victories, "God makes your people completely His own [i.e., brings them into a Christian realm]." Therefore, "I would have you extend from the good treasury of your heart the seed of faith to more remote peoples." Bishop Avitus wants missionary campaigns to those "still situated in a state of natural ignorance," he says. "Be not ashamed or reluctant to send embassies on the matter and to add to the realm of God, who raised up your realm to such an extent."[6]

Bishop Avitus is not recommending Christian "holy war" as a form of evangelization. He simply hopes that Christian "embassies" can tag along with Clovis's expanding European Empire. It is an early form of religious imperialism. Wherever the Merovingian armies went in the next two centuries, the bishops, priests, and deacons would be sent along with them, and new monasteries and churches would be established. A similar approach was adopted by Charlemagne and others in the ninth century, but with greater legal, military, and educational sophistication, as we saw in chapters 14 and 15.

This is all very different from the policy of *persuasion* and *self-sacrifice* advocated by Pope Gregory I, Augustine of Canterbury, Eligius, Boniface, Bishop Daniel, Willibald, Alcuin, and others through roughly the same period. As is so often the case in church history, things are not uniform. Just when you think Christians are at their best, they do something shockingly awful. Just when they seem like the greatest of bullies in the playground, a reformer rises up and calls the church back to its founding traditions.[7]

In time—at about the halfway point between Jesus and today—Europe would be conquered for Christ, partly through "soft power" and partly through "thuggery." It is hard to resist the observation that as the church converted the warrior aristocracy of pagan Europe—now *Christian* Europe—the church itself was drawn to a more militaristic vision of life. The conversion of Europe involved a complex negotiation of cultures that eventually made the notion of Christian "holy war" entirely plausible. By the time the Byzantine emperor Alexius I pleaded with western Christendom in the 1080–1090s to come defend eastern Christendom from the march of Islam, the church was ready to be the "knight of Christ."

From "Just War" to "Holy War"

The celebrated Oxford medievalist Christopher Tyerman has probed the multiple influences leading to the church's full embrace of "holy war." Among the key factors, of course, were the events in faraway Byzantine, as Islamic armies knocked on the door of Constantinople (more about that in chapter 18). He also notes the much earlier development of Saint Augustine's theory of "just war" in the 400s and how this was transformed by medieval thinkers into a theory of "holy war."[8]

One factor in the church's growing acceptance of violence is often overlooked. Part of the cultural negotiation between Christianity and pagan Europe was the church's growing approval of the warrior tradition at the heart of Frankish and Saxon (Germanic) society. European tribal groups sustained themselves either by annual raids on neighbours and distributing booty to their kin, or (for the less powerful) by submitting themselves by treaty to dominant warlords. Plundering and tribute were the key means of achieving social and economic cohesion. It was a European tradition going back centuries.[9]

This is the setting the church found itself in between 500 and 900, even as it went about trying to convert everyone. In the process of evangelizing medieval warlords, "the church had no option but to recognize their values," Tyerman explains. The Clovises of the world had to be flattered in order to be persuaded. Their deeds had to be endorsed before they could be reformed. And the economic realities of the warrior tradition had to be accepted if the church was to ride on the backs of the war machine with the message of salvation for all. "In such a world the virtues of the Frankish warrior and the good Christian coincided."[10]

Pretty soon, bishops in these regions were chosen from among warrior elites, just as in fifth-century Rome they had been drawn from the senatorial class. They would appear as great noblemen, complete with their own private war bands.[11] We know of one abbot (head of a monastery) named Ebolus of Saint-Germain (Paris) who was praised for his prowess with the *ballista*, an oversized crossbow. During the Viking Siege of Paris in 885–886, he boldly defended the city. One contemporary monk named Abbo, an eyewitness to the battle, excitedly tells us that Ebolus "was capable of piercing seven men with a single arrow; in jest he commanded some of them to be taken to the kitchen" (in other words, to be eaten for dinner!). The words are part of a poem and engage in obvious hyperbole. But this is something unique: a Christian warrior-priest praised in the language of the classical hero.[12]

The most remarkable sign of this medieval process of Christian militarisation is a ninth-century Old Saxon poem called the *Heliand* or "Saviour." It is a retelling of the Gospels' account of Christ in the style of a pagan heroic saga. Jesus himself is described as a knight, and his apostles are his travelling war band. Running to 5,983 lines and composed in Germanic epic style, the *Heliand* takes key terms from the pre-Christian Saxon myths and assigns them "new meanings for the purposes of Christian mission," notes James Cathey in his commentary on the poem.[13] Even the Sermon on the Mount—usually associated with an ethic of love—is transposed in the *Heliand* to describe the rewards given to the magnanimous warrior. Here is how the opening lines of the Sermon on the Mount (Matt 5:1–10) are repackaged in the *Heliand*:

> Then they stepped nearer to All-saving Christ,
>> such disciples, as he had chosen Himself,
>> the Wielder amid his vassals there.
> And the wise men, the heroes,
>> stood all gladly about God's Son,
>> the war-men most willingly; they awaited his word.
> He spoke to them smoothly; and said those were blessed,
>> the men on the mid-earth, who in their minds,
>> their hearts, were poor for humility's sake.
> Blessed be those who have done good,
>> heroes who justly have judged:
> For their piety they will be plenteously filled
>> in the kingdom of God: such good things will greet them,
>> these world-men who have judged well and justly.
>> Nor will they be cheated.
> Blessed be also such men whose hearts are mild
>> in their heroes' breasts.
> For them will the Holy Lord, the Mighty, be mild.
> They, too, were blessed,
>> those war-men who ever will [to do] right,

and through this willingly suffer
the harm and hatred of richer men.
To them is the Meadow of God's Heaven then given.

—HELIAND 16[14]

Words originally intended to inspire mercy, peace, and non-retaliation are retold in the *Heliand* as a kind of war speech from the head "Wielder" about the rewards due to his good "war-men." The author of the *Heliand* is obviously attempting to modify the pagan warrior ethic in the direction of justice, but the modifications involve some accommodation to the warrior culture itself. "In mediating between the Christian message and Germanic values," concludes Christopher Tyerman, "the vocabulary of Christianity itself adopted appropriate images accessible to warrior elites."[15] Within this context, Christian discipleship could, without too much of a stretch, be extended to include real physical violence for Christ's cause. Think of the *ballista*-wielding Ebolus. And given that monasteries in this period occasionally needed to be protected from violent brigands and invading pagans, monks were happy to describe the noble knights who defended them as "true servants of God."[16]

When Pope Urban II announced the First Crusade in November 1095, the stage had long been set for a Europe-wide response, which harnessed the ancient warrior tradition and repurposed it for Christ. When the crowds in Clermont that day replied with "God wills it," they were not—in their minds—taking a shocking new turn in the Christian life. They were expressing the fulfilment of centuries of cultural fusion between the universalistic vision of Christianity and the heroic tradition of a warrior elite. The result was Christian "holy war," fighting the enemies of God with a full papal guarantee that such violence was not only permissible but *redemptive* for the sincere "knight of Christ."

The "Armour of God"

In such a mood, it seemed entirely plausible for an accomplished monk like Bernard of Clairvaux (AD 1090–1153) to write about *sacred* violence. He was best known in his day for treatises on love for God. But in the wake of the First Crusade, he penned his famous *In Praise of the New Knighthood*. It assures the soldiers of the newly established Knights Templar that fighting in a Crusade is not the same as fighting for worldly honour. Bernard criticises traditional forms of knighthood, which aimed at wealth and glory, and contrasts it with being Christ's knight:

> But the knights of Christ may safely do battle in the battles of the Lord, fearing neither the sin of smiting the enemy nor danger of their own downfall, inasmuch as death for Christ, inflicted or endured, there is no taint of sin, but deserves abundant glory. Surely, if he kills an evildoer, he is not a mankiller, but, if I may so put it, an evil-killer. Clearly he is reckoned the avenger of Christ against evildoers, and the defender of Christians.[17]

I should add that Bernard—or *Saint* Bernard as he is known in the Catholic tradition—goes on in the text to exhort the Crusaders to act with justice, to dress modestly, and to pursue peace and frugality rather than earthly glory. In theory, this was a highly *moral* form of warfare. Abuses such as we occasionally see among special forces today—whether among Australian or US troops—would have been regarded as damnable, literally damnable. Still, Bernard's full-throated defence of "holy" violence is unmistakable and (for me) utterly depressing.

I am particularly struck by the way Bernard of Clairvaux took New Testament military *metaphors* and *concretized* them. In Paul's letter to the Ephesians, the first-century apostle likens the Christian life to "warfare" against temptation and persecution. The symbolic nature of the paragraph could hardly be clearer:

> Therefore put on the full armor of God, so that when the day of evil comes, you may be able to stand your ground, and after you have done everything, to stand. Stand firm then, with the belt of truth buckled around your waist, with the breastplate of righteousness in place, and with your feet fitted with the readiness that comes from the gospel of peace. In addition to all this, take up the shield of faith, with which you can extinguish all the flaming arrows of the evil one. Take the helmet of salvation and the sword of the Spirit, which is the word of God. (Eph 6:13–17 NIV)

Paul's armour of God is metaphorical. He even explains each item: the belt *is truth*, the breastplate *is righteousness*, and so on. But a thousand years after

Paul, Saint Bernard alludes to this same New Testament imagery to endorse *actual* armour and weaponry. "The knight who puts the breastplate of faith on his soul in the same way as he puts a breastplate of iron on his body is truly intrepid and safe from everything," writes Bernard. "So forward in safety, knights, and with undaunted souls drive off the enemies of the cross of Christ," that is, Muslims in the Holy Land.[18]

Bernard of Clairvaux made an extraordinary interpretive manoeuvre. I noted in chapter 12 that even Jews in the period of Jesus believed that the "holy wars" of the Torah (the Old Testament) did *not* justify expansionist holy wars in their day. We also saw that Christians went a step further and allegorized the battles of Joshua to be pictures of spiritual warfare, as in Paul's metaphor above. But a millennium after Jesus and Paul, Bernard re-concretizes Old Testament "holy war," and he turns Paul's "spiritual warfare" upside-down and inside-out, in an effort to encourage soldiers to fight Muslims in the east. Christopher Tyerman puts it well: "It is a measure of the pragmatism, sophistication, some might say sophistry, and sheer intellectual ingenuity, that there was an ideology of Christian holy war at all."[19]

Christina "the Astonishing"

Bernard was by no means the only charismatic leader making the spiritual case for holy war. A generation after him, right around the time of the Fourth (AD 1198–1204) and Fifth Crusades (AD 1213–1229), an astonishing woman rose to prominence as the mouthpiece for God, many believed. She, in fact, came to be known as Christina the Astonishing (AD 1150–1224). Born in Belgium and orphaned at a young age, Christina suffered regular seizures, one of which nearly killed her in her twenties. In her near-death experience, she said she glimpsed the horrors of hell, and she emerged convinced that her mission was to save others, both through her preaching and through her own suffering. She believed she had to bear the purgatorial punishments of others (something that would not pass as good theology today!). And she suffered quite a lot. Some punishments were self-inflicted—beatings, starvation, extended periods outside in the freezing cold. Locals often thought she was insane or demon-possessed—they ridiculed her and, on occasion, placed her in iron chains. Once, she was mauled by a pack of dogs.

Yet, Christina proclaimed Christ to all she met. She took Communion every Sunday. She visited the dying and wept in public over the sins of society. Many started to see her as some kind of "oracle." Ten years after Christina's death in 1224, her biographer, the scholar-monk Thomas of Cantimpré, wrote, "By the example of life and with many words, with tears, lamentations and boundless cries she taught more and shouted louder than anyone we have known about the praise and glory of Christ."[20] Much of the *Life of Christina the Astonishing* is dismissed by contemporary historians as hagiographical nonsense, but the general, spooky thrust of her public persona is plausible enough. And her wholesale endorsement of the Crusades (which is why I mention her at this point) is entirely believable. In 1187, when Saladin recaptured Jerusalem, Christina openly rejoiced: "I exult because today Christ the Lord rejoices with the angels," she proclaimed. Why? "Know that today the Holy Land has been handed over into the hands of the ungodly, and through this event a great occasion for salvation has been given . . . they [Crusaders] shall be turned to the path of justice from the path of injustice, and men shall shed their blood in this affair of the Holy Land and they, in turn, shall repay the death of Christ with great devotion."[21] As bizarre as all this sounds, Christina is simply endorsing the Crusader theology of the day: remission of sins through sacred combat. She saw the Crusades as an opportunity for sinful, hell-bound men in Europe to win their salvation. Her wide reputation as a divine mouthpiece may well have contributed to the deep fervour that we know was associated with crusading in just this period (early AD 1200s). By pure coincidence—true story—I happen to have written these last two paragraphs on Christina's designated memorial day (24 July). Make of that what you will.

By the end of the first millennium, Christianity had filled the west to an extent not even reached by the Roman Empire. It survived the fall of Rome and the collapse of Gaul. It found new converts and benefactors. It taught kings the way of Christ, and it learnt new ways of commending and adapting its message. But aspects of the church became so attuned to its surrounding culture that they were eventually indistinguishable from that culture. If, by the 500s, being Christian was indistinguishable from being Roman, by the 1000s being

Christian was indistinguishable from being Frankish or Saxon. Europe and the church found themselves *converted* to each other's ways.

It would, however, be a misrepresentation to suggest that this was the *leading* story of the church in the Middle Ages, as if the main thing going on in the period was the work of theologians like Bernard and charismatics like Christina urging Europeans to become "knights of Christ." The fact is, much of the old work of the church was still going on. And there were plenty of genuine prophets popping up and accusing the church of being a pack of hypocrites.

Prophets and Hypocrites

Medieval Monasteries, Charities, and Reforms

Do what they say, but not what they do.

—BENEDICT OF NURSIA

I t remains a thing of wonder—if that's the right word—that a thousand years after Jesus Christ, *violence* was viewed as an acceptable part of Christian devotion. But it would be wrong to imagine that this was the main business of the church in the medieval period. The main business was the normal business we observed about earlier times: evangelization followed up with the establishment of churches, monasteries, hospitals, charities, and schools. And we know the names of enough individuals in this period who aimed for Christian integrity that we can also conclude that even in the gloomiest moments of church history, the flame of Christ still flickered, exposing the darkness and igniting reforms.

The tradition of prophets denouncing hypocrites and calling them back to the right path begins, of course, in the Jewish Scriptures. The prophets frequently demanded that Israel drop the pretence of *religion*, with its prayers and fasts and ceremonies, and instead pursue true spirituality. "Is this not the fast that I choose," says the prophet Isaiah on behalf of the Almighty: "to loose the bonds of injustice, to undo the thongs of the yoke, to let the oppressed go free, and to break every yoke?" (Isa 58:6). Christ said many similar things: "Woe to you, scribes and Pharisees, hypocrites! For you tithe mint, dill, and cummin, and have neglected the weightier matters of the law: justice and mercy and faith" (Matt 23:23); "You hypocrite, first take the log out of your own eye, and then you will see clearly to remove the speck out of your neighbor's eye" (Matt 7:5). The term *hupokritēs*, "hypocrite," basically means "actor." It occurs seventeen times in the Gospels (from the lips of Jesus), four of them in the Sermon on the Mount. In theory, Christianity has an in-built self-corrective mechanism in the life and teaching of Christ. The modern secular charge that the church is full of hypocrites is a historical echo of the original teaching of Christ.

Through all of the centuries that followed, there were Christian "prophets" who made the church look bad and called it back to its foundations. I have already mentioned Bishop Eligius (AD 600s), who gave away his wealth to liberate foreign slaves and taught his converts to do the same. We met Boniface (AD 700s), for whom persuasion and suffering were the true weapons of Christ's mission. Then there is the incomparable Alcuin (also AD 700s), who not only guided a European renaissance but also used his privileged position as the "only person who could contradict Charlemagne"[1] to beg the king to deal gently with the Saxons. The lives of such medieval figures could fill a book. I will give them just a chapter.

Jerome and the Priestly Womanizers

I mentioned Jerome of Bethlehem (AD 342–420) in chapter 17. He was the great scholar of the late fourth and early fifth century who felt he had come to love classical literature *too much*, especially Cicero, and so gave up reading secular books for about fifteen years. Many of his writings seek to expose the laziness and materialism that had crept into the church in the late fourth century, as more and more wealthy elites walked out of the wings of the church into its centre.

One of his celebrated letters—more like an essay—castigates "presbyters" (that is, priests) who use the church to pursue money and women. The mind boggles. It was written in the year 384 to his friend Eustochium, a young, high-born Roman woman who had decided to devote herself to the contemplative Christian life. Jerome advises her to watch out for hypocritical clergy, who "put on a mournful face and pretend to make long fasts, which for them are rendered easy by secret nocturnal banquets." Some of the young clergy were the worst:

> There are other men . . . who only seek the office of presbyter and deacon that they may be able to visit women freely. These fellows think of nothing but dress; they must be nicely scented, and their shoes must fit without a crease. Their hair is curled and still shows traces of the tongs; their fingers glisten with rings; and if there is wet on the road they walk across on tiptoe so as not to splash their feet. When you see these gentry, think of them rather as potential bridegrooms than as clergyman.[2]

In other words: Run, dear Eustochium, *run!* Jerome himself set a very different standard, and he had a genuine impact on people's idea of how a true presbyter was meant to behave—gentle, scholarly, pastoral, unworldly, and pure.

Every century needs a Jerome, someone to call out the excesses of the church. Another one was soon required. He turned up, right on cue.

The Humanitarian Rule of Benedict

Perhaps the most influential religious figure of the early Middle Ages was the Italian monk Benedict of Nursia (AD 480–550). Educated in Rome, Benedict became disillusioned with the decadence he saw all around him, and he withdrew to a contemplative Christian life in Subiaco, forty miles east of Rome. Many started to gather around him, drawn by his personal discipline and reforming zeal. He founded a few monasteries in short order and gained wide fame. A few church authorities were wary of his call to a simpler version of Christianity, and they publicly opposed him. He moved south, halfway between Rome and Naples, and established a community, Montecassino Abbey, on the summit of a hill overlooking the town of Cassino. In this period southern Italy was still largely pagan. Many were converted by his preaching. Large numbers joined his movement. Before his death in the middle of the sixth century, he had founded twelve monastic communities.

Benedict's guidelines for the life of a monk are known as the *Rule of Saint Benedict*. They had an incalculable impact on European Christianity, setting the standard for all monastic orders in the centuries that followed. As a result, he is known as the "patron saint of all Europe."[3] Benedict's "rule" explicitly forbade the accumulation of possessions—an attempt to prevent greed in the church. It demanded five hours a day of productive labour, whether farming, building, or craftsmanship. It set a minimum of two hours private reading each day (oh, bliss!), several periods of daily prayer, and the regular performance of charitable works.

In the section of the *Rule* titled "The Instruments of Good Works," Benedict offers seventy-two pithy descriptions of the life expected of a member of his community. The contrast with the Maxims of Delphi, those 147 aphorisms of ancient Greek morality (discussed in chapter 7), could not be greater. In Benedict's list we naturally find *theological* virtues: "To love God," "Never to despair of God's mercy," and so on. But it is his *humanitarian* virtues that leap out to us as so different from Greek and Roman ethics and yet so recognisable to us today: "To relieve the poor," "To clothe the naked," "To bury the dead," "To help in trouble," "Not to forsake charity," "To love one's enemies," "Not to return evil for evil," "Not to curse those who curse us," and many more just like these.

There are also some very *practical* items in the seventy-two "instruments of good works": "Not addicted to wine" (Benedictines tended vineyards), "Not to love much talking," "To make peace with one's adversary before the sun sets," and—referring to hypocritical church superiors—"Do what they say, but not what they do."[4] This was a key principle for Benedict and those who followed him: the leaders of the church may not always follow the way of Christ, but Benedictines *must*, and they must also try to lead others back to the right path through persuasion and example. That is exactly what Benedict himself did, with a legacy in Europe that is difficult to overstate.

The *Rule of Benedict* continued to call people back to the "instruments of good works" for centuries. Thousands of monasteries (for men and for women) were established throughout France and Germany over the next five hundred years. Many of them were modelled, at least loosely, on Benedict's vision of a community marked by prayer, study, productivity, and a life of charity. More than three hundred medieval manuscripts of the *Rule* have survived. Other than the Bible, few documents survive in more than a handful of manuscripts.

Every now and then, individuals from these monastic communities would notice that Christendom had drifted away from its founding ideals, and they would call everyone back to the faith. Enter: Odo of Cluny.

Odo the Reformer

For much of the 600s, 700s, and 800s, the church experienced wide missionary and political success. But things took a turn for the worse in the mid-to-late ninth century, when Saracen attacks on Italy (AD 846) and Viking attacks in the heart of Europe (Paris, AD 885) left Christendom feeling vulnerable and many churches and monasteries in ruins. Worse than these external factors, however, was the degradation the church brought on itself through its own increasing politicization and secularization. Great Abbeys were bought and sold for profit. The position of bishop—which came with quite a few perks by this time—was often sold to the highest bidder or given as a reward for military exploits.[5] By AD 909, some leaders were in deep despair at the state of the church. They called a council at Rheims, northeast of Paris, where bishops recorded their lament for posterity: "every man does what pleases him, despising the laws of God and man and the ordinances of the church. The powerful oppress the weak, the land is full of violence against the poor." This was not judgmental self-righteousness. The bishops went on to blame themselves: "God's flock perishes through our charge. It has come about by our negligence, our ignorance and that of our brethren (i.e., monks and priests)."[6] Wherever there is this kind of honesty in the church there is hope, and the honesty was soon rewarded.

Shortly after the Council at Rheims, a remarkable reform movement arose, led in large part by a man named Odo (AD 879–942), the Abbot of Cluny in southeast France. As a teenager Odo had trained to be a fighting man, a warrior in the court of Duke William of Aquitaine. After a sudden realization of his duty before God, he abandoned his commission, at nineteen years of age, and pursued a religious life. He studied in Paris with the renowned scholar Remigius of Auxerre (AD 841–908), an expert in ancient Greek and

Latin literature and a shining example of the lasting impact of the Carolingian Renaissance in the previous century. Remigius was a Benedictine, and he influenced Odo greatly.

When Odo became the Abbot of the monastery at Cluny in 927, he quickly reshaped life there, which he believed had become lax. He brought it into line with the *Rule of Benedict*. He was a blistering humanitarian in the style of Jesus Christ, and he denounced violence and greed with gusto. In one of his works titled *Life of St. Gerald of Aurillac*, he provided a model of a soldier who only ever fought to defend the weak, who refused to shed blood, and who pursued humility toward everyone. This is a far cry from the *ballista*-wielding monk, Ebolus of Paris, forty years earlier. In Odo's other great work, *Collationes* or *Conferences*, he castigates proud and wealthy Christians: "How then are these robbers Christians, or what do they deserve who slay their brothers for whom they are commanded to lay down their lives? You have only to study the books of antiquity to see that the most powerful are always the worst. Worldly nobility is due not to nature but to pride and ambition. If we judged by realities, we should give honor not to the rich for the fine clothes they wear but to the poor who are the makers of such things."[7]

A contemporary of Odo, John of Salerno, wrote the biography of his beloved master sometime in the 950s, ten or fifteen years after Odo's death. He offers numerous firsthand snapshots of the personality and behaviour of this medieval reformer. "Whenever I went out with him," John of Salerno writes, "he was always careful to ask if we had something for the poor." And when he met the poor, "he gave to all who asked of him."[8] Sometimes, when Odo suspected someone was poor but unwilling to ask for anything, he would try to preserve their dignity by asking them if they would sing a song for him. When they did, he paid them handsomely for the performance. "They deserved, he would say, no small remuneration."[9] He did the same with poor farmers selling their meagre fruits on the streets. He demanded they increase their price for him, and only when they agreed to some absurd amount would he make the purchase: "And so Odo enriched these men under the pretence of paying the price."[10] Odo sometimes found cheeky ways to drive his points home to his attendants and students:

The blind and the lame, Odo said, would be the doorkeepers of heaven. Therefore no one ought to drive them away from his house, so that in the future they should not shut the doors of heaven against him. So if one of our servants, not being able to put up with their shameless begging, replied sharply to them or denied them access to the door of our tent, Odo at once rebuked him with threats. Then in the servant's presence he used to call the poor man and command him, saying, "When this man comes to the gate of heaven, pay him back in the same way." He said this to frighten the servants, so that they should not act in this way again, and that he might teach them to love charity.[11]

John of Salerno admits that people sometimes took advantage of Odo, and Odo let them. A thief made off with his warm coat in the middle of an Italian snowstorm.[12] On another occasion, while on a peace envoy in Rome to resolve a violent siege, someone attempted to mug Odo, just to steal his water jar. Locals stepped in to save him, and Odo insisted on giving the man some money, since he obviously needed it. The incident was promptly reported to the local governor, Alberic, who arrested the man and ordered that his hand be cut off. Odo intervened and "begged strenuously that this should not be done, and dismissed the yokel safe and unhurt."[13]

Story after story could be told about Odo. The key point, however, is that his way of life, and the life he demanded at the monastery of Cluny, rapidly became the model of a disciplined Christian life. Monks disillusioned with their own communities flocked to Cluny to learn from Odo. The result was a transformation of monastic life all over Europe. Odo was given authority to reform centres at Romainmôtier (AD 929), Aurillac (AD 930), Fleury (AD 930), Sarlat (AD 930), Tulle (AD 930), Saint-Allyre of Clermont (AD 933), Saint-Pierre-le-Vif (AD 938), St. Paul Major (Rome) (AD 936), St. Elias in Nepi (AD 940), Farfa (AD 940), St. Mary on the Aventine (AD 940), the original Benedictine monastery at Montecassino (AD 940), and Saint-Julien of Tours (AD 942).[14] Odo's reforms helped reshape Christian leadership, and therefore Christianity, in Europe for another century.

The Prophetess Hildegard

Two centuries later, we continue to see periodic transformations in the church inspired by outstanding individuals. One such reformer was Hildegard of

Bingen (AD 1098–1179). Hildegard lived as a Benedictine Abbess, the ruler of a community of devout women living by the *Rule of Benedict*. She was born to a noble family in west Germany. From a young age she was recognised as a "prophetess," a term that meant something more like *inspired preacher* than a person who predicts the future.

Hildegard was charismatic, zealous, and scholarly. "She achieved a level of learning and expression enjoyed by few in her day, male or female," says Andrea Dickens of Arizona State University in her *The Female Mystic: Great Women Thinkers of the Middle Ages*, "and her writings show a breadth and originality not found in many others."[15] She wrote of her spiritual visions in the manner of a mystic, but she also produced philosophical and medical works, and even published a commentary on the *Rule of Benedict*.

At the heart of Hildegard's project was renewal. Upset at the worldliness of some of her church superiors, "her work was aimed at the reform of her community and the church, and her reforming agenda parallels that of various schoolmen of her time." She was not only the leader of her own community of women, "she conducted preaching tours, wrote songs," Dickens notes, "and fought for the rights of her monastery's independence from the protecting male monastery."[16] Hildegard advised some of the most powerful clergy in Europe, warning them, for example, about the heresy of Catharism (also known as Albigensianism, mentioned on page 17). She is even known to have addressed clergy directly in her various preaching campaigns, in the year 1160 in Franconia, Lorraine, Schwaben, and Werden, and in 1163 in the major city of Cologne.[17]

Catherine of Siena: Adviser to the Pope

A similar reforming spirit can be seen two centuries later in Catherine of Siena (AD 1347–1380). From a young age Catherine felt she had been called by God to increase devotion to God in the church. In one early vision Christ himself appeared to her, she claimed, with the following complaint about the state of his church: "In these latter days there has been such an upsurge of pride, especially in the case of men who imagine themselves to be learned or wise, but my justice cannot endure them any longer."[18] It was Catherine's mission to remedy the situation. Her parents had other ideas and desperately tried to marry her off. But at age seventeen she caught a pox. She refused treatment, and it left her "disfigured, physically undesirable and hence unmarriageable," says Andrea Dickens. She gained her wish and devoted herself "to the care of the sick and poor and the conversion of sinners."[19]

She soon gained a large following of men and women, clerical and lay. I think of her—and Hildegard—as a medieval religious version of talk show host Oprah Winfrey or climate activist Greta Thunberg, women who have little structural authority in society but whose personal gifts compel the masses and gain the ear of rulers. In Catherine's case, people were drawn to her personal sanctity and spiritual wisdom. We get a sense of her personality in her 383 letters that survive. Her correspondents included friends, abbesses, prostitutes, popes, queens, and various local authorities. She once boldly wrote to Pope Gregory XI—who, like many other popes of the time, was living in Avignon in the south of France—urging him to return to the spiritual centre of Rome. He obeyed her advice.[20] She was also involved in local politics, acting as the mediator between warring factions in Siena, and even becoming an adviser in a conflict between the Vatican and the city of Florence.

Catherine's central concern was that people should live in response to Christ's sacrifice on their behalf. "The bond of payment for human sins was written on nothing less than lambskin, the skin of the spotless Lamb," she wrote. "He inscribed us on himself and then tore up the lambskin! So let our souls find strength in knowing that the parchment our bond was written on has been torn up."[21] In Catherine's view, Christ's love for us in dying on our behalf should inspire devotion to him and love for one another. Whatever we make of that theology, she is a good example of how the original moral logic of Christianity, the beautiful tune, often found concrete expression in the sacrificial lives of men and women, even during times when the church itself was better known for an upsurge of pride.

Francis of Assisi: "Make Me a Channel of Your Peace"

By anyone's estimation, Francis of Assisi (AD 1181–1226) is one of the most remarkable figures of the Middle Ages. His legacy has attracted all sorts of weird and wonderful tales—stories of miracles, stigmata, communicating with animals, and much more. Behind it all, there is an authentic history to tell. The central, undoubted plotline of Francis's life is clear: He was born into a wealthy merchant family in the central Italian town of Assisi. Following a brief career as a solider in various inter-city battles, he experienced some kind of meltdown in his early twenties, which has been likened to post-traumatic stress disorder.[22] In any case, Francis entered a period of deep gloom for the next few years.

Francis's conversion experience is not dramatic, but it is strange. In the winter of 1206 he was wandering the snowy woods outside Assisi when he came across a small group of lepers. *Leprosaria* or leper shelters had been a feature of the landscape in Christianized regions for centuries, and there were several in Francis's part of Italy. Previously, he had despised lepers, mocking them: "he would look at their houses only from a distance of two miles and he would hold his nostrils with his hands," says our earliest source for his life.[23] On this occasion, however, inexplicably, he felt compelled to talk with them, touch them, and even offer to wash their wounds. "The Lord himself took me among them, and I showed mercy to them. And on leaving them, what seemed bitter to me had turned for me into sweetness of body and soul."[24] The experience was life changing.

This was not a simple *moral* conversion from wealth to poverty, or from soldiery to charity. For Francis, it was a spiritual revolution. "As Francis showed mercy to these outcasts," writes Augustine Thompson of the University of Virginia, "he came to experience God's own gift of mercy to himself. . . . The startled veteran sensed himself, by God's grace and no power of his own, remade into a different man."[25] Here is Christ's original melody line having its effect: "Be merciful, just as your Father is merciful" (Luke 6:36). Animated by a sense of divine mercy toward himself, Francis renounced wealth and violence and pursued a life of single-minded devotion to the poor, the sick, the unconverted, and the thousands who joined his movement.

The story of the growth of the Franciscan movement is beyond the scope of this book, but it is remarkable. Suffice it to say that by the time Francis died in 1226, there were already three thousand men and women who had formally embraced his manner of life. It is one thing to establish a church of that size over a twenty-year period—I have several US friends who have achieved that. Francis somehow convinced three thousand people to give up everything and devote themselves full-time to a life of poverty and service. He dubbed his movement the *Fratres Minores* or "Lesser Brothers" (it included sisters from the beginning). Today we call them the Franciscan Order.[26]

Much could be said about Francis's own preaching missions, the missionaries he sent into pagan lands, his charitable projects, and his (sometimes tense) relationships with bishops and Pope Innocent III. One event in his life illustrates well his adventurous or entrepreneurial spirit, as well as his zeal to do good in the world. He attempted to make peace in the middle of the Fifth Crusade.

Francis's name is often associated with "peace." For many people, the only thing they know about him is his famous Peace Prayer: "Make me a channel of your peace. Where there is hatred let me bring your love. Make me a channel of your peace. Where there's despair in life let me bring hope," and so on. Sadly, this is one of those myths that got attached to Francis. Despite being named the "Prayer of St. Francis" all over the Internet, the poem or prayer has nothing to do with Francis. It is anonymous, and it first appeared in French in 1912.[27] That said, Francis did attempt to be a "channel of peace" in 1219 when he made an unorthodox appearance in northern Egypt on the frontline of the Crusade.

Francis was not a pacifist in the strict sense. He would have accepted Augustine's principle of "just war": state violence is tragically necessary to defend the weak from an aggressor. And we know that many leaders of the Crusades believed their project was designed to halt Muslim aggression against formerly *Christian* lands.[28] The "material sword," said Jacques de Vitry (AD 1180–1240), one of the key advocates of the Fifth Crusade, "was the Church's answer to pagan and Saracen violence."[29] While probably not a pacifist, "Francis may have inclined to pacifism," says Oxford's Christopher Tyerman. He hoped to overcome the threat of Islam "through reasoned evangelism . . . by conversion, not conquest."[30]

Francis preached to the Crusaders in Egypt. He declared that it was God's will to convert the Muslims, as an alternative to war. He was mocked by the Christian soldiers. "To the rough Crusader troops, he became something of a joke," notes Augustine Thompson; "to their leaders, he seemed a feckless threat to morale."[31] Francis responded by predicting that the Crusaders would fail in their campaign to take the Islamic stronghold of Fariskur, twenty miles down the Nile River from the Mediterranean Sea. Whether a lucky guess or something else, he was proved right in August 1219.[32]

As a result of his successful "prophecy," Francis was given permission to cross over into enemy territory and plead with the Islamic forces to become Christians and make peace. The Crusader leadership washed their hands of him. Over several days Francis of Assisi attempted to convert the Muslim army. Sultan al-Malik al-Kamil received Francis cordially, at first. He was given a large audience, and Francis made his case—through translators—on behalf of Christianity. The sultan's religious advisers gave a response, and Francis was invited to embrace Islam. When it became clear that Francis had no intention of becoming a Muslim, and indeed that he was eager to convert them, the sultan's advisers recommended that Francis (along with the monk colleague he had brought with him) be executed for preaching against Islam. After being "insulted and beaten" and receiving "threats of torture and death," Francis was dismissed by the sultan, lucky to escape with his life.[33]

Francis presumably had no spiritual impact on Muslims, but he did leave a personal impression. One of Sultan al-Kamil's advisers, the Islamic lawyer Fakhr ad-Din al-Farisi, had his involvement in the "affair of the monk" recorded on his tombstone.[34] On returning to the Crusader camp, several priests were so impressed by Francis's conviction and bravery, they immediately joined his movement.[35] People would continue to flock to Francis over the next seven years, until his death near Assisi on 3 October 1226. His renewal movement would continue to grow throughout Europe for centuries. The Franciscans did not always live up to Francis's high ideals. Serious disputes and schisms over leadership emerged from time to time, and laxity crept into the Order as its material prosperity grew. But as with Christianity itself, the "Lesser Brothers" had a self-corrective mechanism built in, which often led to moments of reform and renewal.[36]

Hospitals, Charities, and the Birth of Modern Welfare

Quite apart from the reforming work of remarkable individuals like Benedict, Odo, Hildegard, Francis, and others, the medieval church throughout Europe continued its traditional work of establishing charities and building hospitals. Perhaps I will bore readers at this point, because much of what occurs in Europe at this time is simply a rerun, or extension, of the same activities we witnessed throughout the Mediterranean in the first few centuries. In the next chapter, we will discover that the Byzantine Empire did the same, on an enormous scale. Still, one benefit of outlining the charitable services of late medieval Europe is that it becomes easy to see exactly how these ancient *Christian* traditions slowly became our modern *secular* traditions.

For the entire medieval period, the obligation to assist the poor fell to the church, specifically to *bishops* as regional church leaders, *priests* as leaders of individual parishes, and *deacons,* who often did the face-to-face work with the impoverished. This was not simply a vague moral duty. Bishops enshrined it into legislation. Here is one of the odd things for us to contemplate today: church courts ran in parallel with secular courts through much of the Middle Ages. This goes back to a law of Constantine in the fourth century, which allowed bishops to decide certain civil disputes. In any case, the Council of Orléans in 511 ruled that bishops should set aside a quarter of their diocesan income for hospitality to the poor and to travellers. Another law from Clermont in 535 declared that any church official caught stealing funds intended for the poor would be "excommunicated."[37] That might not sound like much to us, but to a medieval bishop, priest, deacon, or layperson, excommunication was a shocking punishment that potentially threatened one's eternal salvation. Councils in Rome in 853 and Quierzy (northern France) in 858 insisted that bishops had a special obligation to maintain hospitals in their districts.[38] One indication of the centrality of the church in public welfare is seen in the fact that, by the end of the 600s, the bishop of Rome, the pope, was charged with ensuring the water supply to the city and maintaining the aqueducts.[39] There were certainly abuses of the system. Bishops with bad motives could enrich themselves unimaginably—this is no doubt what prompted the Clermont canon law of 535, just mentioned. Yet, there would not have been a city in western Christendom that was unaware of the obligation of church leaders to be the chief defenders of the poor.

The mention of hospitals above opens up a vast topic of research. The first public hospital we know about, as we saw in chapter 10, was the one built by Basil the Great around AD 370 in faraway Cappadocia (central Turkey). But ever since Fabiola's institution for the sick and dying near Rome twenty years later, there was a "cascade of hospitals" in the west, to use the expression of medievalist James William Brodman in his *Charity and Religion in Medieval*

Europe.[40] There was an early Christian hospital in Arles in the south of France by 540, and another in Clermont, two hundred and fifty miles north, just a short time later. It could shelter twenty patients at a time. Later that century, we know of six such foundations in the town of Le Mans (southwest France), founded by three successive bishops and a wealthy husband-wife benefactor team.[41]

The same was true in Spain. We have a brief biography of the much-loved Bishop Masona of Mérida (died ca. 605), written by an anonymous deacon of the charitable institution a few decades after its founding. Masona "built a *xenodocium* [hospital], enriching it with a large patrimony and appointing ministers and doctors to serve travellers and the sick, giving them this command: that the doctors should go through the entire city without ceasing and whoever they found that was sick, be they slave or free, Christian or Jew, they were to carry in their arms to the *xenodocium*, and having prepared there a well-made bed, set the sick man on it and give him light and pleasant food until, with God's help, they returned the patient to his former heath." Understandably, the townsfolk "burned with love" for Masona, and "through his sweet affection he drew the minds of all the Jews and pagans to the grace of Christ."[42] The building where all this took place has likely been identified in the ruins of the town.

In the following centuries we have similar centres for the sick in Rouen, Amiens, Reims (Rheims), Metz, Orléans, Nevers, Paris, Cologne, Augsburg, Bremen, and throughout the entire Carolingian Empire.[43] By the thirteenth century there are literally thousands of European hospitals, *leprosoria*, and similar shelters for the needy.[44]

Increasingly through the Middle Ages, charitable work was a key part of theological and legal reflection within the church. The most influential theologian of this period (my Catholic friends might say the most influential *ever*) was Thomas Aquinas (AD 1225–1274). He was gifted with unusual intellectual powers and was able to integrate classical philosophy with Christian theology, in a tradition known as Thomism. It remains a major philosophical movement to this day.[45] One of his peculiar talents was what we would call a *photographic memory*: "whatever he had once read and grasped he never forgot," says one of our earliest descriptions of him.[46] In any case, in his major work known as *Summa Theologiae* he devotes 123 pages (in the edition on my shelf) to an analysis of "Charity," its character, motivations, limits, obligations, and benefits. Eighteen pages of the section are dedicated to "almsgiving" alone (i.e., direct gifts to the poor). By way of comparison, Aquinas gives just six pages to the topic of "War."

This theology was reflected in church law of the time. By the eleventh and twelfth centuries, there was a vast legal literature—canon law—summarising authoritative rulings from the previous centuries. The most important of these were the *Decretum*, compiled around the year 1140 by the Italian scholar-monk Gratian, and the *Glossa Ordinaria* by Joannes Teutonicus around 1216. These were hugely important for the development of the western legal tradition. Church courts, as I have said, could decide a range of cases relating to marriage and family law, property law, and inheritance and financial law. They could not send you to prison, let alone execute you, but they could impose certain spiritual disciplines (penance), withhold Holy Communion/Eucharist, and excommunicate offenders. People took the courts seriously.

The standard work on canon law as it relates to charity is *Medieval Poor Law* by the celebrated historian Brian Tierney of Cornell University.[47] His detailed account of the evidence leaves me (Tierney doesn't say this) feeling that much church law in this period would be described today as "leftist." In fact, I posted some of this material on social media recently, and someone asked if I was outing myself as a socialist or even a communist! Medieval church lawyers insisted that the poor had genuine "rights"—and they called them *rights*[48]—not only to the resources of the church but also to the resources of wealthy citizens. Against much ancient (and some modern) opinion, the starting point of their thought was that "poverty was not a kind of crime."[49] Nor was it a sign of moral defect, whether laziness or foolishness. It was a tragedy. Church lawyers knew that people did sometimes game the system, preferring charity to hard work. In these cases, it was right to "deny alms to such individuals when they were known."[50] Yet, the system itself should not be premised on a cynical approach to the poor. As Joannes Teutonicus put it succinctly in the 1200s, "In case of doubt it is better to do too much than to do nothing at all."[51] As Tierney notes, it is almost as if the medieval canonists were trying to head off the later Enlightenment laws, such as the English Poor Act of 1834, which "assumed that if a man was destitute he was probably an idle lout who deserved punishment."[52]

By contrast, the *Decretum* and the *Glossa Ordinaria* are peppered with lines such as: "Feed the poor. If you do not feed them, you kill them"; "Our superfluities belong to the poor"; "Whatever you have beyond what suffices for your needs belongs to others"; "A man who keeps for himself more than he needs is guilty of theft."[53] These canonists went so far as to teach that "a man in extreme need who took the property of another was not guilty of any crime. He was not stealing what belonged to another but only taking what properly belonged to himself."[54] And Joannes Teutonicus argued that a poor person who was neglected by a rich neighbour could appeal to church courts. Those courts could compel the wealthy offender to be more generous by threat of church sanction or even excommunication.[55] And to make it easier for the poor to go to court, the church waived court fees for those without means. Pope Honorius III (AD 1216–1227) even laid down that "litigants too poor to provide themselves with legal counsel were to be supplied with free counsel by the court,"[56] something that happily still exists in secular courts today.

Church law about charity slowly became *secular* law. We can see this happening in a series of legislative changes in England in the fourteenth to the sixteenth centuries. This, of course, is a period when monarchs are gradually surrendering some of their powers. The Magna Carta of 1215 first declared certain limits on royal authority. Then a Parliament was established, first made up of nobles and bishops (AD 1275), and then also commoners (AD 1327), all deliberating with the monarch. In the following two centuries, various Acts of Parliament strengthened and then absorbed canon law. In 1391 a law of Richard II mandates what was already church law, namely, that "a convenient sum of money should be paid and distributed yearly to the poor parishioners of the said churches, in aid of their living and sustenance for ever; and also that the vicar be well and sufficiently endowed."[57] This is the state allying itself with the church to ensure that the poor are looked after. "Fourteenth-century parliaments were quite aware that a system of public poor relief was necessary," writes Brian Tierney, "but they did not seek to create one by statute because they assumed that such a system already existed and was adequately defined in the canon law of the Church."[58]

An Act of Edward VI in 1552 "for the provision and relief of the poor" contained legislation allowing the poor to denounce a miser to the local bishop. The bishop was then to "induce and persuade him or them by charitable ways and means,"[59] whatever that included. An Act of Elizabeth I of 1563 laid down that "if the bishop's exhortations were unsuccessful, a compulsory contribution could be assessed and collected under pain of imprisonment."[60] And this mechanism seems to have been widely used during Elizabeth's reign, even after she had also legislated in 1572 that justices of the peace should determine the number of the destitute in a given parish and determine how much the local inhabitants were required to pay to look after those in need.[61] This law, and another in 1598, are the origins of the English tradition—therefore, the US, Canadian, Australian, and New Zealand tradition—of redirecting our taxes to the poor of society.[62] Fiscal conservatives today who see such taxes as "theft" have the church to blame. Medieval bishops and church lawyers, of course, would have replied that the *true thief* is any wealthy person who does not give some of their surplus to the poor.

This is the century, the sixteenth century, when the English state absorbed the church. And so "the system of dual coequal authorities which was characteristic of the Middle Ages came to an end."[63] In taking over the church, says Tierney, "the state necessarily became responsible for the system of public poor relief which until then had been regulated by canon law."[64] Churches today often continue to be heavily involved in welfare work. But the main responsibility for the social safety net, in the English-speaking world and elsewhere, especially throughout Europe, is gladly borne by governments. What was once an exclusively Christian calling is now shared by all of us in our secular society.

It is a striking fact that in precisely the period when Christians were developing a theory of "holy war" and putting it into practice against Muslims (and others), they were also continuing and refining their more ancient traditions of feeding the hungry, establishing schools, building hospitals, and crafting legislation on behalf of the poor that still exists today. These tensions in church history sometimes give me a headache. Plenty of people were beautifully singing the original melody of Christ. Plenty of others were badly out of tune. Sometimes it was the same people doing both. That is the story of the church in the west for the first thousand or so years—and today.

But now it is time to press PAUSE on the western story—the story of the development of Christendom from Rome to Britain. There is another story to tell, briefly, and it is often overlooked. In the east, the Roman Empire did not end with the collapse of Rome in the fifth century. The church's history in this region—Greece, Turkey, Syria, Palestine, Egypt, and North Africa—is a very different one. It is not part of our western consciousness, but it certainly deserves a chapter in this book. And at the end of that story, as Europe rallied to confront the rise of Islam, the church of the West and the church of the East came together in a shared purpose (the Crusades) for the first time in centuries.

The Eternal Empire of the East

The Forgotten Byzantines
from the 500s to the 1400s

We prohibit the teaching of any subject by those who suffer from the insanity of the unholy pagans.

—EMPEROR JUSTINIAN

In chapters 13 to 17 we tracked the western church from the 500s to the 1000s and beyond, from the collapse of Rome to the conversion of Europe and the rise of the Crusades. I want to rewind the tape and press PLAY for the *eastern part* of the empire, from the fall of Rome to the Crusades. The history is totally different and yet strangely similar.

The claim that Charlemagne was the "emperor" of a new (Holy) "Roman Empire" in the west raised eyebrows in the east among the Byzantines. For them, the actual Roman Empire never ended. They still had real emperors. The ancient ideal of *Roma aeterna*, "eternal Rome," still seemed entirely plausible.

Justinian the Great: Scholar, Builder, and Legislator

In chapter 13 I mentioned the eastern emperor Justinian (AD 483–565), who liberated Italy and North Africa following the barbarian takeovers in the late 400s. His regime provided stability for the Vatican to continue its work westward into pagan Gaul and England, as we have seen. Justinian was viewed as a "second Constantine," not just because of his important military victories and lengthy reign but mostly because he was a staunch supporter of the Christian Church. And he is credited with transforming the Roman Empire in the east into a thoroughly Christianized regime—that was *not* fully achieved in the west before the western empire fell. But whereas Constantine favoured Christianity in an official mood of *toleration* toward the old religions, Justinian did so with prejudice and severity.

From Constantinople Justinian ruled a vast region from Italy to Syria and from Palestine to Egypt—and some other parts of North Africa. While his borders were never wholly secure from barbarians in the north or Persians in the east, he managed to create a politically stable and economically standardised empire during his almost forty-year reign (AD 525–565). In his day you could pick up a cheque in Egypt and confidently have it cashed in Constantinople. That is a financial feat that would not be replicated until thirteenth-century China.[1] Gold coins from his reign have been discovered in Sweden and Beijing. That is mind-blowing. And Byzantine ships from Alexandria in northern Egypt sailed on trading expeditions to faraway Cornwall in the south of England.[2]

Justinian's empire was cosmopolitan and learned. In his court you could hear Latin, Greek, and Syriac. While he displayed open contempt for pagan professors in his realm, he demanded from his Christian courtiers the highest standards of classical secular learning. During his reign one of the greatest intellects of the late Roman world arose, John Philoponus (AD 490–570), a name rarely heard today outside of the obscure fields of Byzantine history and the history of science. In addition to treatises on Christian subjects like the Trinity, Philoponus produced detailed commentaries on Aristotle and wrote the first full-blown critique of Aristotle's concept of an eternal cosmos. His argument was not that the Bible said so ("In the beginning when God created the heavens and the earth," Gen 1:1). Philoponus made his case for a time-bound, contingent universe—created *ex nihilo* (out of nothing)—on purely philosophical and logical grounds. His work touching on physics and metaphysics influenced early western scientists such as Galileo Galilei.[3]

Byzantine's intellectual tradition continued into the following centuries, where "a classical elite survived," writes Peter Brown. "Most of our finest manuscripts of the [Greek] classics were produced in medieval Constantinople. Indeed, if it were not for Byzantine courtiers and bishops of the ninth and tenth centuries onwards, we should know nothing—except from fragments in papyrus—of Plato, Euclid, Sophocles, and Thucydides. The classical Greek culture that we know is the Greek culture that continued to hold the interest of the upper classes of Constantinople throughout the Middle Ages."[4] Alcuin and the Carolingian Renaissance in the west (AD 700s–800s) preserved many classical works in Latin (their copies of Greek philosophers like Plato were mostly only Latin translations). The Byzantines preserved the works of the Greeks in their original form.

The norm in the Byzantine Empire was to study *all* available secular and Christian texts. The library of Constantinople at the time of Justinian housed one hundred and twenty thousand works.[5] By comparison, Oxford University's famous Bodleian Library only surpassed one hundred and twenty thousand works sometime in the eighteenth century.[6] In his *Byzantium: A Very Short Introduction*, Peter Sarris points to the stunning example of Photius I (AD 810–895), the patriarch of Constantinople, which is the eastern equivalent of the Catholic pope. Photius left us some notes about his own recommended reading in a document known as the *Bibliotheca*. It is a bit like the way some of my nerdier friends today post their reading plans on Facebook. Photius summarizes and reviews three hundred and eighty books that he advises people read. Some of the entries are just five hundred words long, and some are ten times that. As we might expect from the leader of the Orthodox Church, 233 of the recommended works are Christian, including many of the authors we have met in this book, such as Eusebius, Athanasius, Basil the Great, Gregory of Nyssa, and so on. And 147 of them are pagan or secular works, including Herodotus, Arrian, Plutarch, Philostratus, and so on. He frequently notes his disagreement with an author, whether pagan or Christian. He nonetheless recommends the reading of each one. About half of the works he summarises are now lost to us or exist only in tiny fragments. It is only because of the work of people like Photius, and the scholars and clergy he directed, that so much ancient Greek literature survives today.[7]

Western Europe experienced a couple of renaissances of classical learning, one in the 700s–800s under Charlemagne, as we have seen, and another in the 1300s among Italian humanists, as we will see in the next chapter. But these intellectuals of the eastern empire did not need any renaissance. For the Byzantines, the classical Greek past was a living part of their ongoing curriculum.[8]

Building was also important for Byzantine emperors, especially for Justinian. He employed the legendary architects and mathematicians Anthemius of Traelles and Isidorus of Miletus to assist in the design and construction of the Hagia Sophia, a church which, at the time, was the largest building in the world and an architectural marvel. It later became a mosque (AD 1453), then a museum (AD 1934), before reverting to a mosque again in July 2020.[9] Numerous other buildings from this period express the same geometrical sophistication and artistic detail (e.g., the Hagia Irene), establishing "Byzantine architecture" as a category in the textbooks. The style embodies all of the monumentalism of classical Rome but with greater mathematical and aesthetic complexity, especially in the use of domes.[10]

Justinian and his wife Theodora were culturally and economically flamboyant. Theodora even travelled with an entourage of four thousand attendants.[11] But they were zealous Christians, and both are regarded as "saints" in the Eastern Orthodox Church. Justinian himself worked and studied so hard—often until dawn—that he earned the nicknames "the sleepless one" and the "many-eyed emperor."[12] It was said that if conspirators ever wanted to kill him, they would have no trouble finding him every evening in the alcove of the great palace, discussing the intricacies of the faith with theologians and bishops.[13] Even if we are tempted to call the western centuries between 500 and 1300 the "Dark Ages," there is no justification for describing these eastern centuries as "dark."

One of Justinian's first acts as emperor was to codify Roman law. He commissioned archivists and lawyers to collate the valid decrees and laws of emperors from the second century up to his own day. He wanted to standardize and harmonize Roman law. On my bookshelf, the *Codex of Justinian* extends to three large volumes, each of about eight hundred pages. The Code influenced later canon law (church law), which in turn influenced the wider western legal system.

One of the more interesting laws ratified in the *Codex of Justinian* confirms churches as "places of refuge" for runaway slaves, victims of revenge, or refugees fleeing danger.[14] The idea originally came from the Jewish Scriptures, as is so often the case. The book of Joshua speaks of "cities of refuge" to which people could flee if they were accused of manslaughter and liable to become victims of revenge (Josh 20:1–6). In any case, centuries later, Justinian formalised the practice, so that anyone fleeing danger would be protected—with the full force of Roman law—if they could make it to the precinct of a church. And that's the other thing that is striking about the legislation quoted below: churches were frequently campuses, not just stand-alone buildings on the street corner. They often included dining rooms, hostels, poor houses, hospitals, and even baths, as well as the church proper (designated the "temple" in the legislation). The law of 23 March AD 431 reads:

> The space lying between the temple, which is enclosed in the manner that we have described above, and the first doors of the church beyond the public grounds, whether these consist of houses, gardens, courtyards, baths, or porticos, shall protect refugees that enter them just as the temple itself; and no one shall lay sacrilegious hands on them.[15]

This sanctuary law was in effect for centuries, in the east and the west. Indeed, the common law of England maintained the status of churches as places of refuge right up until 1623 for criminal cases and 1773 for civil cases.[16] In a conscious echo of the ancient practice, churches in the USA in the early 1980s joined with Salvadoran activist groups to provide food and shelter for refugees fleeing violence in El Salvador.[17] The famous "sanctuary city" movement then followed (AD 1986), and today more than five hundred cities in the US are considered sanctuaries for asylum seekers. Individual churches continue the practice even today. While sanctuary law does not have legal effect, authorities are usually loath to raid churches looking for illegal immigrants.[18]

Byzantine Hospitals

Charity was a big part of the story of the Byzantines, especially medical charity. In chapter 10 we explored history's first public hospital, established in about 370 by Basil the Great in Cappadocia. The idea caught on quickly, and in the sermons and treatises of the Byzantine clergy, practising medicine came to be regarded as the epitome of love of neighbour. The reasoning was simple. While the church could not heal the sick miraculously, as Christ is said to have done in the Gospels, it could follow the Lord's example using what resources it did have—money, buildings, physicians, and volunteers.[19]

Timothy Miller, Professor of History at Salisbury University in Maryland, has written the history of Byzantine hospitals from the time of Basil in the fourth century to the year 1204. It is a remarkable story of charity, professionalism, and expansion. One such facility was founded in Constantinople by the physician and holy man Saint Sampson sometime before 400. It was destroyed by fire in 532, but Justinian quickly restored it and "maintained an elaborate staff of physicians and surgeons."[20] The hospital even accepted middle-class patients, not just the poor.[21] We know of at least four other such facilities in the same city around the same time: the Euboulos, the St. Irene, the Kosmidion, and the Christodotes Xenon. Justinian worked to professionalize these institutions so that everyone, whether poor or rich, could access "the top echelon of the medical profession."[22] Similar developments occurred in other major cities under Justinian's rule, including Antioch, Jerusalem, and Alexandria. By the 600s in Alexandria, there were several hospitals and even an official association of medical workers. Both official canon law and Justinian's imperial legislation made clear that local bishops were duty bound to maintain facilities and staff to care for strangers, the poor, and especially the sick "in all provinces of Our Empire."[23]

Hospitals were fast becoming not just extensions of the church's charity but key facilities of government—a prelude to the common practice today of government-subsidised faith-based hospitals. "Hospitals assumed a central place in the Christian notion of a city," writes Timothy Miller. A "true polis [city] had to have first its church, but next its hospital, followed by other philanthropic institutions. . . . [B]oth the civil government and the official church channeled sufficient resources to assure the survival of well-staffed hospitals," right through to the 1200s.[24] One of those hospitals, the Pantokrator Xenon in Constantinople, had a full-time staff of nineteen physicians and thirty-four nurses, as well as numerous servants and administrators.[25]

The hospitals of the Byzantine Empire are a fitting tribute to the fusion of classical learning and Christian faith. The knowledge and technology for such medical facilities came from the pagan Greek tradition of the physician Galen (AD 129–200), among others. The inspiration for opening the facilities to everyone—rich and poor alike—came from Christian bishops like Basil and emperors such as Justinian, who saw such charitable services as following the life and teaching of Jesus Christ. The words "Go and do likewise" from the parable of the Good Samaritan, not to mention the self-sacrifice of Christ's crucifixion itself, loomed large in the minds of these ancient Christians. A lovely testament to this blend of ancient Greek medicine and Christian charity is found in the discovery of a thousand-year-old Greek manuscript of the Hippocratic Oath in which the text of this ancient pagan oath is written out in the shape of a cross.[26] In a further example of inter-religious sharing, these Byzantine hospitals were exported to or absorbed by the Islamic world following the Muslim conquests of the seventh and eighth centuries.[27]

Yet for all his passion for the way of Christ—and perhaps partly because of it—Justinian was less than "liberal" in his attitude toward pagan *religion*. While he and other Byzantine emperors celebrated the gifts of secular Greek wisdom, they despised the superstitions of Greco-Roman worship. Justinian was as zealous in his attempts to sideline paganism as he was diligent in establishing charities.

The End of Paganism

Justinian and his successors in the east used the law to shape a Christian society, as they saw it. Not only did he introduce legislation against blasphemy and gambling—both of which showed up in later western law—he effectively banned non-Christian religion. Pagans and Jews were outlawed, subjected to "official persecution, and to forced baptism—to compulsory 'integration' in the Christian society."[28] One Byzantine law declares:

> Those who have not yet been deemed worthy of worshipful baptism must make themselves known, whether they live in this Imperial City or in the provinces, and go with their wives and children and their whole household to the most holy churches to be taught the true Christian faith. . . . If they despise these things, they shall know that they shall have no part in Our Empire, nor shall they be permitted to be owners of movable or immovable property.[29]

Another law around the same time (AD 529) closed the famous philosophical academy of Athens, which at one time had been the most venerable in the ancient world. Previous Christian emperors made no move against the academy. Indeed, some of the most famous Christian thinkers of the fourth century had been students there (Gregory of Nazianzus, Basil the Great, and possibly Gregory of Nyssa), and one of them, Prohaeresius the Armenian, had been the head of the school when Emperor Julian's policies forced him to resign back in AD 361. Justinian's law 168 years later was not directed at classical learning itself, as Catherine Nixey mistakenly suggests in *A Darkening Age: The Christian Destruction of the Classical World.*[30] As Edward Watts shows in the *Journal of Roman Studies,* Justinian was attacking certain practices of divination which had crept into the school under the leadership of a certain Damascius.[31] It had nothing to do with any criticism of secular philosophy and was viewed at the time as unremarkable.[32] In any case, in a weird indication of how mixed all this history is, Christian leaders and scholars were still studying Damascius centuries later. In the 800s the legendary patriarch of Constantinople, Photius I, mentioned earlier, regarded Damascius as "impious and godless" but nonetheless recommended that people read him for "concise, clear, and agreeable" prose.[33]

More significant by far, in my view, was a law of Justinian shortly afterwards aimed at ending the influence of pagan professors, whom he believed could infect students with pagan religion. The law reads:

> We prohibit the teaching of any subject by those who suffer from the insanity of the unholy pagans, lest thereby they pretend to teach those who wretchedly attend their classes, while in truth they destroy the souls of their pupils. Nor shall they enjoy a public salary.[34]

It is important to be clear about what this despicable law means—and doesn't. It was not an assault on classical learning itself, as Catherine Nixey assures her readers. That is an impossible interpretation of the evidence. Classical learning thrived in Justinian's court, and for centuries afterwards in the Byzantine Empire, which is why, as I said a moment ago, we possess such fine Byzantine copies of Plato, Thucydides, and other important pagan works. Justinian's law is *religious,* not academic. It is a flat-out ban on "non-Christians" teaching academic subjects at the highest level. Those roles were henceforth to be carried out only by Christian professors. Justinian's expulsion of pagan professors from the academies was no more an attack on classical learning than Emperor Julian's ban on *Christian* professors was seven decades earlier. Both were inspired by religious bigotry, not opposition to Greek and Roman learning.

Two hundred years after Constantine, the Mediterranean world saw itself not just as a society in which Christianity was the dominant religion; it now considered itself "a totally Christian society."[35] Temples had long been closed. Distinctively pagan laws had been rewritten. Pagan professors had to resign. Bishops had replaced town mayors as heads of cities. And, here in the east, all were required to be instructed and baptised in the Christian faith. Culture, education, and charitable institutions all thrived in the Christian Byzantine Empire, but *freedom of religion* was sadly gone.

Within a generation or two of Justinian, a new superpower emerged in the east, which swept through many of Byzantium's provinces and reduced the "Roman Empire" to a much smaller state encompassing just Turkey and Greece.

The Rise of Islam

Muhammad ibn Abdullah was born in AD 570, just five years after the death of Emperor Justinian. By the time Muhammad himself had died in 632, he was regarded as prophet and ruler from Mecca to Medina and beyond.

The terrific success of Islam took everyone in the ancient Near East by surprise. A few years after Muhammad's death, his armies defeated the eastern Roman/Byzantine army on the Golan Heights (AD 636) near the border of modern Israel and Syria. They moved south, taking Jerusalem and Palestine in 637, and all of Egypt in 642. Marching west across North Africa, Islamic forces took Carthage in 698 and then the Visigoth regions of Spain in 711. And then there are the countless victories further east beyond Persia (Iran) and into central Asia. In less than a century, Islam had conquered a land mass equal to that of the Roman Empire at its height. "Nothing like this had happened since the days of Alexander the Great (died 323 BC)," writes Peter Brown. "It was the greatest political revolution ever to occur in the history of the ancient world."[36]

The Byzantine Empire held onto its greatly reduced territory in Greece and Turkey until the mid-eleventh century, at which time Islamic forces pressed deep into Turkey and threatened the capital Constantinople itself. This is what prompted Emperor Alexius I Comnenus in the 1080–1090s to plead for help from the pope and western Christendom. The result was the Crusades. Constantinople's rich Byzantine tradition was preserved throughout the Crusader period (mostly), until it finally fell to the Ottomans in 1453. Few other societies in world history can claim a continuity of imperial rule lasting more than fifteen hundred years.

The Gifts of Byzantium

The eastern Roman Empire, Byzantium or the Byzantine Empire, is little discussed in western accounts of history, but it was nonetheless culturally significant for both east and west. For one thing, it gave the world its own hermetically sealed version of Christianity, known as Orthodoxy. The term "orthodoxy" comes from the Greek *orthos* or "correct" and *doxa* or "opinion." Following the fourth-century Arian innovation of seeing Christ as a bridge between humanity and divinity, "orthodoxy" came to refer to the older—*correct*—view of Christ as fully divine, as articulated in the Nicene Creed.

In this sense, the western church was also "orthodox." It's just that the more common usage in the west was "catholic," meaning "universal" (from the Greek *kata* + *holos* or "according to the whole"). The Roman Catholic Church was simply the universal church based in Rome, which had mainly spread westward. But the eastern church was also "catholic" in the sense that it was part of the universal church, just as the western church was also "orthodox" in the sense that it held to the Nicene Creed.[37] To complicate things further, even the later mainstream Protestant churches may be described as both "catholic" and "orthodox," for the simple reason that most of them—Lutherans, Anglicans, Presbyterians, and many others—affirm the Nicene Creed. (By the way, this is why Protestants often call Catholics "Roman Catholics", to make the point that Catholics don't own the term "catholic"). In any case, my point is: the Orthodox Church—Greek Orthodox, Syrian Orthodox, Russian Orthodox, and so on—is the eastern form of Christianity, now found throughout the world, with its own distinctive prayers, rituals, and leadership structures while maintaining the same Bible and the same central Creed.

The Byzantine Empire also bequeathed to the east and the west a far more secular gift—though the Byzantines themselves would not have thought of it as "secular." Byzantium provided the west with its vast repository of classical Greek literature and learning. I have already mentioned the copies of classical Greek texts preserved by Byzantine clergy and scholars in the ninth and tenth centuries. How did this material get to the west? In two ways.

From the time of Islamic expansion into Byzantine territories (AD 600s–700s) through to the Fourth Crusade's takeover of Constantinople (AD 1200s), many citizens of Byzantium fled westward to Italy and elsewhere. They took their literature and learning with them, much to the delight of Italian intellectuals at the beginning of the Renaissance (AD 1300).[38]

Less well understood is the more circuitous path by which Byzantine learning made its way to the west. It got to the west courtesy of Muslim intellectuals. In the seventh and eighth centuries, Greek and Syrian Christian teachers passed on their accumulated philosophical traditions to Arab scholars during the period of Islamic expansion.[39] The formerly Christian regions of Syria and Iraq were absorbed by Islamic society. As a result, the long-enduring Greek learning of the clergy of these regions "fed the courtiers of Harun al-Rashid [the fifth Abbasid Caliph] with translations of Plato, Aristotle and Galen."[40] Christian cleric-philosophers, such as Sergius of Reshaina (died ca. AD 536) and his later successor Ḥunayn ibn Isḥāq (died ca. AD 873), were both schooled in the Byzantine traditions of Alexandria. And they translated these Greek traditions into Syriac. These Syriac renditions of Greek works were then translated into Arabic. When Islam took *physical possession* of former Byzantine territory, in other words, it also inherited Byzantine's rich *intellectual deposit* of philosophical and medical knowledge. As the *Brill Encyclopaedia of Islam* notes, it was this Greek Byzantine learning that "deeply influenced the development of those fields [philosophy and medicine] in the Muslim world."[41]

In time, Baghdad would itself become a new Alexandria or Athens, boasting some of the greatest scholars of the period. These men translated, taught, and extended the insights of Plato, Aristotle, Galen, and John Philoponus. The celebrated Baghdad School of the ninth and tenth centuries was made up mostly of Arabic-speaking Christians from the Alexandrian intellectual tradition. This included the school's founder Abu Bishr Matta (died ca. AD 940) and his famous student and the most prolific Arabic translator of Aristotle,

Yahya Adi (died AD 974). Matta's most famous student, however, was the revered Muslim scholar al-Farabi (died AD 950). Muslims call al-Farabi the "second teacher" of philosophy, after Aristotle.

The impact of figures like Sergius of Reshaina, Matta, and al-Farabi was enormous. Islamic philosophical and medical learning flourished in the Middle Ages in a manner not seen in western Europe (even under Charlemagne) until these Arabic translations of Greek classical texts were brought to Muslim-controlled Spain sometime before the twelfth century. It was here in Spain that the Muslim scholar Averroes (AD 1126–1198) wrote extensive commentaries on Aristotle in Arabic, which were then translated into Hebrew by Jewish scholars and into Latin by Christian scholars. These renditions then made their way into Europe in the thirteenth century, before being picked up by the immensely influential Italian philosopher-theologian Thomas Aquinas (AD 1225–1274). Aquinas single-handedly sparked a revival of Aristotelean thought throughout Europe in the decades just before the dawn of the Renaissance in the 1300s.

The story is complicated but it can be simply summarised. First, classical Greek texts were preserved by Byzantine scholars and handed directly to Europeans when Byzantines moved west. Second, classical Greek texts were also translated into Syriac by Byzantine-trained monks, whose proteges put them into Arabic, before Muslim scholars took them to Spain where Christians translated them into Latin in the century before the Renaissance (AD 1300). Simple!

It turns out, both the Muslim east and the Christian west have the Byzantine Empire to thank for preserving the best of ancient Greek intellectual life. In this sense, the Roman Empire of the east really was "eternal."

At the launch of the First Crusade in 1095, the two Christendoms could hardly be more different. The east had preserved the cultural, legal, and intellectual traditions of more than a millennium, transposing the Greco-Roman world into a full blown "Christian society." By contrast, western Christendom had endured the almighty disruptions of the fall of Rome, the conquest of barbarians, and the disintegration of Roman Gaul and yet somehow managed to exert its influence through missions, monasteries, and churches. The two grand churches came together in the shared mission of the Crusades in the eleventh to the thirteenth centuries, but the outcome was far from happy. It did not lead to a grand "Christian Empire" from England to Persia, as some imagined it might. These "holy wars" were ultimately a military failure, as we have seen.

Following the failure of the Crusades, the city of Constantinople, ancient Byzantium, itself fell to the Muslim Ottomans in 1453. Byzantine culture would virtually disappear from the earth, except as it can be glimpsed in the rich traditions of the Orthodox Church throughout the world. Western Christendom would mostly forget about the Islamic world after the Crusades and go back to building its own society based on the loose amalgamation of ancient Roman traditions, Germanic warrior culture, and the message of the man from Nazareth.

So with all this action in the medieval period, when were the so-called Dark Ages? They probably never existed. This is not an example of historical revisionism, as is sometimes claimed. In fact, it has become clear to contemporary historians that the very notion of a "dark" period between the fall of ancient Rome and the birth of the modern world was itself a "revision" and, indeed, a highly effective piece of propaganda.

Inventing the "Dark Ages"

The Seeming Catastrophe of the 500s to 1200s

There followed, as is well known, a long period of ignorance and crime, in which even the ablest minds were immersed in the grossest superstitions. During these, which are rightly called the Dark Ages, the clergy were supreme.

—HENRY THOMAS BUCKLE, 1857

The criticisms of the church in recent years from Richard Dawkins, Christopher Hitchens, and many others are part of a trend in sceptical circles to "curate" the evils of Christendom in a way that often comes close to propaganda. But it is not new. "Every age necessarily reinterprets—and rewrites—the past in accord with its own interests, ideals, and illusions," notes historian-theologian David Bentley Hart.[1] We tend to overstate and skew the failings of yesteryear, Hart argues, in order to present our time and place as the high point of humanity and the culmination of history—and "the good" in it.

In this brief chapter I want to explore one of the most successful reinterpretations of the past ever attempted: the designation of the period from the 500s to the 1200s as "the Dark Ages." It will serve as a good reminder of the power of rumour and sloganeering to convince a culture about something that simply is not true—or, at least, is *mostly* not true.

Judging Our Ancestors

Exaggeration and selectivity can happen on a small scale, such as when we talk about how pent-up and conformist the 1950s were compared to the "liberation" that came in the 1960s and 70s, or when we describe nineteenth-century Victorian England as stiff and prudish in comparison to the "Roaring Twenties." Our pictures of these periods can become cartoonish. This no doubt assists us to categorise historical epochs into neat patterns—the Classical Period, the Dark Ages, the Modern World, the Digital World, and so on. It also helps us to feel better about our particular time and place. But it almost always makes for bad history, and it never leads us to a fair assessment of our mothers and fathers from two, ten, or fifty generations ago (AD 500 was almost exactly *fifty* generations ago).

If nothing else, noticing our habit of judging the past and elevating the present should at least prompt us to wonder how our descendants ten generations from now, in the 2320s, will evaluate us in these 2020s. Reflection on this point has led me to a fun personal policy. Whenever I come across something puzzling or objectionable from the past, I try to do what I do when I travel to a foreign culture, whether rural China or outback Australia. I force myself to imagine *how their unfamiliar ways might be right* and *my familiar ways might be wrong*. Even if I cannot quite achieve this (though I often do), the thought experiment itself usually helps me feel less judgmental about alien cultures or distant ancestors.

In any case, an exaggerated and selective kind of storytelling about the past happened on an industrial scale in Europe during the Renaissance (fourteenth–fifteenth centuries) and the Enlightenment (late seventeenth–eighteenth centuries). This is when artists, intellectuals, and even clergy popularised the expression "the Dark Ages" to describe the period after the collapse of the western Roman Empire, when the church rose to prominence in Europe and apparently inaugurated an era of ignorance, superstition, cultural stagnation, and brutality. Thankfully, however, we were all rescued from this colossal human tragedy by a *rebirth*—the meaning of "Renaissance"—of classical learning in the 1300s and an "Enlightenment"—the word says it all—in the 1700s.

The story is neat and artificial. After some excellent historical detective work from European and American scholars in the early twentieth century, we now know that the very term "dark ages" was developed as a piece of propaganda, disconnected from a fair assessment of the centuries more politely called the Middle Ages. The contrast between *darkness* and *light* was deliberate and effective. But it was also an exercise in self-flattery and historical slander.

The Renaissance "Humanists" (1300–1500)

In two highly persuasive investigations, Wallace Ferguson (b. AD 1939) and Theodore Mommsen (b. AD 1942) traced the origin of our use of the language of "darkness" to describe the period roughly from 500 to 1300. It turns out, the first person to employ the image was one of the humanist fathers of the Renaissance, the Italian scholar-poet Francesco Petrarch (AD 1304–1374). As early as 1341, he had expressed his desire to write a comprehensive account of the glories of ancient Rome, up to the time of the last western emperor Flavius Romulus Augustus (AD 460–476). Petrarch believed that the great men of antiquity, especially people like Cicero, Virgil, and Seneca, were the true intellectual forebears of his fourteenth-century Italian intelligentsia. In a letter of 1359 he laments that the great Roman statesman and scholar Cicero (106–43 BC) could not look down the centuries to Petrarch's own time and see "the end of the darkness (*tenebrae*) and the night of error" and "the dawn of the true light."[2] For Petrarch, the epoch immediately following the fall of Rome was "dark" not because it was unknown but because it was "worthless," says Mommsen, and "the sooner the period dropped from man's memory, the better." Petrarch resolved to "bury it in oblivion."[3]

Curiously, Petrarch's use of the era of "darkness" was not at all intended as a critique of the church or Christendom. He seems to have been quite devout, and he had a direct line to the pope (Urban V). He once wrote to his friend Giovanni Colonna, "we are to read philosophy, poetry, or history, in such a fashion that the echo of Christ's Gospel, by which alone we are wise and happy, may ever be sounding in our hearts." Christ, he said, is "the firm foundation of sound learning."[4]

So, what did Petrarch mean by an era of "darkness"? He blamed *the barbarians*. The Visigoths and Ostrogoths had sacked Rome and fractured Gaul, and so had put an end to the progress of classical Roman learning—and it was this learning that he and his humanist colleagues were hoping to revive. The light of Christ had shone throughout the barbarian era, Petrarch thought, but now the glorious literary achievements of ancient Rome must also shine in a revived Italy. "The father of humanism," writes Mommsen, was also "the father of the concept or attitude which regards the Middle Ages as the 'Dark Ages,'" even though Petrarch himself would *not* have thought to blame the church for the darkness.[5]

In the generation following Petrarch, Italian scholars such as the poet Boccaccio, the architect Villani, and the artist Ghiberti increasingly contrasted their age with what came before, and the dark-light contrast gained wider currency. Most of these humanists also wrote histories of their field, whether of art or architecture, in which they tended to downplay the contributions of the Middle Ages and emphasize their own achievements. In so doing, they created the "medieval bogeyman," as the *Brill Encyclopedia of the Middle Ages* puts it.[6] In his classic article "Humanist Views of the Renaissance," published in *The American Historical Review*, Wallace Ferguson notes that the humanists were "of one mind in ignoring almost all cultural and political development outside of Italy, as well as the most characteristic institutions and cultural contributions of the Middle Ages." Instead, all that mattered to them was the observation that "there was a decline of ancient civilisation with the decline of Rome and that this decline led to a period of barbaric darkness." Only the literary and cultural work of their day deserved the accolade "renaissance."[7]

The Enlightenment (1650–1800 and Beyond)

The slogan "the Dark Ages" reached its zenith in the age of Enlightenment during the seventeenth and eighteenth centuries: "the very name of that period [*light*] was a manifest declaration of war against the era of 'darkness' and its scale of values," writes Theodore Mommsen.[8] Thinkers such as the Scottish philosopher David Hume and the American political theorist Thomas Paine revelled in drawing contrasts between the ignorant age of the church and the new "Age of Reason" (the title of Paine's famous work).

We can see the same tendency in what is probably the most learned work of history written in the English language during the Enlightenment. Edward Gibbon's multi-volume *The History of the Decline and Fall of the Roman Empire* was published in six volumes during 1776–1789 (now happily available in a single eBook!). No one doubts Gibbon's peerless expertise in handling the evidence of the Roman world available to him in the eighteenth century. But his contribution has not aged well. This is partly because he could barely contain his contempt for Christianity and the church throughout his work. In chapter 7 I mentioned his (admittedly humorous) quip about the poor monk Telemachus whose protest and death in the Roman arena in AD 404 led to the end of gladiatorial sports: "Telemachus' death was more useful to mankind than his life."[9] Gibbon's work is replete with such witticisms at the church's expense. And he was not shy about speaking in the preface to the first volume of "the darkness and confusion of the middle ages"[10] and, again, of "the dark ages which succeeded the translation of the empire."[11]

It was not long before pretty much everyone was using the slogan "the dark ages" to describe the Middle Ages. In the 1911 edition (the eleventh edition) of the ever-popular *Encyclopaedia Britannica*, trusted by students and families all over the English-speaking world, the era between the fifth and tenth centuries is declared "the dark age," and we are told that "the dark age was a reality."[12] This *Britannica* edition roughly coincides with the work of scholars, like Fergusson and Mommsen, who were tracing the invention of the concept of the "dark ages." By the time Mommsen published his article on the topic (in 1942), he was able to note that the fourteenth edition of *Britannica* no longer contained the expression. The editors had performed a backflip. The relevant entry in the encyclopedia notes, "The contrast, once so fashionable, between the ages of darkness and the ages of light has no more truth in it than have the idealistic fancies which underlie attempts at mediaeval revivalism."[13] Mommsen adds his own insight: "The expression 'Dark Ages' was never primarily a scientific term, but rather a battle-cry, a denunciation of the mediaeval conception of the world, of the mediaeval attitude toward life, and the culture of the Middle Ages."[14] Recent books such as Catherine Nixey's *A Darkening*

Age: The Christian Destruction of the Classical World[15] owe more to this sceptical "battle-cry" than to the discipline of history found in universities today.

Even the more polite description "the Middle Ages" causes some historians to wince, because it is a kind of chronological snobbery. In her *Middle Ages: A Very Short Introduction*, Miri Rubin, Professor of Medieval History at the University of London, explains that the term "Middle Ages" "suggests that this was a time of arrested motion, a time between two other important epochs that define its middle-ness." Indeed, "those who coined the term Middle Ages possessed a tremendous sense of their own worth and good fortune as members of a later age." It was, in other words, a kind of self-flattery among scholars, artists, and even priests who "celebrated their times and their cities, and above all each other." She asks us to set aside "Middle Ages" and "Renaissance" as descriptions and simply use these standard expressions "as a point of reference for people and places in different times."[16]

The Protestant Reformation (1500–1700)

There is one final culprit I must blame for the huge popularity of the "Dark Ages" slogan: the church itself, or part of it. The Renaissance humanists and Enlightenment freethinkers were assisted—in the century in between them—by the Protestant Reformers of the sixteenth and seventeenth centuries. This is my own "tribe," and I can attest that this attitude toward the Middle Ages is often still present in contemporary sermons and books that touch on the period before Protestantism.

Protestants, led by the Catholic scholar-monk Martin Luther (AD 1483–1546), rejected certain Roman Catholic "errors," such as the singular authority of the pope and the practice of indulgences (earthly contributions to one's heavenly pardon). In making the case against such things, Protestants soon joined the Renaissance humanists in describing the period before them as an era of spiritual ignorance and darkness. Following the fall of Rome in the fifth century—or perhaps even earlier—the church went astray, according to many Protestants, and so only a remnant of genuine Christians survived until the Reformation: "The true Church," said Martin Luther, was "hidden from men's sight." Using the biblical imagery of "darkness" to great effect, he described the church itself—not the unbelieving world—as lost in darkness. He cites the Gospel of John (1:5), "The light shines in the darkness, and the darkness did not overcome it," and then declares, "It is therefore not astonishing that in divine things men of outstanding talent through so many centuries have been blind. In human things it would be astonishing. In divine things the wonder is rather if there are one or two who are not blind, but it is no wonder if all without exception are blind."[17]

The same language of "darkness" was employed in a book that, in England in the generation immediately following Luther, rivalled the Bible in sales. John Foxe's 1563 *Actes and Monuments of These Latter and Perillous Dayes* (often shortened to *Foxe's Book of Martyrs*) detailed the persecution of true believers by the "satanic" Catholic Church. Through a complex calculation (the details of which don't matter here) Foxe believed that the year 1360 was "the time wherein the Lord, *after long darkness*, beginneth some reformation of his church."[18] That darkness was overcome finally in the Reformation of the sixteenth century.

The idea of the church *gone astray into darkness* was an exact parallel to the humanist notion that culture and learning had fallen into darkness in the same period. This became the default way of thinking and speaking about church history among Protestants in the decades and centuries that followed, and sometimes still today. It finds clear expression in the works of the influential American Puritan clergyman and intellectual Cotton Mather (AD 1663–1728), the classic seventeenth–eighteenth century "man of letters." Writing at the conclusion of the Reformation, he spoke of the "incredible darkness [that] was upon the western parts of Europe two hundred years ago: learning was wholly swallowed up in barbarity," until, he says, the Byzantine learning came back into the west in the Renaissance. And this "occasioned the revival of letters there, which prepared the world for the Reformation of Religion too, and for the advances of the sciences ever since."[19] The role of Protestants from Luther to Mather in promoting this historical slander is summed up well by Professor Francis Oakley of Williams College in Massachusetts in his introduction to *The Medieval Experience*:

> The very idea, then, of a middle age interposed between the world of classical antiquity and the dawn of the modern world was ultimately of humanist vintage. What it lost in simplicity it gained in firmness during the Reformation

era, drawing added strength from the Protestant depiction of the thousand years preceding the advent of Martin Luther as an age of moral turpitude, religious superstition, and untrammelled credulity. Even more clearly than their humanist predecessors, the reformers saw their own era as one of revival and restoration, though restoration this time not simply of the arts, of learning, and of 'good letters,' but also of the Christian faith to its original purity.[20]

It is an odd thing to ponder: One wing of the church aided and abetted one of the most misleading pieces of storytelling about the *Christian* past ever told. I suppose Protestants (like Cotton Mather) could count on their audience being able to make a clear historical distinction between the Roman Catholic era and the Reformation era. But that is no longer the case. People today lump all Christians together into one large "Christendom," which stumbled around in darkness until the Enlightenment delivered us into the light. In taking aim at the Catholic Church of the Middle Ages, Protestants not only contributed to a falsehood, they shot themselves in the foot.

Few other examples of secular storytelling rise to the level of writing off a millennium of human culture in a single slogan: "Dark Ages." But numerous individual accounts of Christian bad behaviour certainly do contribute to our modern perception of "What happens when you let those religious nuts have a bit of power!" Many of the stories told about the historic church are half-true and truly awful. But sometimes the half that is not true says as much about modern fears and prejudices as the true bit tells us about Christianity. A good example is the Inquisition, which is often put forward as the epitome of all that is cruellest in the human heart, especially when bewitched by superstition. This cliche is about *half* right.

The Inquisition

Heresy Trials from the 1100s to the 1500s

How many saints do you suppose the minions of the Inquisition alone have burned and murdered during the last few centuries?

—MARTIN LUTHER, 1525

Nobody expects the Spanish Inquisition!

These words date me. They come from Monty Python's 1970 comedy hit *The Flying Circus* (I saw it on repeats, not at the time!). Episode 2 of Season 2 is titled "The Spanish Inquisition," and it lampoons the real-life, three-hundred-and-fifty-year Spanish Inquisition (AD 1480–1834), turning it into a comedic punchline remembered by a generation of Brits and Aussies. In scene 2 of the sketch an elderly woman in a modern loungeroom sits on a couch with a younger woman going through old family photos—"There's grandpa. There's Uncle Ted," and so on. She comes to a final image and nonchalantly says, "Oh, and there's the Spanish Inquisition hiding behind the coal shed." "Oh," says the younger woman, "I didn't expect the Spanish Inquisition," at which point three Cardinal Inquisitors, led by beloved English actor Michael Palin, burst through the door with corny horror movie music blaring. Palin menacingly announces, "Nobody expects the Spanish Inquisition!" And suddenly we are treated to a thirty-second cartoon history of the Inquisition, complete with images of hangings and torture racks. "In the early years of the sixteenth century," says the classic British documentary voice, "to combat the rise of religious unorthodoxy, the pope gave Cardinal Ximinez of Spain leave to move without let or hindrance through the land, in a reign of violence, terror and torture that makes a smashing film. This was the Spanish Inquisition." Then it's back to the modern setting, where grandma is "tortured" with "the pillow" and "the comfy couch," as she is called upon to "confess!"

With this classic Monty Python sketch (which is worth Googling if you have never watched it) we reach the zenith of criticism of this late medieval church practice. When something passes from outrage, disdain, and denunciation to simple jest on national TV, you know the process of cultural critique is complete. A comedy sketch like this would have been impossible in the eighteenth or nineteenth centuries, when the memory of church inquisitions throughout Europe was still raw, and a vast critical literature had developed—including philosophical critiques, theological histories, and even the Gothic novel—condemning this as the darkest hour of the church's Dark Ages, a period when, as one Australian journalist I know claims, "millions" of secular martyrs met their cruel deaths.[1]

It turns out, the history of the Inquisitions has been largely unknown—even to experts—until the last fifty years, when the archives of the relevant European governments and church institutions were opened up to researchers. A significant step in this process occurred when Pope John Paul II opened the archives of the Holy Office to historians only in 1998. And it turns out, happily or otherwise, that the Inquisition was freakishly detailed in its reporting: "Its meticulously investigatory methods," writes Professor Edward Peters of the University of Pennsylvania, one of the most influential Inquisition scholars of the last forty years, "have produced the largest and most important body of personal data for any society in early modern Europe."[2] The earlier secrecy around the details of procedures, cases, and executions meant that the "history" of the Inquisitions was largely left to popular retellings and philosophical critiques. And, again, I am embarrassed to say that the contemporary horror or scorn at the thought of the Inquisitions owes a lot to the preachers and pamphleteers of the sixteenth–seventeenth-century Protestant Reformation, who took rhetorical delight in highlighting and amplifying the evils of Catholic Christendom.

Let me be clear: the Inquisitions, and especially the *Spanish* Inquisition, were sometimes as horrific and corrupt as the most exaggerated retellings suggest. They *are* a blight on church history, and it was right that Pope John Paul II publicly apologised for them in a ceremony on 12 March 2000.[3] Still, in a fair-minded history of violence from the Middle Ages to today, the Inquisitions would not even make the Top Ten. Let me explain why.

Heresy

The word "inquisition" today has wholly negative connotations. If we dislike a line of questioning, we describe it as an "inquisition"—as in the title of a recent *New York Times* article about alleged illiberal trends in liberal universities, "These Campus Inquisitions Must Stop."[4] But the original word *inquisitio* just meant an inquiry or inquest and referred originally to various inquiries established by the Roman Church in the twelfth and thirteenth centuries to discover and root out "heresies."

The word "heresy" is another mocked and misunderstood term today. While its root meaning is something like "choice," in church usage it refers to *choosing to reject* some aspect of Christian belief and promote something else as the truth of Christianity. Other religions, therefore, are not considered "heresies," since the word only refers to counterfeit "Christian" claims. Although we rarely use the term in a secular context today, we certainly do have heresies, in the sense of *choices* some people make to reject the truths of equality and human rights: think of anti-Semitism or white supremacy. These things rightly elicit from mainstream society the same kind of disapproval and denunciation that "heresy" once received in the Christian society of the Middle Ages.

We also have "correct doctrines" today. Socialists, by definition, hold that the state should control most means of production for the good of society. Conservatives believe that the state should keep out of the means of production and focus instead on shaping good laws and keeping the peace. Libertarians go a step further and assert that, beyond law and order, government should have very little role in shaping society. Belonging to any one of these political or philosophical traditions involves affirming these central doctrines. Fortunately, no one is interrogated or harmed for rejecting such "truths." Shaming and "cancelling" our heretics is about as far as most of us will go.

An entire book could be written on the kinds of heresies the church of the Middle Ages was trying to root out. There were classic ones, like Arianism (described in chapter 7), which denied the full divinity of Jesus. Then there were more exotic ones, such as Catharism or Albigensianism (mentioned in chapter 2).[5]

The First Inquisitions

The first Inquisition was announced by Pope Lucius II in 1184, but it was not until Pope Gregory IX fifty years later (AD 1233) that it really got going and a formal team of inquisitors was assembled, a crack squad of theologians mainly from the Dominican Order of the Church. Their role was to travel to the heresy hotspots of Europe (mainly France, initially) and interview alleged heretics, such as the Cathars, and convince them to return to the fold. As implausible as it sounds in light of our popular imaginings, the vast majority of these inquests in the towns and villages of Europe engaged only in *persuasio*, simple persuasion, to bring people back to correct doctrine. Even when the pope decided to adopt ancient Roman law and authorise the use of torture in 1252, evidence suggests the measure was rarely employed. (Don't get me wrong: I consider a single act of torture in the name of Christ as a blasphemy.)

The "persuasion" of the Inquisitions certainly involved intimidation. The process in a typical town went as follows: inquisitors gave a public sermon on heresy and true doctrine; they announced a thirty-day "period of grace" during which people could confess their wanderings or inform on known heretics; the formal inquiry itself involved interviewing witnesses and defendants; finally, inquisitors gave a public announcement of restoration or ongoing guilt. Those who were restored had to perform some penance, whether set prayers, a pilgrimage, temporary confinement in prison, or the wearing of a special cross for a period of time (sometimes for life). Those who resolutely refused to stop advocating heresy were declared guilty and handed over to state authorities for sentencing. In this period state authorities saw heretics as traitors to good order and eagerly executed them, usually by burning them alive while tied to a pole in the ground ("burning at the stake"). While the vast majority of recorded cases resulted in little or no consequences, the threat of being handed over to authorities certainly made this unlike any *persuasion* we could tolerate today.

The first Inquisition was controlled by the Vatican, but it was not long before there were local *ecclesiastical inquisitions* launched by regional bishops and *state inquisitions* controlled by government authorities in their own campaigns for doctrinal purity. Often in the Middle Ages, state authorities were more fanatical and less subtle in furthering "Christ's kingdom" than were church officials (think of Charlemagne). State rulers frequently saw heresy as a cancer to social cohesion, which had to be mercilessly cut out. Church inquisitors, on the other hand, normally saw themselves—so the primary documents reveal—as doctors sent to heal sick heretics and their communities. As farfetched as it sounds to modern ears, "When we read what people say about the Inquisitions in the Middle Ages, the biggest criticism," says Professor Thomas Madden, Director of the Center for Medieval and Renaissance Studies at Saint Louis University, "is that they are lenient, that they take too much time, that they are too worried about rules of evidence, and meticulousness of ensuring that everyone is treated fairly. And this was a source of great frustration to secular rulers."[6]

One place where inquisitors were *not* always accused of being lenient was in Spain. The Spanish Inquisition is a story all its own, which is why when people speak of "the Inquisition," they usually mean the three-hundred-and-fifty-year Spanish Inquisition (AD 1478–1834).

The Spanish Inquisition

In 1478 the king of Spain, Ferdinand V, asked Pope Sixtus IV for special permission to conduct his own inquisition to deal with the "problem" of Jewish converts to Christianity known as *conversos*. In the centuries before King Ferdinand, Spain had been a unique amalgam of Jews, Christians, and Muslims. Many Jews had become Christians, some entirely freely, others by coaxing, and still others by coercion. In earlier times Pope Gregory I (late sixth and early seventh century) had demanded that Jews in Christian states were to be protected, never harassed, and "should be brought to the unity of faith by mildness and generosity, by admonition and persuasion," he wrote. "Otherwise men who might be won to believing by the sweetness of preaching and the fear of the coming judgement will be repulsed by threats of pressure."[7] That approach was not to last.

In the centuries that followed, many European regions ignored Pope Gregory's instruction. The relative success and separateness of Jewish communities fuelled an already-present anti-Semitism and led to widespread actions against the Jews in thirteenth- and fourteenth-century Europe. In 1209 England deported all Jews from its territories. France did the same in 1306. In Spain, riots erupted in the hot summer of 1391, blaming the privileged classes and especially the Jews for economic distress. Hundreds of Jewish residents in Seville and Valencia were murdered. According to Jewish letters of the time, many city governors and nobles sought to protect their Jewish neighbours. However, their efforts proved futile, and huge numbers of Jews were forced to "become Christians," henceforth known as *conversos*. Various theologians and even royal officials declared such conversions invalid and decreed that Jews should return to Judaism if they wished. But in many places—for example, in Barcelona and Mallorca—these *conversos* felt it was safer for their families to remain Christians. They still endured anti-Semitic suspicion from the broader community, but they were at least *officially* protected.[8]

The descendants of the *conversos* were also called *conversos*. They were a distinctive community, fully accepted neither by the Jewish community nor by the wider Christian community. It was not long before rumours emerged that Jewish-Christians were part of a larger Jewish conspiracy to infect all levels of society and government (King Ferdinand had both Jews and *conversos* in his court) and eventually take over Spain. This is the context in which Ferdinand gained the pope's permission for an inquiry into the true state of these potentially dangerous half-Christians. The king would be directly in charge of the Spanish Inquisition, reporting to the pope as appropriate. Urged on by a paranoid populace, Ferdinand appointed local church officials to conduct the investigations on his behalf in a highly centralised and ever-expanding way. Pope Sixtus IV himself, who allowed many *conversos* and Jews to live in the Italian papal lands, protested in an extraordinary papal bull of 1482 "that in Aragon, Valencia, Mallorca and Catalonia the Inquisition has for some time been moved not by zeal for the faith and the salvation of souls, but by lust for wealth." He claims that too many "have been thrust into secular prisons, tortured and condemned as relapsed heretics, deprived of their goods and property and handed over to the secular arm to be executed, to the peril of souls, setting a pernicious example, and causing disgust to many."[9]

I wish I could say that was the end of it. It was really just the beginning. King Ferdinand—the most powerful man in Europe—rebuked the pope in a somewhat threatening letter, in which he concluded, "But if by chance concessions [from the pope] have been made through the persistent and cunning persuasion of the said *conversos*, I intend never to let them take effect. Take care therefore not to let the matter go further, and to revoke any concessions and entrust us with the care of this question."[10] Pope Sixtus IV acquiesced, thereby granting the Vatican's "blessing" to the Spanish Inquisition.

A turning point came with Ferdinand's appointment in 1483 of Tomás de Torquemada (AD 1420–1498) as Inquisitor General. Torquemada quickly set about investigating, arresting, interrogating, torturing, and killing many Spanish *conversos*. Whatever stories we may have heard about the horrors of the Inquisition very likely come—assuming they are accurate stories—from this awful period. Over the next two decades, Torquemada and his henchmen not only convinced the king to expel all Jews from Spain (AD 1492) but launched a reign of terror against *conversos*, seeking to expose them as heretical Christians who held onto Jewish faith and allegiance. Because an early confession of fault would result only in the punishment of some act of penance, many offered themselves up "to be reconciled." But many of them were genuine Christians and could hardly believe their own church would allow them to be treated this way. One *converso* woman from Cuenca wept, declaring "God must be really put out that the revered fathers do these things, they are devils and are not acting justly"[11]—an understatement, if I have ever heard one. Another resident of the same city declared, "I would rather see all the Muslims of Granada enter this city than the Holy Office of the Inquisition."[12]

Witches and Protestants

After the "problem" of the *conversos* was resolved, the Spanish Inquisition remained officially active by broadening its scope to include all manner of heresies, including witchcraft. The Inquisition could be brutal toward alleged and confessed witches. Six witches, for example, were burned alive in Logrono on Sunday, 7 November 1610. But the more striking part of the evidence is the broad scepticism of inquisitors toward popular claims of witchcraft. Records show that key investigators, such as Francisco Vaca (AD 1549) and Alfonso Salazar (AD 1611), insisted that most accusations and personal confessions of sorcery were either entirely false or the result of mental illness and/or small-town hysteria. "I have not found the slightest evidence from which to infer that a single act of witchcraft has really occurred," wrote Salazar in his report of April 1611. "Indeed, my previous suspicions have been strengthened by new evidence from the visitation: that the evidence of the accused alone, without external proof, is insufficient to justify arrest." Further, "in the diseased state of the public mind every agitation of the matter is harmful and increases the evil. I deduce the importance of silence. . . . [T]here were neither witches nor bewitched until they were talked and written about."[13]

The Spanish Inquisition had a somewhat enlightened approach to sorcery, at least compared to the thousands of witch trials and executions—perhaps as high as fifty thousand—carried out in Germany, France, and England during the 1500s and 1600s.[14] Witch trials certainly had the support of churches. However, "thanks to archival studies since the 1970s," writes Malcolm Gaskill, Professor of Early Modern History at the University of East Anglia, "it is clear that the 'witch-craze' was essentially a secular legal phenomenon."[15] The reason is clear. Witchcraft was viewed as a public menace, and even as a deadly weapon. It was incumbent on secular authorities to protect the populace. It is no wonder that the peak periods of witch hunting (AD 1620s–1650s) roughly coincided with wars, plagues, and the failure of harvests. Public panic laid the blame on witches, 80 percent of whom, according to our records, were women.[16]

In addition to witches, the Spanish Inquisition also turned its attention to Protestants, who from the mid-to-late sixteenth century were trying to make inroads into Spain. The Protestant Reformation, which began in Germany in the early sixteenth century, rejected the authority of the pope and emphasised that salvation depended solely on Christ's atoning death for sins and not on personal works of charity or church-prescribed penance or payments. It is too big a story to tell in this book, and we will meet the Reformation again in the next chapter, but suffice it to say the Spanish Inquisition investigated and executed

Protestants as heretics in a series of public ceremonies known as *autos de fe* ("acts of faith") held at Valladolid on Sunday, 21 May 1559, at which fourteen people were executed, and again on 8 October when twelve Protestants were killed. One of them was the influential nobleman Carlos de Seso who, upon realising his dreadful fate, affirmed his convictions in highly Protestant terms: "in Jesus Christ alone do I hope, him alone I trust and adore, and placing my unworthy hand in his sacred side I go through the virtue of his blood to enjoy the promises that he has made to his chosen."[17] Seso was burned alive. The Inquisition was highly effective at keeping Protestantism out of Spain in any significant numbers.[18] Even today, Protestants make up only 1.7 million or 3.4 percent of the country's total population of forty-nine million.[19]

After the Protestant "threat" subsided in the late sixteenth and early seventeenth centuries, the Spanish Inquisition had much less to do. It occasionally dealt with heresy, but most of its work focused on things like bigamy (20 percent), offences by clergy (19 percent), blasphemy (15 percent), superstition/magic (11 percent), and horse theft (2 percent).[20] Hardly anyone was executed in this period. The norms were a moral lecture from an inquisitor and a demand for various penitential acts. One woman in Barcelona in 1599 was denounced before the Inquisition for prostitution. Records reveal the inquisitors dismissed the case, urging the woman "to learn the catechism [which involved memorising at least the Creed and The Lord's Prayer or Our Father], and come to the Inquisition every two weeks until she has learnt it."[21] A little more serious—but still not punishable by death—was a case in 1608 where a parish priest in Valencia was tried for attempting to seduce twenty-nine women.[22] Even egregious offences like this rarely led to the death penalty.

For most of its history—leaving aside the awful campaign led by Torquemada—the Spanish Inquisition was known for leniency. It was "widely hailed as the best run, most humane court in Europe," notes Professor Madden from Saint Louis University.[23] There are even contemporary records of prisoners in regular state prisons deliberately making "heretical statements" or pretending "to be a judaizer" (i.e., a *converso*) just so they would be transferred to the prisons of the Inquisition.[24] State authorities themselves sometimes made requests that prisoners in their squalid and overcrowded prisons be transferred to the Inquisition prison, which, according to one such record, was "spacious, supplied abundantly with water, with sewers well distributed and planned to serve the prisoners, and with the separation and ventilation necessary to good health. It would be a prison well suited to preserve the health of prisoners."[25] In his monumental four-volume history of the Spanish Inquisition, the eminent twentieth-century American historian Henry Charles Lea (who was no fan of the Inquisition) after reviewing the evidence remarked: "On the whole we may conclude that the secret prisons of the Inquisition were less intolerable places of abode than the episcopal and public gaols. The general policy respecting them was more humane and enlightened than that of other jurisdictions, whether in Spain or elsewhere."[26]

In any case, the Spanish Inquisition waxed and waned in cultural and legal importance throughout the next century or so, before it was abolished (AD 1808), then restored (AD 1814), and then finally disbanded in 1834.

The Death Toll of the Spanish Inquisition

How many people were executed by the Spanish Inquisition? Precise numbers are impossible to calculate. While records from some cities are near complete, evidence from others is patchy or non-existent. We know, for example, that in the intense early years of the Inquisition managed by Tomás de Torquemada and his immediate successors (AD 1480–1530), some one thousand executions took place in the tribunals of Castille, one hundred and thirty in Saragossa, two hundred and twenty-five in Valencia, and thirty-four in Barcelona. It is by extrapolating such figures to other cities—where we know tribunals were held but for which we do not have surviving evidence—that a total number of deaths can *tentatively* be reached. After reviewing the various scholarly estimates for the first harrowing fifty years of the Inquisition, Henry Kamen, a professor of history working with the Higher Council for Scientific Research in Barcelona, concluded, "it is unlikely that more than two thousand people were executed for heresy by the Inquisition."[27]

Don't get me wrong: two thousand human beings executed for Christian truth is two thousand too many. And we must add to this figure the executions that took place in the remaining, less bloody, three centuries of the Inquisition (up to AD 1834). These can also be calculated thanks to the scrupulous record keeping of inquisitors, now readily available to researchers. Edward Peters in his celebrated *Inquisition* concludes that "The best estimate [for the three hundred years after 1530] is that around three thousand death sentences were carried out in Spain by Inquisitorial verdict."[28] I hope I'm not speaking out of turn by mentioning that when I first started researching the Inquisitions about ten years ago, I contacted Professor Peters to ask for some details about these numbers. At first, he assumed I was a journalist attempting to *inflate* the death toll. And he swore at me! (Few academics have better reason to be grumpy at journalists than scholars of *medieval history*.) I explained that I was a historian—if only an ancient one—and that I was hoping to do a half-decent job of outlining both the best and the worst of Christian history. He was then extremely polite and helpful and confirmed that the total number of men and women executed by the three-hundred-and-fifty-year Spanish Inquisition is approximately five–six thousand, that is, two thousand for the first fifty years, as reported by Henry Kamen, and three thousand for the remaining three hundred years, as detailed by Peters himself.

As a modern Christian—as a human being—the wrongful killing of six thousand men and women leaves me speechless (despite having just written a few thousand words on the topic). But there is a reason I claimed at the outset that the Inquisition would not make the Top Ten of any fair-minded account of human brutality. The scale of cruelty found in the scrupulous inquisitorial documents is wholly dwarfed by what we know of "secular courts" of the same period, and long after. These church "courts" were criticised by the general public as *too lenient*, as I said earlier, mainly because people were comparing inquisitions not to modern Australia, where capital punishment was abolished as recently as 1967, but to their experience of the broader justice systems in Spain and throughout Europe, where stealing a loaf of bread could get you hanged.

The Inquisition executed eighteen people a year across its three-and-a-half centuries (much more in its first fifty years, much less in the remaining three hundred years). Again, that is eighteen per year *too many*. My point is: the Spanish Inquisition would hardly register a blip on the radar of a history of human violence. And yet it looms larger in the modern mind than most other examples of cruelty.

The Reign of Terror

Compare the record of the Inquisition with the death toll of an entirely secular movement from a slightly later period. The French Revolution (AD 1789–1799) had its famous secular catch-cry, *liberté, égalité, fraternité*, or liberty, equality, and fraternity. It represented "the triumph of the Enlightenment," writes William Doyle in his Oxford *A Very Short Introduction* to the subject. "Quite literally, nothing was any longer sacred. All power, all authority, all institutions were now provisional, valid only so long as they could be justified in terms of rationality and utility."[29] The founding document of the revolution, "The Rights of Man," was a powerful Enlightenment statement of individual liberty and democracy—at least for property owners, who alone could vote.

In the name of liberty and rationality, the governing convention (elected to provide a new constitution after the overthrow of the monarchy) decided that many had to die. Leaving aside the two hundred thousand people killed in the civil wars and street rioting, and the approximately ten thousand who died in prison without trial, the convention sanctioned the execution of anyone who did not support the revolutionary cause. Mere suspicion was grounds for arrest. During the so-called Reign of Terror from September 1793 to July 1794, "the government arrested tens of thousands of individuals on the slightest pretext and executed many of them after a meaningless trial," observes Thomas Kaiser of the University of Arkansas. "The convention enforced revolutionary discipline in the provinces, often with great brutality; a de-Christianization campaign wrecked hundreds of churches and other religious sites."[30] In the build up to the Terror, across the Channel in London the front page of *The Times* reported:

> The streets of Paris, strewed with the carcases of the mangled victims, have become so familiar to the sight, that they are passed by and trod on without any particular notice. The mob think no more of killing a fellow-creature, who is not even an object of suspicion, than wanton boys would of killing a cat or a dog.[31]

"Are these 'the Rights of Man'?" *The Times* article asked. "Is this the LIBERTY of Human Nature?" Some seventeen thousand men and women were "tried" and put to death during the Reign of Terror, whether by gunshot, drowning, or the newly invented guillotine.[32] The public drowning of about two thousand men and women in the Loire River near the town of Nantes was coldly dubbed by officials "the national bath" and "republic baptisms."[33]

In any case, the numbers are hard to fathom. In just *nine months*, the newly enlightened revolutionaries executed *three times* as many people as the Spanish Inquisition had killed in *over three centuries*.

Those in command of the Revolution—all of them Enlightenment rationalists—insisted that what they were doing was "virtuous" and that the result of this policy of terror would be a "virtuous France." The great leader of the revolution at the time of the Terror, Maximilien Robespierre, famously argued that "Terror is nothing other than justice, prompt, severe, inflexible; it is therefore an emanation of virtue; it is not so much a special principle as it is a consequence of the general principle of democracy applied to our country's most urgent needs."[34] The Terror is a disturbing reminder that neither religion nor rationalism is protective against the human propensity toward cruelty.

Let me be clear. My point here is *not* that secular liberty is more dangerous than religious dogmatism. Nor am I offering a kind of *whataboutism*. I wish only to highlight a fascinating historical phenomenon, a paradox: while no one today rails against the "ferocity of secular liberty" or the "viciousness of the French," a great many of us (me included) have grown up decrying the legendary brutality of the Inquisition, as if it epitomized all that is worst in humanity and all that is wrong with religion. How this paradox developed is a story worth retelling. It turns out that my mob—Protestant Christians—may well be largely to blame for fashioning the *legend* of the Inquisition.

The Legend of "The Inquisition"

Given its effectiveness in keeping the Reformation out of Spain, it is no wonder that the Spanish Inquisition became an important feature of the Protestant case against the Catholic Church more generally. As early as 1521 Martin Luther declared: "No one spills more Christian blood than the most holy father, the pope. Nowadays he tends the sheep of Christ with sword, gun, and fire." True Christianity, however, is a way of peace, he says: "Isaiah 2 and 11 portray the Christian church as free from bloodshed."[35] Again, in 1525, Luther asked the question in one of his most famous works (*The Bondage of the Will*), "How many saints do you suppose the minions of the Inquisition alone have burned and murdered during the last few centuries?"[36]

Luther's question was rhetorical, but it was not long before others filled in the gory details. Lurid stories of inquisitorial murders of the "saints" became a stock part of Protestant arguments. By 1563 John Foxe had published his *Actes and Monuments of These Latter and Perillous Dayes* (*Foxe's Book of Martyrs*) chronicling the evils of the medieval church, the murderous Inquisitions of Spain and elsewhere, and the recent persecution of Protestants in England. In Section 159, which describes "the execrable Inquisition of Spain," he tells how innocent victims without due process are condemned "in darkness palpable, in horrors infinite, in fear miserable, wrestling with the assaults of death." He speaks of "the injuries, threats, whippings, and scourgings, irons, tortures, and racks which they endure."[37] Foxe's work was an instant sensation. In fact, it rivalled the English Bible in sales, and Queen Elizabeth I (AD 1533–1603) arranged for a copy of the book to be placed in every church in England.[38]

The *Actes and Monuments* was followed soon after by another wildly popular book throughout Europe, *A Discovery and Plaine Declaration of Sundry Subtill Practices of the Holy Inquisition of Spain* (1567) written by a certain Montanus (a pseudonym). The author claimed to be a Spanish Protestant who had barely escaped the clutches of the Inquisition. Montanus "consistently emphasises the deviousness and trickery of the interrogation techniques, the variety of horrors in its torture chambers," observes Edward Peters. "Taking some of the most extreme of inquisition practices as the norm, Montanus portrays every victim of the Inquisition as innocent, every Inquisition official as venal and deceitful, every step in its procedure as a violation of natural and rational law."[39] This book was reprinted, excerpted, and retranslated for the next two centuries. In their day—and it was a very long day indeed—the books by Foxe and Montanus were more famous than any book you could name today (with the obvious exception of the Bible). Their influence is hard to exaggerate.

In the judgment of a good many experts today, the Protestants of the sixteenth and seventeenth centuries played a part in fashioning the image of the Inquisition that most of us hold in our minds to this day, just as they assisted, it seems, in establishing the myth of a "Dark Ages." Enlightenment thinkers in the next century had little work to do, then, in consolidating the modern picture of the murderous dogmatism of the church and contrasting that picture with the spirit of *toleration* that characterised the new age of reason.

Interestingly, one of the most important thinkers in this criticism of medieval Catholicism and shift to Enlightenment pluralism was another devout Protestant, a French Calvinist or Huguenot. Pierre Bayle (AD 1647–1706) was a professor of philosophy at Rotterdam. He was able to promote the ancient Christian notion of religious freedom, found in the Edict of Milan and elsewhere, in a more sophisticated way for his sceptical audience. As Edward Peters notes, "Bayle had seen enough of persecution to adopt many of the religious and philosophical arguments of his predecessors, and to broadcast them in language that reached a far wider audience."[40] He argued that "No person or group may force the conscience of another, no matter how certain one may be of the truth of one's own claims." For Bayle, "even 'erring consciences' must be considered sincere and therefore be respected."[41] Part of his project involved contrasting this enlightened *toleration* with the *brutality* of the Catholic Church and its Inquisitions. He wrote:

> The communion of Rome has never permitted anyone to contradict her, without exterminating by iron and fire anyone who dared to assume such a liberty. It made great efforts to establish everywhere the tribunal of the Inquisition, the most infernal, and the most shameful instrument for the maintenance of its authority that was ever displayed by the human spirit.[42]

The same argument was soon taken up by fiercely anti-religious Enlightenment thinkers in France, such as the legendary François-Marie Arouet, better known by his pen name Voltaire (AD 1694–1778). Voltaire frequently referred to "the Inquisition" in his writings, holding it up as the epitome of what is wrong with hateful religion. He was one of the most widely read authors of the eighteenth century, and he is a pivotal figure in the transition to our secular world. He took ideas that started life as a Protestant critique of medieval Catholicism and recast them as Enlightenment ideas for all: religion results in inquisitions, but reason results in freedom and peace.[43] Voltaire's framing of these ideas greatly influenced the American tradition of liberty, right alongside a more Christian expression of religious freedom advocated by early American thinkers like the founder of Providence, Rhode Island, Roger Williams (AD 1603–1683).[44]

The Galileo Affair

Finally, the famous Galileo affair also contributed to an inflated view of the Inquisition's severity and stupidity, as Edward Peters has argued in detail.[45] Galileo Galilei (AD 1564–1642) had endorsed the view of Copernicus (AD 1473–1543) that the earth revolves around the sun, not the other way around, as was widely believed in scientific and theological circles. Galileo promptly found himself suppressed, tortured, and banished by the anti-scientific Inquisition in Italy for daring to challenge the truth of Scripture. The affair underscores the deep conflict that exists between science and religion.

At least, this is the story many of us have picked up today. In broad terms, this retelling of the Galileo affair derives from two great nineteenth-century works on the history of science, John Draper's *History of the Conflict between Religion and Science* (1875) and Andrew White's *A History of the Warfare of Science with Theology in Christendom* (1896).[46] Their titles say it all: the church opposes science. And Exhibit A is Galileo. But contemporary historians of science generally reject this Enlightenment tale of noble science versus the dogmatic church. For example, writing in the *Cambridge History of Science*— the peerless eight-volume compendium of the discipline—Rivka Feldhay of Tel-Aviv University says the entire Draper-White narrative "rests on a selective, and highly moralized, presentation of a few episodes." The true history of the relationship between science and the church in the sixteenth and seventeenth centuries, she says, was, in fact one of "symbiotic coexistence."[47]

But what of the Galileo affair itself? It is true that the Inquisition opposed Galileo's work and banned his 1632 book *Dialogue Concerning the Two Chief World Systems*. On the other hand, his greatest supporters had always been, and remained, high-ranking members of the church. Yet, given that Galileo's ideas were also opposed by some leading university professors of the time, the church felt free to admonish him on theological grounds. If Galileo's views had been demonstrable in the seventeenth century, things would have turned out very differently. It had been a principle as old as Augustine in the fifth century and Aquinas in the thirteenth century that, if a proven fact about the world con-tradicted something apparently said in the Bible, the church should seek a new, and more truthful, way to read the relevant passage of Scripture.[48] But Galileo's arguments had not yet met that threshold, so the church held its ground. It also did not help that in his *Dialogue Concerning the Two Chief World Systems* Galileo directly insulted his former friend and the current pope, Urban VIII, casting him as a simpleton. In 1633 the Inquisition convicted Galileo of "strong suspicion of heresy." There was no torture. And his "imprisonment" amounted to a short stay in the home of the Archbishop of Siena, Ascanio Piccolomini. He was allowed to move home later that same year to live under house arrest in his own villa in Florence. He died ten years later.[49]

The church's actions against Galileo were undoubtedly misguided and grossly unfair. But the story has been blown out of proportion, adding fuel to the fire—as it were—of our outrage at the Inquisition's hateful dogmatism. As Rivka Feldhay notes, "the trial of Galileo was transformed from a historical event into a powerful cultural symbol, which loomed large in the 19th-century treatments of Draper and White." However, "20th-century investigations of the trial on the basis of the inquisitorial documents," she adds, "have pointed out the importance of the specific historical and political circumstances in which the trial took place. Without reaching agreement about the causes of the trial, such studies have been effective in eroding, though not erasing, the belief in an inevitable conflict between science and religion that grew out of the 19th-century understanding of the trial of Galileo."[50] Interestingly, the late-twentieth-century examination of the documents of Galileo's trial not only led historians of science to question the science-versus-religion interpretation of events, it led the church itself to admit its mistake. In 1992 Pope John Paul II publicly acknowledged that the Inquisition was wrong to have judged Galileo the way it did.[51] Better late than never.

None of what I have written in this chapter could excuse or minimize the cruelty of the Inquisitions. At the time they were unremarkable—"lenient" even—but by the values of today they are rightly considered deplorable. And it is appropriate that the pope felt the need to apologise.[52]

But there is a more obvious point. It is against the backdrop of Christ's life and teaching that the Inquisitions take on their darkest complexion. It may or may not be fair to evaluate the Inquisitions by the standards of medieval

Spain or by the values of revolutionary France or by the ideals of our secular democracy. But it is undoubtedly fitting to judge the church's use of violence in service of the truth by the teachings found in the Gospels. And by *those* standards, the Inquisitions stand condemned. They probably would not make the Top Ten of any fair-minded list of humanity's most barbaric deeds, as I have said. But placed alongside the words "Love your enemies; do good to those who hate you; bless those who curse you," the Inquisitions are a blasphemy.

In this sense, the Protestants were not wrong to fulminate against this "most infernal . . . most shameful instrument" of church authority, as Pierre Bayle put it.[53] It is just that they should have recognised themselves—all humanity—in the description. Protestants also killed people, just like inquisitorial Catholics and French revolutionaries. And in the next chapter I want to turn to one of the weirdest, and therefore most misunderstood, examples of Protestants killing Catholics, Catholics killing Protestants, and Protestant and Catholics joining forces to kill other Catholics and Protestants. I am talking about the Thirty Years' War, the greatest of the so-called Wars of Religion.

The Reformation "Wars of Religion"

More Bloody Battles in the 1600s

A complete peace within the disputed Christian religion shall be attained only by Christian, friendly, and peaceful means.

—PEACE OF AUGSBURG, 1555

"Religion starts most of the wars of history!" This was the firm claim of the man sitting opposite me at a sumptuous lunch at a friend's house overlooking Sydney's lovely Middle Harbour. The conversation started, as they often do in my life, with my acquaintance asking me what I did for a living. I mumbled something about researching history and religion (at the time I had just released a book about the five major world faiths). He explained that he didn't have much time for faith, and when I asked him why, he told me plainly: "Religion starts most of the wars of history!" I naturally probed a little. "Which ones?" He paused, thought about it for a moment, and replied, "Well, there's the Crusades." Another pause. "And the Troubles of Northern Ireland, too!" They were his only two examples. I think I have to give him the Crusades. As we saw in chapters 1 and 2, there is no avoiding that these really were religious wars, *Christian* wars, and they were awful.

I will say something in the next chapter about the other "religious war" mentioned by my new friend—the Irish Troubles—but for now it is worth just noting how common the view is: Religion is a unique contributor to the wars of history. Religion, we are told, can excite such passion, and "sanctify" any behaviour, it is no wonder that it lies behind much human conflict. As Richard Dawkins puts it, "Religious wars really are fought in the name of religion, and they have been horribly frequent in history. I cannot think of any war that has been fought in the name of atheism."[1]

There is another devasting series of battles my new friend at lunch might have mentioned. It is one that eclipses the Crusades and the Troubles—*put together*—in terms of brutality and lasting effect. In the history books it is known as the Thirty Years' War of 1618–1648, but it sometimes even goes by the name "The Wars of Religion." It was a period of unparalleled bigotry and violence.

The Thirty Years' War was a Europe-wide conflagration following the sixteenth-century Reformation, a movement in which huge numbers of Christians in Germany, France, Denmark, Holland, and elsewhere broke with the Roman Church and established their own vision of what it means to follow the way of Christ. It was one of the most tumultuous intellectual revolutions of history, and it profoundly unsettled the city-states of Europe, from Italy to England. Let me briefly explain the Reformation, and then turn to the three-decade long "war of religion."

The Humanists and Martin Luther

There has always been a self-reforming spirit within Christianity. It goes back to Jesus's own warnings against religious hypocrisy and his call for self-assessment ("Take the log out of your own eye"). I have already mentioned numerous reform movements through the Middle Ages, but there were many others that would deserve our attention if this were a proper "history of the church." The sixteenth-century Reformation is undoubtedly the most famous of all the reformations in Christian history, partly because it resulted not so much in the *renovation* of church institutions as the *founding* of entirely new churches, which still called themselves "catholic" (in the sense of being *ortho-dox*) but were no longer connected to Rome and the pope.

In some ways the Reformation grew out of the fourteenth-century Italian Renaissance. As we saw in chapter 19, the Renaissance involved the redis-covery and renewed appreciation of the classical texts of ancient Greece and Rome. It inspired a kind of "back-to-sources" movement throughout Europe in the decades that followed. One of the greatest of the later humanists was the Dutch scholar Desiderius Erasmus of Rotterdam (AD 1466–1536). Erasmus did excellent work in—among many other things—reviving an interest in the original *Greek* text of the New Testament, instead of the more common Latin translation. This renewed interest in the primary sources did not wipe out respect for the church traditions of the centuries, but it did inspire a mood of criticism toward perceived excesses of tradition that contradicted the original documents of Christianity. The loudest critic of the time, himself a great admirer of Erasmus, was an Augustinian monk in Germany named Martin Luther (AD 1483–1546). His public critique of the beloved church would rip western Christianity in two (eventually in three, four, five . . . leading to the endless number of Protestant denominations we have today) and transform Europe within his own lifetime.

Luther's debating points—his famous Ninety-Five Theses—were nailed to the door of a church of Wittenberg, in the usual manner of debates of the time, on 31 October 1517. While this is often thought to be the dramatic start-gun of the Reformation, Luther and others saw it as an invitation to discuss certain criticisms of mother church. His principal critique revolved around indul-gences, the medieval church practice of promising repentant believers relief from the penalties due to them for their temporal sins. The logic was that those sins were forgiven by God, on account of Christ's death and resurrection, but that various punishments or disciplines were still necessary to purify the person to make them ready for eternal life. You can either endure those punishments later in purgatory—a purifying holding place in the afterlife—or you can do something now to receive an indulgence. Crudely, a certified indulgence will state the number of purgatorial days one has been remitted on account of the receiver's sacred act or financial gift. The practice was open to abuse, of course. And Martin Luther wrote to the Archbishop of Mainz in 1517 complaining about the local sale of indulgences to finance the building of a new cathedral:

Papal indulgences for the building of St. Peter's are circulating under your most distinguished name. . . . I grieve over the wholly false impressions which the people have conceived from them; to wit, the unhappy souls believe that if they have purchased letters of indulgence they are sure of their salvation; again, that so soon as they cast their contributions into the money-box, souls fly out of purgatory.[2]

The centre of Luther's argument is the heartbeat of all Protestant denominations today. Christ's death and resurrection are *wholly* sufficient to remove the guilt and punishment due to sinners. Neither good deeds, nor *especially* indulgences, could possibly atone for our sin. It is the grace of Christ *alone* through our faith *alone* that guarantees redemption.

Luther's critiques soon spread throughout Germany, helped massively by the recent invention of the printing press in the mid-1400s. The church tried to discipline this rogue scholar-monk, but Luther just became more strident in his charges of church errors. Key among those errors, he said, was the church's teaching that the bread and wine of the Mass—the body and blood of Christ—were *re-sacrificed* by the priest for the sins of the people. As the Catechism of the Catholic Church puts it, in the Mass itself Christ gives the church "a visible sacrifice by which the bloody sacrifice which he was to accomplish once for all on the cross would be re-presented, its memory perpetuated until the end of the world, and its salutary power be applied to the forgiveness of the sins we daily commit."[3] For Luther, Christ's death for sins was a one-off event in the past, which won complete forgiveness for all who have faith. Christ is truly *present* in the bread and wine, Luther said (something many later reformers would doubt), but the Mass or Holy Communion was in no sense a re-presentation of Christ for our sins. It was, rather, God's means of *feeding* and *nourishing* believers in their *communion* with the Saviour. Luther also increasingly rejected the authority of the pope, seeing him simply as one local bishop in Rome among many. He even called Pope Leo X the *Antichrist*.[4]

Things came to a head in April of 1521 when a kind of judicial assembly was called in the town of Worms, at which Luther unsuccessfully defended his writings of recent years against the charge of heresy. The event took place over several weeks in the presence of the Holy Roman Emperor, Charles V. (Remember, the Holy Roman Empire was the union of European states founded in the year 800 with Charlemagne as the first emperor.) This was a big deal. Luther refused to recant. "Lutheranism" was formally condemned. And the Reformation officially took off.

The Reformation had political as well as religious ramifications. Many of the ruling princes of Germany supported Luther's ideas. They chose to give him immediate protection from authorities, both papal and imperial. This allowed Luther to continue to publish, preach, and organise. In a matter of a few years, Luther's writings were available everywhere in continental Europe and England. His rejection of papal authority—and by implication the jurisdiction of the Holy Roman Empire—suited regional princes perfectly. Region after region, especially in Germany, Denmark, and Sweden, declared themselves supportive of the Lutheran reforms and therefore at *spiritual* odds with the Vatican and *political* odds with the Holy Roman Empire.

I am a proud Protestant. I think Luther's account of "salvation" is truer to the New Testament. But I am ashamed of some of the other things he wrote. I mentioned in my prelude to this book that I do not think Protestants can distance themselves from the bad behaviour of the church of the Middle Ages just because their particular tradition was not around until the sixteenth century. Some of the same bigotry and violence reared its ugly head pretty much as soon as there were Protestants. I will offer one egregious example.

Martin Luther's tract *On the Jews and Their Lies* published in 1543[5] was exactly what the title suggests, an anti-Jewish tirade. It begins with the words, "I had made up my mind to write no more either about the Jews or against them. But since I learned that these miserable and accursed people do not cease to lure to themselves even us, that is, the Christians, I have published this little book, so that I might be found among those who opposed such poisonous activities of the Jews." It goes downhill from there. His relentless description of Jews as deceitful, hateful, and avaricious was a form of anti-Semitism. It was not the *racial* anti-Semitism of early twentieth-century Germany, where Jewish *bloodline* rather than religion was the key defect. Yet, Luther's writings cannot have failed to promote deep prejudice against the Jewish community. Consider his following caricature:

> Therefore, dear Christian, be advised and do not doubt that next to the devil, you have no more bitter, venomous, and vehement foe than a real Jew who earnestly seeks to be a Jew. . . . Therefore the history books often accuse

them of contaminating wells, of kidnaping and piercing children. . . . They, of course, deny this. Whether it is true or not, I do know that they do not lack the complete, full, and ready will to do such things.[6]

After a formidable biblical argument in favour of seeing Jesus as the promised Jewish Messiah and Lord of the world, Luther ends with seven shameful practical recommendations:

> First, to set fire to their synagogues or schools. . . . Second, I advise that their houses also be razed and destroyed. . . . Third, I advise that all their prayer books and Talmudic writings, in which such idolatry, lies, cursing, and blasphemy are taught, be taken from them. . . . Fourth, I advise that their rabbis be forbidden to teach henceforth on pain of loss of life and limb. . . . Fifth, I advise that safe-conduct on the highways be abolished completely for the Jews. For they have no business in the countryside, since they are not lords, officials, tradesmen, or the like. Let them stay at home. . . . Sixth, I advise that usury be prohibited to them, and that all cash and treasure of silver and gold be taken from them and put aside for safekeeping. . . . Seventh, I recommend putting a flail, an ax, a hoe, a spade, a distaff, or a spindle into the hands of young, strong Jews and Jewesses and letting them earn their bread in the sweat of their brow.[7]

I hardly know what to say, except—to any Jewish readers—I am sorry you had to read this. How someone so captivated by a sense of God's love in Jesus Christ—Luther's central teaching—could so blatantly advocate bigotry toward other human beings is, I suppose, the puzzle at the heart of this book. I am glad today that some Protestant leaders of the time—Melanchthon, Osiander, and Bullinger—criticised Luther for this treatise.[8] But nothing can remove the stain this leaves on Luther's memory and on the many who echoed his sentiments in the centuries that followed.

The Calvinists

A similar reform movement, inspired by Luther, was led by the scholar and theologian Ulrich Zwingli (AD 1484–1531) in Zurich, Switzerland. And in

Swiss Geneva a few years later, a French lawyer and theologian named John Calvin (AD 1509–1564) established a rigorous extension and modification of Reformation ideas. Because of his legal expertise, Calvin was able to incorporate his system into an almost theocratic model of government in this city from 1541. Many supporters of the Reformation fled the still-Catholic lands of England, Scotland, and France to find refuge in Geneva. There, they aimed to build a new society based on the best of humanist learning, Calvin's reformed theology, and a more "Christianized" legislative agenda.

How did Luther and Calvin differ? Luther, as we saw, was adamant that "good deeds" cannot save you. Only Christ can save. But his argument left "good deeds" with a somewhat vague status. What is the point of living a good life if Christ had already saved you from every sin? Luther certainly insisted that Christians should do good works, but the *logic* of doing the deeds was not clear. Calvin reinstated the "good life" into the centre of the Christian experience. He agreed with Luther that human works cannot save anyone. But he argued that our deeds were the "evidence" that we had truly experienced the grace of God. Good deeds were not the *basis* of salvation, but they were *signs* of salvation.[9]

Much more can and should be said about the Protestant Reformation. But here I am mainly interested in the enormous war, or series of wars, that erupted following the Reformation. The typical story we hear in popular retellings of events is that Protestants and Catholics immediately started fighting each other to impose their brand of Christianity throughout Europe, climaxing in the deadliest conflagration the world had ever seen, the Thirty Years' War of 1618–1648,[10] which wiped out as much as 15 percent of the population of the German lands. And, according to some accounts, religion was squarely to blame. In his *Cosmopolis: The Hidden Agenda of Modernity,* British philosopher Stephen Toulmin writes, "There were many who would kill and burn in the name of theological doctrines that no one could give any conclusive reasons for accepting. The intellectual debate between Protestant Reformers and their Counter-Reformation opponents had collapsed, and there was no alternative to the sword and the torch."[11]

The Thirty Years' War was certainly "Europe's Tragedy," the title of Peter Wilson's unsurpassed book on the topic.[12] Indeed, in social surveys conducted in the 1960s, Germans still rated the conflict of 1618–1648 as the "greatest disaster" they had ever faced, ahead of both world wars of recent memory![13] But was it a religious war, as is often claimed?

The Peace of Augsburg, 1555

The start date of the conflict (AD 1618) is our first clue to why most experts today do not think of the Thirty Years' War as a conflict between Catholics and Protestants over their religion. The Reformation had established itself in Europe within four decades of Luther's famous Ninety-Five Theses of 1517. While the process had been painful, and various riots and inter-state conflicts arose in this early period, on 25 September 1555, more than sixty years before the outbreak of the war, the Catholic Holy Roman Empire granted freedom of religion to individual German princes and their land, in the extraordinary declaration known as the "Peace of Augsburg," which in part stated: "We [the Holy Roman Empire and the German princes] will not make war upon any estate of the empire on account of the Augsburg Confession [i.e., Lutheranism] and the doctrine, religion, and faith of the same. . . . Nor shall We, through mandate or in any other way, trouble or disparage them, but shall let them quietly and peacefully enjoy their religion. . . . Further, a complete peace within the disputed Christian religion shall be attained only by Christian, friendly, and peaceful means."[14]

The Reformation had provoked turmoil throughout Europe, hence the need for a "peace." But even the Peace of Augsburg was not principally about religion. The *religious* aspects of the settlement take up just *eight* of the 141 paragraphs of the document. Most of it concerned issues of defence, justice, police, and monetary policy.[15] In any case, the Peace of 1555 "proved remarkably successful," writes Peter Wilson. "It gave the empire sixty-three years of freedom from major conflict, the longest period of peace in modern German history. It was not matched until 2008, by the absence of hostilities since 1945."[16]

Out the Window

After more than six decades of peace, there was much more on the minds of European rulers than religion, as each sought to negotiate their position within or alongside the Holy Roman Empire. Dissatisfied with their place in the political equilibrium of the empire, Bohemian Protestant dissidents in Prague threw three Catholic officials out of a negotiating meeting held in Hradschin Palace on 23 May 1618. They literally *threw* these Catholic officials out of the window of the castle—the event is known as the "Defenestration of Prague" in the history books. The officials survived, notes Oxford's Peter Wilson, but this was "a deliberately provocative act"[17] and an unofficial trigger for war.[18]

The Protestant rebels in Prague were dealt with in 1620 by the revered military leader of the Holy Roman Empire, Johann Tserclaes, Count of Tilly. General Tilly, as he is often known, did more than restore the proper allegiances in the region. He captured further Protestant territory, such as the city of Heidelberg in 1622, where he sought to reestablish the Catholic religion. At a later stage Tilly would be responsible for one of the greatest atrocities of the era. He sacked the Protestant city of Magdeburg in Germany, resulting in twenty thousand deaths out of a total population of just twenty-five thousand.

So far, this may all sound like a classic "war of religion." As the years rolled on, however, it became clear that this was really a conflict over land and the ongoing influence of the Holy Roman Empire in Germany and elsewhere. This becomes obvious when the Swedes enter the war in 1630, led by their great military monarch, King Gustavus II Adolphus (AD 1594–1632). Worried about the increasing power of the Holy Roman Empire in the Baltic regions (modern Poland), he landed his army at Pomerania in 1630 and established control. The official declaration of war makes clear that King Gustavus's motivation was principally *commercial* and *political*, not religious (even though he himself was a Lutheran).[19] What's more, his move against the region was supported, even brokered, by Cardinal Richelieu (AD 1585–1642), a Catholic theologian and key political statesman in France.[20] Why would a Catholic cardinal support a Lutheran king against Catholic territories in the Baltic? The answer provides a key to understanding the nature of these conflicts. France itself, while a faithful Catholic nation, was suspicious of the ambitions of the ruling family of the Holy Roman Empire, the Habsburg family. France's *religious* loyalties were certainly with the pope in Rome, but its *political* commitment was to strong territorial borders. With French support, King Gustavus eventually defeated General Tilly and the forces of the Catholic League at Breitenfeld near Leipzig in 1631.

A War of Religion?

In the final and most violent stage of the war (AD 1635–1648), France actually joined with Sweden in the military campaigns, putting the lie to the notion that these were wars over which religion should have prominence. These were wars of European city-states trying to secure their interests and lands in the face of the monolithic Habsburg Holy Roman Empire. Religion played a part—as it did in everything in this period—but this conflict "was not primarily a religious war," writes Peter Wilson:

> Most contemporary observers spoke of imperial, Bavarian, Swedish, or Bohemian troops, not Catholic or Protestant, which are anachronistic labels used for convenience since the nineteenth century to simplify accounts. The war was religious only to the extent that faith guided all early modern public policy and private behaviour.[21]

Wilson points out further that roughly 20 percent of marriages in this period were cross-confessional, that is, Catholics married to Protestants. Catholic soldiers often fought in armies dominated by Protestants, and the other way around. And the messages people were receiving in the pulpits throughout Europe were highly critical of the wars. "There are no calls to arms," Wilson observes. "On the contrary, they're told that this is your sinfulness, and you need to be obedient and pious, and eventually God will take the war away."[22]

Before God did "take the war away," the Thirty Years' War exacted a heavy penalty on the citizens of Europe. Estimates of the death toll vary, but we are probably justified in accepting the middle-range data presented by Wilson that indicates that about five to eight million people, or around 15 percent of the population, lost their lives between 1618 and 1648 as a result of the conflict, making it "the most destructive conflict in European history."[23] The devastation was experienced differently in different locations and times. The people around Prague, for example, lost at least 50 percent of the population, well above the average, whereas the towns of Görz and Gradisca in Austrian territory experienced well below 15 percent losses. A significant proportion of losses resulted from disease. Troop movements and limited hospital services in wartime meant that epidemics did their worst, accounting for at least half the total death count of five–eight million. Something similar occurred in World War I, when around twenty million people died as a result of an influenza outbreak known as the Spanish Flu.

The significant thing about the war of 1618–1648 was its *length*. While both World War I (AD 1914–1918) and World War II (AD 1939–1945) had much higher annual death rates in Europe *per capita*, these were relatively brief wars and so led to the deaths of only about 6 percent of Europe's population (twenty-seven million deaths and thirty-four million deaths, respectively).[24]

Despite the horrors, unprecedented length, and wide geographical stage of the Thirty Years' War, this was a war fought conventionally. The purpose was not to exterminate one's opponent (with the exception of the Battle of Magdeburg, just mentioned) but to force one's opponent to accept appropriate terms of peace. All sides could have continued fighting. There were sufficient resources and fighters to go on and on. But by the late 1640s the interested parties had made sufficient gains in securing their own lands and political sway. It was felt that hostilities could end.

The Peace of Westphalia, 1648

On 24 October 1648 the warring parties signed the so-called Peace of Westphalia, accompanied by a seventy-gun salute. It detailed new territorial agreements, which are sometimes seen by modern political scientists "as the birth of the modern international order based on sovereign states," writes Peter Wilson.[25] More than forty thousand copies of the Peace were printed to be distributed to a thankful public over the coming months.[26]

The Peace of Westphalia also reiterated and extended the principles of *religious toleration* found in the earlier Peace of Augsburg of 1555. Three confessions were now formally recognised: Catholic, Lutheran, and Calvinist. Other minorities (Protestantism was by now splintering into many "denominations") were not granted formal recognition, but neither were they to be persecuted. Such theoretical commitments, combined with more pragmatic considerations such as the need to repopulate territories, led to a growing acceptance of religious diversity throughout the German lands and beyond. This was not a process of "secularization." Everything in this period—whether in war or in peace—was still couched in highly religious terms. These were all Christians of varying stripes and commitments coming to a collective realization that city-states were here to stay, that the Catholic and Protestant churches were here to stay, and that the Holy Roman Empire could continue to thrive in a new Europe. The last of these convictions proved false. While the Holy Roman Empire was strong in 1648, it would decline thereafter, and Napoleon I abolished it in 1806.

The nineteenth century was "when myths about this war are constructed," observes Ulinka Rublack, Professor of Early Modern European History at the University of Cambridge. Characteristic of the Enlightenment's habit of shunning religion, intellectuals began to see the Thirty Years' War as a conflict *about religion* instead of just *involving religion*. However, the scholarly consensus of the last generation is quite different. "We now think of the Thirty Years War as not primarily motivated by religious division," notes Professor Rublack, "but primarily as a conflict about the nature of governance in the German lands and the balance of power in Europe."[27] Oxford's Peter Wilson agrees: "The various armies appeared not as Protestants or Catholics, but as Swedes, Bohemians, Bavarians or Imperialists."[28]

None of this is to suggest that religious disagreement played no part in the fighting. As David Bentley Hart writes, "Catholics and Protestants often hated one another quite sincerely and ferociously." And religious passion is an effective tool in the hands of rulers. "But," Hart adds, "there is something inherently absurd in persistently speaking of these Habsburg wars and nationalist wars and wars of succession as 'wars of religion.'"[29] Something similar must be said about the Northern Ireland "Troubles."

The "Troubles"

Confessional Conflict in the 1700s to 1998

I appeal to you, in language of passionate pleading. On my knees I beg you to turn away from the paths of violence and to return to the ways of peace.

—POPE JOHN PAUL II, DROGHEDA,
29 SEPTEMBER 1979

For the inimitable journalist and atheist Christopher Hitchens, just as for my friend at the Sydney Harbour luncheon mentioned at the beginning of the previous chapter, the period of the "Troubles" in Northern Ireland (AD 1968–1998) provides strong evidence that *religion poisons everything*. "In Belfast I have seen whole streets burned out by sectarian warfare between different sects of Christianity," Hitchens writes early in his book *God Is Not Great*. He says he interviewed people "whose relatives and friends have been kidnapped and killed or tortured by rival religious death squads, often for no other reason than membership of another confession."[1]

Growing up in faraway Australia at the time of the Troubles, I always thought of them as both *prolific* and *all about religion*: Protestants killing Catholics for being Catholics, and vice versa. The reason the conflict loomed so large in my mind was partly the frequent media coverage of terrorist bombings and kidnappings and partly because my favourite band at the time—the biggest band in the world in the early 1990s—was Ireland's U2. They were touring the world singing their hit song "Sunday Bloody Sunday," all about the massacre of thirteen unarmed Catholic protestors in Bogside, Northern Ireland.

My impressions of the conflict were so potent that I can vividly remember where I was—standing in the aisle of a supermarket—when I received a phone call from a clergyman in Northern Ireland inviting me to Belfast to give a series of public talks. I am embarrassed to say my first thought was: *No way!* I politely probed, "But, umm, how are things over there nowadays?" He laughed, reminded me about the Good Friday Agreement ratified a couple of years earlier (AD 1998), and, sure enough, a year or so later my family and I ended up spending a terrific few weeks in Northern Ireland and the Republic of Ireland. During my time there, I met all sorts of fascinating people—both Catholics and Protestants—who had lived through the worst of the Troubles, including one gentleman, a former police officer, who had lost an eye, a cheekbone, and part of his forehead in an attempted assassination in the 1980s. To my surprise, not one person I spoke to felt that the thirty-year Troubles had been a conflict *about* religion.

The "Plantations" and the Seeds of Conflict

The roots of the Northern Ireland conflict go back well before the rise of the Protestant Reformation—as far back as the twelfth century, in fact, when the English crown routinely sought to assert its lordship over the unruly Gaelic chieftains across the Irish Sea. These tensions reached a climax in the Act of Kingly Title of 1541, when Henry VIII proclaimed his direct kingship over Ireland, stipulating that the country was henceforth "united and knit to the imperial crown of the realm of England."[2] The act was not made a reality until decades after Henry's death. Key to the subjugation was a tactic known as "plantation," the deliberate emigration of English and Scottish citizens into the Ulster region of Ireland, basically what is now Northern Ireland. This was used to great effect in 1606 and again in 1608. The crown gave these foreign "settlers" significant tracts of land in Ulster and urged them to breed and build a society based on English law, settled agriculture and commerce, and the newly dominant Protestant faith, which had been made the official faith of England just a few years earlier in the reign of Elizabeth I (AD 1558–1603). "The plantation was a considerable success," writes Marc Mulholland in his Oxford introduction to Northern Ireland, "the settlers proving industrious and determined."[3] This left the indigenous Irish of Ulster, all of whom were Catholics, resentful at the growing number and power of the English and Scottish (Protestant) upstarts in their ancient land.

Rebellion was perhaps inevitable. Reports of Irish massacres of English settlers led to brutal recriminations from England's armies in the late 1640s, under the command of the English general and statesman Oliver Cromwell (AD 1599–1658). A series of punitive laws was also enacted against the indigenous Catholic majority in Ulster, and major land holdings were confiscated. Tensions simmered just beneath the surface, frequently bursting into acts of violence on both sides. Meanwhile, both populations grew. Belfast was mainly Protestant in the century after the plantations, but in the 1800s the city's Catholic community rose from four thousand residents to one hundred thousand—almost a third of the population.[4] Economic inequalities exacerbated problems. Due to employment discrimination, most Catholics belonged to the lower income group, and although they were a third of the population of Belfast, they formed only 5 percent of the skilled workforce, which by then was focused on the famous shipyards (the Titanic was later built there).

Home Rule and Partition

All of this lies in the background of what emerges as the key issue of Irish politics in the period: Catholic *nationalists* increasingly wanted England to grant them "home rule," whereas Protestant *unionists*, fearful of losing their sway in the country, insisted upon the ongoing union of England and Ireland under the English crown (which is why they are also called "loyalists"). In the early twentieth century, as the English parliament contemplated granting home rule to Ireland, Ulster unionists (Protestants loyalists) begin to arm themselves to the hilt! We get a sense of their thinking in a bold declaration signed by two hundred and fifty thousand loyalists in September 1912:

> Being convinced in our consciences that Home Rule would be disastrous to the material well-being of Ulster . . . [we] do hereby pledge ourselves . . . to stand by one another in defending for ourselves and our children our cherished position of equal citizenship in the United Kingdom and in using all means which may be found necessary.[5]

The great compromise was Partition. In 1920 the British Parliament granted home rule to much of Ireland in the south but excluded most of the counties of Ulster in the north. This created the southern Republic of Ireland and the new state called Northern Ireland. Catholics within the new Northern Ireland were in a vulnerable position: cut off from their mainly Catholic neighbours in the Republic of Ireland. And so they found themselves in an awkward standoff with the dominant Protestant population of Ulster. Civil unrest was the result. In the few years following the 1920 Partition, 257 Catholics were killed, 157 Protestants, and 37 members of the security forces. Many more Catholics (11,000) were made jobless, and over 4,500 Catholic-owned shops and businesses were looted or destroyed.[6]

The "Uprising" and the Peace

The twentieth century saw the establishment and growth of deadly paramilitary groups in Ireland. There was the Irish Republican Army (IRA), often described as the military wing of the Catholic nationalist political party *Sinn Féin* ("Ourselves Alone"). On the other side was the Ulster Volunteer Force and the larger Ulster Defence Association, along with various other Protestant splinter groups. As the political strength of the Protestant loyalists began to diminish in the 1960s, the paramilitary groups increasingly came into play. The loyalists had always had a population advantage in the region, which translated into a majority of seats in the parliament of Northern Ireland (known as the Stormont). This was aided by the fact that poorer non-rate-paying citizens, many of them Catholics, were excluded from voting in local elections ("one person, one vote" was a relatively new concept, anyway). But as the old Protestant political bloc began to diminish, and riotous protests demanding equal rights increased, the powder keg that was Ulster exploded.

In January 1969 nationalist Catholic protests descended into outright violence, with numerous confirmed reports of police brutality. This resulted in further riots. Soon the Protestant loyalist groups were targeting Catholic buildings with explosives and smashing windows in Catholic streets, forcing locals to flee to safer districts. In August that year a siege took place in Catholic Bogside in the town of Derry. Locals put up a strong defence, even pelting police and the Protestant volunteer groups with petrol bombs from their high-rise flats. The British Army was called in. Protests and riots erupted across Catholic suburbs, in Belfast and elsewhere, to show support for the besieged Bogsiders in the north. A later military report makes clear that these events were interpreted by British officials as "an armed uprising" on the part of Catholic separatists. British forces used Browning machine guns mounted on armoured cars. Several people were killed. Protestant unionists began burning down houses in Catholic areas. The "Troubles" had officially begun.[7]

The details of back-and-forth violence over the next thirty years, from August 1968 to April 1998, probably do not progress the theme of this book very much, other than to underline the human capacity for hatred. Suffice it to say that muggings, kidnappings, gun battles, assassinations, and terrorist bombings, combined with occasional brutality from British forces, such as the Bloody Sunday massacre of 30 January 1972, marked this bloodiest era of modern Irish history. In typical Irish understatement, the whole period was euphemistically dubbed "the Troubles."

After many ceasefires and false "peaces," a roadmap to the end of hostilities was eventually found in the Belfast Agreement, accepted by all parties on 10 April 1998, which happened to be Good Friday, hence it is best known as "The Good Friday Agreement." According to the thirty-five-page Agreement—downloadable from the UK government website[8]—power was to be justly shared between Catholic and Protestant districts of Ulster. Any new legislation would require bipartisan agreement or a 60 percent majority. Ministers had executive authority in their departments—overseen by subcommittees—but were not obliged to agree with each other in the cabinet. The subcommittees overseeing departments had to be truly representative of the relative electoral power of the various parties. The agreement further stipulated that prisoners from paramilitary groups on both sides were to be released within two years. At a cultural level, the agreement states the importance of "the Irish language, Ulster-Scots and the languages of the various ethnic communities, all of which are part of the cultural wealth of the island of Ireland."[9] Employment law was also to be reformed, ending discrimination.[10]

The human toll of the thirty-year Troubles has been well documented. The IRA was responsible for approximately one thousand, eight hundred deaths, including the killing of five hundred British soldiers. The British military itself was responsible for almost three hundred deaths. Protestant loyalist paramilitaries killed about one thousand people, including over seven hundred targeted Catholic civilians. Various other splinter groups on both sides were responsible for the remaining deaths. The final death toll of the Troubles was just over three thousand, six hundred people, with another forty thousand people injured, including the man I met in Belfast who had lost much of his face.[11] The Good Friday Agreement explicitly recognised this human cost and pledged to work for peace in honour of those who lost their lives: "It is recognised that victims have a right to remember as well as to contribute to a changed society. The achievement of a peaceful and just society would be the true memorial to the victims of violence."[12]

"Religiously Inspired Cruelty"?

Christopher Hitchens famously included the Troubles in his list of the "religiously inspired cruelty" that he had witnessed in his long career as a journalist. For him, it is evidence of the almost endless capacity of religion to wreak havoc on individuals and nations. But this is an argument out of all proportion to the facts. Even if we were to accept that the Troubles were "religiously inspired," I doubt they would rate a mention in any history of cruelty of the last five hundred years, or even the last one hundred years. With the deepest affection for my friends in Northern Ireland, thirty-six hundred deaths over a thirty-year period hardly supports the thesis that *religion poisons everything*. Naturally, *one* killing in the name of Christ is a blasphemy, but the scale of loss in the Troubles was a tiny fraction of the losses encountered in conflicts during exactly the same period (AD 1968–1998). Think of the Vietnam War, the Six-Day War, the Soviet-Afghan War, the First Gulf War, the Yugoslav Wars, and the Rwandan Genocide. And to recall an earlier historic example, the Terror of the French Revolution executed almost five times as many people in nine months as the Troubles did in thirty years. The Terror killed more people than did the Troubles and Spanish Inquisition combined.

In any case, the Troubles cannot really be said to be "inspired" by religion. Religion certainly laid the groundwork for the conflict. The bitter disputes of the Reformation were imposed on the Irish by successive "plantations" in the seventeenth century. The Irish (Catholic) identity was thus set in opposition to the English and Scottish (Protestant) identity. But after more than three centuries, disputes over religion per se were not at the forefront of anyone's mind. The words "Catholic" and "Protestant" now marked out distinct *communities*, living in separate areas, with very little meaningful interaction with one another (rarely intermarrying, for example). Religious identity had morphed into political identity: *Catholic* meant Irish nationalist or separatist; *Protestant* meant British loyalist or unionist.

It is fascinating to wander around Belfast, as you can do freely today, and look at the many surviving murals from the Troubles. Hardly any of them contain religious imagery or language. It is tribal and political, not at all theological. It is even more striking to read through the Good Friday Agreement and note how little mention there is of anything religious. The topic is not avoided. The word "religion" appears twice and "religious" just once in the thirty-five-page text—each time in connection with the principle of political and spiritual "liberty." The words "Catholic," "Protestant," "church," and so on do not appear at all. Instead, reference is made to Irish "nationalists" and "unionists." It is overwhelmingly a political, judicial, and cultural document, not a settlement about religion.

One of the things Belfast locals like to point out is that Pope John Paul II visited Ireland in the middle of hostilities and pleaded with everyone to end the violence and follow the way of love. One-third of Ireland's population turned out to see him! The pope's speech in the town of Drogheda, thirty miles south of Belfast, on Saturday, 29 September 1979, is quite something—worth reading even if you don't much like religion. After referencing Saint Patrick, the fifth-century founder of Christianity in Ireland, John Paul II thanks church leaders from both Catholic and Protestant congregations for their kind invitation to visit their ancient land. He then confronts the proverbial elephant in the room by mentioning the "sufferings" of recent years and insists "that the tragic events taking place in Northern Ireland do not have their source in the fact of belonging to different Churches and Confession; that this is not—despite what is so often repeated before world opinion—a religious war, a struggle between Catholics and Protestants." On the contrary, he says, the shared message of all churches is the love of Christ:

> Now I wish to speak to all men and women engaged in violence. I appeal to you, in language of passionate pleading. On my knees I beg you to turn away from the paths of violence and to return to the ways of peace. . . . In the name of God I beg you: return to Christ, who died so that men might live in forgiveness and peace. He is waiting for you, longing for each one of you to come to him so that he may say to each of you: your sins are forgiven; go in peace.[13]

The pope's visit to Ireland was in 1979. It would be two more decades before the warring parties would sign a lasting peace. I doubt the pope had much, if anything, to do with the final outcome, despite a 2018 documentary suggesting otherwise.[14]

Yet, there *was* a priest who *did* play a role in brokering the peace. Father Alec Reid's face was plastered on newspapers all over the world when he was photographed kneeling over the bloodied and near-naked body of a murdered British soldier, giving him the last rites. According to the BBC, the soldier had been tortured and shot in broad daylight after driving into the path of a republican funeral.

The photo was published everywhere, but no one knew at the time that Father Reid was carrying with him that day an envelope containing secret documents outlining a potential roadmap to peace. Father Reid had been acting as a go-between to get the parties together and to convince the IRA to "renounce violence in favour of negotiation."[15] His actions led to the Belfast Agreement, and Reid was present to witness the decommissioning of the IRA's arsenal—watching as members turned in their weapons for destruction. In an article in the *New York Times*, then-Irish Prime Minister Charles Haughey is said to have regarded Father Reid as "the most important person in the entire peace process, bar none."[16]

◆

The pope's words—and Father Reid's actions—underscore the importance of not racing to conclude that a conflict with superficially religious language— "Catholic" and "Protestant"—has much to do with religion itself.

Yet, there are other evils in this same period that cannot be so easily explained. They threaten to make all the explanations—*all the good*—of Christian history collapse under the weight of evidence of the church's perversion, cruelty, and cover-ups. And this story, too, begins in Ireland.

Moral Reckoning

Child Abuse in the Modern Church

It would be better for you if a millstone were hung around your neck and you were thrown into the sea than for you to cause one of these little ones to stumble.

—JESUS OF NAZARETH

J ust as the "Troubles" of Northern Ireland were coming to their peaceful end, news was breaking in northwest Ireland that would shock the world and lead to the greatest moral reckoning for the church in a thousand years, perhaps ever.

County Donegal is an implausible setting for such dramatic revelations. "It is this unlikely corner of the country," writes Kimiko de Freytas-Tamura in her *New York Times* report, "where among rolling hills of wild heather, castles and bucolic fishing villages, predatory priests terrorized children with impunity for decades."[1] Just one hundred and sixty thousand people live in Donegal, but it has one of the worst records of church abuse ever exposed. The first sign of the horror emerged in 1998, the year of the Good Friday Agreement. Semi-retired detective Martin Ridge had seen his fair share of bombings and bloodshed in the previous decades, but what he found in this beautiful part of the world was "worse than the I.R.A.," he said. A priest, Father Greene, had come to Detective Ridge accusing a local man of blackmailing him over "false" (said Greene) allegations of sexual abuse. Ridge's inquiries, however, revealed that Greene had, in fact, abused the boy.

Martin Ridge's investigations uncovered further allegations of misconduct, and in 1998 he arrested Father Greene. Suddenly, other witnesses came forward throughout Donegal. Greene was eventually sent to prison for raping and molesting twenty-six boys between 1965 and 1982. In a tragic reminder of the effects of these crimes, eight victims of clerical abuse are buried in the churchyard at Gortahork, Donegal, having taken their own lives.[2]

Some readers may want to put this book down and perhaps speak to a trusted friend before going any further. With precious friends who have been abused by clergy, I have had glimpses of the trauma such discussions can cause.

A Global Crisis, an Intimate Tragedy

The Donegal case was the first widespread investigation and publication of clerical sexual abuse of children. It resulted in the 1999 documentary "States of Fear," which revealed the extent of pedophile priests throughout Irish schools and institutions managed by religious orders. Following the documentary, the government established the Residential Institutions Redress Board, which has since compensated more than one hundred and forty thousand victims.[3] Tragically, Ireland has the highest rate of clergy abuse in the world, a fact that may be connected to the unusual education system in the country, where "90 per cent of primary schools are under church patronage."[4]

Compounding the evil of the abuse itself were the secrecy and cover-ups that often followed. But those secrets were brought to light not just in Ireland, but—pretty soon—all over the world.

The *Boston Globe*'s famous "Spotlight investigations" between 2001 and 2003 found that "under an extraordinary cloak of secrecy" the Archdiocese of Boston, in the ten years prior to publication, had quietly settled child molestation claims against at least seventy priests. They had sometimes reassigned known pedophiles to other parishes or parallel ministries in hospitals or prisons. Some of these priests offended again.[5] By the end of 2002, the *Globe* reported that the pope had accepted the resignation of Cardinal Bernard Law, the man who had led the diocese—and therefore the cover-ups—since 1984.[6] It was a huge victory for justice and journalism, and a sign of hope for many victims.

The *Globe* reports triggered a raft of other investigations around the United States and the world. The largest US study on the abuse of minors by Catholic priests was conducted by the John Jay College of Criminal Justice in 2004, commissioned by the United States Conference of Catholic Bishops. It found that 4.3 percent of Catholic clergy had been accused of abuse.[7] Evidence from an even larger investigation, which we will look at next, suggests the number might be higher.

Before drilling down into the extraordinary findings of the world's largest investigation into *institutional* child sexual abuse, it is worth pausing to confront the magnitude of the problem of child sexual abuse more generally. A comprehensive meta-analysis of 217 publications involving 331 independent samples of nearly ten million participants was published in the journal *Child Maltreatment*, a publication of The American Professional Society on the Abuse of Children. The meta-analysis found that the global prevalence of child sexual abuse, or CSA, *for girls* is 19.7 percent as an upper limit and 16.4 percent as a lower limit, and *for boys* is 8.8 percent as an upper limit and 6.6 percent as a lower limit. As the authors of the study note in their closing line, "Even the lower bound estimates are alarming in their demonstration that CSA is a global phenomenon affecting the lives of millions of children."[8] The other confronting finding across a range of studies is that most victims of child sexual abuse were molested by *friends* (55 percent) or *family* (34 percent), not *strangers* (14 percent).[9] This is both a global crisis and an intimate tragedy.

The World's Largest Investigation into Child Sexual Abuse

Child sexual abuse occurs not only in private settings but also in *institutional* contexts, where children have been entrusted to the care of responsible adults, whether in churches, sports clubs, schools, orphanages, or juvenile justice centres. The most extensive and detailed investigation into *institutional* child sexual abuse comes from Australia. In 2012 the federal government announced a Royal Commission into Institutional Responses to Child Sexual Abuse: a "Royal Commission" is Australia's highest form of investigative and legal inquiry on matters of public importance.[10] After five years of investigations, 42,041 calls handled, 25,964 letters and emails received, and 8,013 private interviews held, the seventeen-volume Final Report published in 2017 has given the world the clearest insight into the nature and extent of institutional child sexual abuse. The Commission also made 189 detailed recommendations to better protect children in institutions. Volume 16 of the report concerns religious institutions and is over twenty-five hundred pages long.[11]

The Royal Commission sponsored detailed research that found that *at least* 5 percent of all child sexual abuse occurs in *institutional* settings, whether in churches, schools, orphanages, and so on.[12] The true figure is probably higher, the Commission notes, due to delayed reporting and under-reporting in institutional settings.[13] Yet, even if just 5 percent of instances of child sexual abuse occur in institutions, the Commission estimates this means that at least sixty-nine thousand people in Australia right now—and millions around the world—were molested as a child in an institution. The scale of the heartache is slowly coming to the public's attention.

The Royal Commission found that 41.6 percent of survivors of institutional child sexual abuse were molested in "Out-of-home care" (orphanages, foster care), 31.8 percent of survivors of institutional child sexual abuse were molested in "Schools,"[14] and 14.5 percent of survivors of institutional child sexual abuse were molested in what the Commission categorizes as "religious activities," that is, churches, Sunday schools, and youth groups. That proportion (14.5 percent) is roughly equivalent to the proportion in "youth detention" centres (8 percent) and "recreation, sports and clubs" (5.9 percent) combined.[15] But the true number is more complicated and more disturbing. Many out-of-home care programs and schools are governed by religious bodies. These must also be added to the discussion of what constitutes a religious institution. The Royal Commission has calculated that 58.6 percent of survivors of child sexual abuse were molested in one of 1,691 different *religious* institutions named. Religious bodies, in other words, are responsible for a majority of child sexual abuse in an institution.

The Commission also learnt something about the perpetrators. Virtually all of them (95.3 percent) were adult males. More than half (52.9 percent) of the perpetrators in *religious institutions* were in religious ministry, a priest, a pastor, or equivalent. Other perpetrators in a religious institution included school teachers (23.2 percent), care workers (13 percent), and a variety of other authority figures, such as housemasters, foster carers, volunteers, and others.

Not Just a Catholic Problem

This is not just a Catholic problem. The early high-profile reporting coming out of Ireland and Boston focused exclusively on the Catholic Church. It certainly left a worldwide impression. Australia's Royal Commission has been able to set things in a broader context.

Of the survivors abused in religious institutions (church, school, orphanage, etc.): 61.8 percent were abused in a Catholic institution; 14.7 percent were abused in an Anglican or Episcopalian institution; 7.3 percent were abused in a Salvation Army institution; and the remainder were abused in various Presbyterian, Uniting, Baptist, Pentecostal, Jewish, and other institutions. But these figures leave a somewhat skewed impression. The Catholic Church is also by far the largest denomination in Australia, with 22.6 percent of Australians identifying as "Catholic." "Anglican" is the next largest with 13.3 percent.[16] The Catholic Church is also the country's largest provider of independent schooling, teaching 19.5 percent of Australian students.[17] And the Catholic Church is the largest provider of non-government welfare in the country.[18]

None of this diminishes the scale of the evil perpetrated by Catholic priests, teachers, and volunteers. I hope any readers who are victims of Catholic abuse will bear with my point. I raise all this only to give my fellow *non-Catholic* Christians pause. The Catholic Church provides more institutional services—schools, foster care, orphanages, and churches—than any other non-government agency. It is not surprising that its rates of child sexual abuse are higher than for other denominations. The fact that the Catholic Church is responsible for 61.8 percent of victims of child sexual abuse in some kind of religious institution is "not necessarily a large over-representation," notes Professor Patrick Parkinson, Dean of the University of Queensland School of

Law and one of Australia's leading child protection experts, "since a substantial proportion of all faith-based schools and children's homes were run by Catholic entities in the 60 years after World War Two."[19] There are certainly no grounds for the Protestant smugness I felt in the early 2000s.

There is a feature of the findings of the Royal Commission that will cause Catholics concern. A disturbing number of priests in the Australian Catholic Church are alleged pedophiles. I mentioned earlier that the largest US study on the abuse of minors by Catholic priests was conducted by the John Jay College of Criminal Justice in 2004. It found that 4.3 percent of Catholic clergy had been accused of child sexual abuse.[20] Evidence from the Australian Royal Commission, however, suggests the number—at least for Australia—is higher. Based on sixty years of data, the Commission's conclusion is confronting: "7 per cent were alleged perpetrators."[21]

I suppose someone could reply that this means 93 percent of Catholic priests are likely genuine servants of their people (and God). I certainly agree that it would be unfair—as sometimes happens where I live—to view Catholic priests *generally* with suspicion. Still, 7 percent is higher than the estimated proportion of the general population thought to be pedophiles—between 1 and 5 percent, depending on the study.[22] And it is higher than the proportion of alleged pedophile clergy in the next largest denomination (below 1 percent).[23]

A final important element of the findings of the Australian Royal Commission is that changes can be detected in church practices from the 1990s. "Of the survivors who told us in private sessions about child sexual abuse in religious institutions," the Commission reports, "90 per cent told us about abuse occurring before 1990 and 5.8 per cent told us about abuse occurring from 1990 onwards. Some survivors did not discuss the date of abuse." The report is careful to note that "it would be a mistake to regard child sexual abuse in religious institutions as being historical; as something we no longer need to be concerned about."[24] Moreover, delayed disclosure means that the information gathered by the Commission likely under-represents the number of victims of more recent abuse. "However, it would also be wrong to say that nothing has changed," the report notes.[25] Awareness of the issue of child sexual abuse has increased since 1990. New protocols designed to protect children were brought into government institutions in the 1980s, and these slowly, partially entered into some religious institutions in the 1990s. These had some effect on perpetrators' ability to abuse children undetected. That said, a full fifty-eight of the Commission's 189 detailed recommendations to the government relate specifically to religious institutions.[26] There is *a lot* of work still to do.

"Take Care That You Do Not Despise One of These Little Ones"

The widespread involvement of churches in charitable services—schools, hospitals, orphanages, foster care, as well as their religious activities—partially explains the high incidence of institutional child sexual abuse in specifically religious institutions (58.6 percent). There may be other contributing factors. The Australian Royal Commission controversially mentions compulsory celibacy. "Based on research," the Final Report states, "we conclude that there is an elevated risk of child sexual abuse where compulsorily celibate male clergy have privileged access to children." Celibacy, they note, "is implicated in emotional isolation, loneliness, depression and mental illness. . . . [Compulsory celibacy] may also have contributed to various forms of psychosexual dysfunction, including psychosexual immaturity, which pose an ongoing risk to the safety of children."[27] This has been strongly challenged by both church officials and some academic psychologists.[28]

There is another factor—unrelated to celibacy—that is almost too dark to contemplate. Patrick Parkinson, mentioned a moment ago, has noted that the over-representation of religious bodies in charitable services means that "The church is therefore a community that is likely to attract people with a strong sexual interest in children."[29] He points to research by Joe Sullivan and Anthony Beech from the Department of Psychology at the University of Birmingham, UK. Their study of known "professional perpetrators" found that 15 percent "said they choose their work exclusively to sexually abuse children," and a further 41.5 percent "said abuse was part of their motivation for choosing their job."[30] It is possible, in other words, that a portion of the pedophile clergy in any denomination actually *chose* the ministry in order to molest children. It is a dreadful thought to ponder.[31]

Whatever factors have led to child sexual abuse in the church, the *New York Times* columnist and noted Catholic Ross Douthat is surely right when he says of recent revelations, "No atheist or anticlericalist, no Voltaire or Ingersoll or Twain could have invented a story so perfectly calculated to discredit the message of the Gospel. . . . No external enemy of the faith could have sown so much confusion and dismay among the faithful."[32] This is a disaster the church has brought upon itself. It is an evil for which the church alone is to blame. It is moral reckoning equal to—if not surpassing—the Crusades and Inquisitions.

I hardly need to point out all the ways that child sexual abuse contradicts the message and mission of Jesus Christ. His teaching about sexual ethics alone would rule out any erotic contact of this kind, let alone what he said about the abuse of power: "You know that among the Gentiles those whom they recognize as their rulers lord it over them, and their great ones are tyrants over them. But it is not so among you; but whoever wishes to become great among you must be your servant" (Mark 10:42–43). On several occasions Christ spoke specifically about the mistreatment of children: "Take care that you do not despise one of these little ones; for, I tell you, in heaven their angels continually see the face of my Father in heaven" (Matt 18:10). Whatever we make of the reference to "angels," Jesus's point is that children are represented before the throne of the ultimate Judge. Elsewhere he said, "It would be better for you if a millstone were hung around your neck and you were thrown into the sea than for you to cause one of these little ones to stumble" (Luke 17:2). The word "stumble" is fascinating. It is *skandalizō* in the original Greek. We get "scandalize" from it. Its root idea is to "entrap" or "trip up." I can hardly imagine a more harmful snare than child sexual abuse. Churches are meant to be places not only of sexual self-restraint but of special care for the vulnerable. The abuse of children is an unfathomable scandal. The graves at Gortahork are a silent reminder. Their "angels" continually see the face of God.

To any of my readers who are survivors, or who have loved ones who are survivors, I can only close this chapter by saying, from the depth of my heart, and as a minister in the mainstream church (a church I somehow still love), *I am sorry.*

Social Capital

The Ordinary Work of the Contemporary Church

Religiously observant Americans are more civic and in some respects simply "nicer."

—ROBERT PUTNAM, HARVARD

Several times in the last chapter I spoke of the over-representation of churches in modern charities. I should probably validate that claim. I imagine many of my readers will happily accept that Christianity had a *historical* role in establishing hospitals, sheltering abandoned infants, feeding the destitute, and attempting in their limited way to liberate slaves. But these things are now *secular* activities. There is nothing particularly "Christian" about them. In fact, some readers may even be aware of recent research suggesting that religious believers are *less* altruistic than their secular counterparts. The truth of the matter, as with so many things, is mixed, likely to disturb believer and sceptic alike.

"Religious Upbringing Associated with Less Altruism"

Some studies have underscored the lack of charitableness among contemporary believers. In 2015 the University of Chicago announced the findings of an international study conducted by their Department of Psychology that indicated—to quote their headline—"Religious upbringing associated with less altruism."[1] The results were published in the prestigious science journal, *Current Biology*,[2] and won worldwide media attention for months. The headline in the *Daily Beast* was particularly confronting: "Study: Religious Kids Are Jerks."[3]

The team of researchers, led by Professor Jean Decety at the University of Chicago, gave fun stickers to groups of children aged five to twelve years and then assessed how readily the children shared with kids who had fewer stickers. Next, they showed the children short animations of people being mean to each other and asked the kids about how they felt and what should be done to the bullies. It turned out that children from religious households, mainly Christian and Muslim, "were significantly less likely than children from non-religious households to share their stickers," and this "negative relation between religiosity and altruism grew stronger with age; children with a longer experience of religion in the household were the least likely to share." Religious children were also more likely to demand harsh punishments for the bullies in the cartoons. Religion is not just less charitable; it is more punitive. Professor Decety's conclusion was stark: "Religion negatively influences children's altruism."[4]

It is easy to see why this study attracted so much attention around the world. I read it. I asked a psychologist friend to give me a second opinion. It seemed that Decety had shown what no previous study had revealed: the charitable spirit was *less* prominent in religious households.

I took the study on the chin and started to include its findings in various lectures I gave on the best and worst of Christian behaviour. I often quipped that "If you ever need more stickers, don't go to the Christians!" Mostly, though, I just offered a *mea culpa*: Religion can make our children focus on *what's mine* and *my rights* rather than the good of others. Science is science: Christians do not practise what they preach.

Within twelve months the famous Chicago study was debunked. It turned out to be one of the *thankfully rare* cases of bad data, bad collation, and bad analysis. I was blissfully unaware of all this, and for months afterwards was still offering my *mea culpas* all around the world. An audience member pulled me up one day and asked, "Didn't that study turn out to be junk?" Well, it sure turned out to be wrong. And if you go to the University of Chicago website announcement today, you will find that the study has been retracted, and there is only a sheepish link to the original news story. The online version of the academic article in *Current Biology* (for those with university library access) has the word "RETRACTED" featured in giant red font across every page. It is a credit to academia that errors of fact like this, when discovered, are usually promptly acknowledged. The same cannot be said for the media coverage.

I do not know of any research that supports the conclusion that religious people, or Christians in particular, are less altruistic in the sense that they do not share what they have with those in need. As we will see, overwhelmingly, studies show the opposite—which I suppose is why the Chicago study seemed like such a sensation. Nevertheless, there is one aspect of Professor Decety's contentions that does seem to be widely supported: some forms of religion tend to increase what psychologists call "punitiveness." That harsh and judgmental spirit for which Christians are sometimes famous does have some scientific backing.

Martin Seligman is Professor of Psychology at the University of Pennsylvania and a leader in the Positive Psychology movement over the last thirty years. The key idea in Positive Psychology is that psychological insights can be applied to enhancing healthy mental states, not just mending unhealthy ones. Seligman was the co-editor of a major 2004 volume published by Oxford University Press exploring *Character Strengths and Virtues*.[5] It was a wide-ranging review of the published research to-date on human development in areas such as Creativity (chapter 4), Open-Mindedness (chapter 6), Social Intelligence (chapter 15), Gratitude (chapter 24), Humor (chapter 26), and much more. Seligman's goal is to discover what factors enhance and hinder the attainment of human excellence.

Seligman and his colleagues found a range of published research—none of it retracted!—which suggests that religiosity (mainly Christianity) increased prejudice and harshness. One was a study by Allport and Ross that indicated that those who scored higher on "extrinsic religiousness" tended to be "particularly prejudiced toward African Americans and Jews." These individuals were also "more suspicious and were more likely to perceive the world and those in it as threatening."[6] Seligman points to the work of Leiber and Woodrick who found an association between "biblical literalness" and "correctional punitiveness."[7] In other words, the more strictly or concretely you take the meanings of the Bible, the more likely you are to be an authoritarian law-and-order advocate. The reference above to "extrinsic religiousness" is important. It is used in the literature to refer to those who "use religion or religious affiliation for particular ends as opposed to internalizing and living out religious beliefs," Seligman says.[8] That is fascinating, and suggests that the more someone's faith is a social and political badge, rather than a matter of the heart, the harsher their attitudes will be toward others.[9] I can believe it.

This may chime with research about domestic violence, a scourge outside and inside the church. There is *some* data indicating that men who sporadically attend conservative churches may be more likely to commit intimate partner violence. It is reasoned that the "patriarchal" models of family life taught in such churches may give violent men superficial warrant to treat their wives harshly.[10] It is easy to see how traditional teachings about the "sanctity of marriage" and "male headship" could be used by abusers to trap wives in a harmful relationship, despite explicit biblical commands against spousal abuse.[11] While recent research shows that "highly religious" couples report "the highest levels of relationship quality,"[12] more research is needed before we can claim that intrinsic and frequent religious involvement is in any way "protective" against domestic abuse, specifically. In my own country, my colleagues and I have publicly urged Christian institutions, particularly conservative evangelical ones, to commission a largescale study into domestic violence in our churches and clergy responses to it.[13]

In a range of ways, then, "extrinsic" Christianity—that is, social or political Christianity—could be bad for us all! Better no faith than superficial faith.

Christianity and Mental Health

Extrinsic Christianity may be bad for everyone, but evidence suggests that an internalized version of the faith benefits both the individual believer and our unbelieving society. "A sizable body of research," says Seligman in *Character*

Strengths and Virtues, "has demonstrated a positive link between religiosity, particular religious involvement, and psychological and physical well-being." Seligman, who is not himself religious, briefly reviews fifteen separate studies underscoring this conclusion. For example, "church support and ministerial support," he says, seem to "play crucial roles in people's efforts to cope with adversity."[14]

More striking even than Seligman's review of research is the 2012 *Oxford Handbook of Religion and Health*, which provides a comprehensive meta-analysis of all published studies on the association between religious involvement and medical and mental health. It is a very "western" analysis, I am afraid, focusing mainly on research from countries where Christianity is the main religion (to the degree that religion is practised): the UK, the US, Europe, Canada, Australia, and so on. The findings are nonetheless extraordinary:

Well-being: 78% of more than 300 studies report a positive association between religiosity and well-being.

Optimism: 81% of 32 studies report a positive association between religiosity and optimism.

Meaning and purpose: 93% of 45 studies report a positive association between religiosity and one's sense of purpose and meaning.

Social support: 82% of 74 studies report a positive association between religiosity and one's sense of social support.

Depression: 61% of 413 studies report lower rates of depression or faster recovery from depression in religious individuals.

Suicide: 75% of 141 studies report that religiosity is associated with less suicidal ideation, fewer suicide attempts, or fewer completed suicides.

Social capital (participation in community): 79% of 14 studies report a positive association between religiosity and social capital.[15]

A more recent (2017) review and synthesis of the literature by the director of Harvard's School of Public Health, Professor Tyler VanderWeele, has confirmed and bolstered the conclusion that religious participation is positively associated with a wide range of physical and mental health outcomes, including even lower mortality.[16]

Christianity and Social Capital

The final category mentioned in the above list, "social capital," has been the focus of much research over the last twenty years. It turns out, religion might not poison everything after all. Martin Seligman is sceptical about the power of *extrinsic* religion to promote character and virtue, as I have said. Yet, he thinks there is another story:

> Religiousness (measured as religious participation and religious salience) is associated with lower levels of marital conflict, greater perceived spousal support, more consistent parenting, and less conflictual and more supportive relationships between adolescents and their parents [he then cites the studies]. . . . Religiousness, particularly church involvement, also has been identified as a robust predictor of altruism, volunteerism, and philanthropy [he then cites the studies].[17]

The claim that churches are key providers of social capital was put to the test in a very famous series of studies by Robert Putnam, Professor of Public Policy at the Harvard University John F. Kennedy School of Government. His early work in the 1970s and 80s compared Italian society with US society and was central in the rise of scholarly interest in *social capital*. Putnam defines social capital as the "social networks and the norms of reciprocity and trustworthiness that arise from them."[18]

In his book *American Grace: How Religion Divides and Unites Us*,[19] Putnam (with co-author David Campbell) details the diversity and even divisions that exist in American society, especially when it comes to religion, morality, and politics. He particularly traces the link between religion and political partisanship over the last four decades. No surprises there. What was surprising to many, however, including to Putnam himself, was the evidence that religion is also one of the key factors in American tolerance, volunteering, and philanthropy.

Putnam and his team of researchers completed detailed interviews with three thousand representative Americans. The interviews were, in fact, conducted twice, a year apart, to ensure the robustness of the data. A range of themes was explored: religious participation, involvement in social clubs and charities, philanthropy, politics, and webs of personal relationships, as well as the usual demographic information social scientists need to control for external factors. The results confirm two things that seem to be in tension. First, religious Americans tend to hold more "judgmental" viewpoints than their secular counterparts. They are "less tolerant of dissent than secular Americans, an important civic deficiency," Putnam says.[20] I doubt many readers will be surprised by that. Yet, despite their viewpoint intolerance, religious Americans tend to be concretely more philanthropic and community minded: "Religious Americans are, in fact, more generous neighbours and more conscientious citizens than their secular counterparts," Putnam continues. "[R]eligion boosts total volunteering so substantially that in addition to their higher rate of religious volunteering, regular churchgoers are also much more likely to volunteer for secular causes."[21]

One of Putnam's curious claims is that "theology is not the core explanation for what we shall call the 'religious edge' in good citizenship and neighborliness."[22] In other words, it is not *beliefs* that provide the main effect; it is the *social connectedness* of religious communities. After all, he points out, this bump in neighbourliness also exists among atheists who are involved in church life. It is an intriguing insight. Yet, can it really be that a community's beliefs have no significant impact on the community's activities? Why do we not find these same levels of volunteering and philanthropy in, say, sports clubs or the local theatre company? Surely a religious community's convictions have some impact on the "religious edge"? Theology lifts a religious community to aspire to certain shared ideals. It makes sense that the "lift" will be experienced by atheists in the church, just as it is by believers. Someone does not need to believe that people are made in the "image of God" in order to enjoy serving alongside those who really do believe that.

These are thoughts I was recently able to put to one of Robert Putnam's best known protégés. Dr. Andrew Leigh is Australia's leading researcher and activist in social capital. He did his PhD under Putnam at Harvard before returning to work for a time as an academic at the Australian National University. He is now a Federal Member of Parliament (roughly the equivalent of a US Senator) for the Labor Party (roughly the equivalent of the Democratic Party). He is also an atheist. I only say that because he often does. In fact, in his book on social capital in Australia, he introduces his chapter on religion with a series of caveats so that his readers do not think that his very positive views of religion come from a personal conviction. I have appreciated his work over the years and was able to interview him for my podcast. I quizzed him about his atheism and asked why he thinks churches have this social "edge." Following Putnam, he was clear: "Were an atheist to attend church on a weekly basis, they would probably get all the community benefits that come with church going. It's not in the theology; it's in the community." He kindly allowed me to push back a bit, along the lines just mentioned, and he was terribly good natured about it all.[23]

In any case, the results of Andrew Leigh's research are as clear as those of Putnam, Seligman, and others. His book is titled *Disconnected*, and it laments the measurable decline in social bonds in Australian society over the last forty years. One of the bright spots in the story, however, is church life. "Among churchgoers (those people who attended a religious service in the previous month), 25 per cent also participated in a community service or civic association over the same period," Leigh points out. How does that compare with the general community? "By contrast," he says, "among non-churchgoers, just 12 per cent participated in a community or civic association."[24] The figure is stark. It means that more than *twice* as many churchgoers as non-churchgoers will have done some civic volunteering in the last few weeks. Leigh is quick to point out—as Putnam does—that this effect holds for *secular* volunteering by churchgoers. It does not just refer to the church brass-cleaning roster. These conclusions chime with a 2018 Deloitte Access Economics report, which concluded: "Controlling for a range of observable factors which might affect people's propensity to donate and to volunteer, we find that religious people are more likely to be donors and volunteers than non-religious people."[25]

Churches also founded a lot of major charities, both historically and today. The *Business Review Weekly* once calculated the largest two hundred charities in Australia by revenue: "39 of the top 50 had an official religious affiliation, almost entirely with different Christian denominations," writes Dr. Stephen Judd, himself the chief executive of a major aged-care charity. And "several of the remaining 11 used to have a religious affiliation."[26] It is a common story. Many of our modern charities were started by Christian leaders or church denominations, even if they are now secular from top to bottom. I would not begrudge that for a moment. It is one of the lovely reminders that the original melody of Christ can be heard far outside the walls of the church.

One dimension of Christianity and civic service I would never have predicted is blood donations. Andrew Leigh points to research out of both the

US and Europe indicating that blood donation rates are higher among church-goers than the general population. The US study found that "[t]hose who go to church at least once per week have a 17 percent probability of donating blood as compared to 10 percent for others."[27] Leigh thinks this is highly significant, and he takes the opportunity to challenge Australians, who are not known for their church attending, "One in three of us will need blood at some point in our lives, yet just one in 30 people donate blood. It is just possible that if the rate of churchgoing were higher, the Red Cross would find it easier to meet its targets."[28]

Adding to this "religious edge" is a feature of the church from the beginning. Despite its strident moral and doctrinal claims, churches have always been socioeconomically broad. "Churchgoers are more likely to build friendships with people from a different social class," Andrew Leigh notes. "Those who attend church regularly are more likely to say that they can count among their friends a business owner, a manual worker, or a welfare recipient. Few other institutions in America or Australia are as effective in fostering this 'bridging' social capital between rich and poor."[29] This is something we saw in chapter 9 in connection with the church of fourth-century Rome. Peter Brown believes that a factor in Christianity's attractiveness to many ancient people was the way it provided what he called "a social and moral urban lung." Churches were simultaneously "places of moral zero tolerance," he said, "and places of forgiveness." According to Brown, "this implied the breaking of boundaries, vividly concretized, on a day-to-day basis, by the breaking of social boundaries through outreach to the poor."[30]

It is fascinating to see again the mention of Christian "intolerance" in this context. Whether in the ancient historical studies of Peter Brown and others or the contemporary sociological studies of Putnam and Seligman, the church has often exhibited a strange combination of moral narrowness *and* social openness, of judgmentalism *and* charity. Perhaps these two things go together—in Christianity, at least. One classic study of earliest Christianity emphasized precisely this point. Wayne Meeks, a social historian from Yale University, detailed what he called the strict "boundaries" and the wide-open "gates" of the first Christians: and *both* were necessary to establish the deep bonds of the church while also remaining open to newcomers.[31] Believing that Jesus Christ is the only Saviour of the world probably does lead to a certain intellectual impatience towards contrary views—this sometimes shows up in surveys, and in real life, as bigotry. This must *especially* be so when one's Christianity is "extrinsic." On the other hand, such an uncompromising belief in Christ logically entails embracing Christ's teaching about "love of enemies." Believing that Jesus "died for sinners" is rather narrow, but it also naturally implies that sacrificial love is the heartbeat of reality. A zero tolerance of this kind—one that is almost *fundamentalist* about Christ's love—could be good for the world. I think history reveals that it often has been.

Andrew Leigh, of course, puts this much more soberly: "Churches encourage their members to become more involved in voluntary activities, and provide a structure for civic activism that might otherwise have lain untapped. It seems probable that religious participation produces a positive social benefit, even for non-churchgoers."[32]

Nothing in this chapter is intended to "balance" the previous chapter, let alone tip the scales in favour of the church. My own theology could even accept that Christians were *worse* people than the general public—a "league of the guilty" that is merely *better than it would be* without the Christian faith. Child sexual abuse remains a profound evil that stands on its own. Nothing can moderate it. I am not arguing that we should cut Christendom some slack because it does some really good things. I am suggesting that the degradations of pedophile priests and the shameful cover-ups of a church hierarchy somehow have not prevented millions of humble churchgoers from doing extraordinary collective good. It is not clergyman and academics like me who are doing the heavy lifting of generous philanthropy and community volunteering—that's for sure! It is ordinary Christians who are having this impact. They are the ones who, despite everything—despite *everything*—can still hear the beautiful tune and are quietly humming along.

The "Log in the Eye" of Us All

Hypocrisy in Every Century

Do not judge, so that you may not be judged. For with the judgment you make you will be judged, and the measure you give will be the measure you get.

—JESUS OF NAZARETH

Many of us grow up believing that most things in society are getting better. A champion of this outlook is the Harvard psychology professor and vocal atheist Steven Pinker. One of his recent books captures the sentiment perfectly, *Enlightenment Now: The Case for Reason, Science, Humanism, and Progress.*[1] The book has been much celebrated by those who think of history in evolutionary terms. Humanity has *progressed* through the aeons, from the brutish chaos of the Stone Age, through the "Dark Ages," to the ethical flowering of the Enlightenment, and now to the glorious Online Age. The great Charles Darwin himself (AD 1809–1882) promoted this thought, as his recent biographer, A. N. Wilson, has described in detail (not all of it complimentary[2]). Darwin apparently believed that the evolutionary journey from "savage" to "Englishman" was ethical as well as biological. He wrote in his *Descent of Man*:

> The moral nature of man has reached the highest standard as yet attained, partly through the advancement of reasoning powers and consequently of a just public opinion, but especially through the sympathies being rendered more tender and widely diffused through the effects of habit.[3]

Steven Pinker has sought to give Darwin's insight empirical backing, outlining the numerous concrete improvements in society since the Enlightenment. His work has not been universally praised. Some have pointed to problems in Pinker's facts and figures. Others have noted his ideological singlemindedness. He routinely downplays evils on the "enlightened" side of the equation (the French Terror, for example), and he avoids mentioning the innumerable social goods that have come to us from ancient and religious sources (the explosion of charities and hospitals from the fourth–fifth centuries, for example).[4]

It also very much depends on how we measure morality. If we include such things as the body count of twentieth-century warfare, or our insatiable demand for developing-world sweatshops, or the trafficking of millions of girls for sexual exploitation, then the notion of progress does not seem straightforward (excuse the pun). These things are exacerbated with advancing technologies—they are more deadly, more unequal, and more available. I would not want to reverse Pinker's argument and suggest that things are overall getting worse. I am just a little more democratic when it comes to assessing the human heart. I am with Aleksander Solzhenitsyn in his famous lines from *The Gulag Archipelago*: "The line dividing good and evil cuts through the heart of every human being."[5] I would add: through every human *era*.

I have been saying that Christians should have no problem acknowledging the "log" in their eye, admitting the church's part in the prejudice, hatred, and violence of the human story. The important question, though, is not: *Has the church participated in all that is lamentable in human history?* The answer is obvious. A more interesting question is: *Has Christianity been a unique contributor to evil?* Or to ask an even more revealing question: *What has been Christianity's unique contribution to history?*

"For Good People to Do Evil—That Takes Religion"

Some argue that Christianity's special contribution to history has been its violence and bigotry—the Crusades, Inquisitions, support for slavery, and so on. In a speech titled "A Designer Universe?" the Nobel Prize-winning physicist Steven Weinberg declared, "With or without religion, good people can behave well and bad people can do evil; but for good people to do evil—that takes religion."[6] The statement is often quoted in sceptical circles. It gets a ringing endorsement from Richard Dawkins.[7] And you can even buy T-shirts with the quotation printed on the front (Google: "*Good people doing evil takes religion, Slim Fit T-Shirt*").

The context of Weinberg's quotation is interesting. He is talking about American slavery. He makes the point that Bible preaching on behalf of slavery allowed the "good people" of the south to feel comfortable perpetuating this dehumanizing practice. He mentions the anecdote of Mark Twain, who "described his mother as a genuinely good person," Weinberg says, "but who had no doubt about the legitimacy of slavery, because in years of living in antebellum Missouri she had never heard any sermon opposing slavery, but only countless sermons preaching that slavery was God's will."[8] The Bible makes *good* people do *bad* things.

The argument has difficulties. For one thing, while it is true that Christians were painfully slow in eradicating slavery, every anti-slavery movement we know of—whether in the second, fifth, seventh, or eighteenth centuries—was heavily populated by Christians. And the main arguments against slavery were not economic, political, or scientific. They were *theological*. In chapter 10 I quoted the celebrated slavery scholar David Brion Davis: "The popular hostility to slavery that emerged almost simultaneously in England and in parts of the United States drew on traditions of natural law and a revivified sense of the image of God in man."[9] Even the "natural law" tradition Davis mentions here is quasi-religious. He is not referring to the natural law philosophy of the ancient Greeks—Aristotle had famously argued that Nature intended a slave class.[10] Nor is it a reference to the natural sciences of the nineteenth century, which could be—and *were*—used to demonstrate "the Negro's unfitness for civilisation."[11] The natural law arguments of eighteenth- and nineteenth-century abolitionists were just a desacralized version of the Christian doctrine of the "image of God." It was the view that all humans are equal by virtue of being "endowed by their Creator with certain unalienable Rights."

There is a more obvious problem with the slogan "for good people to do evil—that takes religion." How do we account for the *humanist* heroes of the age who also owned slaves, without any formal religion? Think of Thomas Jefferson (AD 1743–1826), the third President of the United States and a classic Enlightenment free-thinker. He was openly *not* a Christian. Jefferson was also a prolific slaver who owned more than six hundred slaves in his lifetime.[12] It is surely obvious that "good people" (assuming the category is even valid) are well able to do evil *without* the influence of religion.

I do not wish to take my argument any further than to say that Weinberg's famous witticism is difficult to maintain. No historically-informed believer will deny that Christians have participated in all that is worst in human history. But Christianity has not been a *special contributor* to evil. Egypt, Greece, Rome, Gaul, Saxony, and England hardly needed the church to learn violence. All of these societies were doing just fine on the war front—and the slave front—before Christendom. In every part of the world, in every century, there have been divisions and bloody conflicts over land, honour, resources, and revenge, as well as over ideologies.

Unreligious Violence

I do not want to be impolite, but it might also be said that the hatred and violence of the church is utterly dwarfed by the hatred and violence of non-religious causes through history. The Terror of 1793–1794 is such an interesting example not because it resulted in so many unjust deaths but because those killings were justified on *wholly secular* grounds. The beheadings, shootings, and drownings were declared *rational* and even *virtuous* by a French intelligentsia that saw itself as "enlightened," free from the ignorance of monarchy and church dogma.

Think of the greatest wars of history. World War I (AD 1914–1918) resulted in fifteen to twenty million deaths in just four and a half years.[13] No one argues that this was a religious conflict. World War II (AD 1939–1945) led to the deaths of approximately fifty million people in six years.[14] Again, no historian today suggests that religion played even a minor role in the motivations of the war. It is true that both the German and the Allied Forces prayed to the same God for safety, victory, and eventual peace. But this does not make these wars "religious" any more than we can say they were "Enlightenment wars" simply because all sides were steeped in modernity.[15] The occasional attempt to suggest that Adolf Hitler's extermination of millions of Jews was motivated by some form of Christianity faces the impossible task of accounting for Nazism's well-documented hatred of orthodox Christianity.[16]

And this is before we stop to contemplate the decidedly *irreligious* bloodshed of modern history. Joseph Stalin (AD 1878–1953) was responsible for the deaths of fifteen to twenty million people in his Soviet Union[17]—more deaths *each week* than the Spanish Inquisition managed to kill during *three-and-a-half centuries*. One Central Committee Member during Stalin's time described the conduct expected of party officials: "Throw your bourgeois humanitarianism out of the window and act like Bolsheviks worthy of Comrade Stalin. . . . Don't be afraid of taking extreme measures. . . . Better to do too much than not enough."[18] And so they did.

Stalin's true ideological successor—in avowed atheism and applied communism—was China's Mao Zedong (AD 1893–1976). His attempt at a forced industrial revolution, dubbed the "Great Leap Forward," inflicted severe, calculated famines on his people. His Cultural Revolution, designed to purge China of capitalists and traditionalists, stressed precisely Stalin's rejection of humanitarian nonsense. One of Mao's many mottos was, "Mercy to the enemy is cruelty to the people,"[19] which has the ring of Robespierre's revolutionary policy in Paris nearly two centuries earlier: *terror is virtue*. "This combination of large-scale thinking and lack of moral restraints," writes Jonathan Glover in his chilling *Humanity: A Moral History of the Twentieth Century*, "enabled Mao to aim for the total reconstruction of life in China."[20] The result of Mao's "total reconstruction" was between ten and fifty million deaths.[21]

The third atheist regime is the Khmer Rouge in Cambodia led by the Swiss-educated Pol Pot (AD 1925–1998). One of the slogans of his reign of terror says it all: "One or two million young people are enough to make the new Kampuchea."[22] He was not quite as cruel as this adage implied. It is estimated that he killed only two million out of a total population of eight million.[23] As Jonathan Glover writes, "The regimes of Stalin and Mao each killed many more people, but to kill around a quarter of the population seems like the culmination of Stalinism. . . . The shared central project of the three regimes was the total redesign of society, in ways unrestrained by human feelings or morality."[24]

It would not be fair to credit these unprecedented human catastrophes to atheism itself. Richard Dawkins is surely right when he says, "I cannot think of any war that has been fought in the name of atheism. Why should it? . . . [W]hy would anyone go to war for the sake of an absence of belief?"[25] Fair enough. No one has gone to war or slaughtered millions *in the name of atheism*. I doubt that anyone has done anything, good or bad, *in the name of atheism*. But that is not the point. The more interesting question is: Did the atheism of Stalin, Mao, and Pol Pot—their "absence of belief" in a higher moral authority—contribute to their feeling that it was *permissible* to slaughter millions in pursuit of the new society? There is no necessary link between atheism and immorality, but it is equally true that atheism rationally *permits* a Stalin in a way that is not true of religion. Even the strictest Inquisitor never imagined he was *allowed* to kill an innocent.

The Heart of the Problem

I am not suggesting that because atheists are responsible for more bloodshed than Christians the church somehow comes out looking okay! Such a mathematical argument would be perverse. In some ways, Christian cruelty is morally *worse* than atheist cruelty, precisely because it betrays Christian convictions.

My argument is simpler, and hopefully uncontroversial. I am saying that the real problem is neither religion nor irreligion; the problem is the *human heart* in possession of a misdirected passion—a passion for power, land, rights, honour, wealth, or (yes) religion. To redeploy the words of Christ cited earlier in the book:

> Do not judge, so that you may not be judged. For with the judgment you make you will be judged, and the measure you give will be the measure you get. Why do you see the speck in your neighbor's eye, but do not notice the log in your own eye? Or how can you say to your neighbor, "Let me take the speck out of your eye," while the log is in your own eye? (Matt 7:1–4)

Christ originally directed these words to his followers, to those who accepted his teaching about love, mercy, and all the rest. *They* were the ones who were potential "hypocrites"; they were the ones tempted to get all "judgy"; and so they were to focus on the "log" in their own eyes. Much of this book has been devoted to the kind of Christian self-critique Jesus demanded. Yet, I hope I am not being judgy in suggesting that we are *all* tempted to notice the "log" in the eye of others and overlook the "speck" in our own eye.

Condemning the church has become an art form among contemporary sceptics. Secular society is not so good at recognising its own participation in the hatred and violence common to our humanity. We rightly decry the viciousness of the Inquisitions but turn a blind eye to the "virtuous terror" of the Enlightenment. We hold up the Troubles as the epitome of religion's power to divide us but fail to notice what those events actually tell us about the tribalism that lurks in all of us.

The Bible, of course, says that we *all* "fall short" (the strict meaning of the word "sin"): "For there is no distinction," says the apostle Paul in his letter to the very first churches of Rome, "since all have sinned and fall short of the glory of God" (Rom 3:22–23). This applies to the irreligious and religious alike. We fail to live up to our own standards, let alone the standards of the Almighty. If I may put it this way, there is a "log in the eye" of us all.

Well-known British intellectual and Marxist commentator Terry Eagleton has written of the attraction he feels toward the biblical concept of the "fallenness" of humanity, of "original sin," and of "real evil." He is correspondingly scathing of what he calls the "dewy-eyed" optimism of much contemporary atheist chatter about humanity's "progress." He speaks of the "staggeringly complacent belief that we are all becoming kinder and more civilised."[26] Professor Eagleton does not personally accept the Christian account of things, but he hits upon a key Christian point. In recognising the evil in us all—whether the Christian Crusades, the Enlightenment Terror, or modern pornography's complicity in human trafficking[27]—we will become a little more understanding toward our fallen-selves and a little less judgmental of others. The temptation of our age is to elevate our particular time and place as the crescendo of human purity and achievement. And that necessarily involves speaking ill of the past. We talk about the "Dark Ages" partly so we can tell ourselves we live in the light. It is a way of exempting ourselves from the guilt of humanity.

The same self-exonerating tendency was seen in the efforts to deface and destroy various western monuments in the second half of 2020. Personally, I have no problem with removing statues of people whose main contribution was evil. Most of us rejoiced at the removal of the statue of Stalin in Gori, Georgia, in June 2010, or the statue of Saddam Hussein in Baghdad in April 2003. But the current defacings and removals seem more complicated. They involve figures whose *principal* contributions were praiseworthy but whose personal lives were nonetheless marked by the sins and blindspots of their day. The statue of George Washington was toppled by protestors in Portland, Oregon, in June 2020, as was the bronze seated Thomas Jefferson at Jefferson High School. The logic is: because these men owned slaves, they do not deserve recognition for any of the good they achieved.

Far be it from me to tell Americans how they should approach their public memorials. My only thought is that there is something self-righteous in the trend to condemn people of the past. It assumes that a great figure cannot also be deeply flawed. It also assumes that we ourselves are not party to any present evils that later generations could condemn. I am not so sure. When the link between "normal pornography" and human trafficking is fully exposed, will future generations castigate us for making light of porn for the last three decades? When new systems are developed to eradicate poverty, will our descendants pour scorn on us for expecting to live like kings and queens— literally *better* than most kings and queens of history—while hundreds of millions starved? These are nothing but speculations. How would I know what our evils currently are? They are in my blind spot! All I am suggesting is that the more we understand humanity, the more willing we might be to acknowledge the "log in the eye" of us all.

The Beautiful Tune—A Coda

What is Christianity's unique contribution to history? I think the answer is found in chapter 3—and then sporadically in many of the chapters that followed. Jesus took the Jewish doctrine of the *imago Dei* and the Jewish ethic of *love*, and he intensified and universalized them both.

If all human beings bear the image of God—as a child bears the image and love of a parent—then every man, woman, and child is equally and inestimably precious, regardless of talents or usefulness. All Jews believed this, as they do today. But Jesus sent his students out into the world to preach this even among the Gentiles. Jesus also took the command "love thy neighbour" and insisted it also meant "Love your enemies; do good to those who hate you." And the idea was given special force in his death, which was interpreted from the beginning as a death for sinners. "God's love was revealed among us in this way," wrote the apostle John in a passage I quoted in chapter 3; "God sent his only Son into the world so that we might live through him. In this is love, not that we loved God but that he loved us and sent his Son to be the atoning sacrifice for our sins. Beloved, since God loved us so much, we also ought to love one another" (1 John 4:9–11). This is what I called the central moral logic of Christianity: God's love for us must animate our love for all.

I hardly need to repeat that Christians have not followed this moral logic with anything like the consistency we might have hoped for. Nor have they been as quick to acknowledge the "log" in their eye as their Master demanded. Yet, despite everything, the original moral logic of Christianity did make its presence felt in every century on record. Even when the church was at its most cruel, reformers popped up and called everyone to account. They pointed people back to the way of Christ. Enough ordinary believers heeded that call to redouble the Christian effort to preach in new lands, establish charities, build hospitals, and educate the masses. Our world has been demonstrably transformed by it.

Jesus Christ wrote a beautiful composition. Christians have not performed it consistently well. Sometimes they were badly out of tune. But the problem with a hateful Christian is not their Christianity but their departure from it. Albert Einstein put this well when he was asked in 1915 for his opinion of the Great War. He wrote three pages of subtle critique of nationalism, and then ended with the words: "Yet, why so many words, when I can say it all in a single sentence, and indeed in a sentence that is most apt for me as a Jew: Honour your master, Jesus Christ, not only with words and songs but, rather, foremost through your deeds."[1] The antidote to hateful, nationalistic, violent Christianity, Einstein proposed, is *Christianity in practice*. His rationale is the rationale at the heart of this book. Christ's melody remains beautiful—dare I say unique. And when Christians perform it, they leave an indelible mark on the world.

Not for a moment would I suggest that someone needs to believe in Christ in order to pursue the ethics of Christ. In the previous chapter I discussed the work of Andrew Leigh. He is open about his atheism and equally happy to acknowledge that *ethically* he is Christian. "I was married in a church, but am now an atheist," he says. "Yet while I do not believe in God, my values are deeply rooted in the Christian traditions. I find it difficult to think of altruism without reflecting on the Good Samaritan, or reciprocity without the motto 'Do unto others.'"[2] Naturally, I think the Good Samaritan and "Do unto others" make more sense if you believe that the Creator himself is like that. But I can see why an atheist might reject the God part and still find the ethics beautiful.

This seems to be a happy trend among the best secular intellectuals. They have moved past the zero-sum game, the need to deny any good in Christianity. One very recent example—perhaps one still in process—is the well-known British historian, Tom Holland. He is the author of numerous bestselling books on Rome, Persia, and the rise of Islam. It dawned on him a few years ago that the humanitarian ethic he has embraced for most of his adult life cannot have come from Greece or Rome and was certainly present in western culture centuries before the Renaissance or the Enlightenment. The ideas of *love* and *equality* for all, he came to believe, can only have come from "Jerusalem"—that is, from the Jewish-Christian culture that burst westward after Jesus Christ. Holland gave full voice to this discovery in his 2019 book *Dominion: The Making of the Western Mind*. It is, in fact, a far more flattering history of Christianity than the one I have offered.[3] Holland has not had a "Damascus Road" experience. He is not a believing Christian. He has just come to realise that he—like many atheist and agnostic westerners—is *ethically Christian*. In a controversial article announcing his shift in thinking, he explained:

> Today, even as belief in God fades across the West, the countries that were once collectively known as Christendom continue to bear the stamp of the two-millennia-old revolution that Christianity represents. It is the principal reason why, by and large, most of us who live in post-Christian societies still take for granted that it is nobler to suffer than to inflict suffering. It is why we generally assume that every human life is of equal value. In my morals and ethics, I have learned to accept that I am not Greek or Roman at all, but thoroughly and proudly Christian.[4]

Holland is by no means the only "unbeliever" who credits Christianity with the west's notion of intrinsic human value; Raimond Gaita and Samuel Moyn are two others mentioned earlier in the book. I dare say that outside the narrow circles of *evangelistic atheism* it is commonplace to acknowledge this point.

In *A Brief History of Thought*, the atheist professor of philosophy at the Sorbonne and former French Minister for Education, Luc Ferry, laments that when he went to university in France in the 1960s, "it was possible to pass our exams and even become a philosophy professor by knowing next to nothing about Judaism, Islam or Christianity." That now strikes him as "absurd," he says. Ferry is adamant that "Christianity was to introduce the notion that humanity was fundamentally identical, that men were equal in dignity—an unprecedented idea at the time, and one to which our world owes its entire democratic inheritance." Perhaps most surprisingly, given he is a proud Frenchman, Ferry believes that "the French Revolution—and to some extent, the 1789 Declaration of the Rights of Man—[but *not* the Terror] owes to Christianity an essential part of its egalitarian message."[5] I blush. But as history, it seems right.

Violence has been a universal part of the human story. The demand to *love one's enemies* has not. Division has been a norm. Inherent human dignity has not. Armies, greed, and the politics of power have been constants in history. Hospitals, schools, and charity for all have not. Bullies are common. Saints are not.

Notes

Better off without Religion—A Prelude

1. Kully Kaur-Ballagan et al., "Global Study Shows Half Think That Religion Does More Harm Than Good," Ipsos, October 2017, https://www.ipsos.com/en/global-study-shows-half -think-religion-does-more-harm-good.
2. "Veracity Index 2015—All Professions Overview," Ipsos, https://www.ipsos.com/sites /default/files/migrations/en-uk/files/Assets/Docs/Polls/ipsos-mori-veracity-index-2015 -charts.pdf.
3. Sarah Kimmorley, "Ranked: Australia's 20 Most Trusted Professions," Business Insider Australia, May 2015, https://www.businessinsider.com.au/ranked-australias-20-most -trusted-professions-2015-5.
4. "Scores of Priests Involved in Sex Abuse Cases," *Boston Globe*, May 2012, https://www .bostonglobe.com/news/special-reports/2002/01/31/scores-priests-involved-sex-abuse-cases /kmRm7JtqBdEZ8UF0ucR16L/story.html.
5. Christopher Hitchens, *God Is Not Great: How Religion Poisons Everything* (New York: Twelve, 2007), 6, 13.
6. https://www.publicchristianity.org/fortheloveofgod/.

Chapter 1: The Day I Lost Faith in the Church

1. Christopher Tyerman, *God's War: A New History of the Crusades* (London: Penguin, 2007), 157.
2. Letter of Raymond of Aguilers, in *The Crusades: A Reader*, ed. S. J. Allen (Toronto: University of Toronto Press, 2010), 73–78.
3. Christopher Tyerman, *The Crusades: A Very Short Introduction* (Oxford: Oxford University Press, 2005), 2–3.
4. Letter of Raymond of Aguilers, *The Crusades: A Reader*, 73–78.
5. Cited in Tyerman, *God's War*, 67.
6. Cited in Tyerman, *God's War*, 67.

Chapter 2: The Crusades in a Nutshell

1. Tyerman, *God's War*, 79.
2. On the Jewish pogroms, what has been called "the first Holocaust," see Jonathan Riley-Smith, *A History of the Crusades*, 2nd ed. (New Haven: Yale University Press, 2005), 23–25; Tyerman, *God's War*, 55–59.
3. Tyerman, *God's War*, 80.

4. Tyerman, *God's War*, 156.

5. Letter of the year 1100 from Karaite elders of Ascalon (modern-day Ashkelon on the coast of Israel), in S. D. Goitein, "Contemporary Letters on the Capture of Jerusalem by the Crusaders," *Journal of Jewish Studies* 3 (1952). The English translation of the letter appears on pages 171–75. For a discussion of other evidence from the Jewish side of the conflict, see S. D. Goitein, "Geniza Sources for the Crusader Period: A Survey," in *Outremer: Studies in the History of the Crusading Kingdom of Jerusalem*, ed. B. Z. Kedar et al. (Izhak Ben-Zvi Institute, 1982).

6. For a detailed account of the First Crusade and the Outremer kingdoms, see Tyerman, *God's War*, 27–240.

7. Letter of Bernard of Clairvaux, in Allen, *The Crusades: A Reader*, 134–38.

8. For a detailed account of the Second Crusade see Tyerman, *God's War*, 243–338.

9. Imad Ad-Din on the Battle of Hattin, in Allen, *Crusades: A Reader*, 157–58.

10. Cited in Tyerman, *God's War*, 372.

11. Letter of Saladin to the Imam Nassir Del-din-illa Aboul Abbas Ahmed, in Allen, *Crusades: A Reader*, 162–63.

12. For a detailed account of the Third Crusade, see Tyerman, *God's War*, 341–474.

13. For a detailed account of the Fourth Crusade, see Tyerman, *God's War*, 477–560.

14. For an analysis of the event and the sources, see J. M. Powell, "St. Francis of Assisi's Way of Peace," *Medieval Encounters* 13 (2007): 271–80. For a biography of Francis, see Augustine Thompson, *Francis of Assisi: A New Biography* (Ithaca, NY: Cornell University Press, 2012).

15. For a detailed account of the Fifth Crusade, see Tyerman, *God's War*, 606–49.

16. Tyerman, *God's War*, 732–35.

17. For a detailed account of the Albigensian Crusade, see Tyerman, *God's War*, 565–605.

18. The *New York Times* from March 13, 2000, has helpfully excerpted translations of Pope John Paul II's remarkable Homily, https://archive.nytimes.com/www.nytimes.com/library/world/global/031300pope-apology-text.html.

19. Tyerman, *God's War*, 638–39.

20. Tyerman, *God's War*, 902–3.

21. On Luther's views of the Crusades and warfare generally, see Martin Luther, "An Argument in Defence of All the Articles of Dr. Martin Luther Wrongly Condemned in the Roman Bull: The Thirty-Fourth Article," in *Works of Martin Luther*, trans. C. M. Jacobs (Philadelphia: Holman, 1930), 3:105–6. See also Thomas F. Madden, *A New Concise History of the Crusades* (Lanhan, MD: Rowman & Littlefield, 2006), 210; and Kenneth M. Setton, "Lutheranism and the Turkish Peril," *Balkan Studies* 3 (1962): 133–68.

22. For a discussion of Luther's theory and how it played out in the centuries that followed, see John R. Stephenson, "The Two Governments and the Two Kingdoms in Luther's Thought," *Scottish Journal of Theology* 34 (1981).

23. Tyerman, *God's War*, 916.

24. Adam Rasgon, "In Jerusalem, Ramadan Restrictions Last Seen During the Crusades Return," *New York Times*, 15 May 2020, https://www.nytimes.com/2020/05/15/world/middleeast/ramadan-coronavirus-al-aqsa.html.

25. Riley-Smith, *A History of the Crusades*, 306.

26. Cited by Riley-Smith, *A History of the Crusades*, 305.

27. Riley-Smith, *A History of the Crusades*, 305.

28. Tyerman, *The Crusades*, 55.

29. "Was Obama Right about the Crusades and Islamic Extremism?" *Washington Post*, 6 February 2015, https://www.washingtonpost.com/national/religion/was-obama-right-about-the-crusades-and-islamic-extremism-analysis/2015/02/06/3670628a-ae46–11e4–8876

–460b1144cbc1_story.html. And "Critics Seize on Obama's ISIS Remarks at Prayer Breakfast," *New York Times*, 5 February 2015, https://www.nytimes.com/2015/02/06/us /politics/obama-national-prayer-breakfast-terrorism-islam.html.

Chapter 3: The Beautiful Tune

1. https://www.publicchristianity.org/how-to-judge-the-church/.
2. Interview with Einstein, *Saturday Evening Post*, October 26, 1929, 117.
3. I offer a brief account of the sources and methods for studying Jesus in *The Christ Files: How Historians Know What They Know about Jesus* (Grand Rapids: Zondervan, 2010). For a slightly longer assessment of *what we know* of the life of Jesus, see my *A Doubter's Guide to Jesus: An Introduction to the Man from Nazareth for Believers and Skeptics Alike* (Grand Rapids: Zondervan, 2018).
4. Richard Dawkins, *The God Delusion* (London: Transworld, 2016), 283.
5. An important work on the sources and themes of popular morality in the Roman period is Teresa Morgan, *Popular Morality in the Early Roman Empire* (Cambridge: Cambridge University Press, 2007).
6. See my *Humilitas: Lost Key to Life, Love, and Leadership* (Grand Rapids: Zondervan, 2011). On humility in the Greco-Roman world in contrast to the rise of the virtue in early Christian texts, see chapters 5–6.
7. Mishnah Avot 1:12, in Jacob Neusner, *The Mishnah: A New Translation* (New Haven: Yale University Press, 1988), 674.
8. Babylonian Talmud, Shabbat 31a, trans. Philip S. Alexander, "Jesus and the Golden Rule," in *Hillel and Jesus: Comparative Studies of Two Major Religious Leaders*, ed. James H. Charlesworth and Loren L. Johns (Philadelphia: Fortress, 1997), 363–88.
9. David Flusser, *Jesus the Sage from Galilee: Rediscovering Jesus' Genius* (Grand Rapids: Eerdmans, 2007), 65.
10. Flusser, *Jesus the Sage*, 61.
11. The "Original Rough Draft" of the Declaration of Independence can be read on the Library of Congress website, https://www.loc.gov/exhibits/declara/ruffdrft.html.
12. The UN Universal Declaration of Human Rights is online at https://www.un.org/en/universal -declaration-human-rights/.
13. Samuel Moyn, *Christian Human Rights (Intellectual History of the Modern Age)* (Philadelphia: University of Pennsylvania Press, 2015). I should stress that Moyn's thesis is not a laudatory account of the way Christianity saved the day and gave us human rights. He argues that conservative Catholics and Protestants in Europe in the pre-war period were employing "rights" language to impose a conservative moral and family agenda on Europe and elsewhere. In the *For the Love of God* documentary, he says that Jesus and the Church probably *did* advance the notion of human equality in western history but also that the church was often a roadblock to the implementation of that idea.
14. "Rights and Wrongs," Episode 2, *For the Love of God: How the Church is Better and Worse Than You Ever Imagined*, Centre for Public Christianity, 2018, https://www.publicchristianity .org/episode-2-rights-wrongs/.
15. Also from "Rights and Wrongs."
16. There have been various attempts in church history to distinguish between the words "image" (*tselem*) and "likeness" (*demut*) in Gen 1:26. Biblical scholarship today is in broad agreement that there is no significant distinction between the terms. See Ferguson, "Image of God," in *New Dictionary of Theology* (Downers Grove, IL: InterVarsity, 1988), 328.
17. Gordon J. Wenham, *Genesis 1–15*. Word Biblical Commentary, 1 (Waco, TX: Word, 1987), 33.

18. Wolfhart Pannenberg, *Systematic Theology* (Grand Rapids: Eerdmans, 1994), 2:203; Ferguson, "Image of God," 329; Wenham, *Genesis 1–15*, 30–31.

19. Jonathan Sacks, *Morality: Restoring the Common Good in Divided Times* (London: Hodder & Stoughton, 2020), 119–20.

20. Luke 3:38 calls Adam, the first human being, a "son of God." Paul describes humanity as a whole as God's "offspring" in Acts 17:28–29. While "offspring" is an appropriate term for humanity's creaturely relation to God, "son/daughter" are the more apt terms for *redeemed* humanity, especially since they carry the notion of future inheritance. See Rom 8:14–17.

21. Genesis 9 assumes that humanity has retained the *imago Dei*, even after the fall of Gen 3. See Ferguson, "Image of God," 328–29. See also Henri Blocher, *In the Beginning: The Opening Chapters of Genesis* (Downers Grove, IL: InterVarsity Press, 1984), 94.

22. *Letter of Hilarion, Oxyrhynchus Papyri* (ed. B. P. Grenfell and A. S. Hunt). 4:744. Readers can view the letter itself online, together with the above translation and some discussion, http://www.papyri.info/apis/toronto.apis.17/.

23. J. R. Sallares, "Infanticide," *Oxford Classical Dictionary*, 757; Josef Wisehöfer, "Child Exposure," *Brill's New Pauly*, ed. Hubert Cancik et al. (2006), doi: e613990, https://referenceworks.brillonline .com/browse/brill-s-new-pauly.

24. Aristotle, *Politics* 7.14.10 (Rackham, Loeb Classical Library 264), 623. Aristotle adds that having too many children might also be a good reason to discard a child.

25. Philo of Alexandria (25 BC–AD 50), *Special Laws*, 3.9–11, laments that "many nations" regard the practice of infant-exposure as "commonplace."

26. Tertullian (AD 160–225) spoke out against the practice: *Apology* 9; *To the Nations* 1.15. The ministry of the church in collecting foundlings and raising them as their own is detailed by Gerhard Uhlhorn, *Christian Charity in the Ancient Church* (1888; repr., Eugene, OR: Wipf & Stock, 2009), 385–87.

27. For an excellent introduction to this ancient Greek philosophical way of thinking, see Luc Ferry's *A Brief History of Thought: A Philosophical Guide to Living* (Edinburgh: Canongate, 2010), 55–92.

28. Killing an infant became a form of homicide in the law of the Christian emperor Valentinian I in AD 374: *Theodosian Code*, 9.14.1., also ratified in the later *Codex of Justinian*, 8.51.2. See Judith Evans Grubbs, "Church, State, and Children: Christian and Imperial Attitudes Toward Infant Exposure in Late Antiquity," in *The Power of Religion in Late Antiquity*, ed. Andrew Cain and Noel Lenski (London: Routledge, 2009), 119–31.

29. Raimond Gaita, *Thinking about Love and Truth and Justice* (London: Routledge, 2002), 23–24.

Chapter 4: Log in the Eye of the Church

1. D. A. Carson, *Jesus' Sermon on the Mount and His Confrontation with the World* (Toronto: Global Christian, 2001), 18.

2. Francis Spufford, *Unapologetic: Why, Despite Everything, Christianity Can Still Make Surprising Emotional Sense* (London: Faber & Faber), 27.

3. Spufford, *Unapologetic*, 35–36.

4. Spufford, *Unapologetic*, 43.

5. John P. Meier, *A Marginal Jew: Rethinking the Historical Jesus* (New York: Doubleday, 1991), 1:278–85.

6. Spufford, *Unapologetic*, 47.

Chapter 5: Good Losers

1. Judith Ireland, "Religious Discrimination Bill Gives Australians 'Right to Be a Bigot,'" Sydney Morning Herald, January 2020, https://www.smh.com.au/politics/federal/religious-discrimination -bill-gives-australians-right-to-be-a-bigot-20200129-p53vq4.html.

2. "Persecution of Christians Review: Foreign Secretary's Speech Following the Final Report," Gov.Uk, July 2019, https://www.gov.uk/government/speeches/persecution-of-christians-review-foreign-secretarys-speech-following-the-final-report.

3. Wang Yi, "My Declaration of Faithful Disobedience," December 2018, https://www.china partnership.org/blog/2018/12/my-declaration-of-faithful-disobedience/.

4. See Eckhard Schnabel, *Early Christian Mission, Vol. 2: Paul and the Early Church* (Downers Grove, IL: IVP Academic, 2004); James D. G. Dunn, *Beginning from Jerusalem: Christianity in the Making, Vol. 2* (Grand Rapids: Eerdmans, 2008).

5. John P. Dickson, *Mission-Commitment in Ancient Judaism and in the Pauline Communities: The Shape, Extent and Background of Early Christian Mission*, Wissenschaftliche Untersuchungen zum Neuen Testament 2/159 (Tübingen: Mohr Siebeck, 2003). See also W. V. Harris, ed., *The Spread of Christianity in the First Four Centuries: Essays in Explanation* (Leiden: Brill, 2005); Larry Hurtado, *Destroyer of the Gods: Early Christian Distinctiveness in the Roman World* (Waco, TX: Baylor University Press, 2016). Hurtado helpfully outlines what many in the Roman world saw as distinct—negative and positive—in the Christian faith.

6. Claudius (AD 41–54) banished Jewish leaders from Rome in AD 49 because they "constantly made disturbances at the instigation of Chrestus" (Suetonius, *Claudius* 25.4). "Chrestus" is an understandable Latin misspelling of "Christ." On the origins of Christianity in Rome, see Peter Lampe, *From Paul to Valentinus: Christians at Rome in the First Two Centuries* (Philadelphia: Fortress, 2003), 11–16.

7. Candida Moss, *The Myth of Persecution: How Early Christians Invented a Story of Martyrdom* (New York: HarperCollins, 2013).

8. For a critical review, see N. Clayton Croy, review of Candida Moss, *The Myth of Persecution: How Early Christians Invented a Story of Martyrdom, Review of Biblical Literature* (10/13/2013), https://www.sblcentral.org/home/bookDetails/9158.

9. Tacitus, *Annals* 15.44 (Jackson, Loeb Classical Library 322).

10. On the dating of the New Testament documents, the earliest being from AD 50, the latest from around AD 90, see my *Is Jesus History?* (London: The Good Book Company, 2019).

11. My reflections on the incident, while wandering around the Circus of Nero, were caught on film in "War and Peace," Episode 1, *For the Love of God*, https://www.publicchristianity.org /episode-1-war-peace/.

12. For an excellent account of Pliny and his situation in Bithynia-Pontus see Robert Louis Wilken, *The Christians as the Romans Saw Them* (New Haven: Yale University Press, 2003), 1–30.

13. Pliny, *Letters* 10.96 (Radice, Loeb Classical Library 59), 285–91.

14. Wilken, *The Christians as the Romans Saw Them*, 15.

15. In the New Testament there is a three-chapter discussion of the problem of tainted meat. See 1 Cor 8–10.

16. Tertullian (AD 160–225) reports that pagans were complaining in his region (Carthage) that revenues were down in the temples on account of so many people becoming Christians: Tertullian, *Apology*, 42.

17. Pliny, *Letters* 10.96 (Radice, Loeb Classical Library 59), 285–91.

18. Pliny, *Letters* 10.96 (Radice, Loeb Classical Library 59), 285–91.

19. Pliny, *Letters* 10.96 (Radice, Loeb Classical Library 59), 285–91.

20. Pliny, *Letters* 10.96 (Radice, Loeb Classical Library 59), 285–91.

21. Pliny, *Letters* 10.96 (Radice, Loeb Classical Library 59), 285–91.

22. Pliny, *Letters* 10.97 (Radice, Loeb Classical Library 59), 291–93.

23. Wilken, *The Christians as the Romans Saw Them*, 29–30.

24. "Roman Gentleman" is the title of Wilken's chapter on Pliny in *The Christians as the Romans Saw Them*.

25. For an introduction to Ignatius and his letters, as well as the texts themselves with English translation, see Michael Holmes, *The Apostolic Fathers: Greek Texts and English Translations* (Grand Rapids: Baker Academic, 2007), 166–271.

26. A point noted by William R. Schoedel in this commentary on the seven letters, *Ignatius of Antioch* (Philadelphia: Fortress, 1985), 24.

27. Ignatius, *Ephesians*, 10.1–3 (Holmes, *Apostolic Fathers*, 191–92).

28. Tertullian mentions (*To Scapula*, 5, in S. Thelwall, *The Ante-Nicene Fathers, Vol. 3: Latin Christianity* [New York: Cosimo Classics, 2007], 105–8) an earlier non-violent peaceful protest of Christians, when Arrius Antoninus governed the province of Asia (Turkey) about thirty years earlier.

29. Tertullian, *To Scapula*, 5 (Thelwall, *The Ante-Nicene Fathers*).

30. Tertullian, *To Scapula*, 1–2 (Thelwall, *The Ante-Nicene Fathers*).

31. See "Decius," *Oxford Dictionary of the Christian Church*, 460.

32. Tertullian makes this very point to Scapula (Tertullian, *To Scapula*, 5).

33. For much of my discussion of Porphyry, I am following Wilken, *The Christians as the Romans Saw Them*, 126–63. See also his, "Pagan Criticism of Christianity: Greek Religion and Christian Faith," in *Early Christian Literature and the Classical Intellectual Tradition*, ed. W. R. Schoedel and R. L. Wilken (Paris: Editions Beauchesne, 1979), 117–34. Also, Elizabeth dePalma Digeser, "Lactantius, Porphyry, and the Debate over Religious Toleration," *Journal of Roman Studies* 88 (1998): 129–46.

34. These citations from Porphyry's *Philosophy from Oracles* are known to us through the quotations and rebuttal of Augustine, *The City of God* 1919.23. Translation by William Babcock, *Augustine, Saint. The City of God: Books 11–22* (I/7), The Works of Saint Augustine: A Translation for the 21st Century (Hyde Park, NY: New City, 2013). See also Digeser, "Lactantius," 135.

35. Digeser, "Lactantius," 145; Wilken, "Pagan Criticism of Christianity," 130–31.

36. For a discussion of this and other passages from Porphyry, see Digeser, "Lactantius," 129–46.

37. On the combined arguments of Porphyry and Hierocles, see Digeser, "Lactantius," 129–46.

38. Acts of Munatius Felix, in *Proceedings before Zenophilus*, trans. Mark Edwards in *Optatus: Against the Donatists*, Translated Texts for Historians 27 (Liverpool: Liverpool University Press, 1997), 153–56.

39. Raymond Peter Davis, "Diocletian," *Oxford Classical Dictionary*, 471–72. See also "Early Christian Persecutions," *Oxford Dictionary of the Christian Church*, 1257–59.

40. On the question of whether Lactantius is deliberately responding to Porphyry, see Digeser, "Lactantius," 129–46.

41. Lactantius, *Divine Institutes* 6.10.1–8, in *Lactantius, Divine Institutes*, Translated Texts for Historians 40, trans. Anthony Bowen and Peter Garnsey (Liverpool: Liverpool University Press, 2003), 349–50.

42. Lactantius, *Divine Institutes* 6.18.9–11 (Bowen and Garnsey, *Lactantius, Divine Institutes*).

Chapter 6: Constantine and Religious Liberty

1. David Von Drehle, "The Church Is Tempted by Power and Obsessed with Sex," *The Washington Post*, August 18, 2018, https://www.washingtonpost.com/opinions/the-church-is-tempted-by-power-and-obsessed-with-sex/2018/08/17/14467d3c-a24b-11e8-8e87-c869fe70a721_story.html.

2. Eusebius, *Life of Constantine* 33.

3. Eusebius, *Life of Constantine* 1.29 (E. C. Richardson, *The Nicene and Post-Nicene Fathers¹* [Massachusetts: Hendrickson, 2004]).

4. Lactantius, *On the Death of the Persecutors* 44, in *Lactantius, The Minor Works. The Fathers of the Church*, trans. Mary Francis McDonald (Washington, DC: The Catholic University of America Press, 1965), 54:197–98.

5. Eusebius, *Life of Constantine* 1.28 (Richardson, *The Nicene and Post-Nicene Fathers¹*).

6. A. H. M. Jones, *Constantine and the Conversion of Europe* (Toronto: University of Toronto Press, 2003), 85–86.
7. Eusebius, *Life of Constantine* 1.30–31 (Richardson, *The Nicene and Post-Nicene Fathers¹*).
8. Eusebius, *Life of Constantine* 4.47 (Richardson, *The Nicene and Post-Nicene Fathers¹*).
9. The Edict of Milan is preserved in Lactantius, *The Death of the Persecutors* 48 (McDonald, *Lactantius, The Minor Works*). Another version of the edict is found in Eusebius, *Ecclesiastical History* 10.5. On the details of the edict, its sources, meaning, and significance, see Milton Anastos, "The Edict of Milan (313): A Defence of its Traditional Authorship and Designation," *Revue des études byzantines* 25 (1967): 13–41.
10. Tertullian, *To Scapula*, 2 (Thelwall, *The Ante-Nicene Fathers*).
11. Robert Louis Wilken argues the case that Lactantius was a direct influence on the Edict of Milan. Wilken, *Liberty in the Things of God: The Christian Origins of Religious Freedom* (New Haven: Yale University Press, 2019), 22–23.
12. Lactantius, *Divine Institutes* 5.19.6–30 (Bowen and Garnsey, *Lactantius, Divine Institutes*).
13. Digeser, "Lactantius," 129–46.
14. See the excellent discussion of Lactantius's theological rationale for religious freedom in Bowen and Garnsey, *Lactantius, Divine Institutes* 46–48.
15. Libanius, *Oration to Emperor Theodosius* 30.29 (Norman, Loeb Classical Library 452, p. 127).
16. Jones, *Constantine and the Conversion of Europe*, 83–87.
17. *Theodosian Code* 9.16.3, in *The Theodosian Code: A Translation with Commentary, Glossary, and Bibliography*, trans. Clyde Phar (New Jersey: Lawbook Exchange, 2012). Constantine's position amounts to a legal hardening of a traditional Roman—not simply Christian—view. See H. S. Versnel, "Magic," *Oxford Classical Dictionary*, 908–10.
18. The specific law is found in the *Theodosian Code* 16.2.5. For the details of Constantine's laws concerning pagan religion, see John Curran, "The Legal Standing of the Ancient Cults in Rome," in *Pagan City and Christian Capital* (Oxford: Oxford University Press, 2000), 161–217.
19. Eusebius does say the emperor promulgated laws "intended to restrain the idolatrous abominations." Eusebius, *Life of Constantine* 2.44 (Richardson, *The Nicene and Post-Nicene Fathers¹*). For the argument that Constantine banned paganism and (in effect) made Christianity the official religion of the empire, see Timothy D. Barnes, *Constantine and Eusebius* (Cambridge: Harvard University Press, 1981), 210. However, see the review of Barnes on this point by H. A. Drake in the *American Journal of Philology*, 103:4 (1982): 462–66.
20. Eusebius, *Life of Constantine* 2.56–60 (Richardson, *The Nicene and Post-Nicene Fathers¹*). For a careful discussion see John Curran's "The Legal Standing of the Ancient Cults in Rome," 176–78.
21. On the brief persecutions ordered by Licinius, see Jones, *Constantine and the Conversion of Europe*, 110–12.
22. "First Amendment," https://constitution.congress.gov/constitution/amendment-1/.
23. The Jefferson memorial and archive of Monticello website tries to explain the influences behind his views on religious freedom in terms of the Enlightenment and the Baptists of Buckingham County, https://www.monticello.org/site/research-and-collections/thomas-jefferson-and-religious-freedom.
24. Tertullian, *To Scapula*, 2 (Thelwall, *The Ante-Nicene Fathers*).
25. Wilken, *Liberty in the Things of God*, 190.
26. Raymond Peter Davis, "Constantine I," *Oxford Classical Dictionary*, 379.

Chapter 7: Constantine and the Birth of Charity

1. Eusebius, *Ecclesiastical History* 10.5.10–11 (Oulton, Loeb Classical Library 252). A similar order for north Africa is found in 10.5.17.

2. Eusebius, *Ecclesiastical History* 10.5.11. See also Anastos, "The Edict of Milan," 37.

3. Jerusalem had fallen into disrepair and dishonour ever since Emperor Hadrian (AD 117–138) had crushed a second major Jewish revolt in AD 135 and renamed the Holy City Aelia Capitolina ("Aelia" refers to Hadrian's family name; "Capitolina" refers to the god Jupiter to whom Hadrian built a temple in the city).

4. Dan Bahat, "Does the Holy Sepulchre Church Mark the Burial of Jesus?" in *Archaeology in the World of Herod, Jesus, and Paul*, ed. H. Shanks and D. P. Cole (Washington, DC: Biblical Archaeology Society, 1990), 260. The three-volume archaeological report on the Sepulchre (in Italian): V. Corbo, *Il Santo Sepolcro di Gerusalemme: Aspetti archeologici dale origini al period crociato*, 3 vols., Studium Biblicum Franciscanum 29 (Jerusalem: Franciscan Printing Press, 1981–82).

5. Michael H. Crawford, "Population, Roman," *Oxford Classical Dictionary*, 1223; H. A. Drake, "Models of Christian Expansion," in *The Spread of Christianity in the First Four Centuries: Essays in Explanation*, ed. W. V. Harris, Columbia Studios in the Classical Tradition 27 (Leiden: Brill, 2005); Rodney Stark, *The Rise of Christianity* (New York: HarperCollins, 1997), 3–27.

6. *Theodosian Code* 1.27.1. Also, Timothy D. Barnes, *Constantine: Dynasty, Religion and Power in the Later Roman Empire*, Blackwell Ancient Lives (Oxford: Blackwell, 2014), 134.

7. Edwin A. Judge, "The Early Christians as a Scholastic Community" in *The First Christians in the Roman World: Augustan and New Testament Essays*, ed. James R. Harrison, Wissenschaftliche Untersuchungen zum Neuen Testament 229 (Tübigen: Mohr Siebeck, 2008), 526–52. In the same volume, see Judge's "Did the Churches Compete with Cult-Groups?" 597–618.

8. Constantine's letter is preserved in Eusebius, *Life of Constantine* 4.36. On the selection of the four New Testament Gospels, see Martin Hengel, *The Four Gospels and the One Gospel of Jesus Christ* (Norcross, GA: Trinity International, 2000). On the broader question of the development of the canon, see Bruce M. Metzger, *The Canon of the New Testament: Its Origin, Development and Significance* (Oxford: Oxford University Press, 1997).

9. John Dickson, "Old Papers," https://undeceptions.com/podcast/old-papers.

10. Eusebius, *Life of Constantine* 2.56 (Richardson, *The Nicene and Post-Nicene Fathers¹*).

11. Dan Brown, *The Da Vinci Code* (London: Transworld, 2003).

12. E.g., Phil 2:10–11 takes the statement about God in Isa 45:23 and applies it to Jesus.

13. Col 1:15–20.

14. John 1:1.

15. See "Arius," *Oxford Dictionary of the Christian Church*, 104.

16. Fifty years later, the great biblical scholar St. Jerome wrote, "the whole world groaned, and was astonished to find itself Arian," Jerome, *Dialogue Against the Luciferians* 19, in *The Nicene and Post-Nicene Fathers²*, trans. Henry Wallace. (New York: Cosimo, 2007), 6:329. See "Arianism" *Oxford Dictionary of the Christian Church*, 99–100.

17. "Constantine's main interest," the *Oxford Dictionary of the Christian Church* explains, "was to secure unity rather than any predetermined theological verdict." See "Nicaea, First Council of (325)," *Oxford Dictionary of the Christian Church*, 1144; Barnes, *Constantine and Eusebius*, 225.

18. The original sources are *Theodosian Code* 2.8.1; Eusebius, *The Oration of Constantine* 9.10; Eusebius, *Life of Constantine* 4.18. There is debate about how far the ban on work went and how much Constantine was influenced by his Christianity in shaping this law.

19. Sozomen, *Ecclesiastical History* 1.8.13.

20. *Theodosian Code* 9.40.2 (Phar, *The Theodosian Code*).

21. *Theodosian Code* 15.12.1 (Phar, *The Theodosian Code*).

22. On the rise and significance of monasteries and monks, see Peter R. L. Brown, *The World of Late Antiquity* (New York: Norton, 1971), 96–112.

23. Theodoret, *Ecclesiastical History* 5.26, in *The Nicene and Post-Nicene Fathers²*, trans. Blomfield Jackson, (New York: Cosimo, 2007).

24. Edward Gibbon, *History of the Decline and Fall of the Roman Empire* (New York: Random House, 1995), Modern Library eBook Edition, chapter 30, location 22844.

25. On the question of family law in this period see Geoffrey Nathan, *The Family in Late Antiquity: The Rise of Christianity and the Endurance of Tradition* (London: Routledge, 2000).

26. *Theodosian Code* 8.16.1 (Phar, *The Theodosian Code*). See further, Barnes, *Constantine*, 136–37.

27. *Theodosian Code* 3.16.1 (Phar, *The Theodosian Code*). See further, Barnes, *Constantine*, 137–38.

28. *Theodosian Code* 11.27.1–2 (Phar, *The Theodosian Code*).

29. See Nathan, *The Family in Late Antiquity*, 66. Eusebius, *Life of Constantine* 4.28.

30. Eusebius, *Life of Constantine* 4.27 (Richardson, *The Nicene and Post-Nicene Fathers¹*). See also *Theodosian Code* 16.9.1–2.

31. *Theodosian Code* 16.2.4 (Phar, *The Theodosian Code*).

32. Eusebius, *Ecclesiastical History* 10.7.2 (Oulton, Loeb Classical Library 265).

33. For more, see Peter Brown, *Through the Eye of a Needle: Wealth, the Fall of Rome, and the Making of Christianity in the West, 350–550 AD* (Princeton: Princeton University Press, 2012), 31–52; also T. G. Elliott, "The Tax Exemptions Granted to Clerics by Constantine and Constantius II," *Phoenix* 32.4 (1978): 326–36.

34. For example, *Theodosian Code* 16.2.3.

35. *Theodosian Code* 16.2.3 (Phar, *The Theodosian Code*).

36. *Theodosian Code* 16.2.17 (Phar, *The Theodosian Code*).

37. Brown, *Eye of a Needle*, 44.

38. *Theodosian Code* 16.2.6 (Phar, *The Theodosian Code*).

39. Christian leaders, such as Augustine (AD 354–430), even noted how some pagan individuals put Christians to shame in their care for the poor. See Brown, *Eye of a Needle*, 61.

40. For the Greek text and translation of the *Delphic Canon,* see Edwin A. Judge, "Ancient Beginnings of the Modern World," in *Ancient History in a Modern University*, ed. T. W. Hillard et al. (Grand Rapids: Eerdmans, 1998), 473–75.

41. Plotinus, *On Providence* 1.13 (Armstrong, Loeb Classical Library 442), 81–83.

42. Plato, *Laws* 11.936 b–c (Bury, Loeb Classical Library 192), 465.

43. Brown, *Eye of a Needle*, 70.

44. Brown, *Eye of a Needle*, 62. See also Arthur Robinson Hands, *Charities and Social Aid in Greece and Rome* (Ithaca, NY: Cornell University Press, 1968), 26–61.

45. An excellent example of Christian criticism of *euergetism* is found in Lactantius, *Divine Institutes* 6.11.13–19.

46. Morgan, *Popular Morality*.

47. Teresa Morgan with John Dickson, "Moral Classics," *Undeceptions*, season 1, episode 4, 23 September 2019, https://undeceptions.com/podcast/moral-classics.

48. For example, Deut 15:4–11; Isa 58:5–10.

49. Deut 24:19–21. On this text, see Christopher J. H. Wright, *Deuteronomy*, NIBC (Peabody, MA: Hendrickson, 1996), 261.

50. Julian, "To Arsacius, high-priest of Galatia," *Letter* 22.430C (Wright, Loeb Classical Library 157), 71. On the Jewish origins of Christian charity, see Brown, *Eye of a Needle*, 79–83.

51. The parable has occasionally been interpreted as an allegory about eternal life. However, the final line, "Go and do likewise," makes allegory a most unnatural reading of what plainly fits into Jesus's numerous instructions to assist the poor (see esp. Luke 11:41; 12:33; 14:21; 18:22; 19:8).

52. The famine itself is reported in biblical and non-biblical texts (Acts 11:27–28; Josephus,

Jewish Antiquities 20.101). Paul's poverty-relief program is known simply as the "collection" (1 Cor 16:1–4; 2 Cor 8–9; see also Rom 15:25–27).

53. Justin Martyr, *First Apology*, 67, trans. Alexander Roberts et al., in *The Ante-Nicene Fathers* (New York: Cosimo Classics, 2007), 1:186.

54. *Shepherd of Hermas* 50:7–9 (Holmes, *Apostolic Fathers*, 442–685).

55. Recorded in Eusebius, *Ecclesiastical History* 6.43.11 (Oulton, Loeb Classical Library 265), 119.

56. Brown, *Eye of a Needle*, 43.

57. Cyprian, *On Mortality*, 14, trans. Ernest Wallis in *The Ante-Nicene Fathers* (New York: Cosimo Classics, 2007), 5:472.

58. Kyle Harper, "Solving the Mystery of an Ancient Roman Plague," *The Atlantic*, 1 November 2017, https://www.theatlantic.com/science/archive/2017/11/solving-the-mystery-of-an-ancient-roman-plague/543528/.

59. Epistle of Dionysius, in Eusebius, *Ecclesiastical History* 7.22.10 (Oulton, Loeb Classical Library 265).

60. Epistle of Dionysius, in Eusebius, *Ecclesiastical History* 7.22.7–9 (Oulton, Loeb Classical Library 265). Archaic English adjusted in consultation with the Greek text.

61. Acts of Munatius Felix, in *Proceedings before Zenophilus*, in *Optatus: Against the Donatists*, trans. Mark Edwards, 154–55). Direct biblical warrant lay behind giving people clothes: Matt 25:36; Jas 2:14–16.

62. Brown, *Eye of a Needle*, 530.

63. Stephen Judd et al., *Driven by Purpose: Charities that Make a Difference* (Sydney: HammondCare Media, 2014), 55.

64. Jones, *Constantine and the Conversion of Europe*, 197–98.

Chapter 8: Julian the Apostate

1. Julian, "To Porphyrius," *Letter* 38.411c (Wright, Loeb Classical Library 157), 123.

2. Julian, "Hymn to the Mother of the Gods," *Oration* 5 (Wright, Loeb Classical Library 13), 436.

3. Rowland B. E. Smith, "Julian," *Oxford Classical Dictionary*, 800.

4. Julian, "To Atarbius," *Letter* 37.376c–d (Wright, Loeb Classical Library 157), 123.

5. Socrates Scholasticus, *Ecclesiastical History* 3.2–3, in *The Nicene and Post-Nicene Fathers²*, trans. A. C. Zenos (New York: Cosimo, 2007), 2:79.

6. Ammianus Marcellinus (AD 330–400), *History* 22.11.5–10 (Rolfe, Loeb Classical Library 315), 259–63.

7. Socrates Scholasticus, *Ecclesiastical History* 3.3 (Zenos, *The Nicene and Post-Nicene Fathers²*).

8. Ammanius Marcellinus, *History* 22.13.1–3 (Rolfe, Loeb Classical Library 315).

9. Julian, "To Hecebolius," *Letter* 40.424c (Wright, Loeb Classical Library 157), 127.

10. *Theodosian Code*, 13.3.5 (Phar, *The Theodosian Code*).

11. Julian, *Letter* 36.422b–424d (Wright, Loeb Classical Library 157), 117–23.

12. See the Introduction in the Loeb Classical Library edition of Julian's works (pages VII–LXIII).

13. "Armenia," *Oxford Dictionary of the Christian Church*, 106.

14. Julian, *Fragment of a Letter to a Priest* 305b–d (Wright, Loeb Classical Library 29), 337–39.

15. So also Wilmer Cave Wright, *The Works of the Emperor Julian, Vol. 2*, Loeb Classical Library 29 (Massachusetts: Harvard University Press, 1913) 295.

16. Julian, *Misopogon* ("Beard-hater") 363a (Wright, Loeb Classical Library 29), 491.

17. Julian, "To Arcacius, High-priest of Galatia," *Letter* 22.429c–431b (Wright, Loeb Classical Library 157), 67–73.

18. For the documentation and discussion see Wilken, "Christianity as a Burial Society," in *The Christians as the Romans Saw Them*, 31–47.

19. John Bodel, "From *Columbaria* to *Catacombs*: Collective Burial in Pagan and Christian Rome," in *Commemorating the Dead: Texts and Artifacts in Context. Studies of Roman, Jewish, and Christian Burials*, ed. Laurie Brink and Deborah Green (Berlin: de Gruyter, 2008), 177–242.

20. Lactantius, *Divine Institutes*, 6.12.25–31 (Bowen and Garnsey, *Lactantius, Divine Institutes*).

21. Julian, "To Arcacius, High-priest of Galatia," *Letter* 22.429C–431B (Wright, Loeb Classical Library 157), 67–73.

22. Theodoret, *Ecclesiastical History*, 3.20 (Jackson, *The Nicene and Post-Nicene Fathers²*).

23. R. S. O. Tomlin., "Valentinian I," *Oxford Classical Dictionary*, 1576.

Chapter 9: Muscular Christianity

1. Pliny, *Letters* 10.96.9 (Radice, Loeb Classical Library 59), emphasis added.

2. Minucius Felix, *Octavius* 8, trans. Robert Ernest Wallis in *The Ante-Nicene Fathers* (New York: Cosimo Classics, 2007), 4:177.

3. *Inscriptiones Christianae Urbis Rome Septimo Saeculo Antiquiores*, ed. A. Ferrua (Rome: Pontificio Istituto di Archeologia Cristiana, 1971), no. 13655, 5:133, in Brown, *Eye of a Needle*, 37.

4. Brown, *Eye of a Needle*, 45.

5. The canons of this council are translated and analysed in H. Hess, *The Early Development of Canon Law and the Council of Serdica* (Oxford: Oxford University Press, 2002), 221 (for this particular Canon 13).

6. Brown, *Eye of a Needle*, 87.

7. Brown, *Eye of a Needle*, 47–49.

8. On Ambrose and his impact, see Brown, *Eye of a Needle*, 120–47.

9. See *The Fathers of the Church* series published by the Catholic University of America from 2001–2020; also "Doctors of the Church" *Oxford Dictionary of the Christian Church*, 494. The number of official "doctors" has increased to about thirty, including Teresa of Avila, Catherine of Siena, and others.

10. Brown, *Eye of a Needle*, 123.

11. Translation by John Chandler in *Twenty-Four Hymns of the Western Church: The Latin Text, with a Verse Rendering of Each Hymn, a Brief Introduction, Commentary, and Appendices*, ed. Howard Henry Blakeney (London: Partridge, 1930), 6–7.

12. Ambrose, *Epistle* 74.10 in *Ambrose of Milan: Political Letters and Speeches*, ed. and trans. J. H. W. G. Liebeschuetz (Liverpool: University of Liverpool Press, 2005), 101.

13. Ambrose, *Epistle* 74.15 (Liebeschuetz, *Ambrose of Milan*).

14. Ambrose, *Epistle* 74.12 (Liebeschuetz, *Ambrose of Milan*).

15. The event is recounted in several sources, including Sozomen, *Ecclesiastical History*, 7.25. We also have Ambrose's own letter to the emperor, *Extra Collection, Epistle* 11.12–13 (Liebeschuetz, *Ambrose of Milan*, 267).

16. Brown, *Eye of a Needle*, 128.

17. Ambrose, *Epistle* 73.16 (Liebeschuetz, *Ambrose of Milan*, 86).

18. On this incident, see John Curran, "The Legal Standing of the Ancient Cults," 205–8.

19. Brown, *Eye of a Needle*, 45.

20. Brown, *Eye of a Needle*, 527–28.

21. Brown, *Eye of a Needle*, 122.

22. Ambrose, *Epistle* 73.24 (Liebeschuetz, *Ambrose of Milan*, 89).

Chapter 10: Cappadocian Christianity

1. Brown, *Eye of a Needle*, 46–47.

2. Basil of Caesarea, *Letter 197*, "To Ambrose, bishop of Milan," trans. Agnes Clare Way in

Saint Basil. Letters, Vol. 2 (186–368): The Fathers of the Church: A New Translation, 28 (Washington, DC: Catholic University of America Press, 1955), 42–45.

3. Gregory of Nazianzus, *Oration 14*, "On love for the Poor," trans. Martha Vinson in *St. Gregory of Nazianzus: Select Orations* (Washington, DC: Catholic University of America Press, 2017), 39–42.

4. For a full discussion, see Gary B. Ferngren, *Medicine and Health Care in Early Christianity* (Baltimore: Johns Hopkins University Press, 2009), 113–39.

5. Basil the Great, *Homily 6 on "I will pull down my barns" (Luke 12:18)*. The translation is mine based on the Greek text published in *Patrologia Graeca* 31, 277A, ed. Jacques-Paul Migne. 162 volumes, 1857–66.

6. Thomas Aquinas, *Summa Theologiae*, IIa–IIae.32.5. A similar thought is present in John Calvin, *Institutes of the Christian Religion*, Book 2, 8.45. It is a theme I explore in length in chapter 11 of my *Doubter's Guide to the Ten Commandments*.

7. Gregory of Nazianzus, "Funeral Oration on Basil the Great," trans. Leo P. McCauley et al., in *St. Gregory Nazianzen and Saint Ambrose: Funeral Orations. The Fathers of the Church: A New Translation*, 22 (Washington, DC: Catholic University of America Press, 1953), 80–81.

8. Ferngren, *Medicine and Health Care in Early Christianity*, 129. See also Timothy S. Miller, *The Birth of the Hospital in the Byzantine Empire* (Baltimore: Johns Hopkins University Press, 1997).

9. Jerome, "On the Death of Fabiola," *Letter* 77.6 (Wright, Loeb Classical Library 262), 323. Jerome's two letters to Fabiola are no. 64 and no. 78.

10. See James William Brodman, *Charity and Religion in Medieval Europe* (Washington, DC: Catholic University of America Press, 2009). Chapter 11 is titled "A Cascade of Hospitals" (45–88) and tells the story of the Italian, French, and German hospitals in the period AD 400–1000.

11. On the life of Macrina, see Lynn H. Cohick and Amy Brown Hughes, *Christian Women in the Patristic World: Their Influence, Authority, and Legacy in the Second through Fifth Centuries* (Grand Rapids: Baker Academic, 2017), 157–88. For a translation of Gregory's account of her life, see Anna M. Silvas, *Macrina the Younger: Philosopher of God* (Turnhout: Brepols, 2008), 109–48.

12. Gregory of Nyssa, *Life of Macrina*, 26.30. See Judith Evans Grubbs, "Church, State, and Children: Christian and Imperial Attitudes Toward Infant Exposure in Late Antiquity," in *The Power of Religion in Late Antiquity*, ed. Andrew Cain and Noel Lenski (New York: Routledge, 2009), 128–29.

13. *Life of Macrina*, 26.30 (Silvas, *Macrina the Younger*).

14. Cohick and Hughes, *Christian Women in the Patristic World*, 158.

15. For Gregory's catechetical lectures see the translation in *The Ante-Nicene Fathers* (New York: Cosimo Classics, 2007), 5:471–512. See also Juliette J. Day, "Catechesis," *Brill Encyclopedia of Early Christianity Online*, ed. David G. Hunter et al. (2018), https://referenceworks.brillonline.com/browse/brill-encyclopedia-of-early-christianity-online.

16. See, e.g., Anthony Meredith, "Gregory of Nyssa," in *The Cambridge History of Philosophy in Late Antiquity*, (Cambridge: Cambridge University Press, 2011), 1:471–81. The website for the *International Colloquium on Gregory of Nyssa* is https://www.gregoryofnyssa.org/en/.

17. Williams in "Rights and Wrongs," Episode 2, *For the Love of God*.

18. David Brion Davis, *In the Image of God: Religion, Moral Values, and Our Heritage of Slavery* (New Haven: Yale University Press, 2001), 198.

19. Letter, "Frederick Douglass to William Lloyd Garrison" (9 November 1842), in *The Frederick Douglass Papers. Series 3: Correspondence. Volume 1.* (New Haven: Yale University Press, 2009), 1–8.

20. A classic example of this argumentation can be found in Douglass's famous speech, "What to the Slave Is the Fourth of July?" (An Address Delivered in Rochester, New York, 5 July 1852),

in Frederick Douglass, *The Speeches of Frederick Douglass: A Critical Edition* (New Haven: Yale University Press, 2018), 55–92. See also his "Lecture on Slavery, No. 1" (delivered in Corinthian Hall, Rochester, NY, on Sunday evening, December 1, 1850), in *Frederick Douglass: Selected Speeches and Writings*, ed. Philip S. Foner (New York: Lawrence Hill, 2000), 164–70.

21. On the interpretation of 1 Cor 7:21–23, see J. Albert Harril, *The Manumission of Slaves in Early Christianity*, Hermeneutische Untersuchungen zur Theologie 32 (Tübingen: Mohr Siebeck, 1995), 68–128.

22. 1 Clement 55:2.

23. Our earliest evidence for the church fund to free slaves is Ignatius (AD 115), *To Polycarp* 4.3. On the church's "common chest" for manumission see J. Albert Harril, *The Manumission of Slaves in Early Christianity*, 129–92.

24. *Theodosian Code* 4.7.1 (Phar, *The Theodosian Code*). Chris De Wet, "Slave/Slavery," *Brill Encyclopedia of Early Christianity Online*, https://referenceworks.brillonline.com/browse/brill -encyclopedia-of-early-christianity-online. First published online: 2018.

25. Williams in "Rights and Wrongs," Episode 2, *For the Love of God*.

26. Gregory of Nyssa, *Homily 4, On Ecclesiastes (Eccl. 2:7)*, 5.334.4–5.338.22, trans. Stuart George and Rachel Moriarty in *Gregory of Nyssa, Homilies on Ecclesiastes. An English Version with Supporting Studies. Proceedings of the Seventh International Colloquium on Gregory of Nyssa, (St. Andrews, 5–10 September 1990)*, ed. Stuart G. Hall (Berlin: de Gruyter, 1993), 73–75, emphasis added.

Chapter 11: Iconoclastic Christianity

1. Robyn Whittaker, "Trump's Photo Op with Church and Bible Was Offensive, but Not New," *The Conversation*, 5 June 2020, https://theconversation.com/trumps-photo-op-with-church -and-bible-was-offensive-but-not-new-140053.

2. Brown, *Eye of a Needle*, 45.

3. Brown, *Eye of a Needle*, 45.

4. Ammianus Marcellinus (AD 330–400), *History* 22.11.4 (Rolfe, Loeb Classical Library 315), 259.

5. Brown, *The World of Late Antiquity*, 110.

6. Brown, *The World of Late Antiquity*, 103.

7. Rufinus 11.23–24, in *The Church History of Rufinus of Aquileia: Books 10 and 11*, trans. Philip R. Amidon (Oxford: Oxford University Press, 1997). The events are also recounted in Sozomen, *Ecclesiastical History*, 7.15.

8. Philip R. Amidon, *The Church History of Rufinus*, 103.

9. https://www.nytimes.com/2020/06/15/arts/design/fallen-statues-what-next.html.

10. Sozomen, *Ecclesiastical History*, 7.15, in *The Nicene and Post-Nicene Fathers²*, trans. Chester D. Hartranft (New York: Cosimo, 2007), 2:385. For a scholarly attempt to piece together the details of these events, see Amidon, *The Church History of Rufinus of Aquileia*, 103–6; and Ramsay MacMullen, *Christianizing the Roman Empire* (New Haven: Yale University Press, 1984), 99–101.

11. See MacMullen, *Christianizing*, 99.

12. Brown, *The World of Late Antiquity*, 110.

13. Catherine Nixey, *The Darkening Age: The Christian Destruction of the Classical World* (London: Pan Macmillan, 2017). For an excellent account of how Hypatia has been "remembered" in modern works, see Edward J. Watts, *Hypatia: The Life and Legend of an Ancient Philosopher* (Oxford: Oxford University Press, 2017), 135–47.

14. Watts, *Hypatia*, 113.

15. Socrates, *Ecclesiastical History*, 7.14.

16. Watts, *Hypatia*, 115.

17. Socrates, *Ecclesiastical History*, 7.14 (Zenos, *The Nicene and Post-Nicene Fathers²*).
18. Watts, *Hypatia*, 117.
19. Socrates, *Ecclesiastical History*, 7.15 (Zenos, *The Nicene and Post-Nicene Fathers²*).
20. In addition to Socrates Scholasticus quoted above, we have another contemporary Christian writer named Philostorgius (AD 368–439) who likewise lauds Hypatia (Philostorgius, *Church History*, 8.9. trans. Philip R. Amidon [Society of Biblical Literature, 2007], 117). There is also a pagan source from a century later, Damascius, *Life of Isidore*, 106A. Damascius is not as complimentary of Hypatia as these Christian sources are.
21. Watts, *Hypatia*, 46.
22. Pierre (Limours) Hadot, "Hypatia," *Brill's New Pauly*, doi: e519580, https://referenceworks.brillonline.com/browse/brill-s-new-pauly.
23. Watts, *Hypatia*, 154.
24. We can see ambivalence toward pagan temples in, for example, *Theodosian Code*, 16.10.8.
25. So Curran, "The Legal Standing of the Ancient Cults," 208.
26. The evidence for some tolerance of paganism early in Theodosius's reign is detailed in Curran, "The Legal Standing of the Ancient Cults," 209–12.
27. *Theodosian Code*, 16.10.11 (Phar, *The Theodosian Code*).
28. John Curran, "The Legal Standing of the Ancient Cults in Rome," 216.

Chapter 12: "Just War"

1. For a brief overview with a helpful bibliography see "War, Christian Attitude to," *Oxford Dictionary of the Christian Church*, 1719–20.
2. See the helpful online summary, "Military Law," Jewish Virtual Library, https://www.jewishvirtuallibrary.org/military-law.
3. On the development of the allegorical reading in the early Church, see Robert Louis Wilken, *The Spirit of Early Christian Thought: Seeking the Face of God* (New Haven: Yale University Press, 2003), 69–77. On the theological or biblical problem of violence in the Old Testament, see chapter 5 of my *A Doubter's Guide to the Bible: Inside History's Bestseller for Believers and Skeptics* (Grand Rapids: Zondervan, 2015). Also see, John Walton and J. Harvey Walton, *The Lost World of the Israelite Conquest* (Downers Grove, IL: IVP Academic, 2017); William J. Webb and Gordon K. Oeste, *Bloody, Brutal, and Barbaric: Wrestling with Troubling War Texts* (Downers Grove, IL: IVP Academic, 2019).
4. Tertullian, *Apology*, 42.
5. For details of the excavation and inscriptions, see Yottam Tepper and Leah Di Segni, *A Christian Prayer Hall of the Third Century CE at Kefar Othnay (Legio): Excavations at the Megiddo Prison 2005* (Jerusalem: Israel Antiquities Authority, 2006).
6. Hippolytus, *Apostolic Traditions*, 17–19 in *The Treatise on the Apostolic Tradition of St Hippolytus of Rome*, ed. and trans. Gregory Dix, reissued with corrections by Henry Chadwick (London: SPCK, 1968).
7. Lactantius, *Divine Institutes*, 6.20.16 (Bowen and Garnsey, *Lactantius, Divine Institutes*).
8. Canon 12, Council of Nicaea, *The Nicene and Post-Nicene Fathers²*, ed. Philip Schaff (Grand Rapids: Christian Classics Ethereal Library, 2009), 14:84.
9. Augustine, *Confessions* 8.2, in *Saint Augustine. Confessions. Fathers of the Church: A New Translation*, trans. Vernon J. Bourke (Washington, DC: Catholic University of America Press, 1953), 21:199.
10. Augustine, *Confessions*, 8.27–30.
11. Augustine, *Confessions*, 8.29 (Bourke, *Saint Augustine. Confessions*).
12. Augustine, *Confessions* 1.1. I have followed the translation of Vernon J. Bourke (as above) but have changed the masculine "he" to "person" and to "they," in keeping with the gender inclusive meaning of Augustine's Latin.

13. See Hermigild Dressler, et al. (ed.), *Saint Augustine. Letters (6 volumes). The Fathers of the Church: A New Translation* (Washington, DC: Catholic University of America Press, 1956–1989).

14. "Callistus" *Oxford Dictionary of the Christian Church*, 265. His name is also sometimes spelled Calixtus.

15. Augustine, *Letter 10**, "To Alypius," trans. Robert B. Eno, *St. Augustine. Letters 1*–29*. The Fathers of the Church: A New Translation*, 81 (Washington, DC: Catholic University of America Press, 1989), 74–80. (The asterisk indicates newly discovered letters). For an outline of the letter and its significance, see Henry Chadwick, "New Letters of St. Augustine," *Journal of Theological Studies* 34 (1983), 432–43.

16. Augustine, *Letter 10**, "To Alypius" (Eno, *St. Augustine. Letters 1*–29**).

17. Augustine, *Letter 10**, "To Alypius" (Eno, *St. Augustine. Letters 1*–29**).

18. Pelagius, *To Demetrias*, 1, trans. Brinley Roderick Rees, *Pelagius: Life and Letters* (Suffolk: Boydell, 1991), 69.

19. Henry Chadwick, *Augustine: A Very Short Introduction* (Oxford: Oxford University Press, 1986), 112–13. See also Wolin S. Sheldon, *Politics and Vision: Continuity and Innovation in Western Political Thought* (Princeton: Princeton University Press, 2004), 117.

20. Augustine, *To Boniface*, Letter 189.4, in *The Works of Saint Augustine: A Translation for the 21st Century. Letters 156–210*, volume II/3, trans. Roland Teske (New City, 2004), 259–62.

21. Augustine, *To Boniface*, Letter 189.4 (Teske, *The Works of Saint Augustine*).

22. Augustine, *To Boniface*, Letter 220.7 (Teske, *The Works of Saint Augustine*), 72–78.

23. See *The City of God* 4.14–17; 15.4.

24. Chadwick, *Augustine*, 111–12.

25. Chadwick, *Augustine*, 111–12.

26. Augustine, *The City of God*, 19.7, trans. William Babcock in *Augustine, Saint. The City of God: Books 11–22* (I/7), The Works of Saint Augustine: A Translation for the 21st Century (Hyde Park, NY: New City, 2013).

Chapter 13: The Death of Rome and Growth of the Church

1. Brown, *The World of Late Antiquity*, 122.

2. Peter J. Heather, "Theoderic," *Oxford Classical Dictionary*, 1499.

3. Brown, *The World of Late Antiquity*, 125.

4. Brown, *The World of Late Antiquity*, 135.

5. "Sidonius Apollinaris," *Oxford Dictionary of the Christian Church*, 1498.

6. *Sidonius, Vol. 1, Poems, Letters, Books 1–2* (Anderson, Loeb Classical Library 296). *Sidonius, Vol. 2, Letters, Books 3–9* (Anderson, Loeb Classical Library 420).

7. On this dynamic between bishops and their clergy in the fifth and sixth centuries see Brown, *Eye of a Needle*, 481–502. For an excellent overview of Sidonius's life and works see *Sidonius, Vol. 1, Poems, Letters* (Anderson, Loeb Classical Library 296), xxxii–lxvii.

8. Brown, *The World of Late Antiquity*, 126.

9. For an authoritative account of the conversion of Europe, region by region, see *The Cambridge History of Christianity, Vol. 3: Early Medieval Christianities: c. 600–c. 1100*, ed. Thomas F. X. Noble et al. (Cambridge: Cambridge University Press, 2014).

10. Knut Schäferdiek, "Germanic and Celtic Christianities," in *The Cambridge History of Christianity, Vol. 2: Constantine to c. 600*, ed. Augustine Casiday et al. Cambridge: Cambridge University Press, 2007), 63.

11. For a history of the Merovingians, see Ian Wood, *The Merovingian Kingdoms: 450–751* (London: Routledge, 2014), 41–49, for a discussion of Clovis's conversion. For the primary sources of the period, see Alexander Callander Murray, ed., *Roman to Merovingian Gaul: A Reader* (Toronto: University of Toronto Press, 2008).

12. See Schäferdiek, "Germanic and Celtic Christianities," 59–63.

13. Dado's *Vita Eligii* 1.10. It is printed in the original Latin in *Patrologia Latina*, ed. J. P. Migne (Paris, 1844–64), 87:479–594. English translation above is by Jo Ann McNamara, the Fordham University *Medieval Sourcebook*, https://sourcebooks.fordham.edu/basis/eligius.asp.

14. Dado's *Vita Eligii* 1.12 (McNamara, *Medieval Sourcebook*).

15. Dado's *Vita Eligii* 1.10 (McNamara, *Medieval Sourcebook*).

16. Dado's *Vita Eligii* 2.3 (McNamara, *Medieval Sourcebook*).

17. Dado's *Vita Eligii* 2.8 (McNamara, *Medieval Sourcebook*).

18. Dado's *Vita Eligii* 2.38 (McNamara, *Medieval Sourcebook*).

19. "Boniface," *Oxford Dictionary of the Christian Church*, 123–24.

20. Daniel to Boniface 15.23, in *The Letters of Saint Boniface: Translated with an Introduction by Ephraim Emerton* (New York: Norton, 1976), 48–50.

21. Gregory II to Boniface 16.24 (Emerton, *The Letters of Saint Boniface*, 50–52).

22. Wood, *Merovingian Kingdoms*, 251.

23. George W. Robinson, trans., *Willibald: The Life of Saint Boniface* (Cambridge: Harvard University Press, 2013), 84.

24. See Ephraim Emerton, trans., *The Letters of Saint Boniface: Translated with an Introduction* (New York: Norton, 1976).

25. For a history of Charlemagne and his impact on the future of Europe, see Rosamond McKitterick, *Charlemagne: The Formation of a European Identity* (Cambridge: Cambridge University Press, 2013).

Chapter 14: Christian "Jihad"

1. Documentary evidence of this general policy of state wars followed by Christian missions is found in *Letter 39*, "Letter of Bishop Avitus of Vienne to Clovis Regarding the King's Baptism," in Murray, *Roman to Merovingian Gaul*, 261–63.

2. McKitterick, *Charlemagne*, 308.

3. For an authoritative account of Christianity's interaction with, and conversion of, pagan Europe in the early Middle Ages, see Ian N. Wood, "The Northern Frontier: Christianity Face to Face with Paganism," in *The Cambridge History of Christianity*, 3:230–46; in the same volume see also Abrams, "Germanic Christianities," (107–29).

4. McKitterick, *Charlemagne*, 105–6.

5. Einhard, *Life of Charlemagne*, 8, trans. Barbara H. Rosewein, ed., in *Reading the Middle Ages: Sources from Europe, Byzantium, and the Islamic World* (Toronto: University of Toronto Press, 2014), 139.

6. Einhard, *Life of Charlemagne*, 8 (Rosewein, *Reading the Middle Ages*).

7. *Capitulatio de partibus Saxoniae* 8, trans. Dana Carleton Munro, ed., in *Translations and Reprints from the Original Sources of European History, Vol. 5: Laws of Charles the Great* (Philadelphia: King, 1900), 2.

8. For the latter argument, see Yitzhak Hen, "Charlemagne's Jihad," in *Religious Franks: Religion and Power in the Frankish Kingdoms: Studies in Honour of Mayke de Jong*, ed. Rob Meens, et al. (Manchester: Manchester University Press, 2016), 33–51.

9. Robert Flierman, "Religious Saxons: Paganism, Infidelity and Biblical Punishment in the *Capitulatio de partibus Saxoniae*," in Meens, *Religious Franks*, 184.

10. Hen, "Charlemagne's Jihad," 33–51.

11. Hen, "Charlemagne's Jihad," 47.

12. Lactantius, *The Death of the Persecutors* 48 (McDonald, *Lactantius, The Minor Works*).

13. Augustine, *Against the Letters of Petilian the Donatist*, 2.184, in *The Nicene and Post-Nicene*

Fathers¹, St. Augustine: The Writings Against the Manichaeans, and Against the Donatists, trans. J. R. King and rev. by Chester D. Hartranft (New York: Cosimo, 2007), 4:572. See also "Donatism," *Oxford Dictionary of the Christian Church*, 499–500.

14. Letter to Miletus, *Bede's Ecclesiastical History* 2.30 (King, Loeb Classical Library 246), 161–65.

15. Jinty Nelson, "Alcuin's Letter to Meginfrid," in *Penser la paysannerie médiévale, un défi impossible?*, ed. Alain Dierkens, et al. (Paris: Sorbonne University Press, 2017), 122.

16. Nelson, "Alcuin's Letter," 120.

17. Nelson, "Alcuin's Letter," 120.

18. Nelson, "Alcuin's Letter," 120.

19. See Melvyn Bragg, "Alcuin," interview with Mary Garrison, Joanna Story, and Andy Orchard, *In Our Time*, BBC, 30 January 2020, https://www.bbc.co.uk/programmes/m000dqy8.

20. Hen, "Charlemagne's Jihad," 43.

21. This is Alcuin's famous *Epistle 110*, cited in Hen, "Charlemagne's Jihad," 43.

22. Gratian, *Decretum*, Distinctio 45, Canon 3, trans. Robert Chazan, *Church, State, and the Jew in the Middle Ages* (West Orange, NJ: Behrmam House, 1980), 20.

23. Thomas Aquinas, *Summa Theologiae*, IIa–IIae, 10.8. in *Summa Theologiae Secunda Secundae, 1–91*, trans. Laurence Shapcote (Lander, WY: The Aquinas Institute for the Study of Sacred Doctrine, 2012), 104. Also see chapter 2 of Robert Louis Wilken's *Liberty in the Things of God*.

Chapter 15: The Greatest European You've Never Heard Of

1. Stephen Greenblatt, *The Swerve: How the World Became Modern* (New York: Norton, 2011).

2. Greenblatt, *The Swerve*, 43.

3. Greenblatt, *The Swerve*, 36.

4. Greenblatt, *The Swerve*, 50.

5. Greenblatt, *The Swerve*, 7.

6. Representative critical reviews include: Charles Kay Smith in *Kritikon Litterarum* 41 (2014), 112–34; Aaron W. Godfrey in *Forum Italicum: A Journal of Italian Studies* 46 (2012): 203–4; John Monfasani in *Reviews in History* 1283, https://reviews.history.ac.uk/review/1283; Morgan Meis in *N+1 Magazine,* https://nplusonemag.com/online-only/book-review/swerving/; and a blistering but not inaccurate one by Jim Hench, "Why Stephen Greenblatt Is Wrong—and Why It Matters" in *The Los Angeles Review of Books*, December 1, 2012, https://lareviewofbooks.org /article/why-stephen-greenblatt-is-wrong-and-why-it-matters/.

7. Brian Tierney, *Western Europe in the Middle Ages: 300–1475*, 6th ed. (New York: McGraw-Hill, 1992), 143–44.

8. Quoted from discussion about Alcuin between historians Mary Garrison, Joanna Story, and Andy Orchard, Professor of Anglo-Saxon at the University of Oxford, in Bragg, "Alcuin."

9. See Rosamond McKitterick, "The Carolingian Renaissance of Culture and Learning," in *Charlemagne*, 151–66. Also see John J. Contreni, "The Carolingian Renaissance: Education and Literary Culture," in *The New Cambridge Medieval History, Vol. 2: c.700–900*, ed. Rosamond McKitterick (Cambridge: Cambridge University Press, 2008), 709–57.

10. 3200 pages of Carolingian poetry has survived; John J. Contreni, "The Carolingian Renaissance," 753. A study of the poetry of this period from thirty different poets is Peter Godman's *Poetry of the Carolingian Renaissance* (London: Duckworth, 1985).

11. Eleanor Shipley Duckett, *Alcuin, Friend of Charlemagne: His World and His Work* (New York: Macmillan, 1951), 109.

12. Einhard, *Life of Charles the Great* (*Vita Karoli Magni*), 25, in "The Library of Alcuin's York," trans. Mary Garrison, in *The Cambridge History of the Book in Britain*, ed. R. Gameson (Cambridge: Cambridge University Press, 2011), 634. For a modern translation, see David

Ganz, *Einhard and Notker the Stammerer: Two Lives of Charlemagne* (London: Penguin, 2008).

13. See the discussion on this point in Bragg, "Alcuin."

14. Jerome, "To Eustochium," *Letter* 22.30 (Wright, Loeb Classical Library 262), 127.

15. Jerome, "To Eustochium," *Letter* 22.29 (Wright, Loeb Classical Library 262), 125.

16. Arthur Stanley Pease, "The Attitude of Jerome towards Pagan Literature" in *Transactions and Proceedings of the American Philological Association* 50 (1919): 150–67.

17. The rule is clearly laid out in Hippolytus, *Apostolic Traditions*, 16–17.

18. *The Pilgrimage of Egeria*, 46, trans. George E. Gingras, *Egeria: Diary of a Pilgrimage* (Westminster, MD: Newman, 1970), 124. For the details of Egeria, see Cohick and Hughes, *Christian Women in the Patristic World*, 127–56.

19. *The Pilgrimage of Egeria*, 46.

20. On the life and teaching of Cyril, including translation of his lectures, see Edward Yarnold, *Cyril of Jerusalem* (London: Routledge, 2000). On the broader phenomenon of *catechesis* in the early church see M. E. Nelson, "Catechesis and Baptism in the Early Christian Church," *In die Skriflig* 20 (1996): 443–56.

21. Rosamond McKitterick, *The Carolingians and the Written Word* (Cambridge: Cambridge University Press, 1989), 212.

22. Charlemagne's letter to Lectors (church readers) from 786, cited in McKitterick, *Charlemagne*, 315.

23. Einhard, *Life of Charles the Great* (*Vita Karoli Magni*), 25 (Ganz, *Einhard and Notker*, 36).

24. From the *Admonitio generalis* of 789, cited in McKitterick, *Charlemagne*, 316.

25. Contreni, "The Carolingian Renaissance," 721.

26. McKitterick, "The Carolingian Renaissance of Culture and Learning," 157.

27. Hincmar, *Collectio de Ecclesiis et Capellis, MGH Fontes* XIV, C.100. Cited in Contreni, "The Carolingian Renaissance," 717. Also Tierney, *Western Europe in the Middle Ages: 300–1475*, 141.

28. Rolph Barlow, *The Letters of Alcuin* (New York: Forest, 1909), 91.

29. Steven A. Stofferahn, "Changing Views of Carolingian Women's Literary Culture: The Evidence from Essen," *Early Medieval Europe* 8.1 (1999): 70, 72. On women's education in this period, see McKitterick, *The Carolingians and the Written Word*, 226. So also Contreni, "The Carolingian Renaissance," 715–20.

30. McKitterick, *The Carolingians and the Written Word*, 192.

31. Contreni, "The Carolingian Renaissance," 719.

32. Notker, *The Deeds of Charlemagne*, 1.8

33. Notker, *The Deeds of Charlemagne*, 1.3–4 (Ganz, *Einhard and Notker*). So also McKitterick, *The Carolingians and the Written Word*, 222.

34. Cited in Duckett, *Alcuin*, 111.

35. Contreni, "The Carolingian Renaissance," 728–32.

36. Contreni, "The Carolingian Renaissance," 747–51.

37. Charles W. Colby, ed., *Selections from the Sources of English History* (London: Longmans, Green, 1899), 17–19.

38. On this, see McKitterick, "The Carolingian Renaissance," 160–61; Garrison, "The Library of Alcuin's York," 633–64.

39. McKitterick, *The Carolingians and the Written Word*, 179.

40. McKitterick, *The Carolingians and the Written Word*, 163.

41. McKitterick, "The Carolingian Renaissance of Culture and Learning," 153–54.

42. Rainer A. Müller, "Cathedral Schools," *Brill's Encyclopedia of the Middle Ages*, ed. Gert Melville and Martial Staub (2016), https://referenceworks.brillonline.com/browse/brill-s -encyclopaedia-of-the-middle-ages.

43. Rainer A. Müller, *Geschichte der Universität. Von der mittelalterlichen Universitas zur deutschen Hochschule* (Munich: Callwey, 1990); Rainer A. Müller, "Universities," *Brill's Encyclopedia of the Middle Ages*, https://referenceworks.brillonline.com/browse/brill-s-encyclopaedia-of-the -middle-ages.

Chapter 16: Knights of Christ

1. Pew Research Centre. "The Global Religious Landscape," 2012, https://www.pewforum.org /2012/12/18/global-religious-landscape-exec/.
2. Pew Research Centre. "Racial and Ethnic Composition among Christians (US)," 2015, https:// www.pewforum.org/religious-landscape-study/christians/christian/racial-and-ethnic -composition/. I was alerted to these studies by Rebecca McLaughlin, *Confronting Christianity: 12 Hard Questions for the World's Largest Religion* (Wheaton, IL: Crossway, 2019), 36–48.
3. *Epistle to Diognetus* 5.4–6. See Holmes, *Apostolic Fathers*, 686–719.
4. According to the World Religion Database, Boston University (2020), Christianity has 2.5 billion adherents, or 32 percent of the world's population, spread across 234 countries. Islam is not far behind, with 1.9 billion adherents, or 24 percent of the world's population, spread across 218 countries. See https://worldreligiondatabase.org.
5. *Letter 38*, "Letter of Bishop Remigius of Rheims to Clovis," in Murray, *Roman to Merovingian Gaul*, 260.
6. *Letter 39*, "Letter of Bishop Avitus of Vienne to Clovis Regarding the King's Baptism," in *Roman to Merovingian Gaul*, 261–63.
7. Brown, *Eye of a Needle*, 505.
8. Tyerman, *God's War*, 34.
9. Tyerman, *God's War*, 35–36.
10. Tyerman, *God's War*, 37.
11. Tyerman, *God's War*, 36.
12. Abbo of St-Germain, "The Viking Siege of Paris: Odo and Ebolus." The Latin text and English translation appear in Godman, *Poetry of the Carolingian Renaissance*, 312–13.
13. James E. Cathey, ed., *Heliand: Text and Commentary* (Morgantown: West Virginia University Press, 2002), 135.
14. *Heliand* 16 (Cathey, *Heliand*).
15. Tyerman, *God's War*, 39.
16. See Tyerman, *God's War*, 40–42.
17. Bernard of Clairvaux, *In Praise of the New Knighthood*, 3 (Allen, *The Crusades: A Reader*, 197).
18. The citation and translation are from Tyerman, *God's War*, 28.
19. Tyerman, *God's War*, 28.
20. *The Life of Christina of St-Trond by Thomas of Cantimpré*, §56, in *Medieval Saints: A Reader*, ed. Mary-Ann Stouck (Peterborough, Ontario: Broadview, 1999), 452.
21. *The Life of Christina* §33–34 (Stouck, *Medieval Saints*, 445–46).

Chapter 17: Prophets and Hypocrites

1. See Bragg, "Alcuin."
2. Jerome, "To Eustochium," *Letter* 22.28 (Wright, Loeb Classical Library 262).
3. "Benedict, St.," *Oxford Dictionary of the Christian Church*, 182–83.
4. The complete English translation of the Rule is found at Project Gutenberg, http://www.gutenberg .org/files/50040/50040-h/50040-h.html#chapter-1-nl-on-the-kinds-of-monks.
5. Christopher Dawson, *Religion and the Rise of Western Culture* (New York: Doubleday, 1991), 120–21.

6. Rulings of the Council of Rheims (AD 909), cited in Dawson, *Religion and the Rise of Western Culture*, 121.

7. Odo of Cluny, *Collationes*, III, 26–30 (Dawson, *Religion and the Rise of Western Culture*, 123).

8. *Life of St. Odo of Cluny by John of Salerno*, §4 in *St. Odo of Cluny: Being the Life of St. Odo of Cluny by John of Salerno, and the Life of St. Gerald of Aurillac by St. Odo*, Gerard Sitwell, trans. and ed., (New York: Sheed & Ward, 1958), 44.

9. *Life of St. Odo of Cluny by John of Salerno*, §5, 46 (Sitwell, *St. Odo of Cluny*).

10. *Life of St. Odo of Cluny by John of Salerno*, §7, 50 (Sitwell, *St. Odo of Cluny*).

11. *Life of St. Odo of Cluny by John of Salerno*, §7, 47 (Sitwell, *St. Odo of Cluny*).

12. *Life of St. Odo of Cluny by John of Salerno*, §8, 51–52 (Sitwell, *St. Odo of Cluny*).

13. *Life of St. Odo of Cluny by John of Salerno*, §9, 52–53 (Sitwell, *St. Odo of Cluny*).

14. See the excellent summary of his life and contribution by Barbara H. Rosenwein, "Saint Odo of Cluny," Encyclopedia Britannica, https://www.britannica.com/biography/Saint-Odo-of-Cluny.

15. Andrea Janelle Dickens, *The Female Mystic: Great Women Thinkers of the Middle Ages* (London: Tauris, 2009), 26.

16. Dickens, *The Female Mystic*, 26.

17. Dickens, *The Female Mystic*, 30–31.

18. Catherine of Siena, *Dialogue*, 1.26, cited in Dickens, *The Female Mystic*, 151.

19. "Catherine, St., of Siena," *Oxford Dictionary of the Christian Church*, 304–5.

20. Dickens, *The Female Mystic*, 152.

21. Catherine of Siena, *Letter* T69, cited in Dickens, *The Female Mystic*, 155–56.

22. Thompson, *Francis of Assisi*, 177.

23. *Life of St. Francis by Thomas of Celano*, "How Francis Lived in the World before His Conversion," §17, cited in Stouck, *Medieval Saints*, 479.

24. Cited in Thompson, *Francis of Assisi*, 16.

25. Thompson, *Francis of Assisi*, 17.

26. Thompson, *Francis of Assisi*, 88.

27. Thompson, *Francis of Assisi*, ix.

28. See Benjamin, Z. Kedar, *Crusade and Mission: European Approaches toward the Muslims* (Princeton: Princeton University Press, 1984), 126–31.

29. Kedar, *Crusade and Mission*, 129.

30. Tyerman, *God's War*, 638.

31. Thompson, *Francis of Assisi*, 67.

32. Tyerman, *God's War*, 630.

33. For an analysis of the event and the sources, see Powell, "St. Francis of Assisi's Way of Peace," 271–80. For a scholarly but accessible biography of Francis, see Thompson, *Francis of Assisi*.

34. Thompson, *Francis of Assisi*, 69.

35. Thompson, *Francis of Assisi*, 69–70.

36. "Franciscan Order," *Oxford Dictionary of the Christian Church*, 634–35.

37. Brodman, *Charity and Religion in Medieval Europe*, 48.

38. Brodman, *Charity and Religion in Medieval Europe*, 49.

39. Frances J. Niederer, "Early Medieval Charity," *Church History* 21 (1952): 289.

40. Brodman, *Charity and Religion in Medieval Europe*, chapter 11, "A Cascade of Hospitals" (45–88).

41. Brodman, *Charity and Religion in Medieval Europe*, 50–56.

42. *Lives of the Fathers of Merida*, §5.3., in A. T. Fear, *Lives of the Visigothic Fathers*, Translated Texts for Historians, 26 (Liverpool: Liverpool University Press, 2001), 73–75. For the date of the text, see Fear's introduction on pages xxx–xxxi.

43. Brodman, *Charity and Religion in Medieval Europe*, 50–56.
44. Brodman, *Charity and Religion in Medieval Europe*, 85.
45. For a brief account of Aquinas's life and thought, see Fergus Kerr, *Thomas Aquinas: A Very Short Introduction* (Oxford: Oxford University Press, 2009). A more advanced introduction is Denys Turner, *Thomas Aquinas: A Portrait* (New Haven: Yale University Press, 2013). Also see Edward Feser, *Aquinas: A Beginner's Guide* (London: Oneworld, 2009).
46. *Life of St. Thomas Aquinas by Bernard Gui* (1261–1331), §32, in *Life of Saint Thomas Aquinas: Biographical Documents*, ed. Kenelm Foster (Baltimore: Helicon, 1959), 51.
47. Brian Tierney, *Medieval Poor Law: A Sketch of Canonical Theory and Its Application in England* (Berkeley: University of California Press, 1959). See also Charles J. Reid, "The Canonistic Contribution to the Western Rights Tradition: An Historical Inquiry," *Boston College Law Review*, 33:37 (1995): 37–92.
48. See Reid, "The Canonistic Contribution."
49. Tierney, *Medieval Poor Law*, 12.
50. Tierney, *Medieval Poor Law*, 62.
51. Cited in Tierney, *Medieval Poor Law*, 62.
52. Tierney, *Medieval Poor Law*, 48.
53. All cited in Tierney, *Medieval Poor Law*, 37–38.
54. Tierney, *Medieval Poor Law*, 38.
55. Tierney, *Medieval Poor Law*, 38.
56. Tierney, *Medieval Poor Law*, 13–14.
57. Statute 15, Richard II, 1391, Chap. VI, "Provisions for the Poor," cited in Tierney, *Medieval Poor Law*, 129.
58. Tierney, *Medieval Poor Law*, 129.
59. Statues 5 and 6, Edward VI, 1552, "The Provision and Relief of the Poor," in J. R. Tanner, *Tudor Constitutional Documents: AD 1485–1603* (London: Chivers, 1971), 471. On this see Tierney, *Medieval Poor Law*, 127.
60. Statue 5, Elizabeth I, 1563, Chap. 3, in Tanner, *Tudor Constitutional Documents*, 471–72. See also Tierney, *Medieval Poor Law*, 127.
61. Statute 14, Elizabeth I, 1572, Chap. 5, "Vagabonds Act," in Tanner, *Tudor Constitutional Documents*, 471–72. On this see Tierney, *Medieval Poor Law*, 131.
62. Elizabeth I, "Poor Relief Act of 1598." For the full text of the Act, see Tanner, *Tudor Constitutional Documents*, 488–94.
63. Tierney, *Medieval Poor Law*, 131.
64. Tierney, *Medieval Poor Law*, 131. See also Tierney, *Medieval Poor Law*, 132.

Chapter 18: The Eternal Empire of the East

1. Brown, *The World of Late Antiquity*, 145.
2. Brown, *The World of Late Antiquity*, 156.
3. Miira Tuominen, "Late Antiquity: Science in the Philosophical Schools," in *The Cambridge History of Science, Vol. 1: Ancient Science* (Cambridge: Cambridge University Press, 2018), 278–92.
4. Brown, *The World of Late Antiquity*, 177.
5. Peter Sarris, *Byzantium: A Very Short Introduction* (Oxford: Oxford University Press, 2015), 102.
6. See the history of the Bodleian, https://www.bodleian.ox.ac.uk/bodley/about-us/history.
7. Sarris, *Byzantium*, 102. Photius's book summary is known as the *Bibliotheca*. It can be read online, http://www.tertullian.org/fathers/photius_01toc.htm.
8. Brown, *The World of Late Antiquity*, 177.
9. Orla Guerin, "Hagia Sophia: Turkey Turns Iconic Istanbul Museum into Mosque," BBC, 10 July 2020, https://www.bbc.com/news/world-europe-53366307.

10. See "Byzantine Architecture," in *The Oxford Dictionary of Architecture*, ed. James Stevens Curl and Susan Wilson (Oxford: Oxford University Press, 2015), 134–36.

11. Brown, *The World of Late Antiquity*, 152.

12. Brown, *The World of Late Antiquity*, 155.

13. Brown, *The World of Late Antiquity*, 147.

14. Justinian ratified and expanded the earlier laws in *Theodosian Code* 9.44.1–2.

15. *Codex of Justinian*, 1.12.1–2, in *The Codex of Justinian, Vol. 1*, Bruce W. Frier, ed., trans. Fred H. Blume (Cambridge: Cambridge University Press, 2016).

16. See "Sanctuary," in *A Dictionary of British History*, 3rd ed., ed. John Cannon and Robert Crowcroft (Oxford: Oxford University Press, 2009), 574.

17. Hector Perla and Susan Bibler Coutin, "Legacies and Origins of the 1980s US-Central American Sanctuary Movement," in *Refuge* 26.1 (2009): 7–19.

18. Talal Ansari, "Some Churches Offer Refuge from Deportation With 'Sacred Resisting,'" *The Wall Street Journal*, 4 August 2019, https://www.wsj.com/articles/some-churches-offer-refuge-from-deportation-with-sacred-resisting-11564927200.

19. Miller, *The Birth of the Hospital in the Byzantine Empire*, 89.

20. Miller, *The Birth of the Hospital in the Byzantine Empire*, 91.

21. Miller, *The Birth of the Hospital in the Byzantine Empire*, 90–91.

22. Miller, *The Birth of the Hospital in the Byzantine Empire*, 92.

23. For the church laws, see the Arabic Canons of Nicaea, canon 70. Justinian's laws are found in his published *Novellae Constitutiones* or New Constitutions, nos.120, 131. See the discussion in Miller, *The Birth of the Hospital in the Byzantine Empire*, 100–3.

24. Miller, *The Birth of the Hospital in the Byzantine Empire*, 117.

25. Miller, *The Birth of the Hospital in the Byzantine Empire*, 110–17.

26. The manuscript is held in the Vatican Library today. Peregrine Horden, "Sickness and Healing," in Thomas F. X. Noble, et al., *The Cambridge History of Christianity*, 3:420–21.

27. Horden, "Sickness and Healing," 431.

28. Brown, *The World of Late Antiquity*, 174.

29. *Codex of Justinian*, 1.11.10.1 (Blume, *The Codex of Justinian*).

30. Catherine Nixey, *The Darkening Age: The Christian Destruction of the Classical World* (London: Pan Macmillan, 2017), 231–47.

31. Edward Watts, "Justinian, Malalas, and the End of Athenian Philosophical Teaching in A.D. 529," *The Journal of Roman Studies* 94 (2004): 169.

32. Watts, "Justinian," 168. The primary source is Malalas, *Chronical* 18.47. For an English translation of the Chronicle, see *The Chronicle of John Malalas. Byzantina Australiensia, Vol. 4* (Leiden: Brill, 1986).

33. Photius, *Bibliotheca*, 130.

34. *Codex of Justinian*, 1.11.10.2 (Blume, *The Codex of Justinian*).

35. Brown, *The World of Late Antiquity*, 174.

36. Peter Brown, *The Rise of Western Christendom: Triumph and Diversity, A.D. 200–1000*, 2nd ed. (Oxford: Blackwell, 2007), 296.

37. There is one highly technical difference between the Nicene Creed as affirmed by the Orthodox Church and the Nicene Creed as affirmed by Catholics and Protestants. In the third stanza of the Creed, the Orthodox declare that the Holy Spirit "proceeds from the Father," whereas Catholics and Protestants say "proceeds from the Father *and the Son*."

38. Sarris, *Byzantium*, 94–102. See also David Bentley Hart, *Atheist Delusions: The Christian Revolution and Its Fashionable Enemies* (New Haven: Yale University Press, 2009), 34.

39. For this complicated story see Brown, *The World of Late Antiquity*, 194–203.

40. Brown, *The World of Late Antiquity*, 202.
41. Peter Adamson, Oliver Overwien, and Gotthard Strohmaier, "Alexandria, School of," *Encyclopaedia of Islam, Three*, ed. Kate Fleet et al., https://referenceworks.brillonline.com /browse/encyclopaedia-of-islam-3.

Chapter 19: Inventing the "Dark Ages"

1. Hart, *Atheist Delusions*, 31.
2. Theodore E. Mommsen, "Petrarch's Conception of the 'Dark Ages,'" *Speculum* 17 (April 1942): 227.
3. Mommsen, "Petrarch," 234.
4. Cited in Mommsen, "Petrarch," 231–32.
5. Mommsen, "Petrarch," 242.
6. Martial Staub, "Humanism and the Reception of Antiquity," *Brill Encyclopedia of the Middle Ages*, https://referenceworks.brillonline.com/browse/brill-s-encyclopaedia-of-the-middle-ages.
7. Wallace K. Ferguson, "Humanist Views of the Renaissance," *The American Historical Review* 45 (October 1939): 28.
8. Mommsen, "Petrarch," 227.
9. Gibbon, *History of the Decline and Fall of the Roman Empire*, chapter 30.
10. This comes from the "Author's Preface" to volume 1 of Gibbon's *Decline and Fall*.
11. Gibbon, *Decline and Fall*, chapter 13. The same "learned" perspective was expressed in another influential work of the next century: Henry Thomas Buckley, *History of Civilization in England, Vol. 1* (London: Robson, Levey, and Franklyn, 1857; repr., Cambridge: Cambridge University Press, 2011), 558.
12. Cited in Mommsen, "Petrarch," 226.
13. Mommsen, "Petrarch," 226.
14. Mommsen, "Petrarch," 227.
15. Catherine Nixey, *The Darkening Age: The Christian Destruction of the Classical World* (London: Pan Macmillan, 2017).
16. Miri Rubin, *The Middle Ages: A Very Short Introduction* (Oxford: Oxford University Press, 2014), 4–6.
17. This was Luther's argument to a question from the revered humanist scholar Desiderius Erasmus (AD 1469–1536). See Luther's *On the Bondage of the Will*, especially the section referenced as WA 649–661 in the Weimar edition of Luther's Works, which may be found in English translation in Ernest Gordon Rupp, ed., *Luther and Erasmus: Free Will and Salvation* (Louisville: Westminster John Knox, 1969), 154–66.
18. George Townsend, ed., *The Acts and Monuments of John Foxe, Vol. 2* (London: Seeley, 1843), 727.
19. Quoted by Francis Oakley, *The Medieval Experience: Foundations of Western Singularity* (Toronto: University of Toronto Press, 2005), 4.
20. Oakley, *The Medieval Experience*, 1. See also Richard E. Sullivan, "What Were the Middle Ages," *The Centennial Review of Arts and Science* 2 (1958): 171. See also Hart, *Atheist Delusions*, 33–34.

Chapter 20: The Inquisition

1. It is weirdly common to hear people speak of the "millions" killed by the Inquisitions, as Thomas Madden points out. See http://www.nationalreview.com/article/211193/real-inquisition -thomas-f-madden. The "millions" figure is probably out by a factor of a thousand.
2. Edward Peters, *Inquisition* (Berkeley: University of California Press, 1989), 87.
3. "Pope Apologises for Church Sins," BBC News, March 2000, http://news.bbc.co.uk/2/hi /europe/674246.stm.
4. https://www.nytimes.com/2017/06/03/opinion/sunday/bruni-campus-inquisitions-evergreen -state.html?searchResultPosition=6.

5. See "Cathari," *Oxford Dictionary of the Christian Church*, 301.

6. Thomas F. Madden, "Crafting the Myth of the Inquisition," Lecture 12, *Heaven or Heresy: A History of the Inquisition in Modern Scholar Series* (Prince Frederick, MD: Recorded Books, 2008).

7. Cited in R. A. Markus, "Gregory the Great and a Papal Missionary Strategy" (29–38), in *Studies in Church History, vol.6: The Mission of the Church and the Propagation of the Faith* (Cambridge: Ecclesiastical History Society, 1970), 30.

8. On the origin of the *conversos* see Henry Kamen, *The Spanish Inquisition* (New Haven: Yale University Press, 1997), 8–11.

9. Cited in Kamen, *The Spanish Inquisition*, 49.

10. Cited in Kamen, *The Spanish Inquisition*, 50.

11. Cited in Kamen, *The Spanish Inquisition*, 58.

12. Cited in Kamen, *The Spanish Inquisition*, 58.

13. Cited in Kamen, *The Spanish Inquisition*, 274.

14. Malcolm Gaskill, *Witchcraft: A Very Short Introduction* (Oxford: Oxford University Press, 2010), 76.

15. Gaskill, *Witchcraft*, 71.

16. Gaskill, *Witchcraft*, 30. The most famous witch trial in the modern imagination is that from Salem in 1692, made famous in Arthur Miller's *The Crucible* (1953). Between February and October of 1692, twenty people, mostly women, were executed for sorcery (nineteen hanged, one crushed to death). The craze stopped as quickly as it had begun. Church and political figures put an end to it, and apologised for the shameful episode.

17. Cited in Kamen, *The Spanish Inquisition*, 274.

18. On the Spanish Inquisition's effectiveness in rooting out Protestantism from Spain, see Kamen, *The Spanish Inquisition*, 83–102; also Peters, *Inquisition*, 86–90.

19. Reliable statistics for the number of Protestants in Spain are notoriously difficult to find. Here I am relying on the United States Department of State, "Spain 2018 International Religious Freedom Report," 2.

20. These are the case percentages for the Catalans, who represented just over half of the cases dealt with by the Inquisition in this period. See Kamen, *Spanish Inquisition*, 257–60.

21. Kamen, *The Spanish Inquisition*, 266.

22. Kamen, *The Spanish Inquisition*, 267.

23. See Thomas Madden, "The Real Inquisition," *National Review*, 18 June 2004, https://www .nationalreview.com/2004/06/real-inquisition-thomas-f-madden/.

24. Kamen, *The Spanish Inquisition*, 235.

25. Cited in Kamen, *The Spanish Inquisition*, 235.

26. Henry Charles Lea, *A History of the Inquisition of Spain, Vol. 2* (New York: Macmillan, 1906), 534. Lea was accused of being anti-Catholic and even anti-Spanish.

27. Kamen, *The Spanish Inquisition*, 59–62.

28. Peters, *Inquisition*, 87.

29. William Doyle, *The French Revolution: A Very Short Introduction* (Oxford: Oxford University Press, 2001), 80.

30. Thomas Kaiser, "Reign of Terror," in *Oxford Encyclopedia of the Modern World*, ed. Peter N. Stearns (Oxford: Oxford University Press, 2008).

31. *The Times*, September 10, 1792.

32. The death toll is described and explained in the "Reign of Terror" article in the Encyclopaedia Britannica, https://www.britannica.com/place/France/The-Reign-of-Terror.

33. Jonathan Glover, *Humanity: A Moral History of the Twentieth Century* (New York: Random House, 2001), 413.

34. Maximilien Robespierre, "On the Moral and Political Principles of Domestic Policy,"

Internet History Sourcebooks Project. History Department of Fordham University, New York, https://sourcebooks.fordham.edu/mod/robespierre-terror.asp. See also discussion between Mike Broers, Rebecca Spang, and Tim Blanning on the BBC show *In Our Time* with Melvin Bragg (one of my favourite podcasts), "The French Revolution's Reign of Terror," *In Our Time*, BBC, 26 May 2005, https://www.bbc.co.uk/programmes/p003k9cf.

35. Martin Luther, "Defence and Explanation of All the Articles" (1521), 1.34, in *The Works of Martin Luther, Vol. 32: Career of the Reformer*, trans. Charles M. Jacobs, rev. George W. Forell, (Charlottesville, VA: Intelex, 2013), 88–89.

36. Luther, *On the Bondage of the Will*, WA 649–661 in the Weimar edition of Luther's Works; English translation in Rupp, *Luther and Erasmus*, 154–66.

37. George Townsend, ed., *The Acts and Monuments of John Foxe, Vol. 4* (London: Seeley, 1846), 452.

38. So Madden, "Crafting the Myth of the Inquisition."

39. Peters, *Inquisition*, 134.

40. Peters, *Inquisition*, 170–71.

41. Peters, *Inquisition*, 172.

42. Cited in Peters, *Inquisition*, 171.

43. Peters, *Inquisition*, 122–88.

44. See John M. Barry, *Roger Williams and the Creation of the American Soul: Church, State, and the Birth of Liberty* (London: Penguin, 2012); Wilken, *Liberty in the Things of God*, 144–54.

45. Peters, *Inquisition*, 242–54.

46. John W. Draper, *History of the Conflict between Religion and Science* (New York: Appleton, 1875); Andrew D. White, *A History of the Warfare of Science with Theology in Christendom* (New York: Appleton, 1896).

47. Rivka Feldhay, "Religion," in *The Cambridge History of Science, Vol. 3: Early Modern Science* (Cambridge: Cambridge University Press, 2006), 727.

48. Augustine, *The Literal Meaning of Genesis*, 1.19; Aquinas, *Summa Theologiae*, 1a, 68, 1.

49. Peters, *Inquisition*, 249.

50. Rivka Feldhay, "Religion," 746–47.

51. "Vatican Admits Galileo Was Right," *New Scientist*, 7 November 1992, https://www.newscientist.com/article/mg13618460-600-vatican-admits-galileo-was-right/.

52. Papal address to an International Symposium on the Inquisition (§4), on 31 October 1998, http://www.vatican.va/content/john-paul-ii/en/speeches/1998/october/documents/hf_jp-ii_spe_19981031_simposio.html.

53. Cited in Peters, *Inquisition*, 171.

Chapter 21: The Reformation "Wars of Religion"

1. Dawkins, *The God Delusion*, 316.

2. Martin Luther, "Letter to the Archbishop of Mainz, 1517," in *The Works of Martin Luther, Vol. 1*, ed. and trans. Adolph Spaeth et al. (Philadelphia: Holman, 1915), 25–28. Also online at the Fordham University Medieval Sourcebook website, https://sourcebooks.fordham.edu/source/lutherltr-indulgences.asp.

3. Catechism of the Catholic Church, 2.2.3.5 (1366), http://www.vatican.va/archive/ENG0015/_INDEX.HTM.

4. He published a tract in 1520 titled *Adversus execrabilem Antichristi bullam*, "Against the Execrable Bull of the Antichrist."

5. Martin Luther, "On the Jews and Their Lies," (1543) in *Luther's Works, Vol. 47: The Christian In Society IV*, ed. Franklin Sherman, trans. Martin H. Bertram (Philadelphia: Fortress, 1971), 121–306.

6. Luther, "On the Jews and Their Lies," 217.

7. Luther, "On the Jews and Their Lies," 268–70.

8. See the editor's introduction to "On the Jews and Their Lies," 123–24.

9. See Steven Ozment, *The Age of Reform, 1250–1550: An Intellectual and Religious History of Late Medieval and Reformation Europe* (New Haven: Yale University Press, 1980), 374–77.

10. See "Thirty Years War," *Oxford Dictionary of the Christian Church*, 611–12.

11. Stephen Toulmin, *Cosmopolis: The Hidden Agenda of Modernity* (Chicago: University of Chicago Press, 1990), 54.

12. Peter Wilson, *Europe's Tragedy: A New History of the Thirty Years War* (London: Penguin, 2010). On the death toll (and the 15 percent figure), see his chapter 22, "The Human and Material Cost."

13. Wilson, *Europe's Tragedy*, Kindle location, 428.

14. English translation by Emil Reich, *Select Documents Illustrating Mediaeval and Modern History* (London: King & Son, 1905), 226–32, http://ghdi.ghi-dc.org/sub_document.cfm ?document_id=4386.

15. Peter Wilson, "Dynasty, Constitution, and Confession: The Role of Religion in the Thirty Years War," *The International History Review* 30 (Sept 2008): 503.

16. Wilson, "Dynasty, Constitution, and Confession," 503. See also Bragg, "The Thirty Years War," interview with Peter Wilson, Ulinka Rublack, and Toby Osborne, *In Our Time*, BBC, 6 December 2018, https://www.bbc.co.uk/programmes/m0001fv2.

17. Wilson in Bragg, "The Thirty Years War."

18. Wilson, "Dynasty, Constitution, and Confession," 508.

19. Rublack in Bragg, "The Thirty Years War."

20. See "Richelieu, Armand Jean du Plessis," *Oxford Dictionary of the Christian Church*, 1397.

21. Wilson, *Europe's Tragedy*, Kindle location, 499. See also his essay dedicated to the question: Wilson, "Dynasty, Constitution, and Confession," 473–514.

22. Wilson in Bragg, "The Thirty Years War." For the general misunderstandings of the Thirty Years' War, see chapter 1 of Wilson, *Europe's Tragedy*.

23. Wilson, *Europe's Tragedy*, Kindle location, 14139.

24. Wilson, *Europe's Tragedy*, Kindle location, 14126–14278. Slightly lower estimates are offered by John Theibault, "The Demography of the Thirty Years War Re-Revisited: Günther Franz and his Critics," *German History* 15 (1997): 1–21.

25. Wilson, *Europe's Tragedy*, Kindle location, 13477.

26. Wilson, *Europe's Tragedy*, Kindle location, 13,465.

27. This is one of the clearest points of agreement between Rublack, Wilson, and Osborne in Bragg, "The Thirty Years War."

28. Wilson, *Europe's Tragedy*, Kindle location, 14896.

29. Hart, *Atheist Delusions*, 95–96.

Chapter 22: The "Troubles"

1. Hitchens, *God Is Not Great*, 18.

2. Michael J. Braddick, ed., *The Oxford Handbook of the English Revolution* (Oxford: Oxford University Press, 2015), 246; F. N. Forman, *Constitutional Change in the United Kingdom* (London: Routledge, 2002), 32.

3. Marc Mulholland, *Northern Ireland: A Very Short Introduction* (Oxford: Oxford University Press, 2001), 2.

4. Mulholland, *Northern Ireland*, 12–14.

5. Cited in Mulholland, *Northern Ireland*, 19.

6. Mulholland, *Northern Ireland*, 25.

7. Mulholland, *Northern Ireland*, 55–92.

8. Officially titled "The Belfast Agreement," the Good Friday Agreement can be downloaded from https://www.gov.uk/government/publications/the-belfast-agreement.

9. The Belfast Agreement, 24.

10. For the details of the agreement, see Mulholland, *Northern Ireland*, 141–46.

11. Mulholland, *Northern Ireland*, 76–77.

12. The Belfast Agreement, 22.

13. Homily of John Paul II, Saturday, 29 Sept 1979, Holy Mass in Drogheda, https://w2.vatican .va/content/john-paul-ii/en/homilies/1979/documents/hf_jp-ii_hom_19790929_irlanda -dublino-drogheda.html.

14. *John Paul II in Ireland: A Plea for Peace* (2018), written by Navid Naglieri and directed by Marc Boudignon and David Naglieri. See the Internet Movie Database (IMDb) listing, https://www.imdb.com/title/tt8775080/?ref_=ttfc_fc_tt.

15. Peter Crutchley, "IRA Ceasefire 20 Years On: The Priest Who Brokered the Peace," BBC News, 31 August 2014, https://www.bbc.com/news/uk-28812366.

16. Douglas, Dalby, "Alec Reid, Northern Ireland Priest Who Helped Broker Peace Accord, Dies at 82," *The New York Times*, 25 November 2013, https://www.nytimes.com/2013/11/26 /world/alec-reid-priest-who-helped-broker-peace-accord-in-northern-ireland-dies-at-82.html.

Chapter 23: Moral Reckoning

1. Kimiko de Freytas-Tamura, "Pope to Visit Ireland, Where Scars of Sex Abuse Are 'Worse than the I.R.A,'" *New York Times*, 23 August 2018, https://www.nytimes.com/2018/08/23 /world/europe/francis-ireland-sexual-abuse-catholic-church.html.

2. An account of the Donegal investigations has been published by the lead detective, Martin Ridge with Gerard Cunningham, *Breaking the Silence: One Garda's Quest to Find the Truth* (Dublin: Gill, 2008).

3. "'States of Fear' Journalist Mary Raftery Dies," BBC News, January 2012, https://www.bbc .com/news/uk-northern-ireland-16484276.

4. "The Irish Affliction," *The New York Times Magazine*, February 2011, https://www.nytimes .com/2011/02/13/magazine/13Irish-t.html.

5. https://www.bostonglobe.com/news/special-reports/2002/01/31/scores-priests-involved-sex -abuse-cases/kmRm7JtqBdEZ8UF0ucR16L/story.html.

6. "A Church Seeks Healing," December 2002, *Boston Globe*, https://www.bostonglobe.com /news/special-reports/2002/12/14/church-seeks-healing/WJS0tI6gQP8zQAHjAHVhmL /story.html.

7. John Jay College of Criminal Justice report, 2004, "The Nature and Scope of Sexual Abuse of Minors by Catholic Priests and Deacons in the United States, 1950–2002," https://www.usccb .org/sites/default/files/issues-and-action/child-and-youth-protection/upload/The-Nature-and -Scope-of-Sexual-Abuse-of-Minors-by-Catholic-Priests-and-Deacons-in-the-United-States -1950–2002.pdf.

8. Marije Stoltenborgh et al., "A Global Perspective on Child Sexual Abuse: Meta-Analysis of Prevalence Around the World," *Child Maltreatment* 16 (2011): 79–101.

9. Bronwyn Watson and Kim Halford, "Classes of Childhood Sexual Abuse and Women's Adult Couple Relationships," *Violence and Victims* 25 (2010): 518–35.

10. The Australian Royal Commission into Institutional Responses to Child Sexual Abuse 2017, https://www.childabuseroyalcommission.gov.au/final-report. A helpful summary of the findings was provided by Australia's national broadcaster, the ABC, https://www.abc.net.au /news/2017–12–15/royal-commission-child-sexual-abuse-by-the-numbers/9263800.

11. Royal Commission into Institutional Responses to Child Sexual Abuse. https://www.child abuseroyalcommission.gov.au/religious-institutions.

12. L. Bromfield, C. Hirte, O. Octoman, and I. Katz, *Child Sexual Abuse in Australian Institutional Contexts 2008–13: Findings from Administrative Data* (Sydney: Royal Commission into Institutional Responses to Child Sexual Abuse. University of South Australia, 2017), 205–6, https://www.childabuseroyalcommission.gov.au/sites/default/files/file-list/research_report _-_child_sexual_abuse_in_australian_institutional_contexts_2008–13_findings_from _administrative_data_-_causes.pdf.

13. *Final Report, Vol. 2: Nature and Cause* (Royal Commission into Institutional Responses to Child Sexual Abuse. Commonwealth of Australia, 2017), 65.

14. The best data for child sexual abuse in schools comes from a 2014 study commissioned by the US Department of Education which found that 6.7 per cent of public school students have experienced contact sexual abuse from an educator. Charol Shakeshaft, *Educator Sexual Misconduct: A Synthesis of Existing Literature* (U.S. Department of Education, 2004), 16–18, https://www2.ed.gov/rschstat/research/pubs/misconductreview/index.html.

15. The Australian Broadcasting Commission (our national broadcaster) has created a helpful summary of the Royal Commission's findings. See https://www.abc.net.au/news/2017–12 –15/royal-commission-child-sexual-abuse-by-the-numbers/9263800.

16. Australia Bureau of Statistics, Religion in Australia, 2019, https://www.abs.gov.au/ausstats /abs@.nsf/Lookup/by%20Subject/2071.0-2016-Main%20Features-Religion%20Data%20 Summary-70.

17. Australia Bureau of Statistics, Schools in Australia, 2019, https://www.abs.gov.au/ausstats /abs@.nsf/mf/4221.0.

18. See Patrick Parkinson, "Child Sexual Abuse in the Catholic Church: The Australian Experience," Berkley Center, Georgetown University, 25 September 2019, https://berkleycenter .georgetown.edu/responses/child-sexual-abuse-in-the-catholic-church-the-australian-experience.

19. Parkinson, "Child Sexual Abuse in the Catholic Church."

20. https://www.usccb.org/sites/default/files/issues-and-action/child-and-youth-protection/upload /The-Nature-and-Scope-of-Sexual-Abuse-of-Minors-by-Catholic-Priests-and-Deacons-in-the -United-States-1950–2002.pdf.

21. *Final Report: Preface and Executive Summary*, 60–61, https://www.childabuseroyalcommission .gov.au/sites/default/files/final_report_-_preface_and_executive_summary.pdf.

22. Thomas G. Plante, "Keeping Children Safe in the Catholic Church," April 2020, https://www .psychologytoday.com/au/blog/do-the-right-thing/202004/keeping-children-safe-in-the-catholic -church. See also, "Pedophilia," https://www.psychologytoday.com/au/conditions/pedophilia. See also M. Seto, "Pedophilia," *Annual Review of Clinical Psychology* 5 (2009): 391–407. Seto recently revised down his estimate to between 1 and 2 per cent. See https://www.bbc.com/news /magazine-28526106.

23. Patrick Parkinson, R. Kim Oates, Amanda Jayakody, "Child Sexual Abuse in the Anglican Church of Australia," *Journal of Child Sexual Abuse* 21 (2012): 565. See also Patrick Parkinson, "Child Sexual Abuse and the Churches: A Story of Moral Failure?" *Current Issues in Criminal Justice*, 26(1).

24. *Final Report, Vol. 16: Religious Institutions*, 12.

25. *Final Report, Vol. 16: Religious Institutions*, 12.

26. *Final Report: Recommendations*, 50–60.

27. *Final Report: Preface and Executive Summary*, 71. RMIT University in Melbourne has published a controversial study of celibacy's connection to child sexual abuse: Desmond Cahill and Peter Wilkinson, "Child Sexual Abuse in the Catholic Church: An Interpretive

Review of the Literature and Public Inquiry Reports," Centre for Global Research, RMIT University, 2017, https://www.rmit.edu.au/content/dam/rmit/documents/news/church-abuse /child-sex-abuse-and-the-catholic-church.pdf.

28. For example, https://www.psychologytoday.com/au/blog/do-the-right-thing/202004/keeping -children-safe-in-the-catholic-church.

29. Parkinson, "Child Sexual Abuse and the Churches," 119.

30. Joe Sullivan and Anthony Beech, "A Comparative Study of Demographic Data Relating to Intra-and Extra-Familial Child Sexual Abusers and Professional Perpetrators," *Journal of Sexual Aggression* 10 (2004): 46.

31. Sadly, the same may be true of schoolteachers and other professions with access to children. See Alison Gaitonde, "Sexual Abuse in Schools," *British Journal of Psychotherapy* 3 (1987): 315–22.

32. Ross Douthat, *Bad Religion: How We Became a Nation of Heretics* (New York: Simon & Schuster, 2012), 132.

Chapter 24: Social Capital

1. The original announcement of the Chicago study can be found at https://news.uchicago.edu /sites/default/files/story/attachments/2019–10/Decety_Religion_Altruism_Study.pdf.

2. Jean Decety et al., "The Negative Association between Religiousness and Children's Altruism across the World," *Current Biology*, 25:22.

3. Bobby Azarian, "Study: Religious Kids Are Jerks," *The Daily Beast*, April 2017, https://www .thedailybeast.com/study-religious-kids-are-jerks.

4. https://news.uchicago.edu/sites/default/files/story/attachments/2019–10/Decety_Religion _Altruism_Study.pdf.

5. Christopher Peterson and Martin Seligman, ed., *Character Strengths and Virtues: A Handbook and Classification* (Oxford: Oxford University Press, 2004).

6. Peterson and Seligman, *Character Strengths and Virtues*, 610. See G. W. Allport and J. Ross, "Personal Religious Orientation and Prejudice," *Journal of Personality and Social Psychology* 5 (1967): 432–43.

7. Peterson and Seligman, *Character Strengths and Virtues*, 611. See M. Leiber and A. Woodrick, "Religious Beliefs, Attributional Styles, and Adherence to Correctional Orientations," *Criminal Justice and Behaviour* 24 (1997): 495–511.

8. Peterson and Seligman, *Character Strengths and Virtues*, 610.

9. See the review of all these studies in Peterson and Seligman, *Character Strengths and Virtues*, 610–11.

10. See the review article, Steven Tracy, "Patriarch and Domestic Violence," *Journal of the Evangelical Theological Society* 50 (Sept 2007): 583–84. See also Christopher G. Ellison and Kristin L. Anderson, "Religious Involvement and Domestic Violence among U.S. Couples," *Journal for the Scientific Study of Religion* 40 (2001): 269–86.

11. Col 3:19; 1 Pet 3:7.

12. See the 2019 *World Family Map* from the Institute of Family Studies, https://ifstudies.org /blog/the-ties-that-bind. Domestic violence in churches was explored in an important series of articles by respected Australian journalist Dr. Julia Baird. See https://www.abc.net.au /news/2018–05–23/when-women-are-believed-the-church-will-change/9782184.

13. https://www.abc.net.au/news/2015–03–12/moore-dickson-the-church-must-confront -domestic-abuse/6300342.

14. Peterson and Seligman, *Character Strengths and Virtues*, 610.

15. Harold Koenig, Dana King, Verna Carson, ed., *Handbook of Religion and Health*, 2nd ed. (Oxford: Oxford University Press, 2012), 301–6.

16. Tyler VanderWeele, "Religion and Health," in *Spirituality and Religion Within the Culture of Medicine: From Evidence to Practice*, ed., Michael Balboni and John Peteet (Oxford: Oxford University Press, 2017), 357–416.

17. Peterson and Seligman, *Character Strengths and Virtues*, 609.

18. Robert Putnam, *Bowling Alone: The Collapse and Revival of American Community* (New York: Simon & Schuster, 2000), 19. On his important early work, see Sergio Fabbrini, "Robert D. Putnam between Italy and the United States," *Bulletin of Italian Politics* 3 (2011).

19. Robert Putnam and David Campbell, *American Grace: How Religion Divides and Unites Us* (New York: Simon & Schuster, 2012).

20. Putnam and Campbell, *American Grace*, 444.

21. Putnam and Campbell, *American Grace*, 444–45. The data on volunteering was gathered in Putnam's 2006 Faith Matters Survey and is available at http://www.thearda.com/Archive/Files/Descriptions/FTHMATT.asp. See also Arthur Brooks, *Who Really Cares: The Surprising Truth about Compassionate Conservativism* (New York: Basic Books, 2006) and published studies by Tyler VanderWeele of Harvard's School of Public Health, https://www.hsph.harvard.edu/tyler-vanderweele/selected-publications/.

22. Putnam and Campbell, *American Grace*, 444.

23. Andrew Leigh and John Dickson, "Social Capital," *Undeceptions*, Season 1, Episode 5, https://undeceptions.com/podcast/social-capital. Also, Andrew Leigh, *Disconnected* (Sydney: University of New South Wales Press, 2010), 35.

24. Leigh, *Disconnected*, 32.

25. Deloitte Access Economics report, "Economic Value of Donating and Volunteering Behaviour Associated with Religiosity," (May 2018), https://www2.deloitte.com/content/dam/Deloitte/au/Documents/Economics/deloitte-au-economics-donating-volunteering-behavior-associated-with-religiosity-01062018.pdf.

26. Stephen Judd, et al., *Driven by Purpose*, 55. The original article was "Australia's Top 200 Charities," *Business Review Weekly*, June 29–July 5, 2006, 56–59.

27. David J Houston, "'Walking the Walk' of Public Service Motivation: Public Employees and Charitable Gifts of Time, Blood, and Money," *Journal of Public Administration Research and Theory* 16 (2006): 78. The European study is by Kieran Healy, "Embedded Altruism: Blood Collection Regimes and the European Union's Donor Population," *American Journal of Sociology* 105 (2000): 1633–57.

28. Leigh, *Disconnected*, 34.

29. Leigh, *Disconnected*, 33.

30. Brown, *Eye of a Needle*, 46–47.

31. Wayne Meeks, *The First Urban Christians: The Social World of the Apostle Paul* (New Haven: Yale University Press, 1983), 74–110.

32. Leigh, *Disconnected*, 35.

Chapter 25: The "Log in the Eye" of Us All

1. Steven Pinker, *Enlightenment Now: The Case for Reason, Science, Humanism, and Progress* (London: Penguin, 2018); and see his earlier *The Better Angels of Our Nature: Why Violence Has Declined* (New York: Viking, 2011).

2. A. N. Wilson, *Charles Darwin: Victorian Mythmaker* (London: Murray, 2017), 105–6; see also 299–300.

3. Charles Darwin, *The Descent of Man, and Selection in Relation to Sex* (London: Murray, 1871), cited in Daniel J. McKaughan and Holly VandWall, *The History and Philosophy of Science: A Reader* (London: Bloomsbury, 2018), 966.

4. Fellow atheist intellectual John Gray wrote a withering review of *Better Angels* in the UK Guardian, provocatively titled "Steven Pinker Is Wrong about Violence and War," https://www.theguardian.com/books/2015/mar/13/john-gray-steven-pinker-wrong-violence-war-declining. For a theologian's critique, see David Bentley Hart, https://www.firstthings.com/article/2012/01/the-precious-steven-pinker. On Pinker's *Enlightenment Now*, see John Gray's typically scathing review, https://www.newstatesman.com/culture/books/2018/02/unenlightened-thinking-steven-pinker-s-embarrassing-new-book-feeble-sermon. Also see the more mild-mannered assessment by Nick Spencer from the British think tank *Theos*, https://www.theosthinktank.co.uk/comment/2018/02/20/enlightenment-and-progress-or-why-steven-pinker-is-wrong. See also review in *Times Literary Supplement*, https://www.the-tls.co.uk/articles/comfort-history-enlightenment-now/.

5. Aleksander Solzhenitsyn, *The Gulag Archipelago* (New York: Vintage Classics, 2018), 113.

6. Weinberg's original speech is online at PhysLink, https://www.physlink.com/Education/essay_weinberg.cfm.

7. Dawkins, *The God Delusion*, 283.

8. Steven Weinberg, "A Designer Universe," PhysLink, https://www.physlink.com/Education/essay_weinberg.cfm.

9. Davis, *In the Image of God*, 198.

10. Aristotle, *Politics* 1.2.1254b (Rackham, Loeb Classical Library 264), 22–23.

11. James Hunt, *On the Negro's Place in Nature* (London: Trübner & Co., 1863), 52, 60.

12. Henry Wiencek, "The Dark Side of Thomas Jefferson," *Smithsonian Magazine*, October 2012, https://www.smithsonianmag.com/history/the-dark-side-of-thomas-jefferson-35976004/.

13. Authoritative figures for World War I are difficult to find. The following sources offer a number of fifteen–twenty million total (six–nine million civilian) deaths: Rüdiger Overmans, "Military Losses (Casualties)," *Brill's Digital Library of World War I*, https://referenceworks.brillonline.com/browse/brills-digital-library-of-world-war-i; see also Antoine Prost, "War Losses," *International Encyclopedia of the First World War*, ed. Ute Daniel et al. (Freie Universität Berlin, Berlin, 2014–10–08), doi: 10.15463/ie1418.10271, https://encyclopedia.1914-1918-online.net/home/; and John Graham Royde-Smith, "World War I: Killed, Wounded, and Missing," in *Encyclopedia Britannica*, https://www.britannica.com/event/World-War-I/Killed-wounded-and-missing.

14. J. M. Winter, "Demography of War," in *The Oxford Companion to World War II*, ed. I. C. B. Dear and M. R. D. Foot (Oxford: Oxford University Press, 2001), 224–27.

15. This is a point argued at length in William Cavanaugh, *The Myth of Religious Violence: Secular Ideology and the Roots of Modern Conflict* (Oxford: Oxford University Press, 2009).

16. An excellent popular review of Nazi views of orthodox Christianity is found in McLaughlin, *Confronting Christianity*, 87–94. For a detailed academic account of the same, see Richard Steigmann-Gall, *The Holy Reich: Nazi Conceptions of Christianity, 1919–1945* (Cambridge: Cambridge University Press, 2004). See also Glover, *Humanity*, 355–356.

17. Robert Conquest, *The Great Terror: Stalin's Purge in the Thirties* (New York: Random House, 2018), 486.

18. Cited in Glover, *Humanity*, 259.

19. Jung Chang, *Wild Swans: Three Daughters of China* (New York: Simon & Schuster, 2003), 314.

20. Glover, *Humanity*, 297.

21. Even official Chinese sources acknowledge that deaths under Mao reach to twenty thousand. See Lucian W. Pye, "Reassessing the Cultural Revolution," *The China Quarterly* 108 (Dec 1986): 597–612.

22. Glover, *Humanity*, 306.

23. Glover, *Humanity*, 309.

24. Glover, *Humanity*, 309.

25. Dawkins, *The God Delusion*, 316.

26. Terry Eagleton, *On Evil* (New Haven: Yale University Press, 2010), 156.

27. See Catharine A. MacKinnon, "Pornography as Trafficking," *Michigan Journal of International Law* 26 (2005): 993–1012; Allison J. Luzwick, "Human Trafficking and Pornography: Using the Trafficking Victims Protection Act to Prosecute Trafficking for the Production of Internet Pornography," *Northwestern University Law Review* 111 (2017): 137–53.

The Beautiful Tune—A Coda

1. Albert Einstein, "Meine Meinung über den Krieg" ("My Opinion of the War"), paper offered to the Berlin chapter of the Goethebund, 23 October–11 November 1915. The German original is printed in A. J. Kox et al., eds., *The Collected Papers of Albert Einstein, Vol. 6: The Berlin Years: Writings, 1914–1947* (Princeton: Princeton University Press, 1996), 211–13. Translation mine.

2. Leigh, *Disconnected*, 48–49.

3. Tom Holland, *Dominion: The Making of the Western Mind* (Boston: Little, Brown, 2019).

4. Tom Holland, "Why I Was Wrong about Christianity," *The New Statesman*, 14 September 2016.

5. Ferry, *A Brief History of Thought*. All of the quotations above come from chapter 3, "The Victory of Christianity over Greek Philosophy," 55–92. See also the review by Gary Rosen, "How to Think about How to Live," *The Wall Street Journal*, 27 December 2001, https://www.wsj.com/articles/SB1000142405297020455230457711298303327416.

Scripture Index

Genesis

1	31–32
1:1	198
1:26	114, 289
1:26–28	31
3	290
5:1–3	32
9	290
9:6	32

Leviticus

19:18	27

Deuteronomy

15:4–11	295

Joshua

20:1–6	201

Proverbs

8	159
9:1	164

Isaiah

2	230
11	230
45:23	294
58:5–10	295
58:6	180
61:1–9	40
61:8	41

Matthew

5–7	26
5:1–4	38–39
5:1–10	173
5:9	11
5:23–24	33
5:38–48	26
7:1–4	280
7:1–5	41
7:5	180
7:11	38
7:12	28
7:22–23	38
16:18	1
18:10	264
23:23	180
25:36	296

Mark

6:3	42
8:34–35	6
10:42–43	264
12:30	159

Luke

3:38	290
6	26
6:27	xxiv, 9
6:27–36	26
6:28	11
6:31	28
6:35–36	29
6:36	32–33, 188
6:37–42	41

7:33–34. 167
10:30–37. . . . 81
11:41 295
12:13–21 108
12:33 295
12:48 25
14:21 295
15:11–32 32
17:2. 264
18:22; 19:8 . . . 295

John
1:1 294
1:5 216

Acts
11:27–28 295
17:28–29 290

Romans
5:8 29
12:2. 169
12:14–19 127
12:17–21 48
13:3–5 127
13:14 129
15:25–27 296

1 Corinthians
8–10 291
1:26. 97
6:1–6. 71
7:21–23. . . . . 113, 299
9:20–22 168
16:1–4 296

2 Corinthians
8–9 296
8:9, 13 81

Galatians
2:10. 81

Ephesians
6:10–17. 127
6:13–17. 175

Philippians
2:10–11. 294

Colossians
1:15–20. 294
3:19. 315
3:22–4:1 112

1 Timothy
1:9–11 112

James
2:14–16. 296
3:9 32

1 Peter
2:17. 112
3:7 315
3:15–16. 148

1 John
3:16. 29–30
3:16–17. 82
4:8–11 30
4:9–11 . . . . . 283, 296
4:20–21 33

Subject Index

Abdulhamid II, 20
abolitionism, 111
Act of Kingly Title, 249–50
Adam, 32, 290
Admonitio generalis, 149, 169
Ælberht of York, 158, 164
Æthelbert of Kent, 141
Age of Reason, 214, 231
Agora (film), 120
Al-Aqsa Mosque, 2–4, 10, 12, 16, 19, 21
Alaric, 132, 138–39
Albigensian Crusades, 17
Albigensianism, 186, 221
Alcuin of York, 147, 151–55, 157–58, 161–66, 171, 180, 199
Alexander the Great, 205
Alexander of Jerusalem, 52
Alexandria riot, 117–18, 119, 126
Alexius I Comnenus, 5, 9, 13–14, 171, 206
al-Farabi, 208
al-Hariri, Sayyid 'Ali. *See* Hariri, Sayyid 'Ali, al-
al-Kamil. *See* Kamil, al-Malik al-
altruism, 266, 270, 284
Ambrose of Milan, xxiii, 95, 97, 100–7, 111, 114, 117, 124, 126, 129, 130, 135, 139, 164
Ammianus Marcellinus, 89
anti-intellectualism, the beginning of Christian misogyny and, 120
anti-Semitism, 9, 76, 220, 223, 240–41
Aquinas. *See* Thomas Aquinas
Archdiocese of Boston, xxi, 258–59
Arianism, 74, 102, 221
Aristotle, 27, 34, 78, 164, 198, 207, 208, 277, 290
Arius, 73–74

armor of God, 127, 175
Athanasius, 123, 199
atheism, 91, 92, 94, 237, 272, 279, 280, 284, 285
atheists, 91, 124, 271, 280
Augsburg Confession, 243
Augustine of Canterbury, 141, 143, 145, 151, 171
Augustine of Hippo, Saint, 100, 125, 126, 128–36, 141, 153, 160, 164, 172, 189, 233, 295
Augustus, 70
autos de fe, 225–26
Avitus of Vienne, 170–71
Babylas of Antioch, 52
Balthild of Ascania, 143
barbarians, 53, 132, 134, 137–39, 198, 208, 213
Basil the Great, 107, 108–11, 136, 160, 191, 199, 201, 202, 203, 204
Battle of Hattin, 11–12
Battle of Milvian Bridge, 59, 77
Belfast Agreement, 249, 252–53, 254, 255, 258
Benedict of Nursia, 179, 181–83, 190
Berbers, 134
Bernard of Clairvaux, 10–11, 167, 174–76, 178
Black Lives Matter movement, 119
Bloody Sunday, 249, 252
Boniface I, 134
Boniface, Saint, 137, 143–45, 151, 171, 180
Bracciolini, Poggio, 155–57
bread and wine, 82, 239
burial services of the church, 92–93
Byzantine Empire. *See chapter 18* (197–209); *also* 5, 109, 132, 138, 191

Byzantium, xxiii, 70–71, 138, 205, 206–7, 209. *See also* Constantinople; Roman Empire: Eastern

Caecilius Natalis, 97–98

Callinicum, 102, 117

Calvin, John, 242

canon law (or, church law), 99, 153, 193–94, 195, 200, 202

capital punishment, 76, 127, 128, 228

Cappadocian Christianity. *See chapter 9* (106–15)

Cappadocian fathers, 107

Cardinal Richelieu, 244

Carolingian, 141, 145, 148, 157, 162, 163, 164, 165, 169, 184, 192, 199, 200

catacombs, 92–93, 98

Catharism, 186, 221

Catherine of Siena, 186–87, 297

Catholic Church. *See* Roman Catholic Church

Catholicism, xxiii, 23, 232

celibacy, 263

charities, xxiii, 84, 94, 107, 179, 190, 203, 265, 270, 272, 276, 284

charity
the birth of Christian, 80–84
in Greek and Roman society, 78–80

Charlemagne, 141, 145–46, 148–54, 157–58, 162–64, 166, 171, 180, 197, 200, 208, 222, 240

Charles V (Holy Roman emperor), 239

Charles the Great. *See* Charlemagne

children, Greco-Roman killing of unwanted, 34

Children's Crusade, 14

child sexual abuse. *See chapter 23* (257–64)
global prevalence for girls, boys, 259
not just a Catholic problem, 261–63
scandals, xxi, 58
in schools, 314
in specifically religious institutions, rate of, 263
and the teachings of Jesus, 264
the world's largest investigation into, 259–61

China, 45, 168, 198, 279

Chi-Rho symbol, 60–61, 85

Christianity
the antidote to hateful, nationalistic, 284
Cappadocian. *See chapter 9* (106–15)
the central moral logic of, 30, 283
eastern form of, 206
iconoclastic. *See chapter 10* (116–24)
and mental health, 268–69
and slavery, 111–13
and social capital, 270–74

Christian "jihad." *See chapter 14* (147–54)

Christians
the first state-sponsored violent suppression of, 47
currently living in Europe, Latin America, and the Caribbean (percents), 168
and warfare (AD 100–400), 126–28

Christina the Astonishing, 176–78

church
burial services of the, 92–93
child abuse in the modern. *See chapter 23* (257–64)
the conversion of the, 169–71
the death of Rome and the growth of. *See chapter 13* (137–46)
the four traditional "Doctors" of the, 100
law. *See* canon law
persecution of the. *See chapter 5* (44–57)
schooling in the ancient, 159–61
and taxation under Constantine, 76–78

churchgoers, 272–73, 274, 271

church law (or, canon law), 99, 153, 193–94, 195, 200, 202

Cicero, 128, 156, 159, 160, 164, 180, 212

Circus of Nero, 47, 48

cities of refuge, 201

Claudius, 47, 291

Clement of Alexandria, 160

Clothar II, Dagobert, 141

Clovis I, 140–41, 148, 149, 170–71

Code of Hammurabi, 27

Codex of Justinian, 200, 290

communism, 279

Conservatives, 220

Constantine II, 87

Constantine the Great. *See chapters 6–7* (58–86); *also* 46, 87, 88, 96–100, 105, 113, 117, 124, 128, 138, 139, 149, 191, 198, 205, 294

building program of, 70–71
the conversion of, 59–61
humanitarianism and anti-Semitism of, 74–76
illness and death, 85
Constantinople, 5, 9, 13–14, 20, 62, 71, 85, 88, 99, 132, 138, 172, 198–99, 202, 204, 206–7, 209
Copernicus, Nicolaus, 233
Cornelius of Rome, 82
coronavirus/COVID-19, 19–20, 99, 100
Council of Nicaea, 73–74, 101, 128
Council of Serdica, 99, 100
crucifixion, 3, 29, 74, 203
Crusade, origin of the word, 6
Crusades. *See chapter 2* (8–22); *also*, 2, 36, 96, 135, 140, 177, 189, 196–97, 206, 208, 209, 236–37, 264, 277, 281. *See individual crusades (First, Second, etc.) by name*
factors leading to the demise of the, 17–20
legacy of the, 22
religious motivations for the, 4–7
Cyprian, 82
Cyprian Plague, 82–83
Cyril of Alexandria, 120–22, 136
Cyril of Jerusalem, 161
Dado, 141–42
Daniel of Winchester, 143–44, 171
Dark Ages, 6, 22, 133, 138, 139, 141, 156, 165, 166, 200, 209–15, 217, 218, 231, 275, 281
Darwin, Charles, 275–76
Dawkins, Richard, 25–26, 53, 210, 237, 277, 280
dead, Christian care for the (2nd–4th cent.), 92–93
death toll
of the French Revolution, 228–30
under Mao Zedong, 279, 317
of the Spanish Inquisition, 227–28
of the Thirty Years' War, 245
of the Troubles, 253
World Wars I, II, 278
Decius, 52
Declaration of the Rights of Man, 229, 285
Defenestration of Prague, 243–44
Diet of Worms, 239–40
Diocletian, 53–56, 72

Diocletianic Persecution. *See* Great Persecution
Dionysius, 83
Dome of the Rock, 2, 16, 19
Eastern Orthodox Church, 200
Ebolus of Saint-Germain, 172, 174, 184
Edict of Milan, 62–64, 66–68, 151, 232
Edward VI, 194
Einstein, Albert, 25, 284
Eligius, 141–43, 145, 171, 180
Elizabeth I, 194–95, 231, 250
El Salvador, 201
Emeric of Hungary, 13
Enlightenment, 120, 193, 211–15, 217, 229, 230, 231–32, 247, 275, 276, 278, 281, 284
Epicurus, 78
Epictetus, 27, 78
Erasmus, Desiderius, 238
euergetism, 79–80
Eugenius III, 10
Europe
forced conversions in (late 700s). *See chapter 14* (147–54)
400–1100, barbarians and Christians in. *See chapter 13* (137–46)
number of Christians living in, 168
Eusebius, 59–61, 199
Eustochium, Saint, 181
Eutropius, 123
Fabian, 52
Fabiola, Saint, 109–10, 191
fall of Acre, 15–16
fall of Rome, 98, 177, 197, 208, 212, 215
Felix, Mutatius, 54–55
Ferdinand V, 222–24
Fifth Crusade, 14–17, 176, 189
first amendment, 67
First Crusade, 2, 4–10, 14, 19, 174, 208
Floyd, George (slain African American), 116, 119
forced conversions, 9. *See chapter 14* (147–54)
For the Love of God, xxii, 23, 289
Fourth Crusade, 9, 13–14, 176, 207
Franciscan Order, 15, 188–89
Francis of Assisi, 15, 18, 187–90
Franks, 140–41, 145, 150, 165, 169, 170
Frederick II, 15–16
freedom of religion, 44–45, 63–65, 67, 68, 86, 117, 205, 232, 243

French Revolution, 228–29, 254, 285
Galerius, 53–54, 55
Galileo, 58, 123, 199, 233–34
Gaul, 53, 55, 109, 137, 139–40, 142, 149, 161, 162, 169, 170, 177, 198, 208, 213, 278
General Admonitions (*Admonitio generalis*) of Charlemagne, 149, 162
George of Cappadocia, 88
Godfrey of Bouillon, 10
Golden Rule, 28
good deeds, 239, 242. *See also* works
Good Friday Agreement (or, Belfast Agreement), 249, 252–53, 254, 255, 258
Good Samaritan, 25, 81, 83, 203, 284
Goths, 132, 138–40, 142, 213
Gratian, 124
Gratian, 153, 193
Great Leap Forward, 279
Great Persecution, 52–57, 64, 66, 72, 73, 83
Gregory I "the Great", 100, 141, 144, 151, 153, 164, 171, 222–23
Gregory II, 143, 144
Gregory VII, 165
Gregory IX, 221
Gregory XI, 187
Gregory of Naziansus, 107–9, 160, 204
Gregory of Nyssa, xxiii, 106, 107, 110–11, 113–14, 130, 160, 199, 204
Gustavus II Adolphus, 244
Hadrian, 16, 294
Hagia Sophia, 200
Hariri, Sayyid 'Ali, al-, 20
Haughey, Charles, 256
Helena, 71
Henry VIII, 249
heresies, 17, 220–21, 224–25
"heresy," meaning and church usage of the word, 220
heretics, 94, 105, 114, 136, 221–22, 224, 226
Hierax, 121
Hierocles, Sossianus, 53
Hildegard, Saint, 185–86, 187, 190
Hillel, 27–28
Hippocratic Oath, 203
Hitchens, Christopher, xx, xxi–xxii, 53, 210, 248, 253
Hitler, Adolf, 279

Holy Communion, 193, 239
Holy Roman Empire, 15–16, 146, 197, 239–40, 243–45, 247
"holy war," theory of, 19, 172, 195
holy wars
    from the 1000s to the 1200s. *See chapter 2* (8–22)
    of the Torah, NT Jews' feeling about, 176
Honorius, 75
Honorius III, 15, 194
Horace, 159, 160, 164
Hosius Of Córdoba. *See* Ossius
hospitals, xxiii, 33, 109–10, 119, 179, 190–92, 195, 201, 259, 263, 265, 276, 284, 286
    Byzantine, 201–3
    the first public hospital, 108, 109
human being: Judeo-Christian versus Greco-Roman view, 33–36
humanism, 19, 213
humanists, 19, 156, 200, 213, 215, 238
humanitarianism, Constantine's, 74–76
human nature, Jesus' view of, 38
Hume, David, 214
humility, 26, 27, 41, 45, 107, 173, 184
Hussites, 17
Hypatia, 120–23, 136
"hypocrite," meaning and uses of the word, 180
Ibn al-Athir, 12
ibn Ishāq, Hunayn, 207
Imad Ad-Din, 11
imago Dei, 30–33, 56, 283, 290
indulgences, 215, 238–39
infant exposure, 34–35, 76, 290
Innocent III, 13, 14–15, 189
Inquisitions. *See chapter 20* (218–35)
    the First Inquisitions 221–22
    Spanish Inquisition, 218–19, 220, 222–28, 230, 254, 279
intolerance, 86, 271, 273
Ireland, establishment of deadly paramilitary groups in, 251
Islam
    number of adherents, 305
    the rise of, 205–6
Islamic expansion, 207
Islamic period, 123
Islamic State, 21

Israel, establishment of the state of, 16
Istanbul, 5, 71, 138. *See* Byzantium;
  Constantinople
Jefferson, Thomas, 30, 57, 67, 119, 278, 282, 293
Jerome, Saint, 100, 109–10, 159–60, 164,
  180–81, 294
Jerusalem
  Siege of (1099), 2–5, 9, 10, 19, 21
  Siege of (1187), 12, 177
Jesus
  child sexual abuse and the teachings of, 264
  on his log and speck, 41–43
  two of his most distinctive teachings,
  24–36
Jews, 9, 10, 16, 30, 35, 49, 53, 70, 76, 81.
  86, 102–3, 118, 121, 168, 176, 192, 203,
  222–24, 240–41, 267, 279, 283
John Paul II, 17, 219, 220, 234, 248, 254–55
John of Salerno, 184–85
Joseph (father of Jesus), 42
Jovian, 94
Julian the Apostate. *See chapter 8* (87–95);
  also 61–62, 86, 96, 102, 103, 111, 118, 123,
  204, 205
  death and successor, 94
  pagan revival of, 88–90
  welfare program of, 90–92
Justinian, 90, 197, 198–205
Justin Martyr, 82, 160
just war
  theory, 126, 130, 134, 136, 151, 172. See
  in general chapter 12 (125–36)
  what constitutes a "just" war, 134–35
Kamil, al-Malik al-(sultan), 15, 18, 190
Kennedy, John F., 25
Knights Templar, 10, 175
Lactantius, Lucius, 55–56, 60, 64–65, 67–69,
  93, 128, 160
Leo III, 146
Leo X, 239
lepers, 108, 188
Libanius, 65
Libertarians, 220–21
Licinius, 62, 66
love, the centrality of (in Jesus's teachings),
  26–30
Lucius II, 221

Lucretius, 156–57
Luther, Martin, xxiii, 18, 215–18, 230–31,
  237–43
Macrina the Younger, 110–11
Madden, Thomas, 222, 226
Magna Carta, 194
Mao Zedong, 279–80, 317
Masona of Mérida, 192
Maxentius, 59–60, 63
Maximinus Daia, 55
Maxims of Delphi, 27, 78, 182
mental health, Christianity and, 268–69
Merovingian, 141, 144, 145, 148, 162, 169, 171
Middle East, 2, 5, 45
military force, conditions of "just" use, of
  (Augustine), 134–35
Minucius Felix, 97–98
Mizushima, Kenichi, 23–24
Moses, 74
Muhammad, 21, 205
Muslims, 3, 6, 10, 13, 15, 16, 19–20, 123,
  136, 176, 189, 190, 195, 208, 222, 224
misogyny, the beginning of Christian, 120
Napoleon I, 247
natural law tradition, 112, 277
Neo-Platonism, 120
Nero, 47–48
Nicene Creed, 1, 2, 73, 74, 161, 206, 308
Ninety-Five Theses, 238–39, 243
North Africa, Augustine's freeing of slaves in,
  130–32
Northern Ireland conflict. *See* Troubles, the
Obama, Barack, 8, 21–22
Octavius Januarius, 97–98
Odo of Cluny, 163, 183–85, 190
Odoacer, 139
Orestes, 120–22
Origen of Alexandria, 160
Orthodox Church, xxii, 199, 200, 206, 209, 308
Orthodoxy, xxiii, 29, 206
Ossius, 99
Ostrogoths, 139, 213
Ottoman Empire, 20
Ottoman Turks, 16
Outremer, 10
Ovid, 156, 164
paganism, 4, 5, 62, 66, 86, 87, 94, 117, 203

pagans, 17, 64, 66, 74, 86, 94, 101, 104, 105, 118, 119, 133, 142, 143–44, 145, 148, 151, 153, 174, 192, 197, 203–4, 291
pagan temples, 49, 84, 91, 99, 104, 124, 151
Palladius of Ratiaria, 101
parable of the Good Samaritan, 81, 83, 203
Paul, 29, 47–48, 72–73, 81, 97, 127, 129, 139, 168–69, 175–76, 281, 296
Peace of Augsburg, 236, 243, 246
Peace of Westphalia, 246–47
pedophile priests, xxi, 258–59, 274
persecution of the church
    AD 64–312. See in general chapter 5 (44–57)
    today, 45–46
Peter, 81, 139
Peter the Hermit, 9–10
Philo of Alexandria, 35
Philoponus, John, 123, 198–99, 207
Photius I, 199, 204, 307
Plato, 27, 78, 79, 164, 199, 204, 207, 290
Platonists, 123
Pliny the Elder, 164
Pliny the Younger, 48–50, 97
Plotinus, 79, 128
Plutarch, 27, 78, 199
Pol Pot, 279, 280
polytheism, 12, 124, 144
poor, the, 33, 78, 80–81, 84, 89, 91, 94, 97, 98, 101, 104, 105, 107–10, 118, 130, 131, 133, 142, 143, 170, 182, 183–85, 188, 191, 193–95, 202, 273, 295
Poor Act of 1834, 193
popes, 16, 17–18, 58, 103, 187. See individual popes by name
Porphyry, 53, 56, 63
poverty
    Greco-Roman view of, 79
    of spirit, 39–40
Prayer of St. Francis, 189
Protestantism, xxiii, 29, 215, 226, 246
Protestant Reformation, 18, 58, 215–17, 220, 225, 230, 237–38, 240, 242–43, 249, 254
Protestants, xxii, xxiii, 17, 73, 100, 206, 215–17, 225–26, 231, 235, 240, 242, 243, 245, 247, 249, 251, 255, 289, 308, 310
punitiveness, 267, 268

purgatory, 238, 239
Rashid, Harun al-, 207
Raymond of Aguilers, 2–4
Reformation, 18, 58, 215–17, 220, 225, 230, 237–38, 240, 242–43, 249, 254
reformers/Protestant Reformers, 18, 25, 217, 239, 242, 283
Reign of Terror, 228–30, 254, 278, 285
religion
    conflict between science and, 233–34
    freedom of. See next
"religious edge," 271, 273
religious freedom, 44–45, 63–65, 67, 68, 86, 117, 205, 232, 243
Remigius of Auxere, 163, 183–84
Remigius of Reims, 140, 170
Renaissance, 139, 156–58, 200, 207, 208, 211, 212, 216, 238, 284
    humanists, 212–13, 215
resolve, the keys to Christian, 55–57
resurrection, Christ's death and, 3, 15, 52, 57, 238, 239
Richard I, 12–13, 21
Richard II, 194
Richelieu, Armand Jean du Plessis, 244
riots, Christian, 117–19
Roman Catholic Church, xxii, 100, 206, 216, 217, 230, 232, 261–62
Roman Empire, 13, 46, 53, 66, 96, 124, 133, 137–39, 146, 177, 197, 198, 205
    eastern, xxiii, 13, 109, 132, 138, 195–96, 200, 206, 208. See Byzantine Empire; Byzantium
    Holy, 15–16, 146, 197, 239–40, 243–45, 247
    western, 16, 60, 117, 137–38, 139, 140, 145, 149, 169, 198, 211
Rome
    the death of. See chapter 13 (137–46)
    the Goths' sacking of, 132, 138, 213
Romulus Augustus, Flavius, 212
Rufinus of Aquileia, 118
Rule of Benedict, 181–82, 184, 186
Saladin (Salah ad-Din), 11–13, 15, 177
salvation
    the central Christian doctrine of, 29
    good deeds and, 242

true basis of, 225, 239
"sanctuary city" movement, 201
Saxons, 142, 149–50, 152, 153, 157, 158, 169, 180
Scapula, 51–52, 63, 67
schooling in the ancient church, 159–61
schools, percent of survivors of institutional child sexual abuse molested in (per Australian Royal Commission), 260
science, conflict between religion and, 233–34
Second Crusade, 10–11
Seneca, 27, 78, 156, 164, 212
Sergius of Reshaina, 207, 208
Sermon on the Mount, 23, 24–26, 29, 33, 37–41, 173, 180
Sidonius Apollinaris, 140
Siege of Jerusalem (1099), 2–5, 9, 10, 19, 21
Siege of Jerusalem (1187), 12, 177
Siege of Paris, 172
Simplician, 129
slavery, 14, 76, 105, 119, 130–31, 277
    Christianity and, 111–13
    Gregory of Nyssa versus, 113–14
slaves, 33, 49, 50, 55, 72, 76, 79, 103, 104, 112–13, 130–32, 136, 141–43, 180, 200, 265, 278, 282, 299
Sixth Crusade, 16
Sixtus IV, 222–24
social capital, 269, 270–71, 273
Socialists, 220
society, Ambrose's Christian, 103–5
Socrates Scholasticus, 89, 122–23
Spanish Inquisition, 218–19, 220, 222–28, 230, 254, 279
    death toll, 227–28
Stalin, Joseph, 279–80, 282
Synesius, 123
Tacitus, 44, 47
Tamura, Kimiko de Freytas-, 257
taxation, the church and (Constantinian), 76–78
Telemachus, Saint, 75, 214
Temple Mount, 2, 16
temples. See pagan temples
Terror, the (French), 228–30, 254, 278, 285
Tertullian, 51–52, 63–64, 67, 68, 160, 291, 292

Teutonicus, Joannes, 193–94
Theodora, 200
Theodoret of Antioch, 94
Theodoric, 139
Theodosius I, 65, 102, 103, 116, 118, 119, 124
Theodulf of Orleans, 157, 164
Theon of Alexandria, 120
Theophilus of Alexandria, 118
theory
    of holy war, 19, 172, 195
    of just war, 126, 130, 136, 151, 172. See in general chapter 12 (125–36), 65
    of toleration
theurgy, 88
Third Crusade, 11–13
Thirty Years' War, 235, 237, 242–46, 247
Thomas Aquinas, 109, 153, 192, 193, 208, 233
Thucydides, 199, 204
Tiberius, 46, 47
tithes, 150, 152
Titus, 70
toleration, 55, 65, 69, 198, 231–32, 246
Torquemada, Tomás de, 224, 226, 227
torture, 3, 10, 49, 51, 55, 121, 127, 190, 219, 221, 224, 231, 233, 234, 248, 255
Trajan, 48, 50, 97
Trinity, 107, 198
Troubles, the. See chapter 22 (248–56); also, 237, 247, 257, 281
Urban II, 1, 5–6, 8, 9, 10, 14, 140, 174
Urban V, 212
Urban VIII, 234
Valens, 94
Valentinian I, 94–95, 290
Valentinian II, 104
Vatican, 48, 139, 149, 187, 198, 222, 224, 240
Victorinus, 90, 129
violence
    of the church. See Crusades; Inquisition
    domestic, 268
    "gentle," 104, 117
    sacred (or "holy"), 175. See "holy war," theory of; holy wars
    state, 124, 126, 128, 133, 135, 136
    unreligious, 278–80
Virgil, 156, 160, 164, 212
Visigoths, 132, 138–40, 213

Voltaire, 232, 264
warfare, Christians and, 126–28
Wars of Religion. *See* Thirty Years' War
"white" magic, 65
Willibald, 145, 171
wisdom-theology, 158–59, 160

witchcraft, 225
witch trials, 225, 310
works (deeds), 91, 143, 182, 225, 242
World War I, 16, 169, 246, 278, 284
World War II, 169, 246, 278